Sherlock Bones 5

Sherdog & Takeru

Story: Yuma Ando   Art: Yuki Sato

CHARACTERS

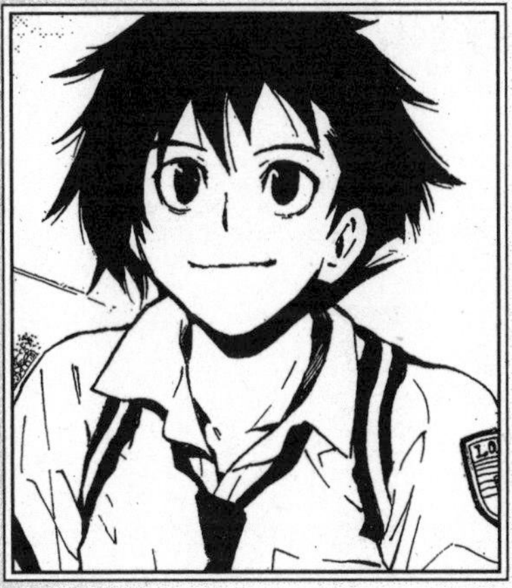

Takeru Wajima

A second-year at London Academy High School, he is an ordinary student who loves dogs. He is Sherdog's owner and the one person who can understand him. He and Sherdog must team up to solve all kinds of difficult cases. He has a crush on his childhood friend Miki.

Sherdog
(Sherlock Holmes)

The mixed-breed puppy that Takeru adopted. His true identity is that of the world-famous detective, Sherlock Holmes. When he has the Wajima family's heirloom pipe in his mouth, he can speak to Takeru. He solves crimes with Takeru, learning about the modern world in the process.

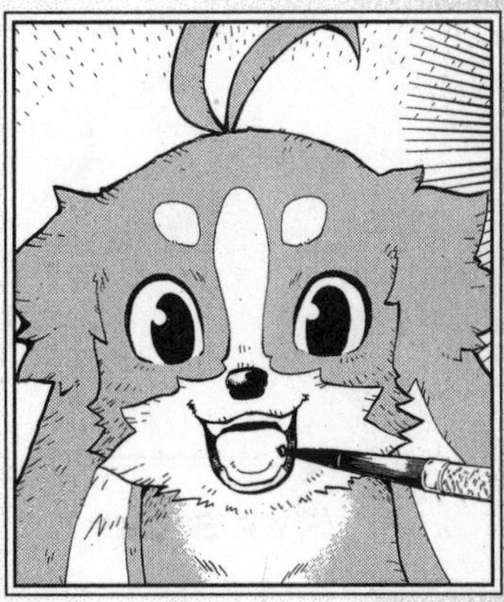

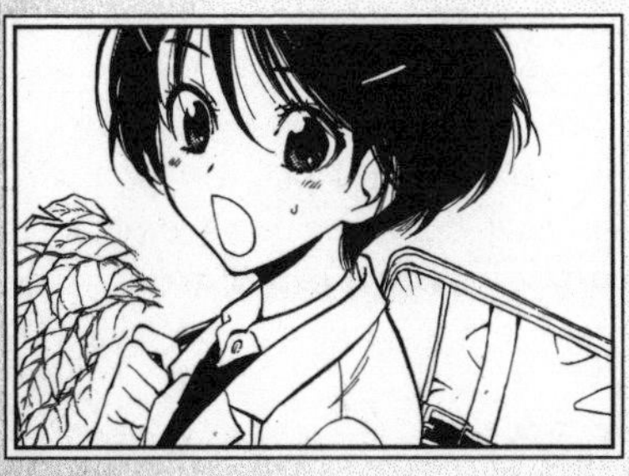

Miki Arisaka

A second-year at London Academy High School. Takeru's friend since childhood, and a member of the school newspaper staff.

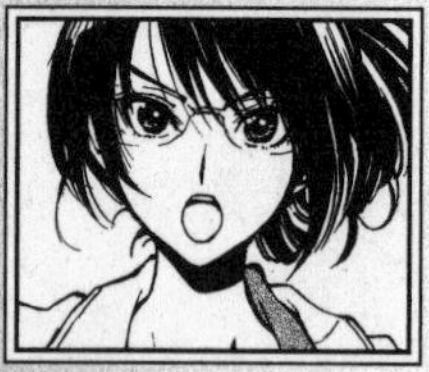

Airin Wajima

Takeru's sister, an inspector in the Violent Crimes Division. Sherdog calls her Irene.

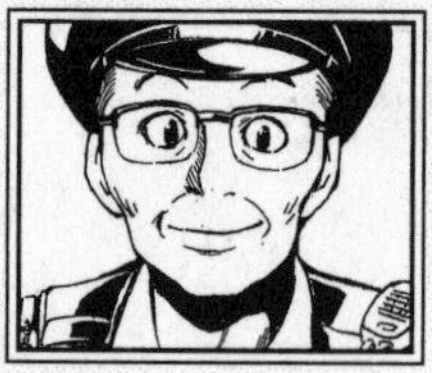

Kosuke Wajima

Takeru's father. A sergeant in the police force.

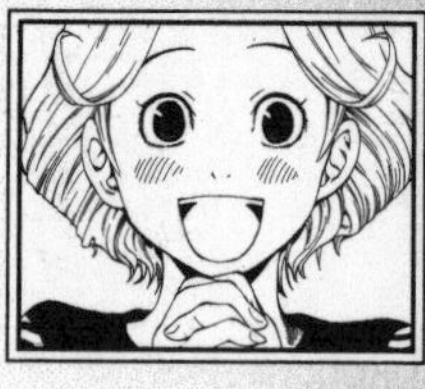

Satoko Wajima

Takeru's mother. She really hates it when Sherdog sits in her favorite rocking chair.

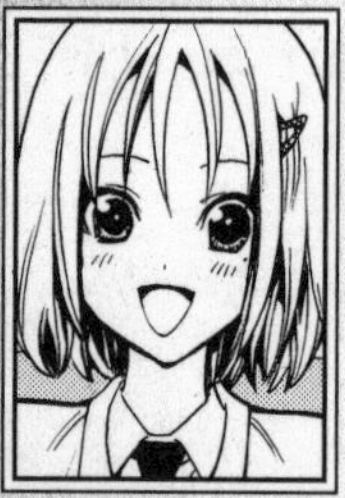

Akane Nanami

A second-year at London Academy High School, and friend of Takeru and Miki. President of the volunteer club.

Mika Takasugi

The mayor of London, she is gaining attention as the "too beautiful mayor."

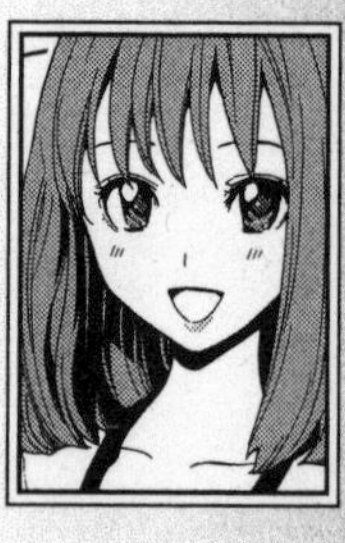

The Story So Far

The puppy Sherdog—reincarnation of Sherlock Holmes—and the ordinary high school student Takeru Wajima team up to solve tough cases! Takeru and company are visiting city hall to interview London's "too beautiful mayor" for the school newspaper. But right before their visit, the mayor was busy killing her former lover...

STORY

Volume.5

CONTENTS

Case 7: ⚜ Hidden from the Press, Part 2

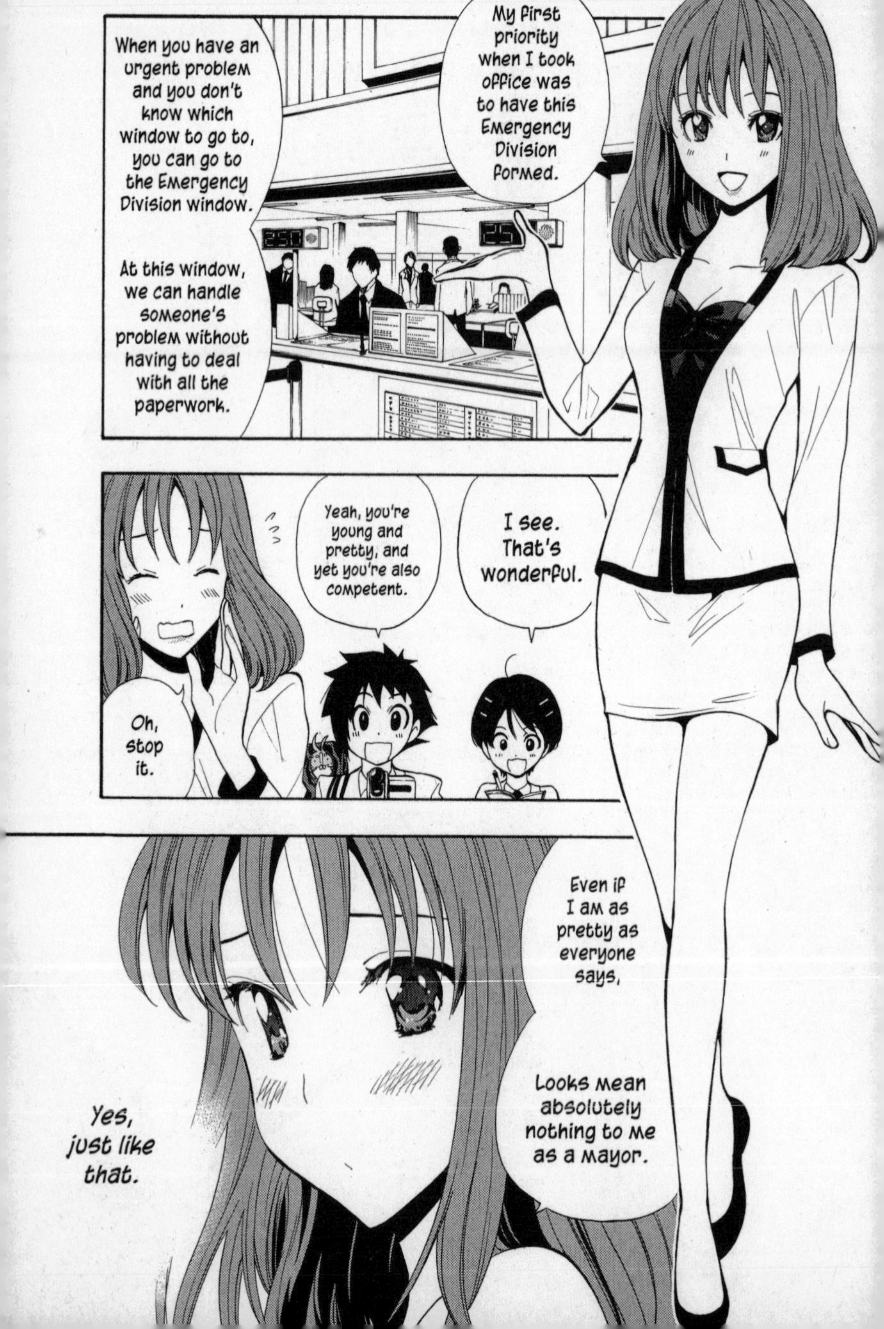
My first priority when I took office was to have this Emergency Division formed.
When you have an urgent problem and you don't know which window to go to, you can go to the Emergency Division window.
At this window, we can handle someone's problem without having to deal with all the paperwork.
I see. That's wonderful.
Yeah, you're young and pretty, and yet you're also competent.
Oh, stop it.
Even if I am as pretty as everyone says,
Looks mean absolutely nothing to me as a mayor.
Yes, just like that.

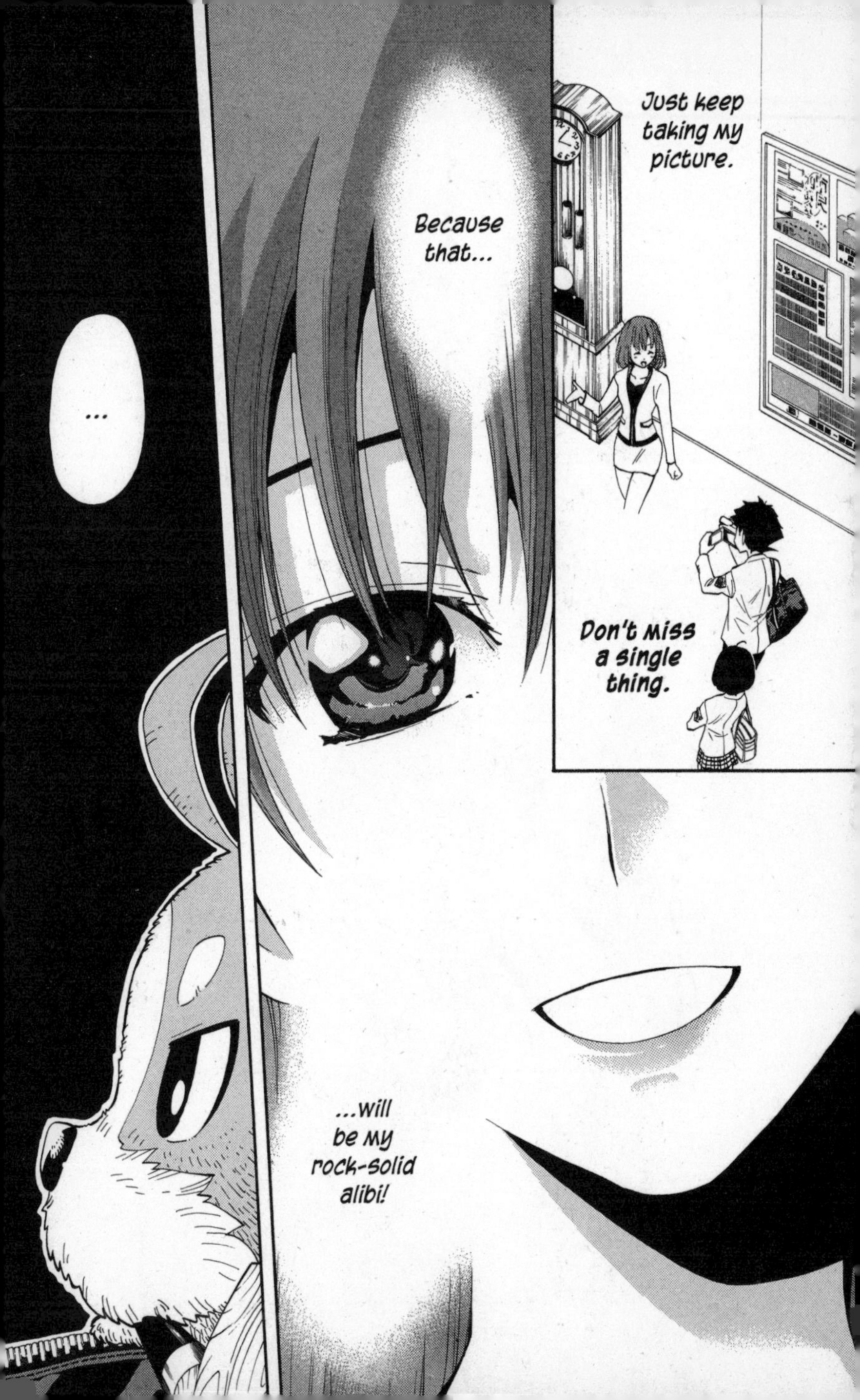
Just keep taking my picture.
Don't miss a single thing.
Because that...
...will be my rock-solid alibi!
...

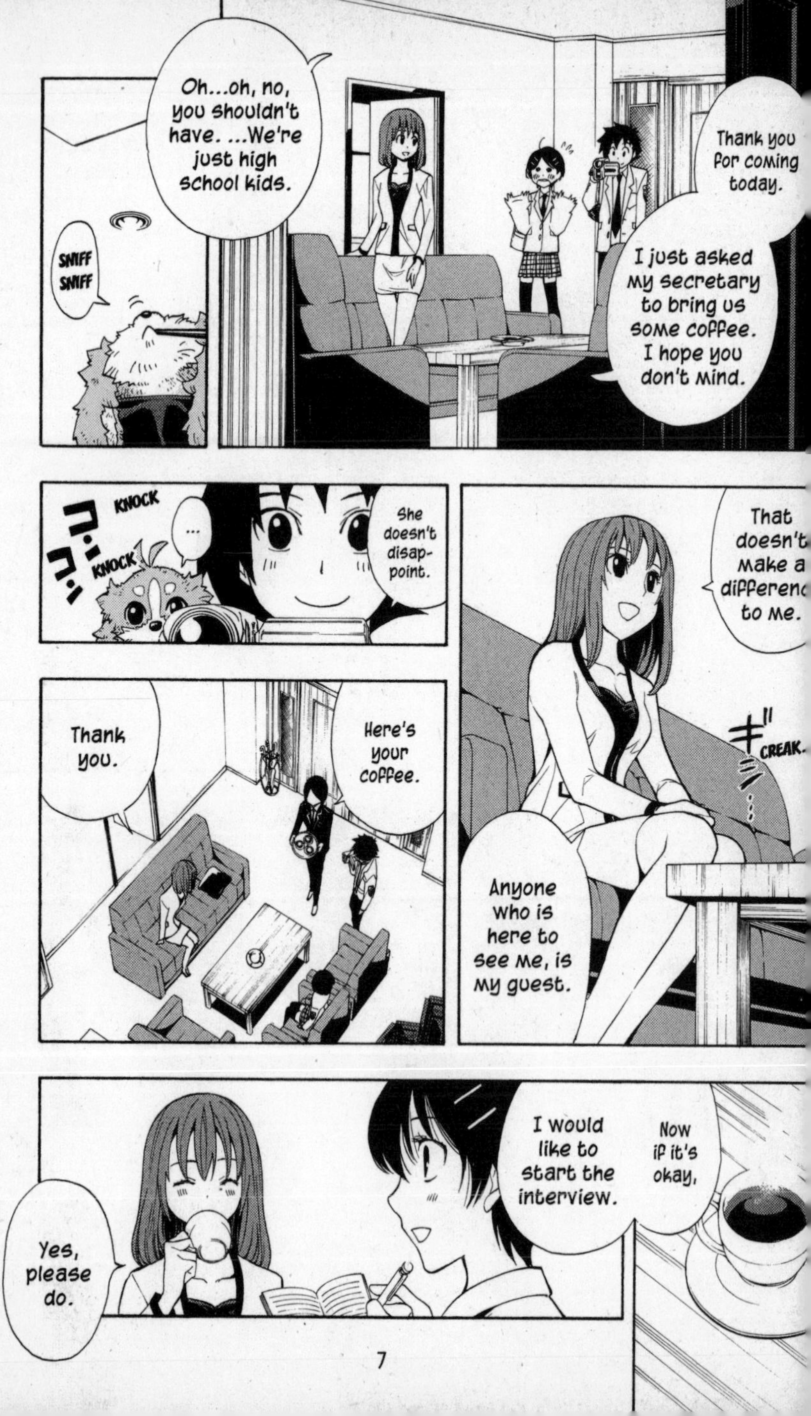
Thank you for coming today.
I just asked my secretary to bring us some coffee. I hope you don't mind.
Oh...oh, no, you shouldn't have. ...We're just high school kids.
SNIFF SNIFF
That doesn't make a differenc to me.
CREAK
Anyone who is here to see me, is my guest.
She doesn't disap-point.
...
KNOCK
KNOCK
Here's your coffee.
Thank you.
Now if it's okay,
I would like to start the interview.
Yes, please do.

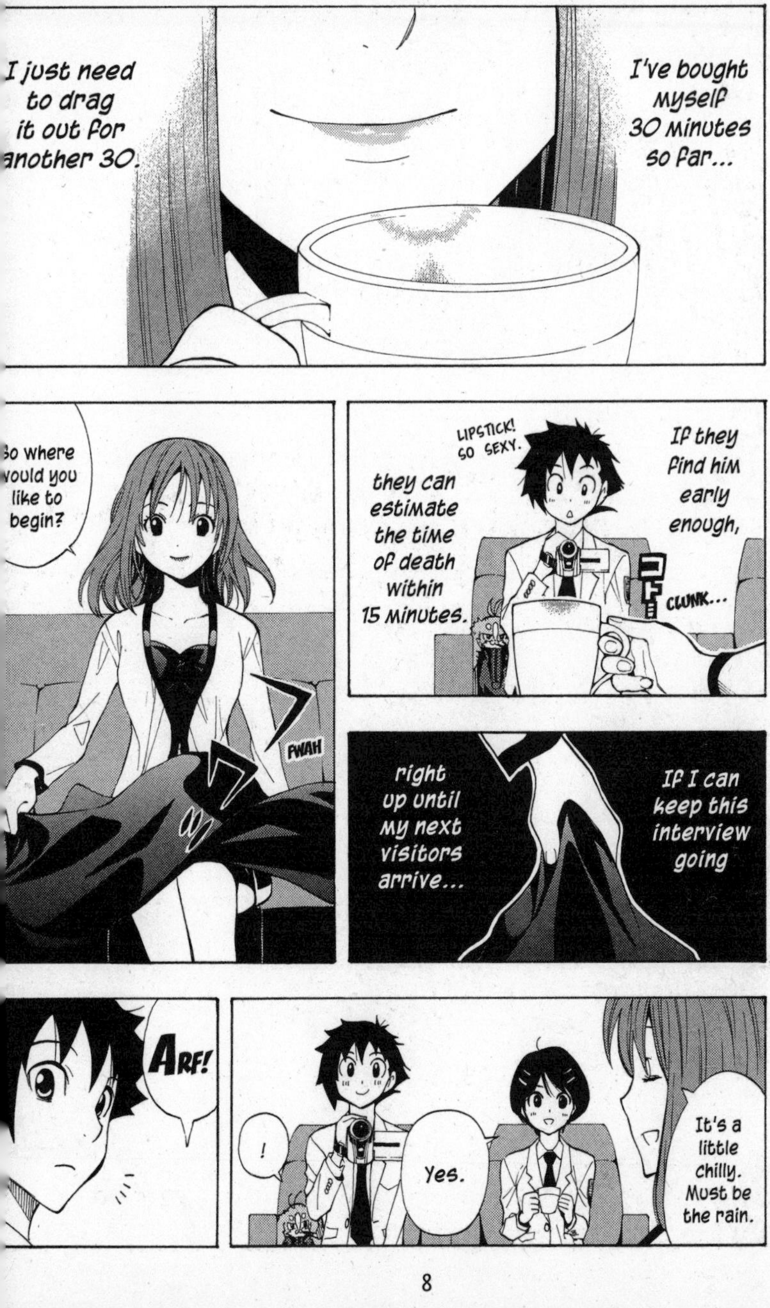
I've bought myself 30 minutes so far...
I just need to drag it out for another 30.
If they find him early enough,
they can estimate the time of death within 15 minutes.
LIPSTICK! SO SEXY.
CLUNK...
If I can keep this interview going
right up until my next visitors arrive...
So where would you like to begin?
FWAH
It's a little chilly. Must be the rain.
Yes.
!
ARF!

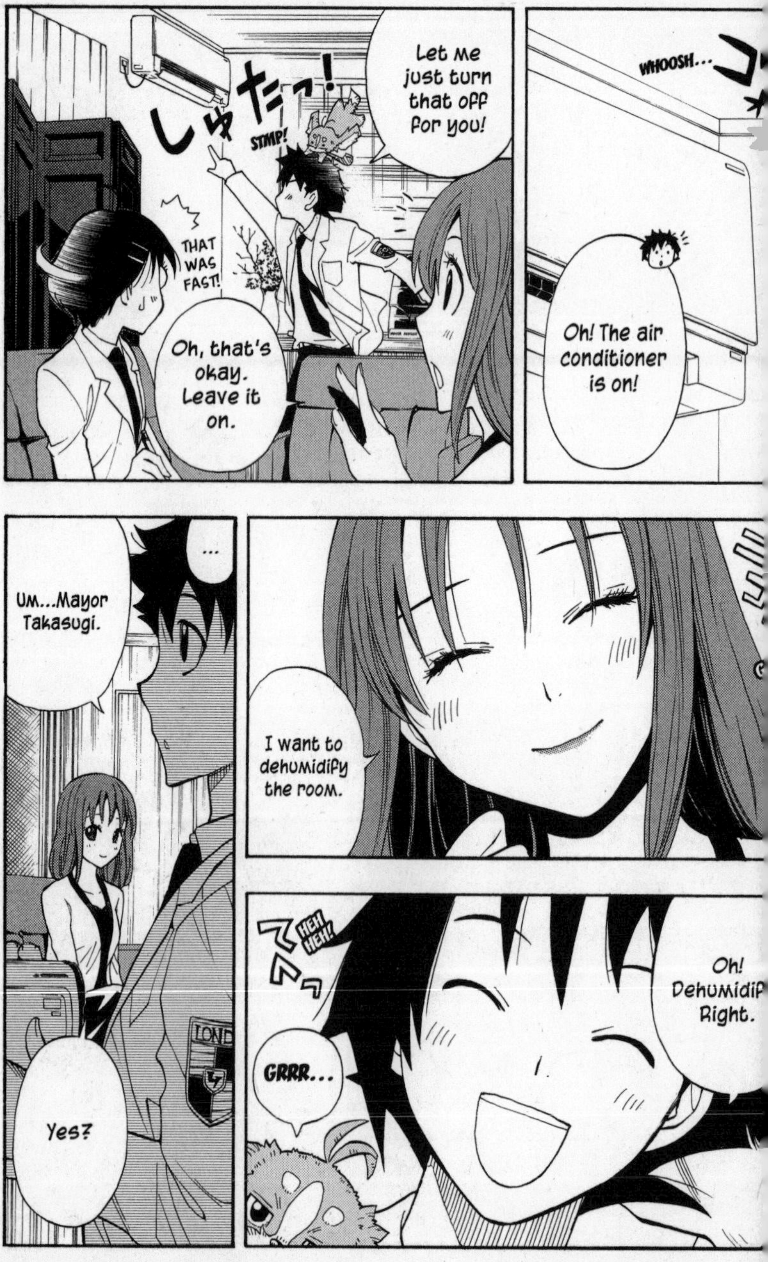
WHOOSH...
Oh! The air conditioner is on!
Let me just turn that off for you!
しゅたっ!
STMP!
THAT WAS FAST!
Oh, that's okay. Leave it on.
I want to dehumidify the room.
Oh! Dehumidif Right.
HEH HEH!
GRRR...
...
Um...Mayor Takasugi.
Yes?

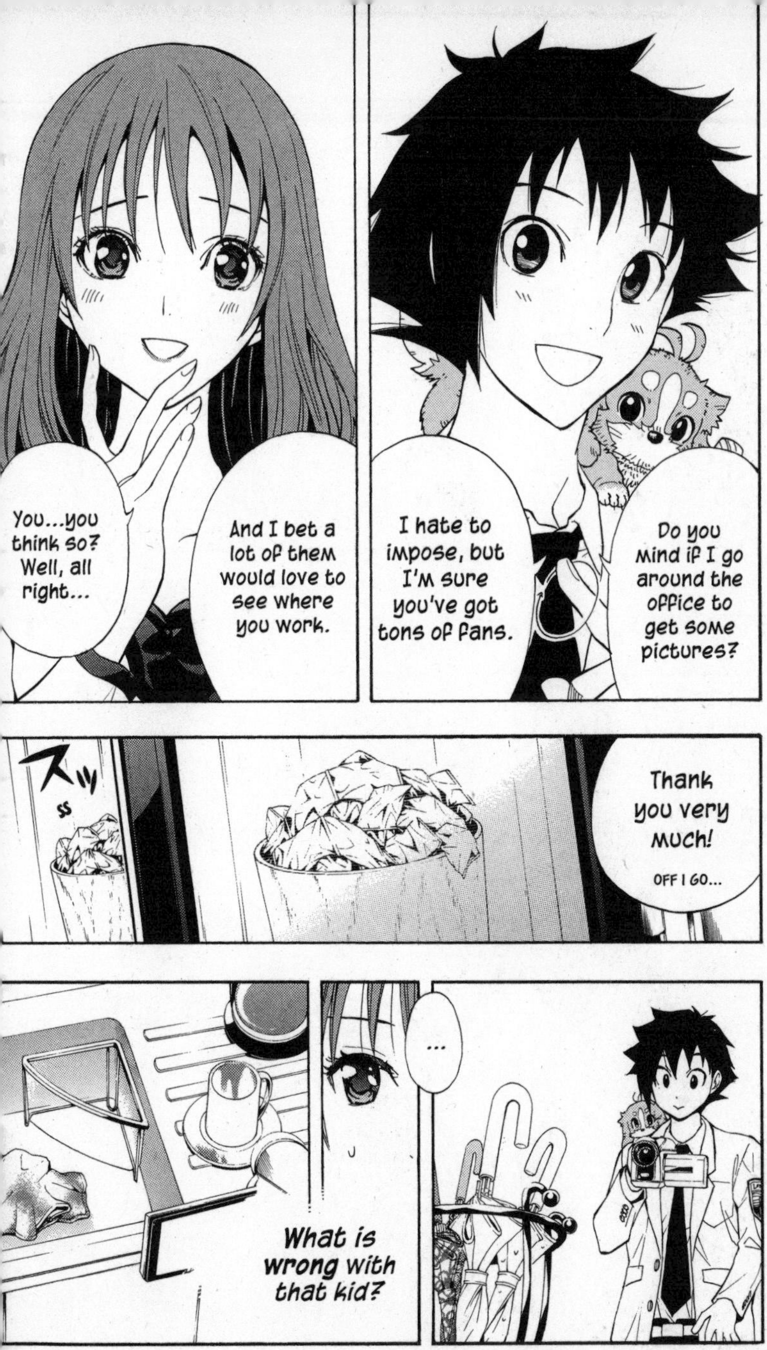
Do you mind if I go around the office to get some pictures?
I hate to impose, but I'm sure you've got tons of fans.
And I bet a lot of them would love to see where you work.
You...you think so? Well, all right...
Thank you very much!
OFF I GO...
スッ
SS
...
What is wrong with that kid?

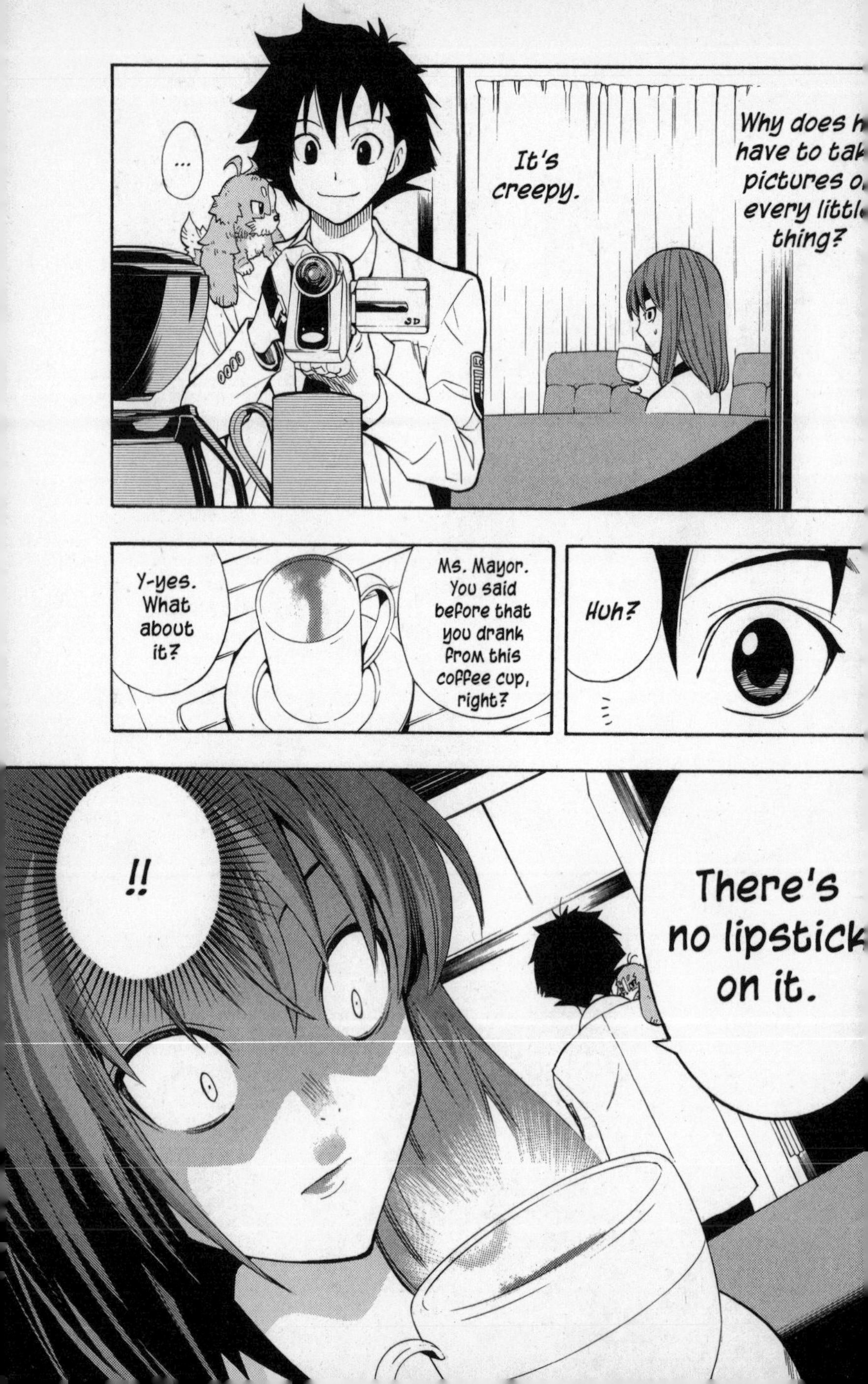
Why does h have to tak pictures o every littl thing?
It's creepy.
...
Huh?
Ms. Mayor. You said before that you drank from this coffee cup, right?
Y-yes. What about it?
There's no lipstick on it.
!!

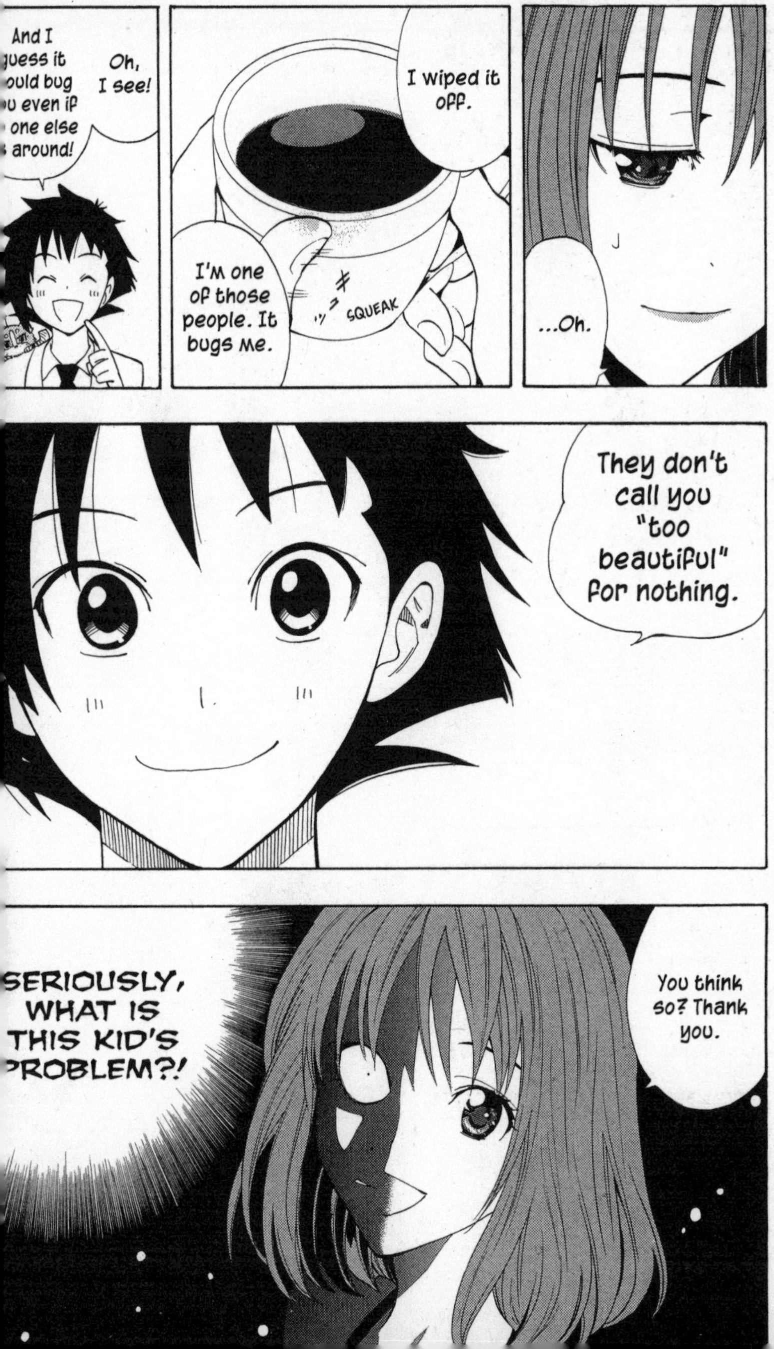
...Oh.
I wiped it off.
I'm one of those people. It bugs me.
SQUEAK
Oh, I see!
And I guess it ould bug u even if one else around!
They don't call you "too beautiful" for nothing.
You think so? Thank you.
SERIOUSLY, WHAT IS THIS KID'S ROBLEM?!

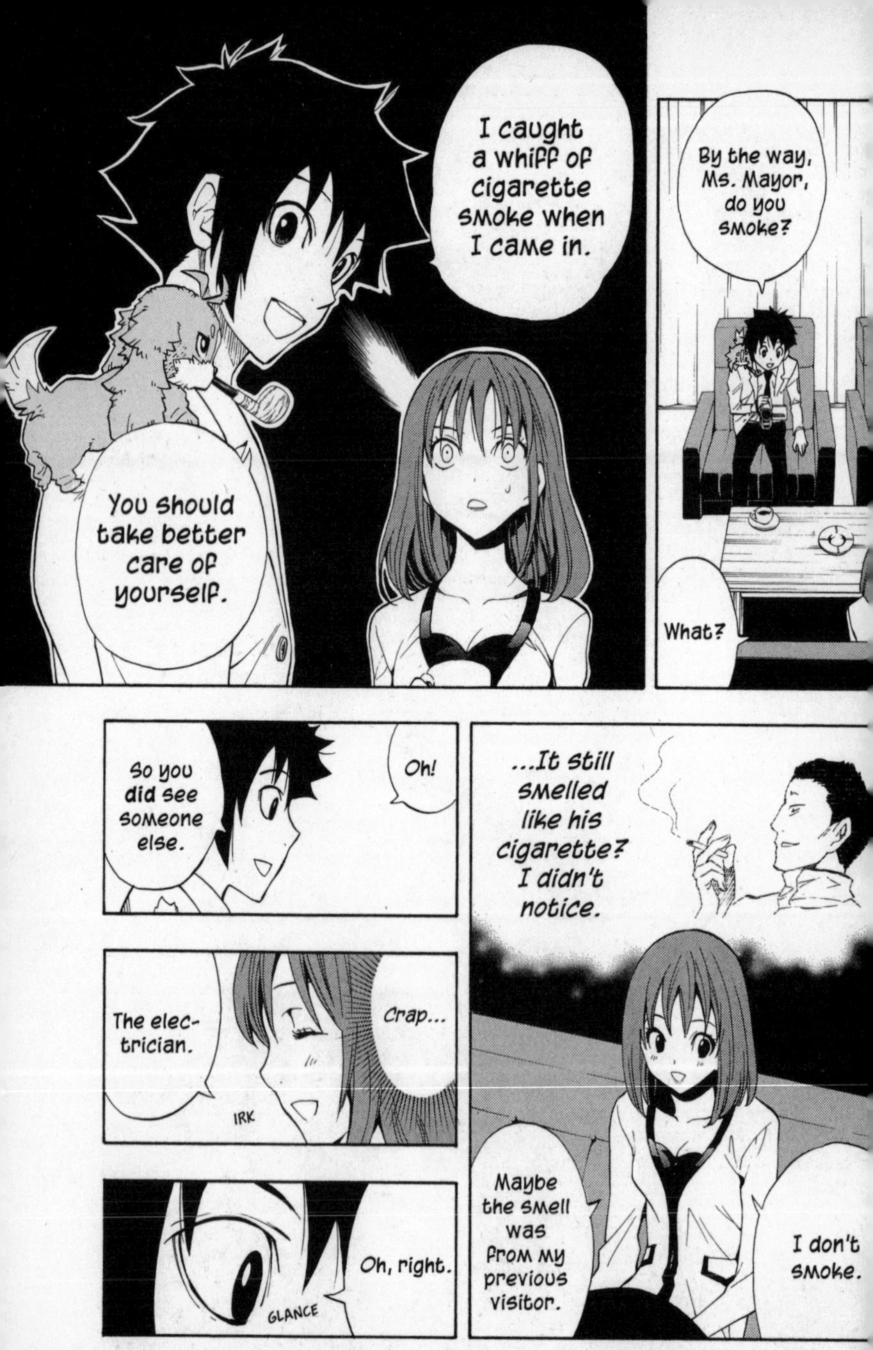
By the way, Ms. Mayor, do you smoke?
What?
I caught a whiff of cigarette smoke when I came in.
You should take better care of yourself.
...It still smelled like his cigarette? I didn't notice.
I don't smoke.
Maybe the smell was from my previous visitor.
Oh!
So you did see someone else.
Crap...
The elec-trician.
IRK
Oh, right.
GLANCE

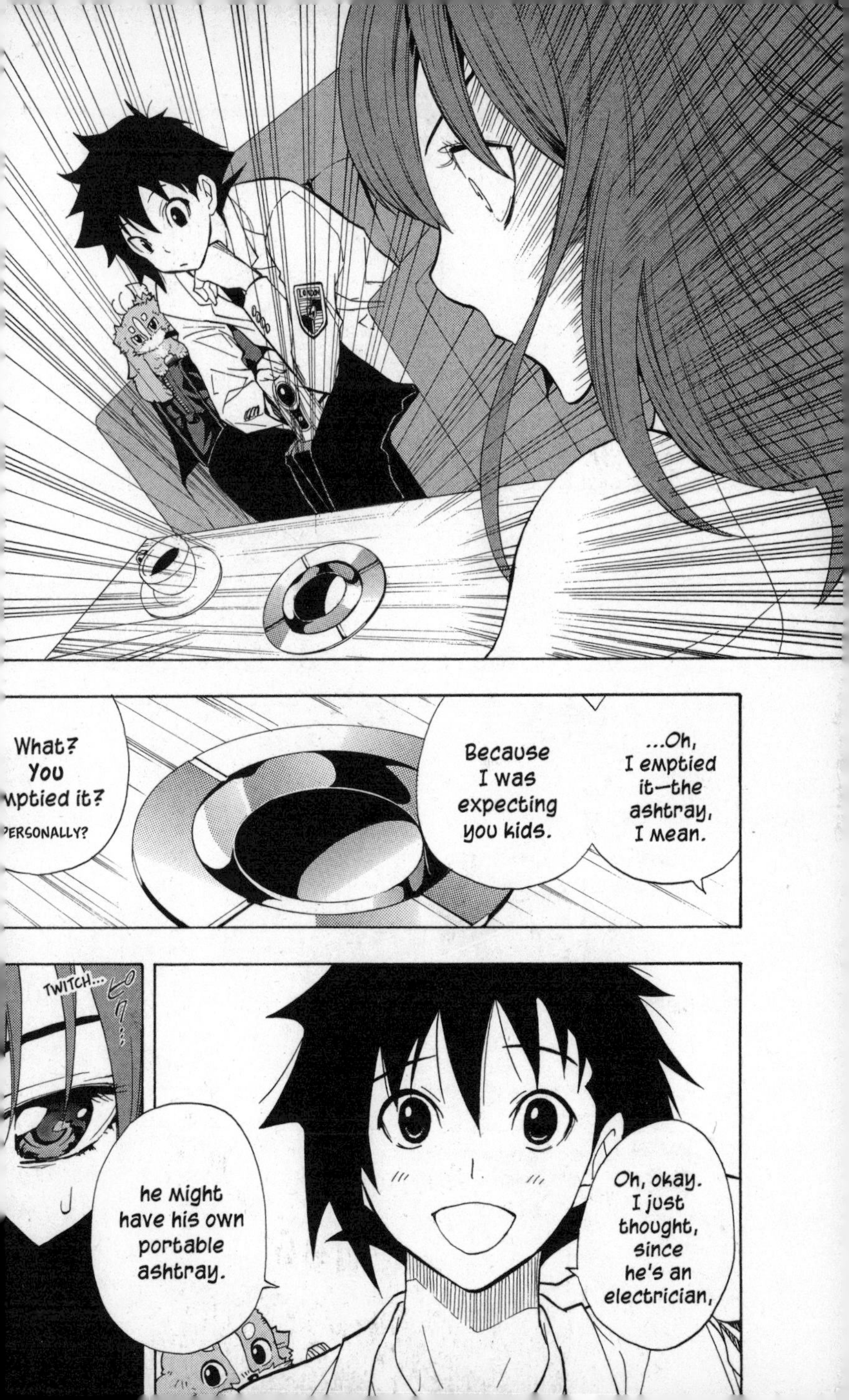
...Oh, I emptied it—the ashtray, I mean.
Because I was expecting you kids.
What? You mptied it?
ERSONALLY?
Oh, okay. I just thought, since he's an electrician,
he might have his own portable ashtray.
TWITCH...
ピク…

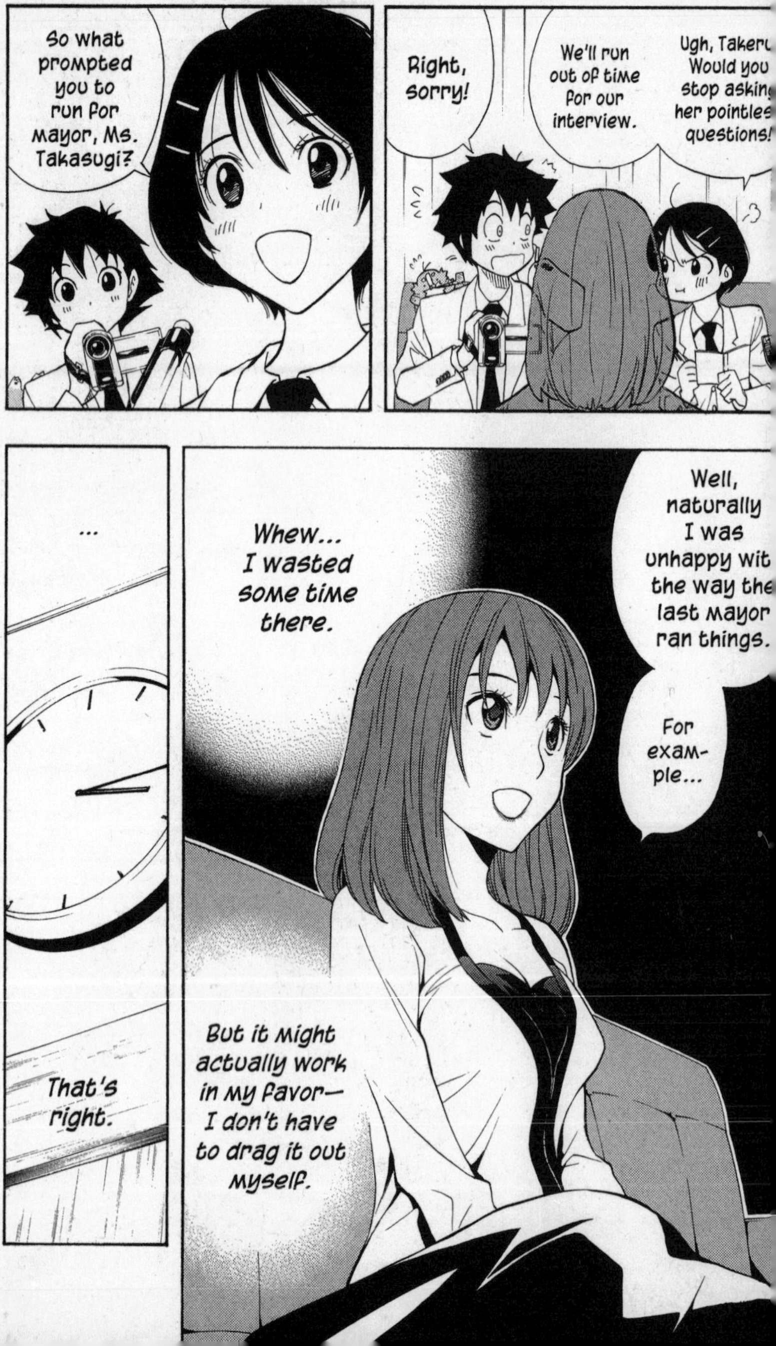
Ugh, Takeru Would you stop askin her pointles questions!
We'll run out of time for our interview.
Right, sorry!
So what prompted you to run for mayor, Ms. Takasugi?
Well, naturally I was unhappy wit the way the last mayor ran things.
For exam-ple...
Whew... I wasted some time there.
But it might actually work in my favor— I don't have to drag it out myself.
...
That's right.

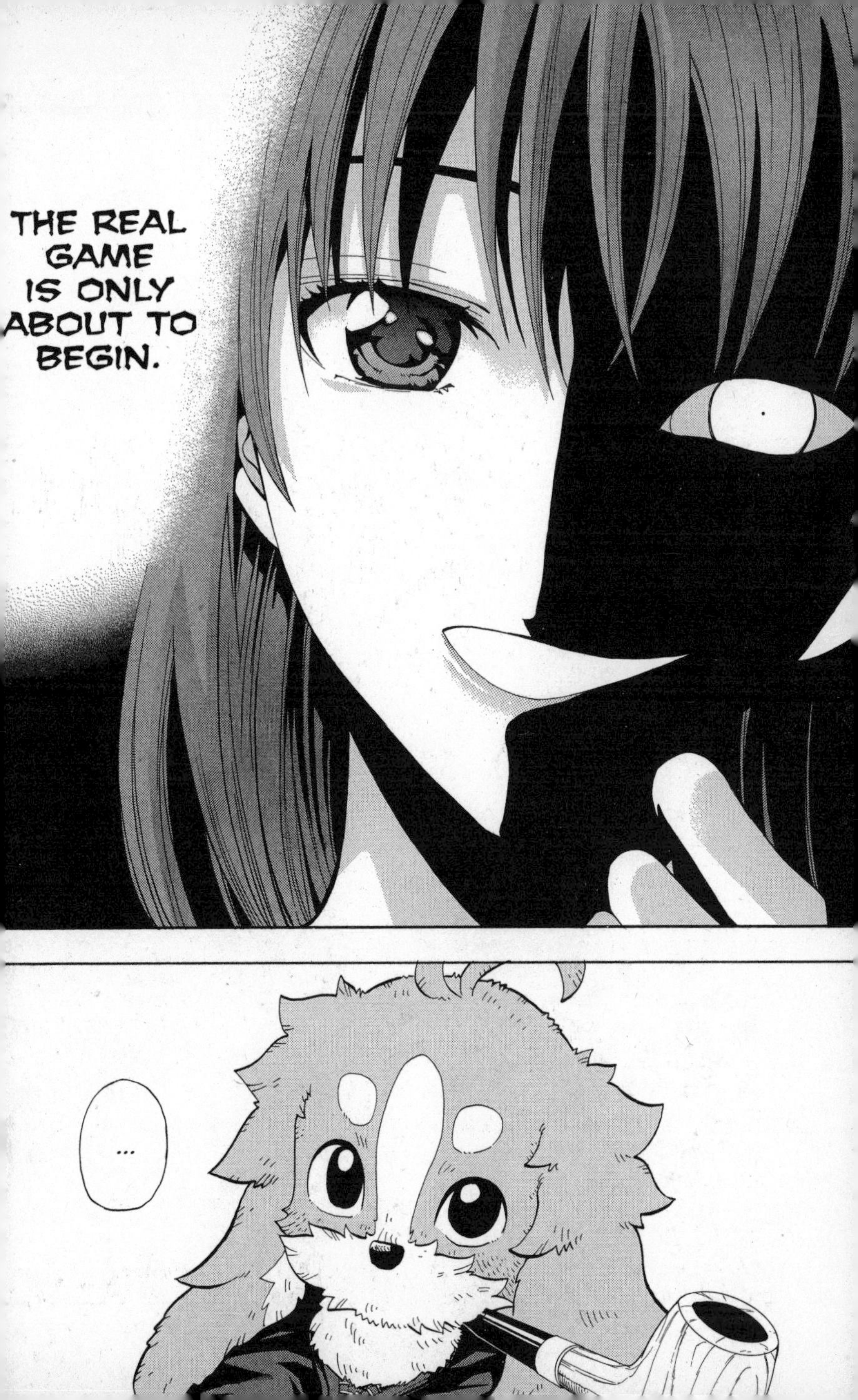
THE REAL GAME IS ONLY ABOUT TO BEGIN.
...

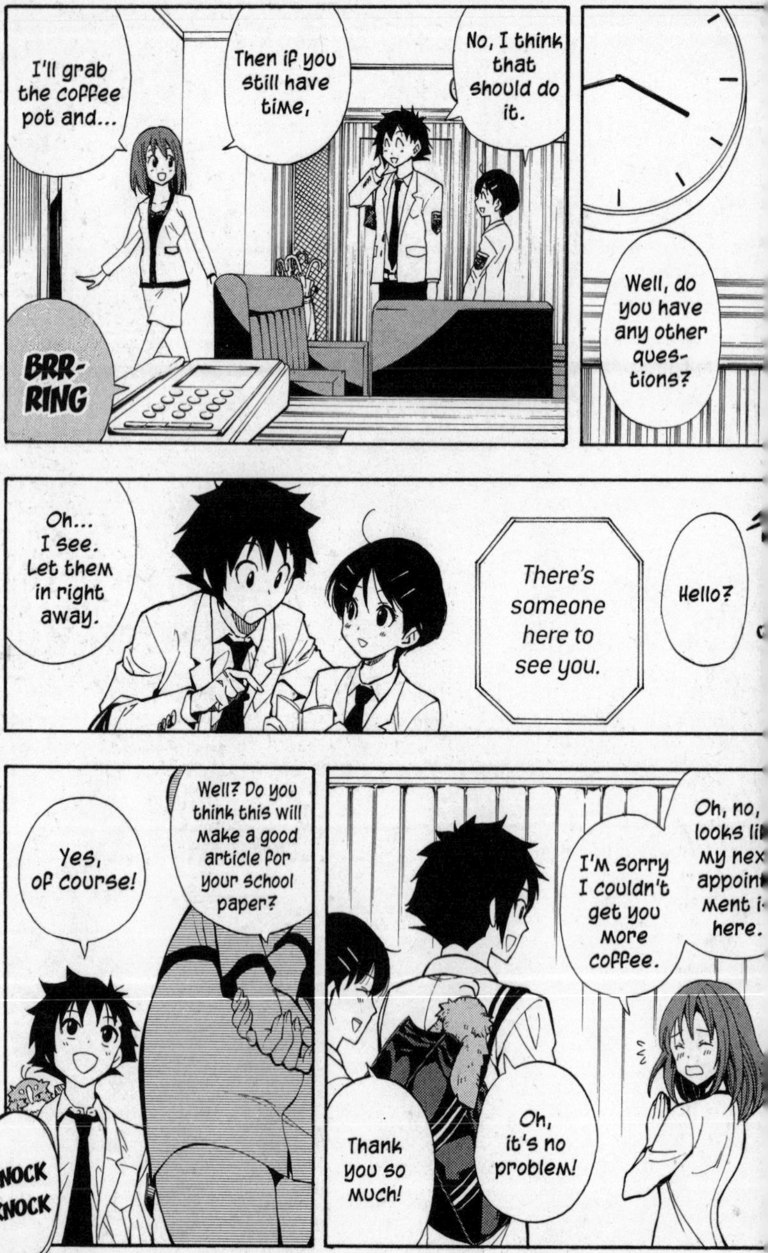
Well, do you have any other ques-tions?
No, I think that should do it.
Then if you still have time,
I'll grab the coffee pot and...
BRR-RING
Hello?
There's someone here to see you.
Oh... I see. Let them in right away.
Oh, no, looks li my nex appoin ment i here.
I'm sorry I couldn't get you more coffee.
Oh, it's no problem!
Thank you so much!
Well? Do you think this will make a good article for your school paper?
Yes, of course!
KNOCK KNOCK

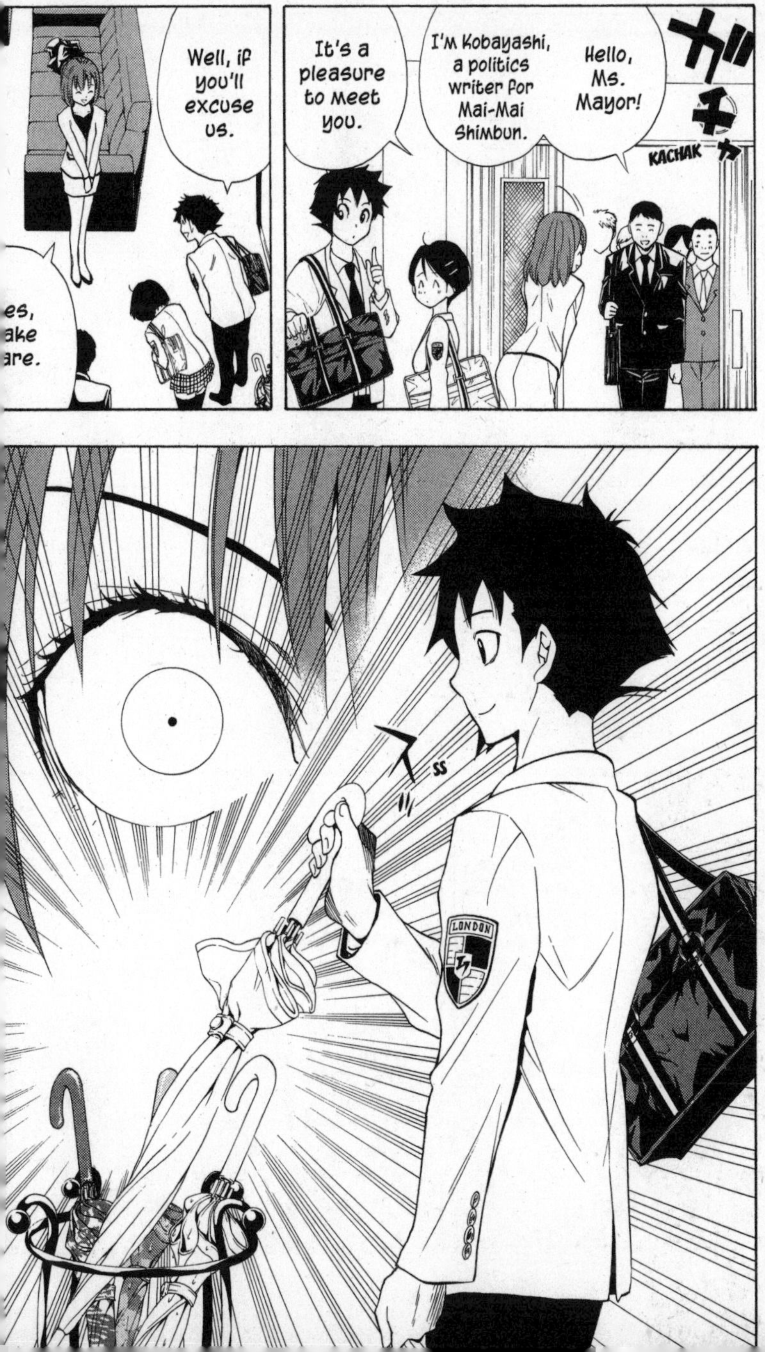
KACHAK
Hello, Ms. Mayor!
I'm Kobayashi, a politics writer for Mai-Mai Shimbun.
It's a pleasure to meet you.
Well, if you'll excuse us.
es, ake are.
SS

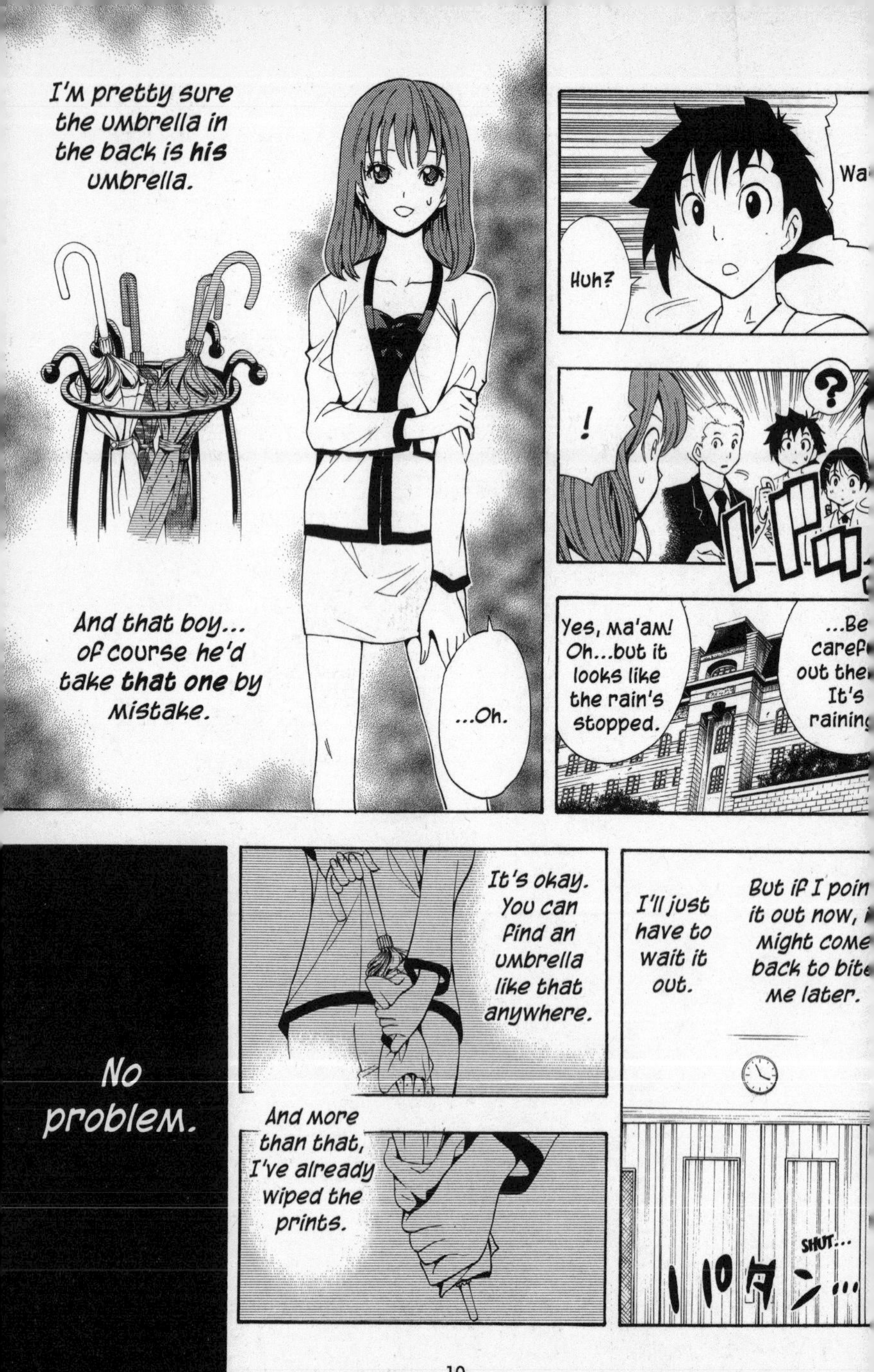
Wa
Huh?
!
?
...Be caref out the It's raining
Yes, ma'am! Oh...but it looks like the rain's stopped.
I'm pretty sure the umbrella in the back is his umbrella.
And that boy... of course he'd take that one by mistake.
...Oh.
But if I poin it out now, might come back to bite me later.
I'll just have to wait it out.
SHUT...
It's okay. You can find an umbrella like that anywhere.
And more than that, I've already wiped the prints.
No problem.

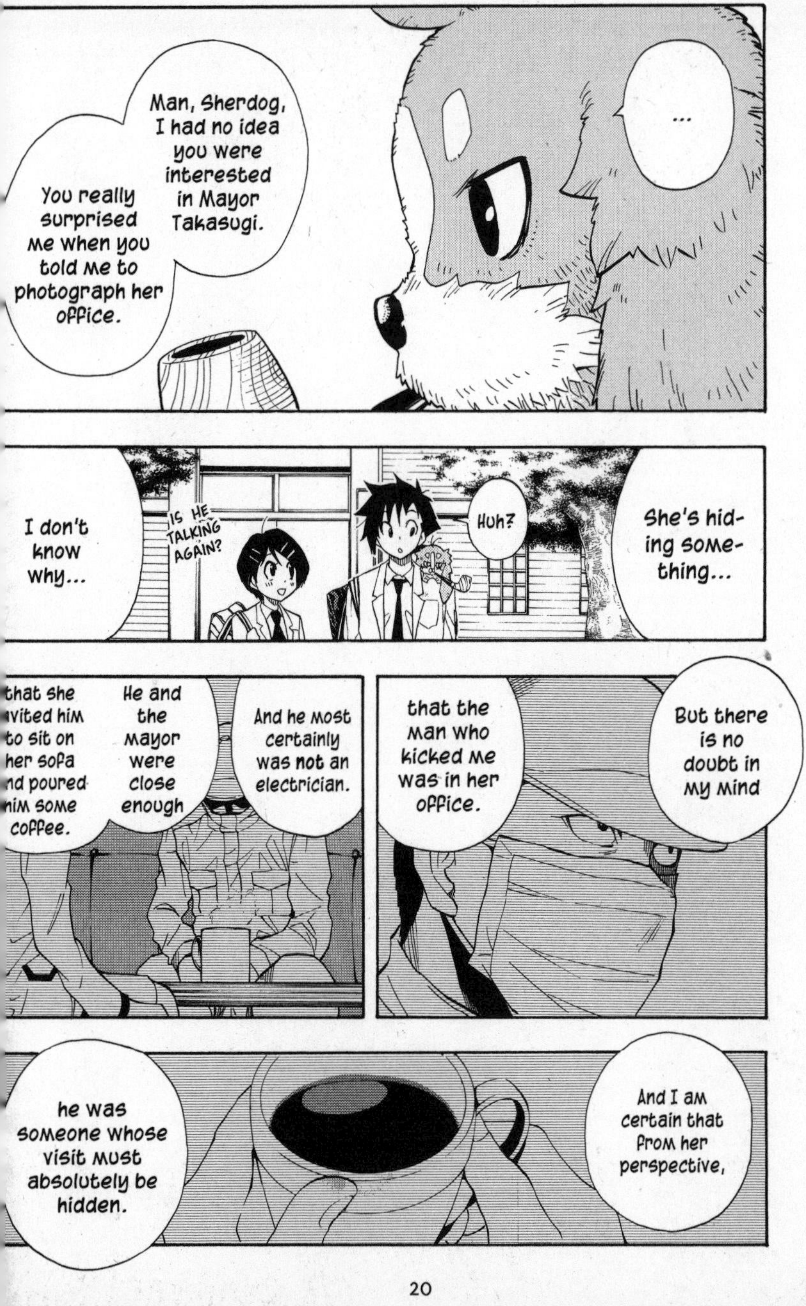
...
Man, Sherdog, I had no idea you were interested in Mayor Takasugi.
You really surprised me when you told me to photograph her office.
She's hiding something...
Huh?
Is he talking again?
I don't know why...
But there is no doubt in my mind
that the man who kicked me was in her office.
And he most certainly was not an electrician.
He and the mayor were close enough
that she vited him to sit on her sofa nd poured him some coffee.
And I am certain that from her perspective,
he was someone whose visit must absolutely be hidden.

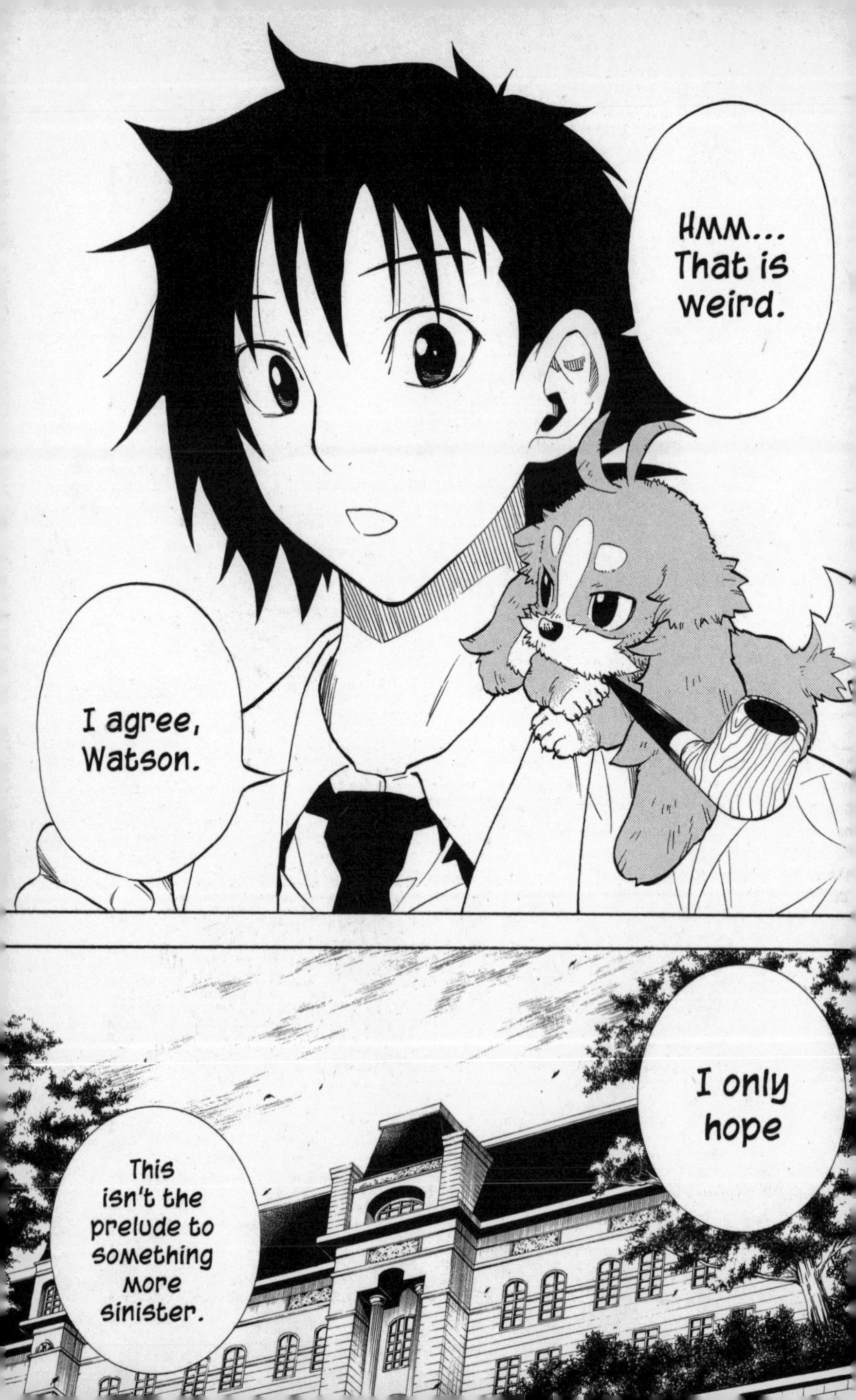
HMM... That is weird.
I agree, Watson.
I only hope
This isn't the prelude to something more sinister.

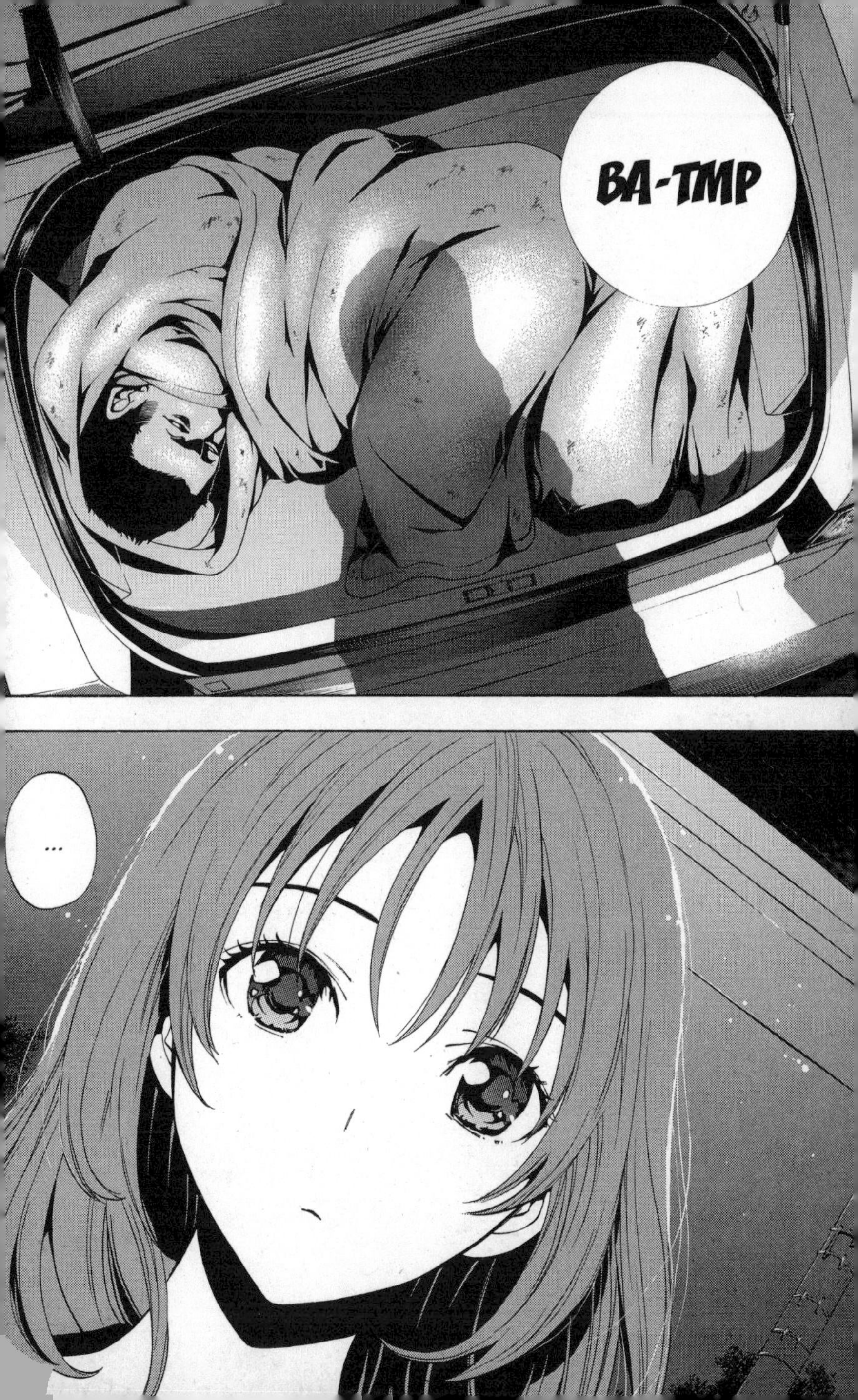
BA-TMP
...

Oof...

ZLRR... ズ ズ ル... ル... ズ ル... ZLRR...

He's heavy!

RUM-MAGE

Whoops...

THU

タム SHUT

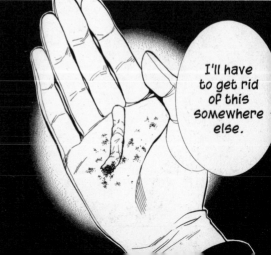

I'll have to get rid of this somewhere else.

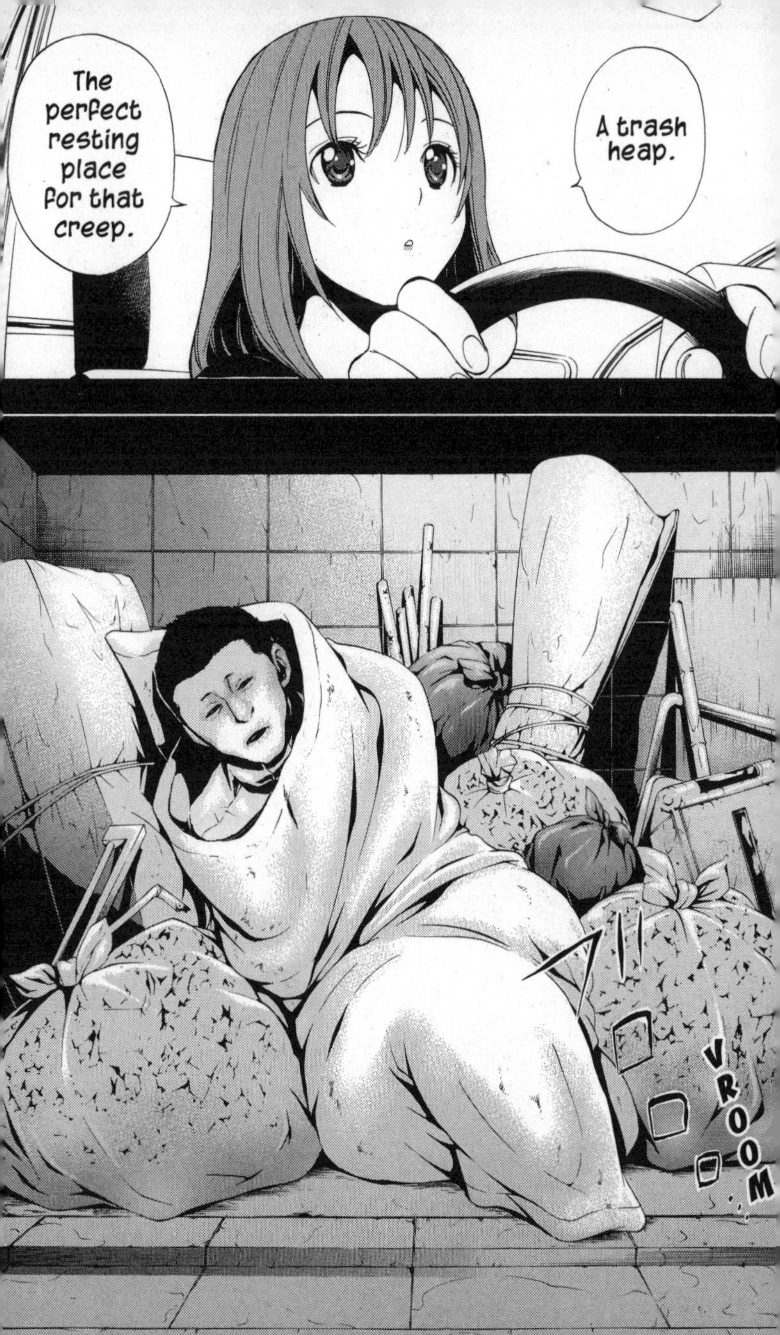
A trash heap.
The perfect resting place for that creep.
VROOM

Case 7: ⚜ Hidden from the Press, Part 3

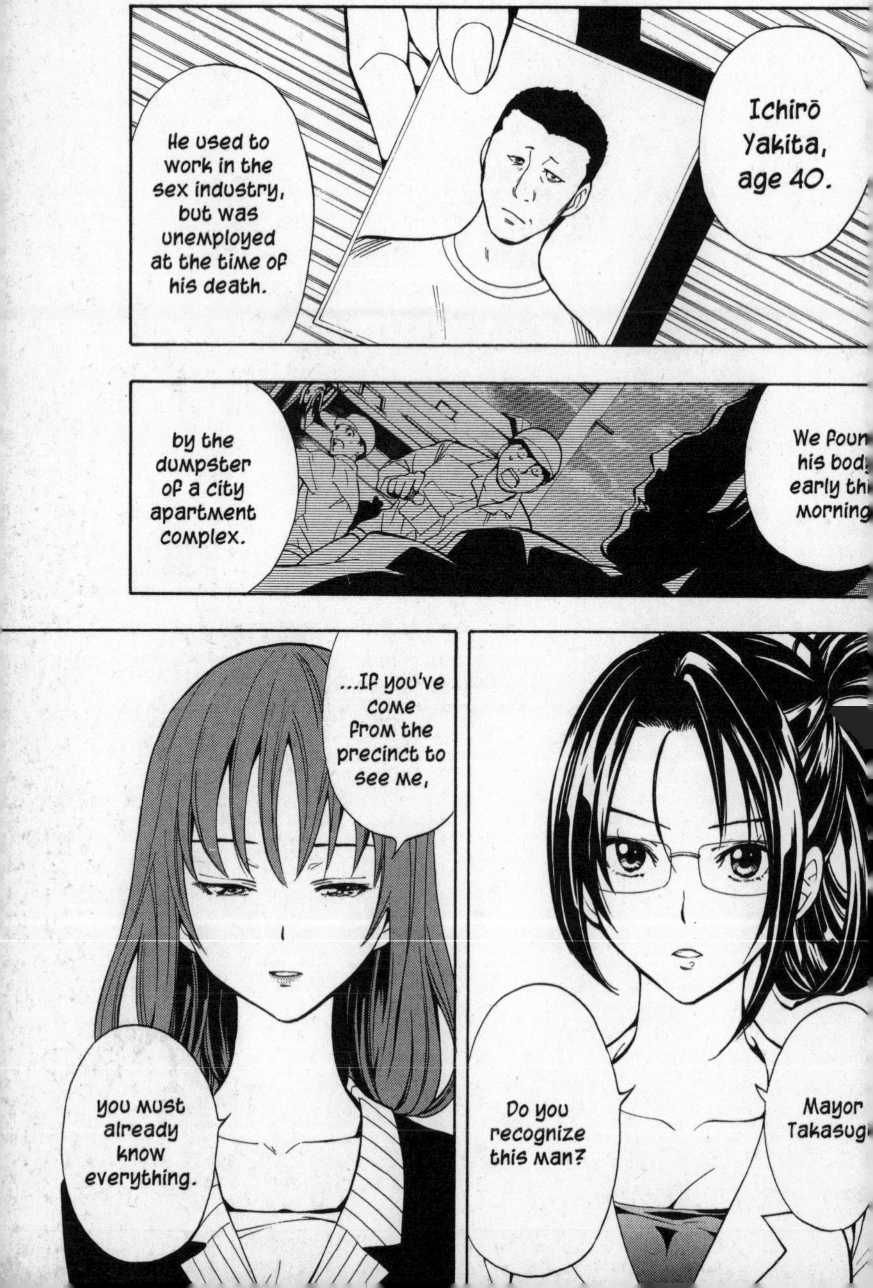
Ichirō Yakita, age 40.
He used to work in the sex industry, but was unemployed at the time of his death.
We foun his bod early thi morning
by the dumpster of a city apartment complex.
Mayor Takasug
Do you recognize this man?
...If you've come from the precinct to see me,
you must already know everything.

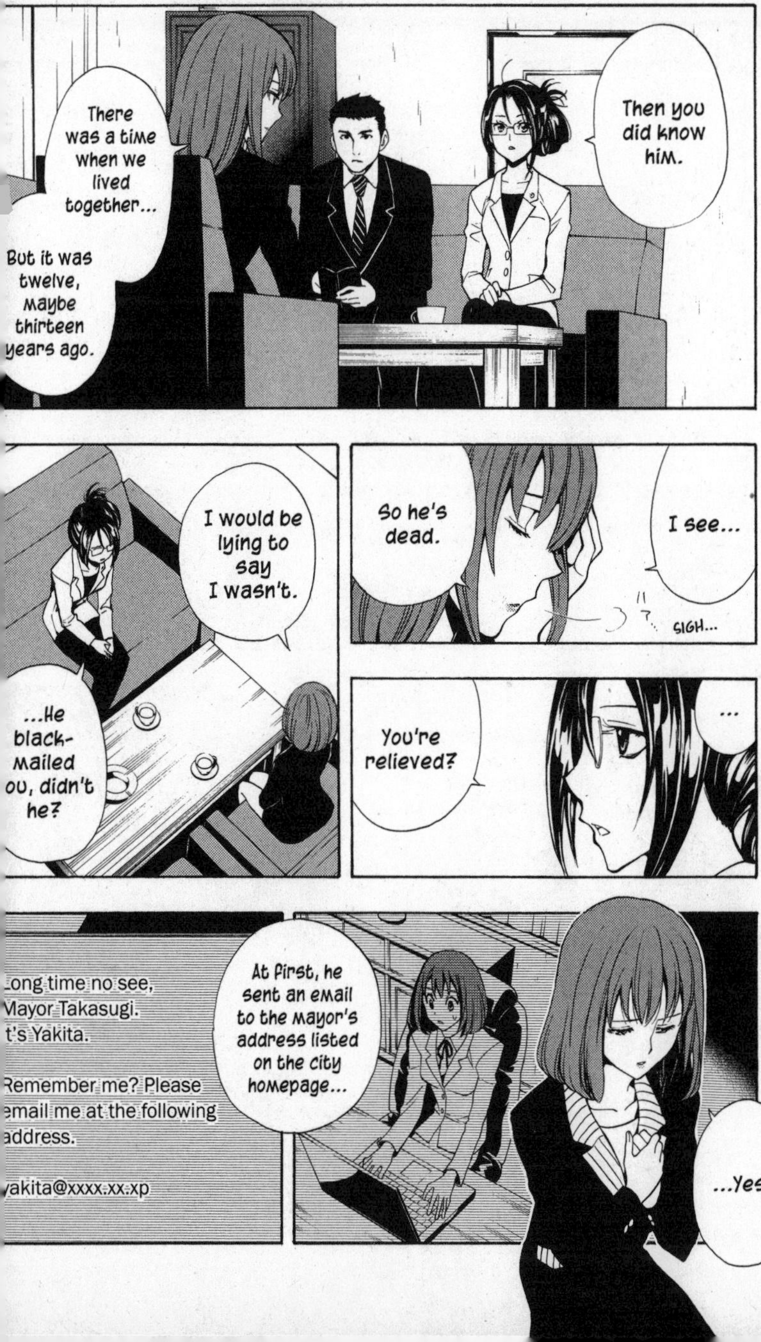
Then you did know him.
There was a time when we lived together...
But it was twelve, maybe thirteen years ago.
I see...
SIGH...
So he's dead.
...
You're relieved?
I would be lying to say I wasn't.
...He black-mailed ou, didn't he?
...Yes.
At first, he sent an email to the mayor's address listed on the city homepage...
ong time no see,
Mayor Takasugi.
t's Yakita.
Remember me? Please
email me at the following
address.
akita@xxxx.xx.xp

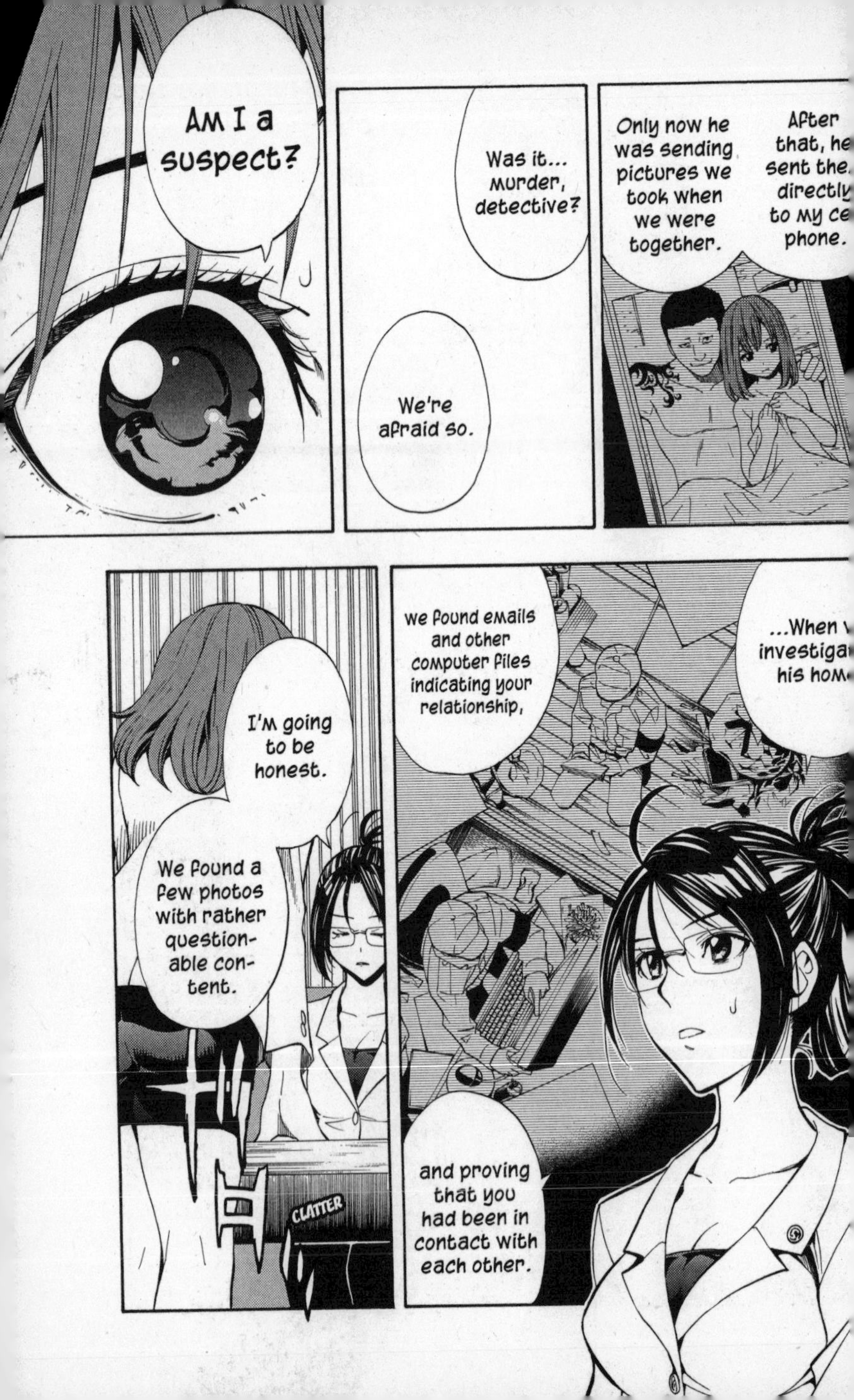
After that, he sent the directly to my ce phone.
Only now he was sending pictures we took when we were together.
Was it... murder, detective?
We're afraid so.
Am I a suspect?
...When investiga his hom
we found emails and other computer files indicating your relationship,
and proving that you had been in contact with each other.
I'm going to be honest.
We found a few photos with rather question-able con-tent.
CLATTER

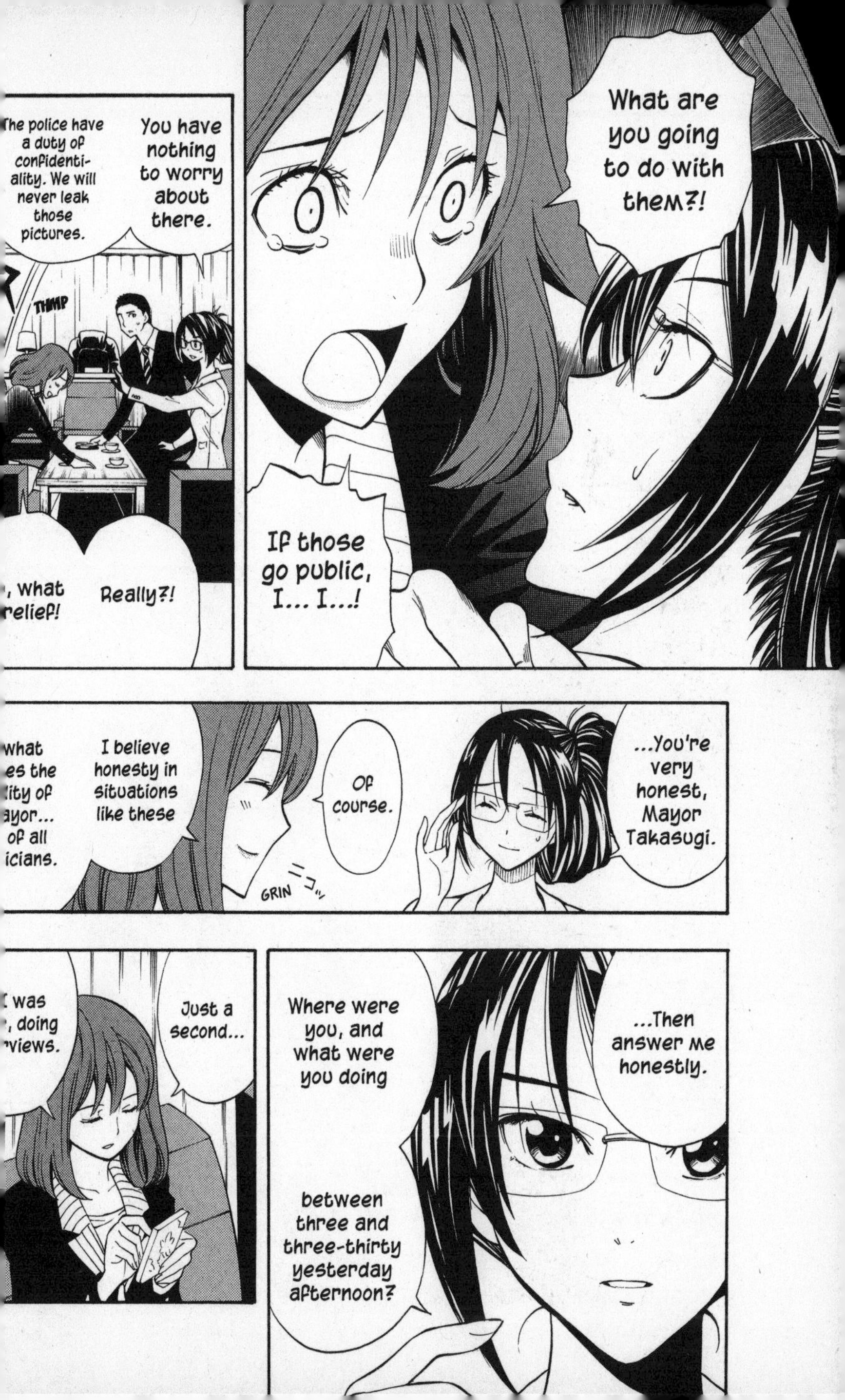
What are you going to do with them?!
If those go public, I... I...!
You have nothing to worry about there.
The police have a duty of confidentiality. We will never leak those pictures.
THMP
Really?!
, what relief!
...You're very honest, Mayor Takasugi.
Of course.
GRIN
I believe honesty in situations like these
what es the lity of ayor... of all icians.
...Then answer me honestly.
Where were you, and what were you doing
between three and three-thirty yesterday afternoon?
Just a second...
I was , doing rviews.

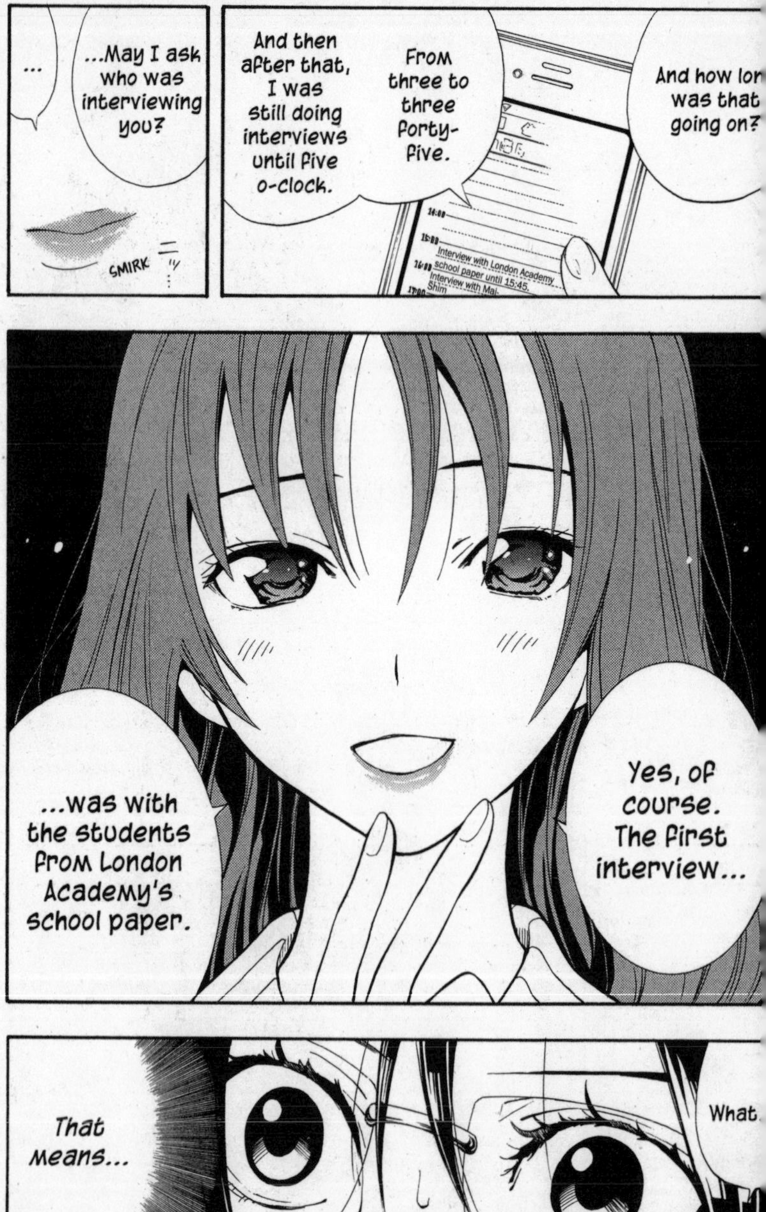
And how lo
was that
going on?
From three to three forty-five.
And then after that, I was still doing interviews until five o-clock.
14:00
15:00
Interview with London Academy school paper until 15:45.
16:00
Interview with Mai-Shim
17:00
...May I ask who was interviewing you?
...
SMIRK
Yes, of course. The first interview...
...was with the students from London Academy's school paper.
What
That means...

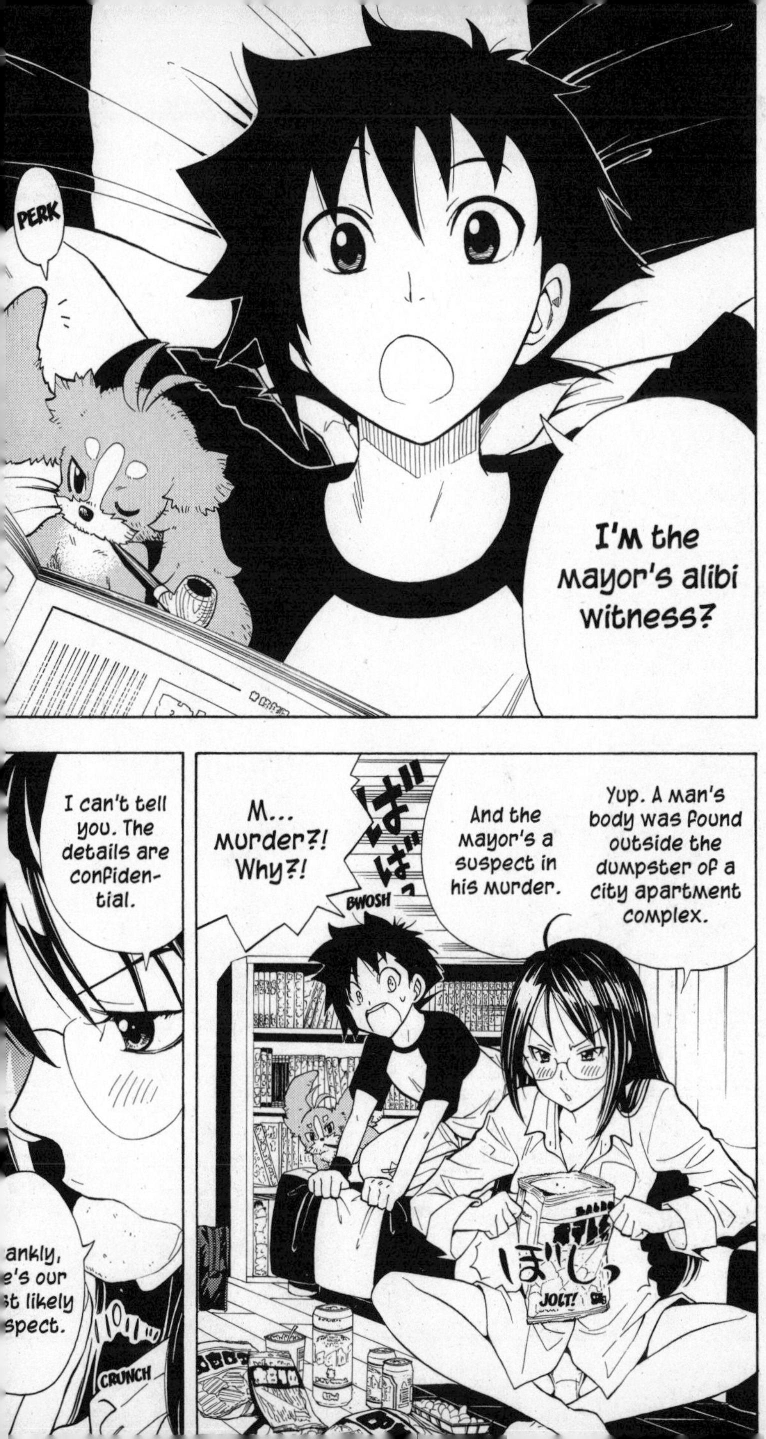
PERK
I'm the mayor's alibi witness?
Yup. A man's body was found outside the dumpster of a city apartment complex.
And the mayor's a suspect in his murder.
ばばっ
BWOSH
M... Murder?! Why?!
ぼりっ
JOLT!
I can't tell you. The details are confidential.
ankly, e's our st likely spect.
CRUNCH

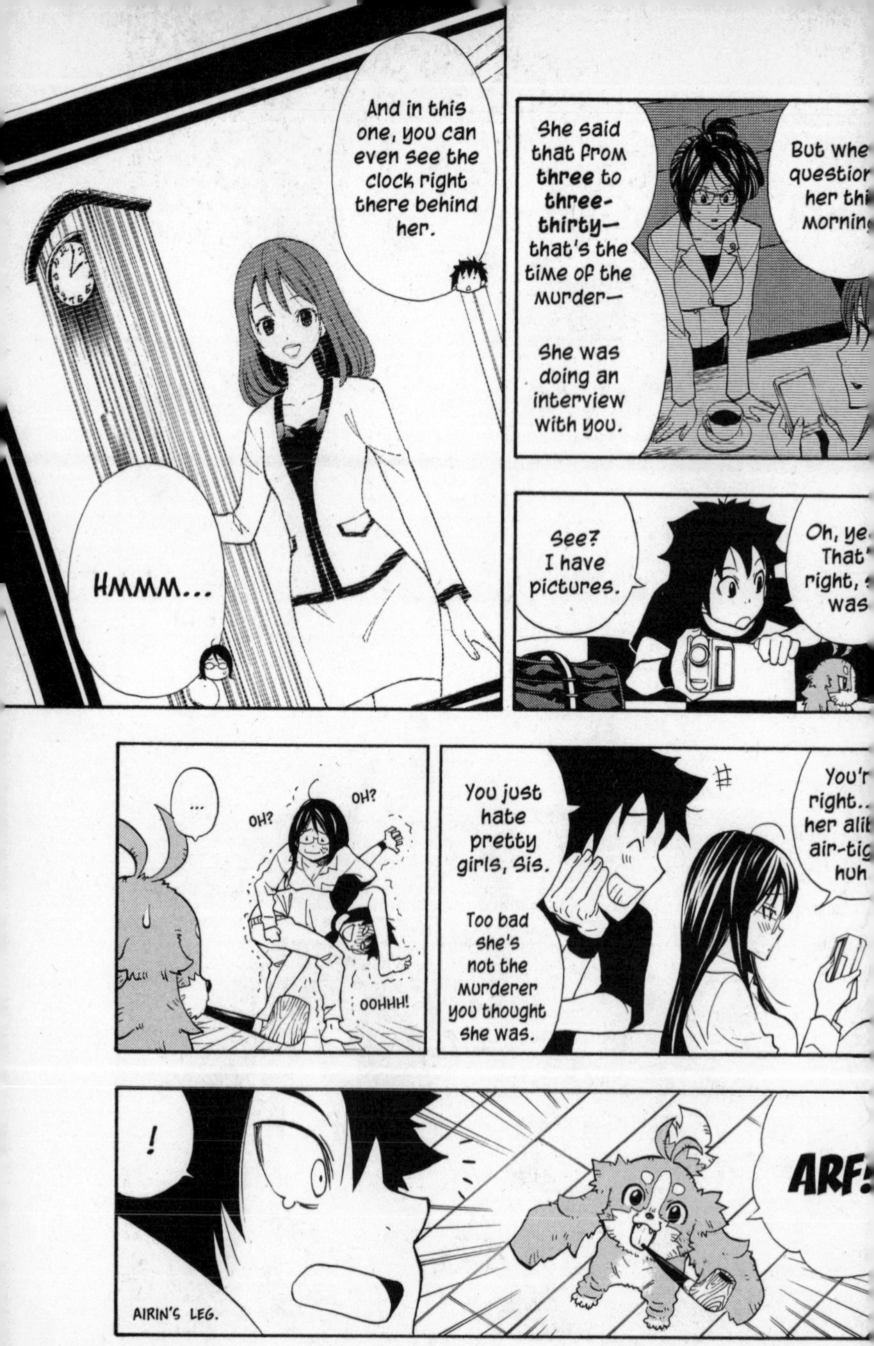
But whe
question
her thi
morning
She said that from three to three-thirty—that's the time of the murder—
She was doing an interview with you.
Oh, ye
That'
right,
was
See? I have pictures.
And in this one, you can even see the clock right there behind her.
HMMM...
You'r
right..
her alit
air-tig
huh
You just hate pretty girls, Sis.
Too bad she's not the murderer you thought she was.
OH?
OH?
...
OOHHH!
ARF!
!
AIRIN'S LEG.

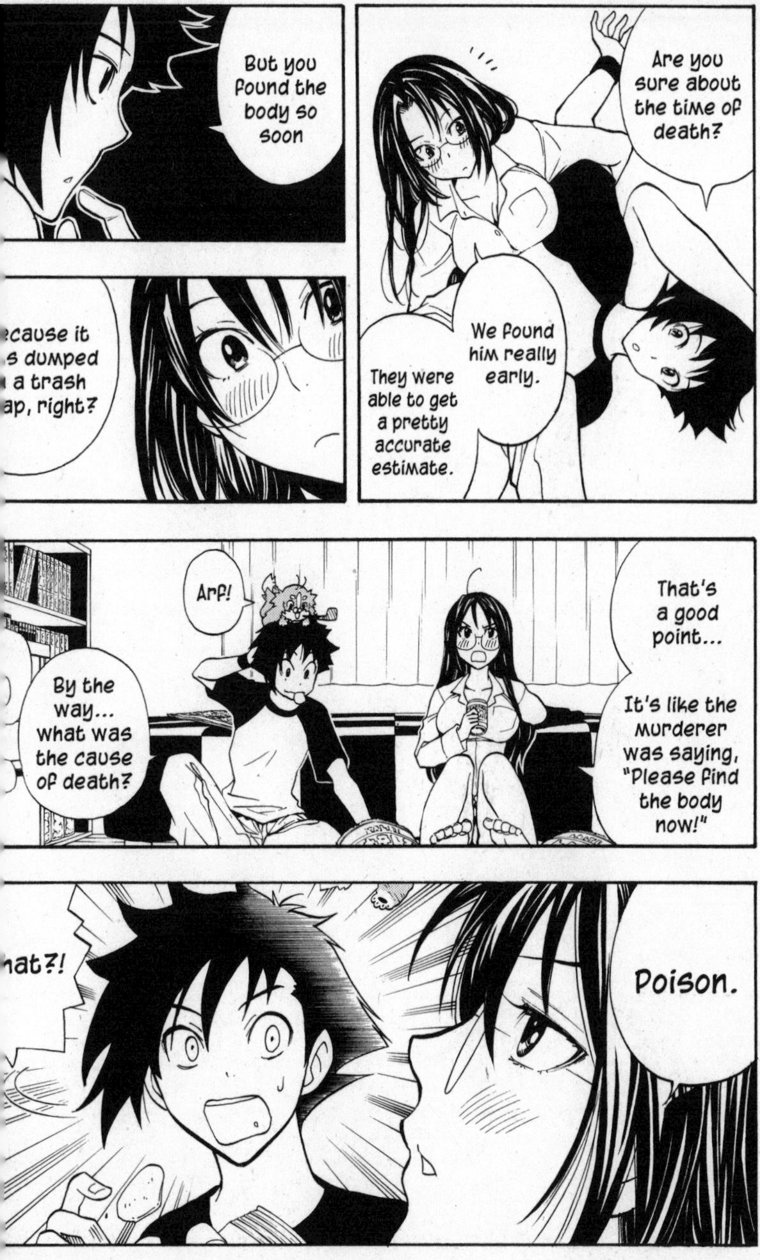

Are you sure about the time of death?
We found him really early.
They were able to get a pretty accurate estimate.
But you found the body so soon
ecause it s dumped a trash ap, right?
That's a good point...
It's like the murderer was saying, "Please find the body now!"
Arf!
By the way... what was the cause of death?
Poison.
hat?!

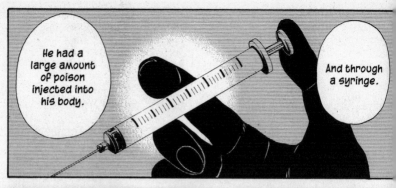

He had a large amount of poison injected into his body.
And through a syringe.
But there' one thing that gets me.
...
What?
↑ JERKY
Normally, if you were goin to inject poison int someone,
you would get him in the arm or the neck.
But Yakita, the victim,
was injected here, in the leg.
I see
...
Even if you suddenly decided to attack him, you wouldn't get him in the shin.
Right, exactly.
...To be honest,

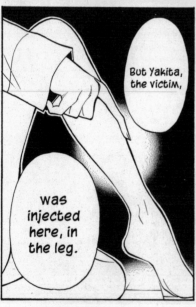

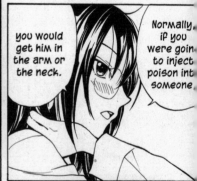

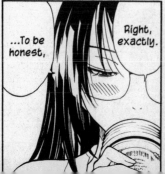

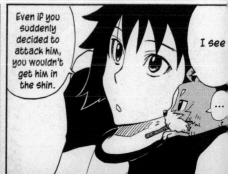

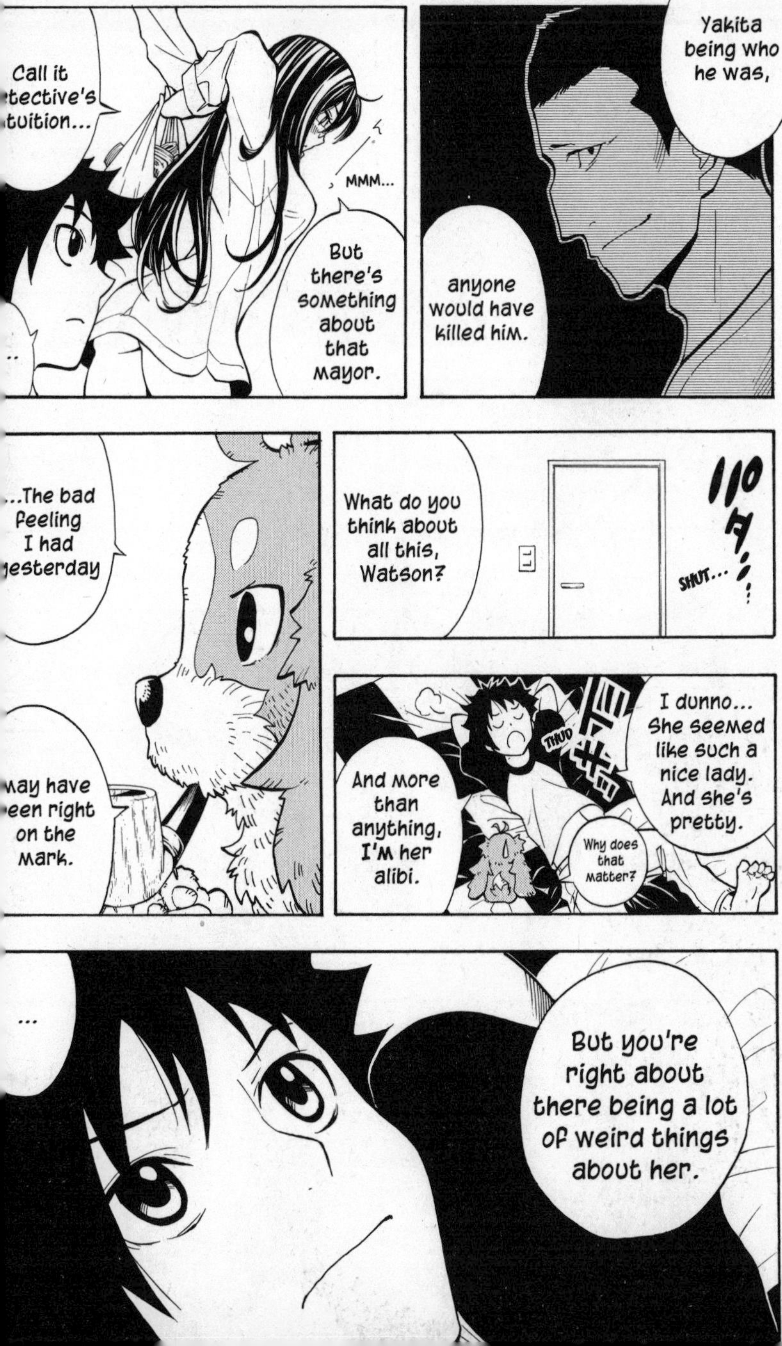
Yakita being who he was,
anyone would have killed him.
MMM...
But there's something about that mayor.
Call it
tective's
tuition...
..
SHUT...
What do you think about all this, Watson?
I dunno... She seemed like such a nice lady. And she's pretty.
THUD
Why does that matter?
And more than anything, I'm her alibi.
...The bad feeling I had
esterday
ay have
een right on the mark.
But you're right about there being a lot of weird things about her.
...

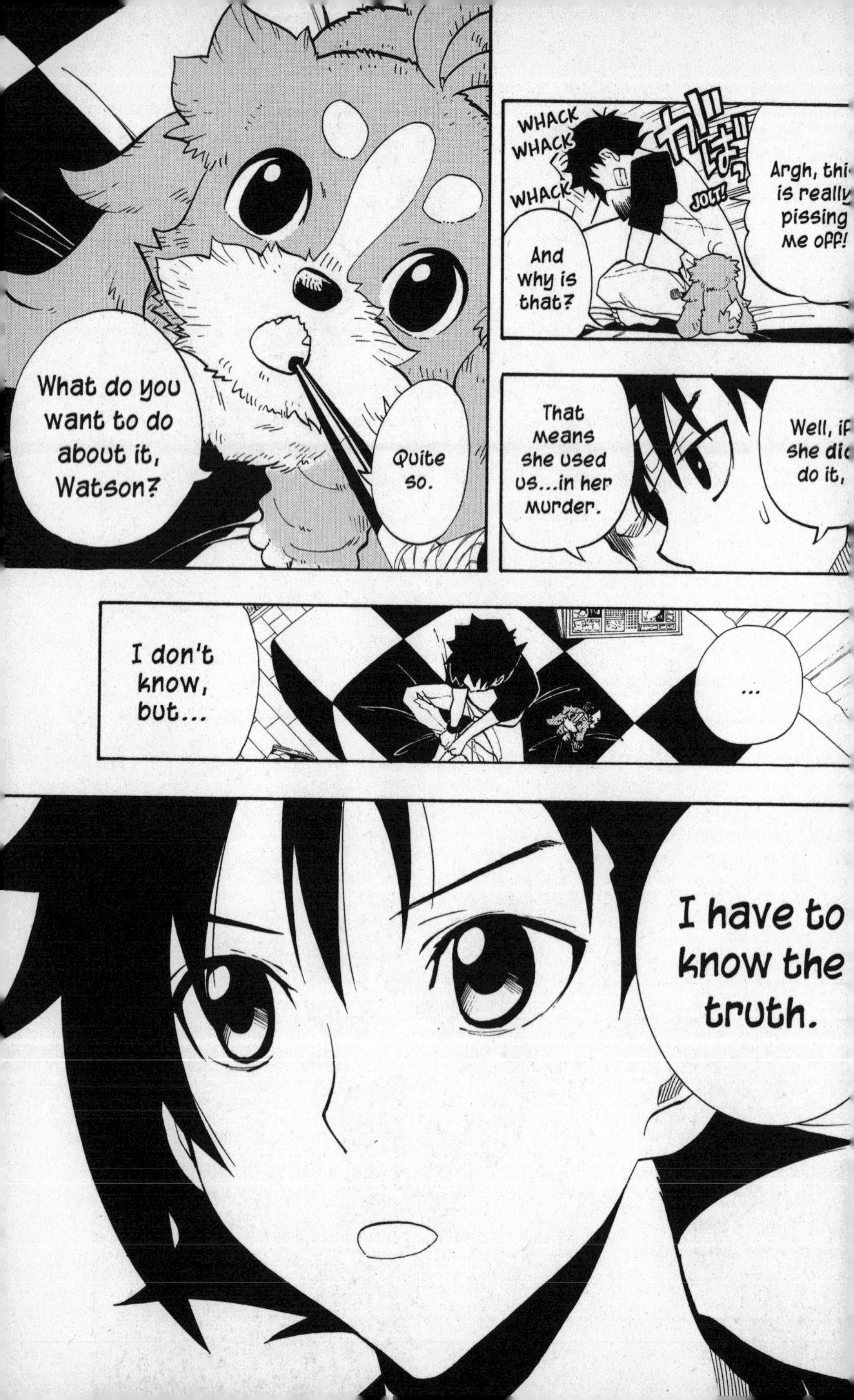

Argh, thi is really pissing me off!
JOLT!
WHACK
WHACK
WHACK
And why is that?
Well, if she di do it,
That means she used us...in her murder.
Quite so.
What do you want to do about it, Watson?
...
I don't know, but...
I have to know the truth.

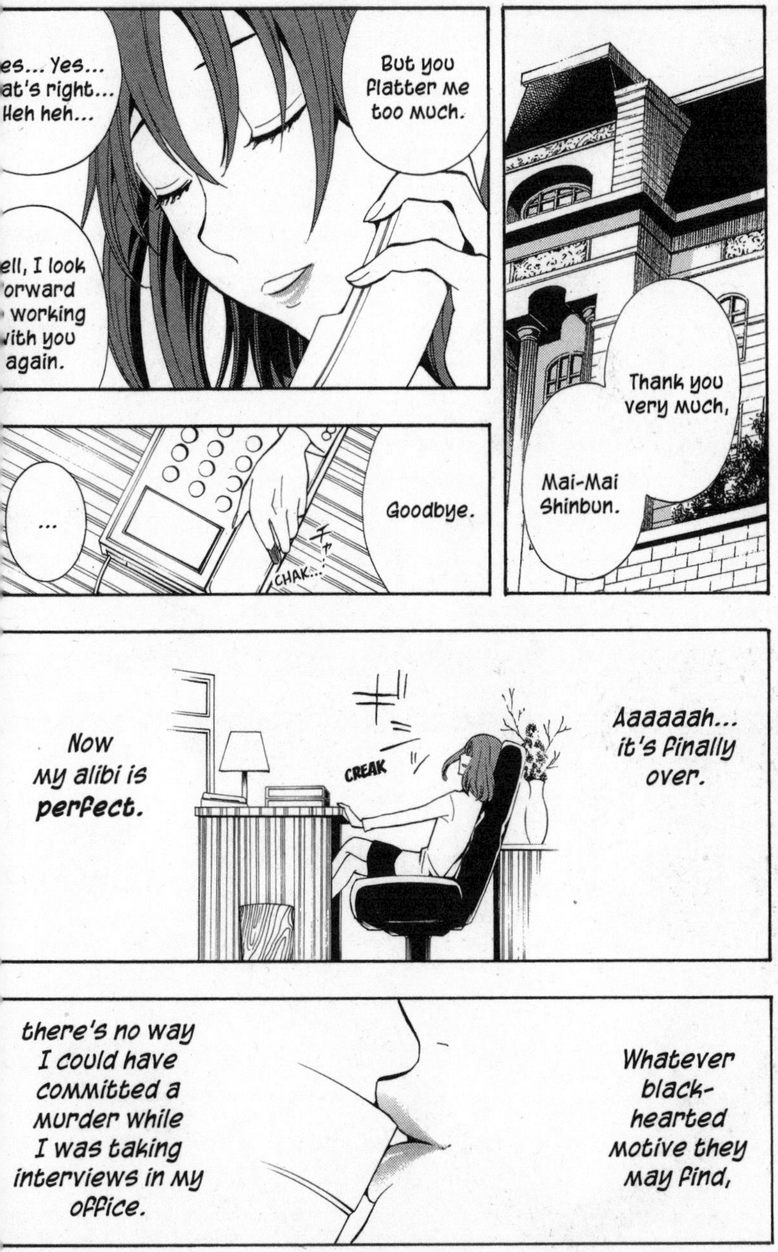
Thank you very much,
Mai-Mai Shinbun.
But you flatter me too much.
es... Yes... at's right... Heh heh...
ell, I look orward working with you again.
Goodbye.
チャ...
CHAK...
...
Aaaaaah... it's finally over.
CREAK
Now my alibi is perfect.
Whatever black-hearted motive they may find,
there's no way I could have committed a murder while I was taking interviews in my office.

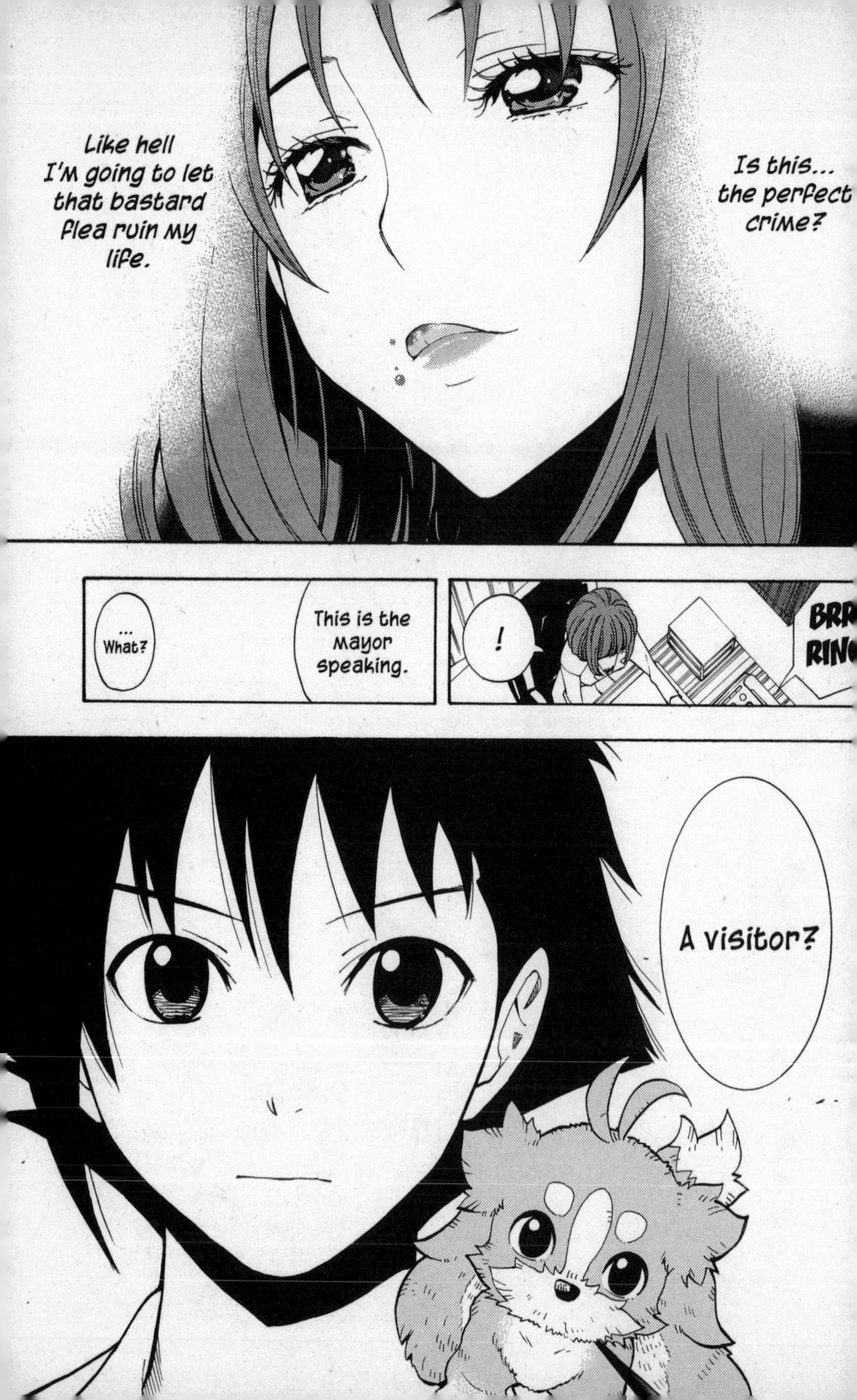
Is this... the perfect crime?
Like hell I'm going to let that bastard flea ruin my life.
BRR
RIN
!
This is the mayor speaking.
... What?
A visitor?

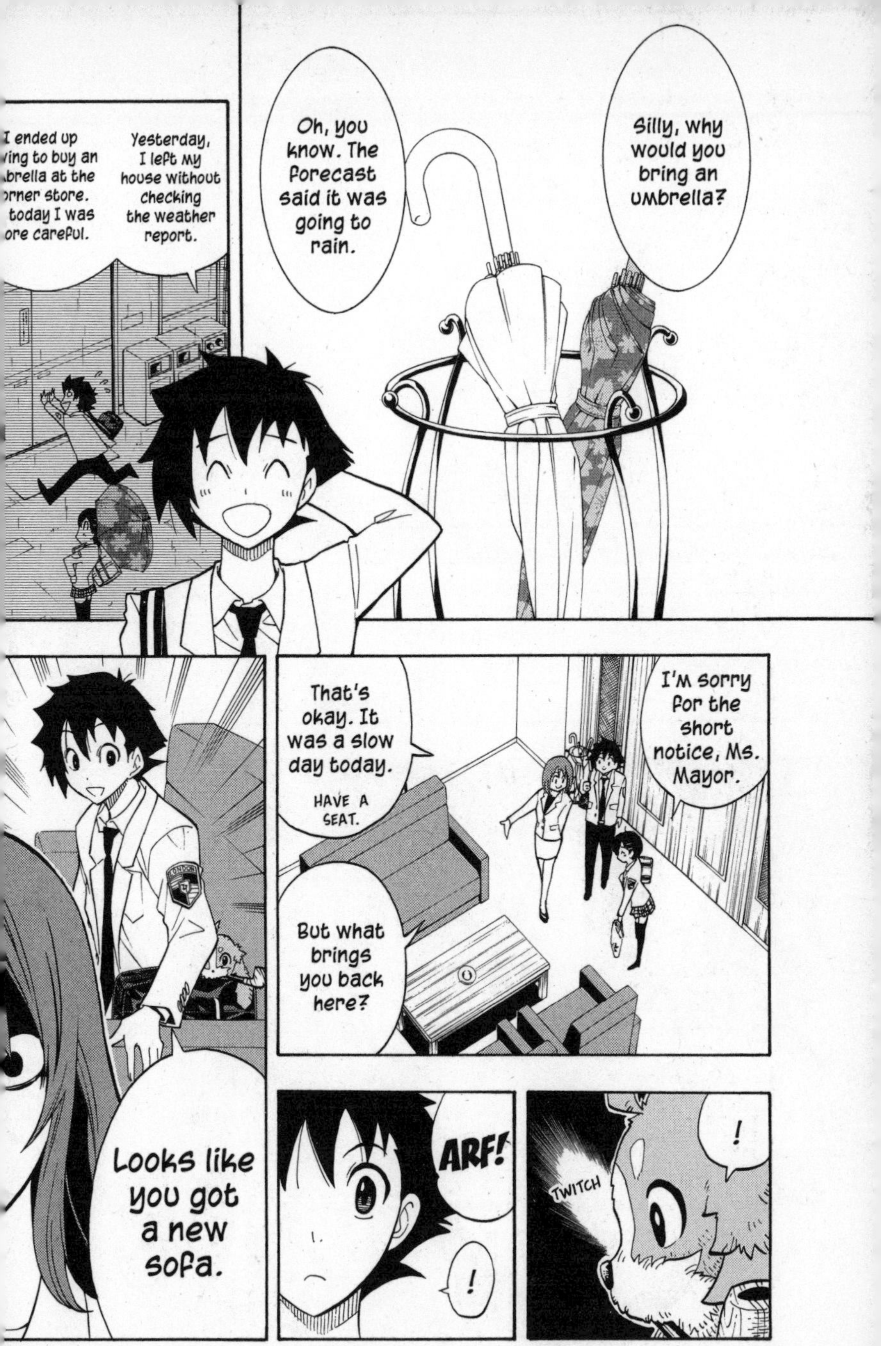
Silly, why would you bring an umbrella?
Oh, you know. The forecast said it was going to rain.
Yesterday, I left my house without checking the weather report.
I ended up ving to buy an brella at the rner store. today I was ore careful.
I'm sorry for the short notice, Ms. Mayor.
That's okay. It was a slow day today.
HAVE A SEAT.
But what brings you back here?
!
TWITCH
ARF!
!
Looks like you got a new sofa.

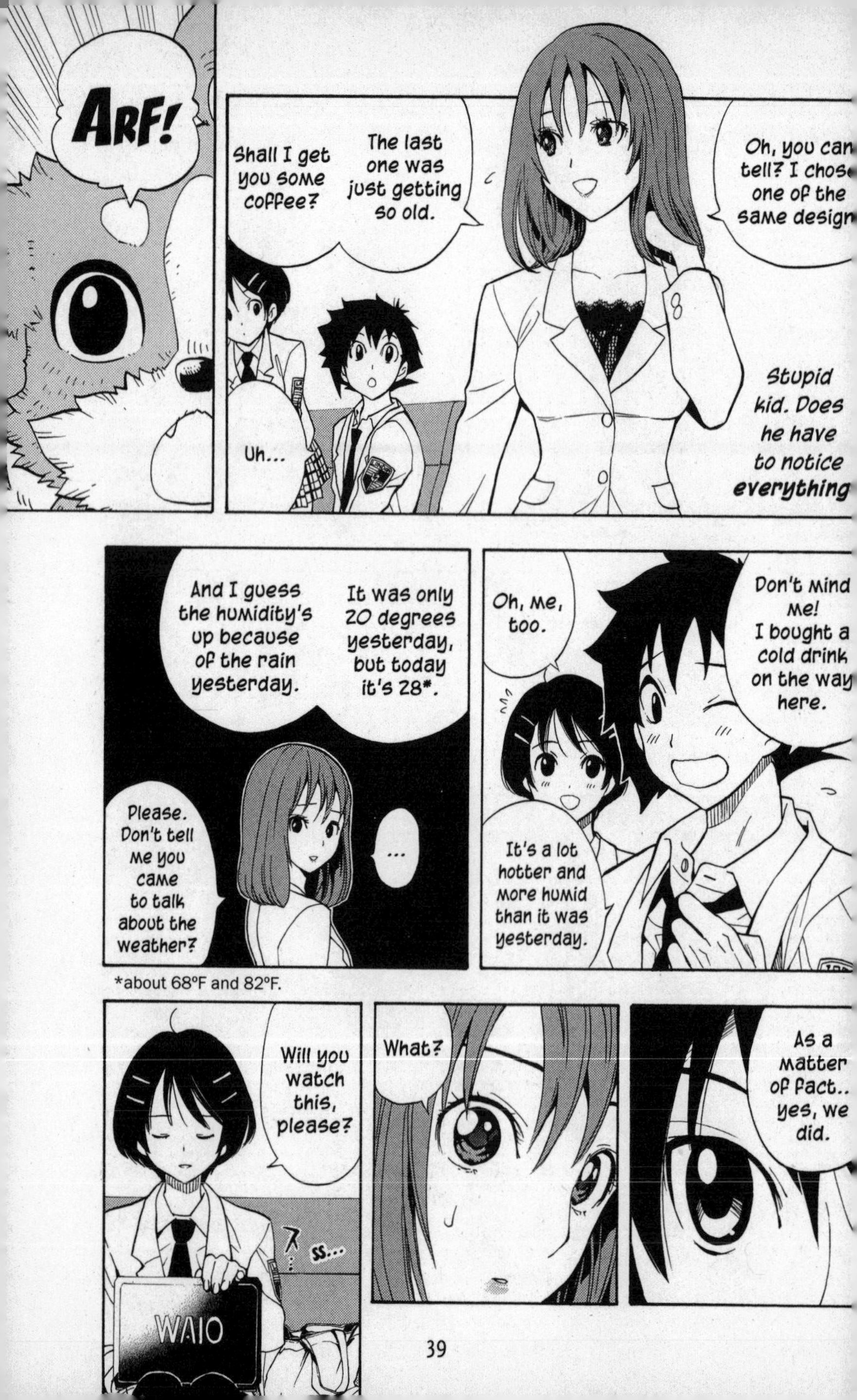

Oh, you can tell? I chos one of the same design
Stupid kid. Does he have to notice everything
The last one was just getting so old.
Shall I get you some coffee?
Uh...
ARF!
Don't mind me! I bought a cold drink on the way here.
Oh, me, too.
It's a lot hotter and more humid than it was yesterday.
It was only 20 degrees yesterday, but today it's 28*.
And I guess the humidity's up because of the rain yesterday.
...
Please. Don't tell me you came to talk about the weather?
As a matter of fact.. yes, we did.
What?
Will you watch this, please?
ss...
WAIO

*about 68°F and 82°F.

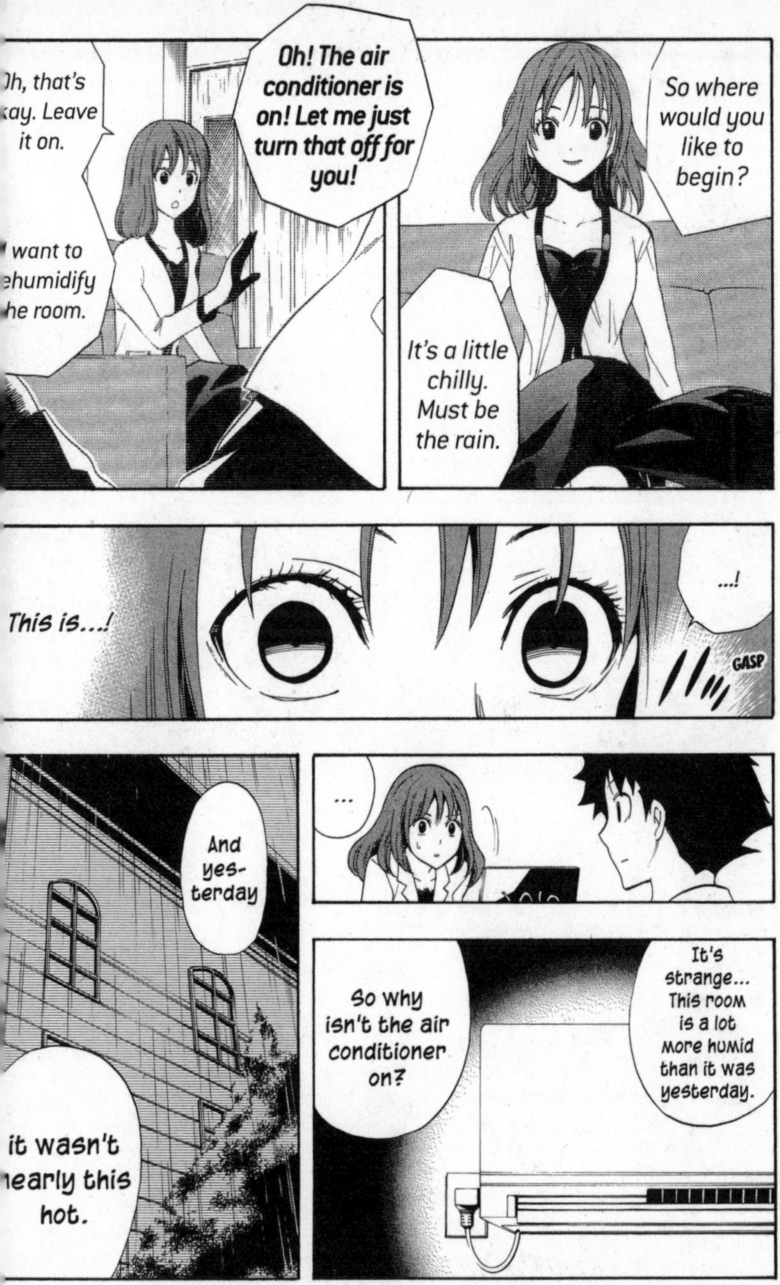
So where would you like to begin?
It's a little chilly. Must be the rain.
Oh! The air conditioner is on! Let me just turn that off for you!
h, that's ay. Leave it on.
want to ehumidify he room.
...!
GASP
This is...!
...
It's strange... This room is a lot more humid than it was yesterday.
So why isn't the air conditioner on?
And yes-terday
it wasn't early this hot.

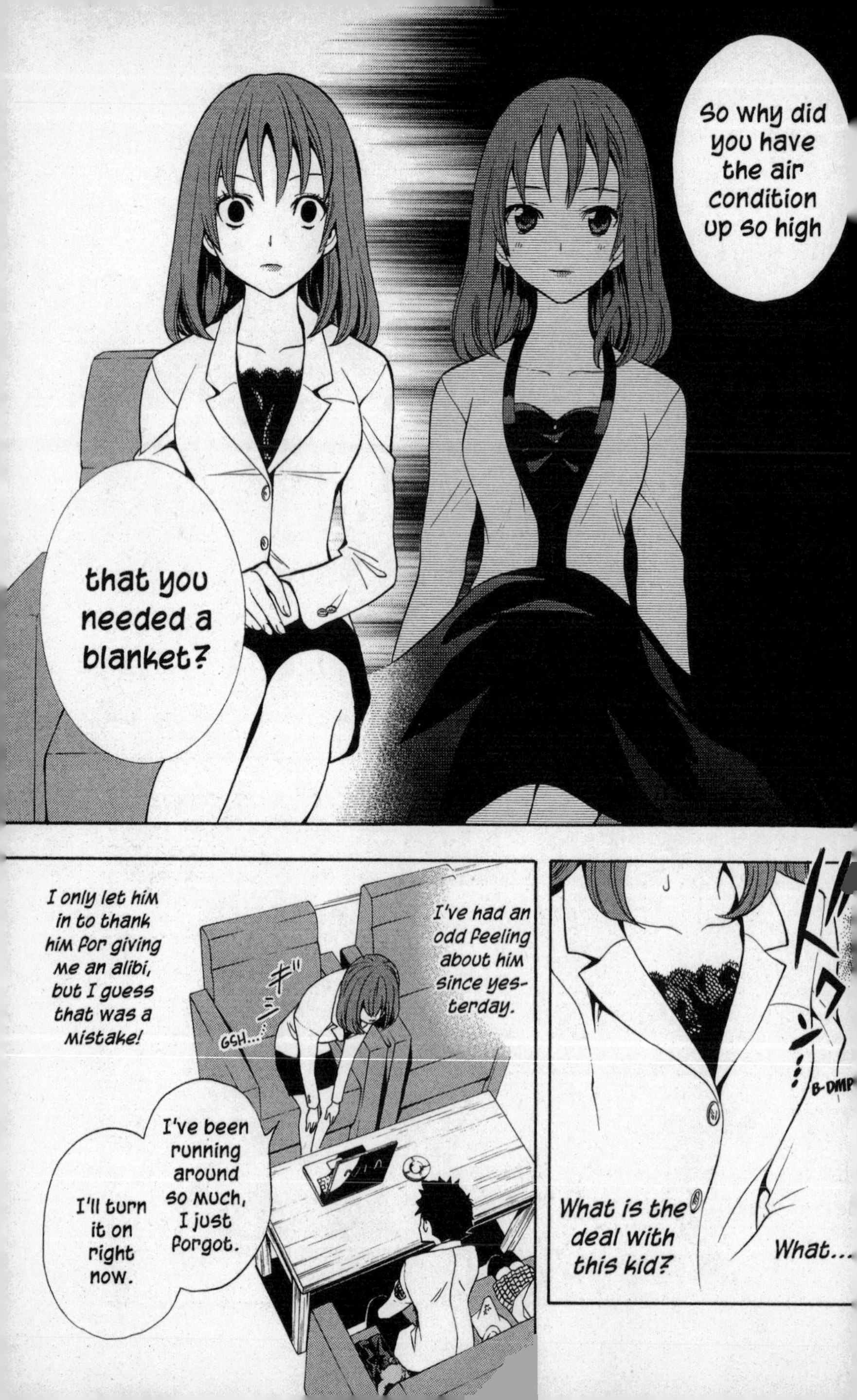
So why did you have the air condition up so high
that you needed a blanket?
B-DMP
What...
What is the deal with this kid?
I've had an odd feeling about him since yesterday.
I only let him in to thank him for giving me an alibi, but I guess that was a mistake!
GSH...
I've been running around so much, I just forgot.
I'll turn it on right now.

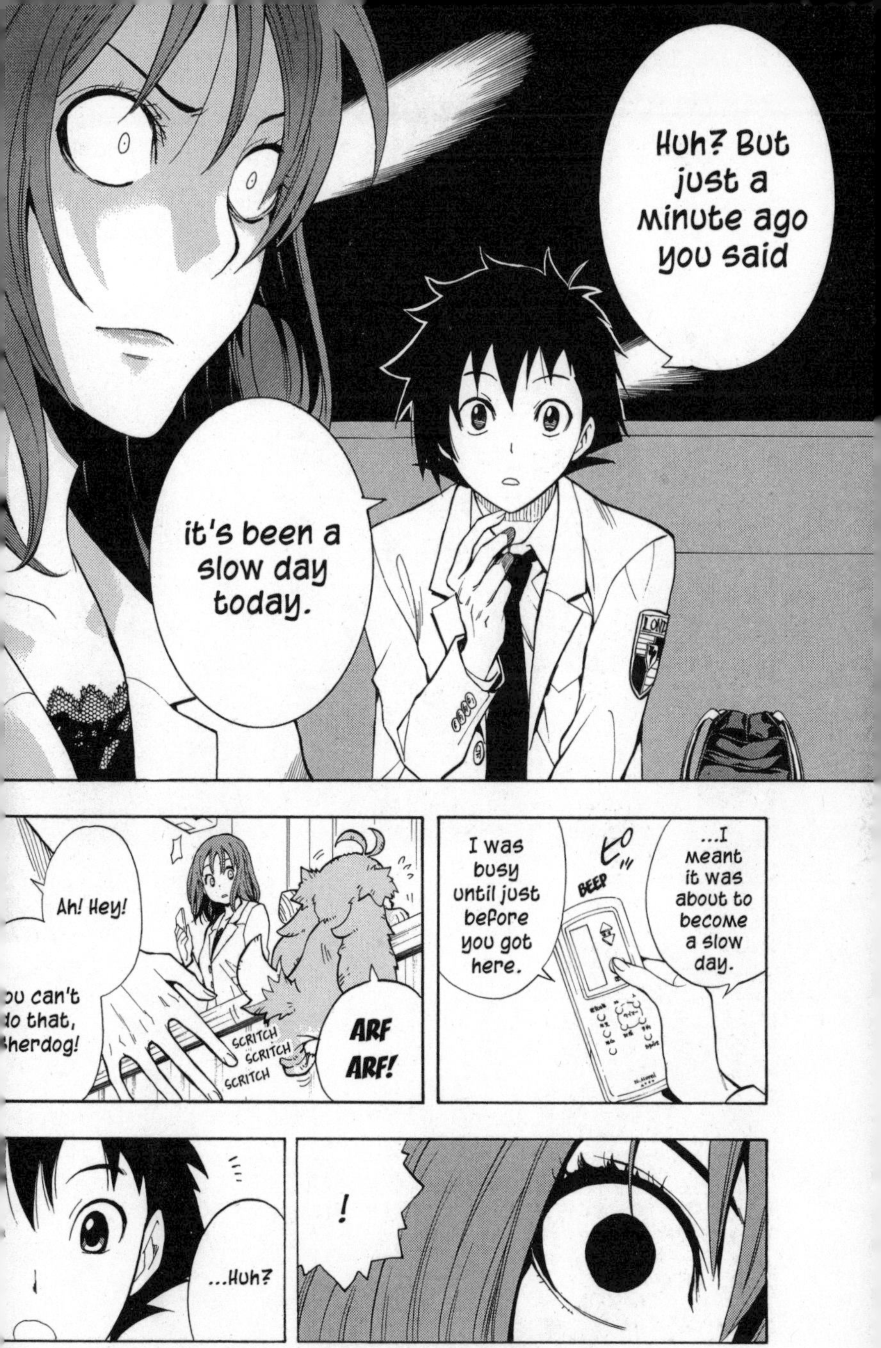
Huh? But just a minute ago you said
it's been a slow day today.
...I meant it was about to become a slow day.
BEEP
I was busy until just before you got here.
Ah! Hey!
ARF ARF!
SCRITCH SCRITCH SCRITCH
ou can't o that, herdog!
!
...Huh?

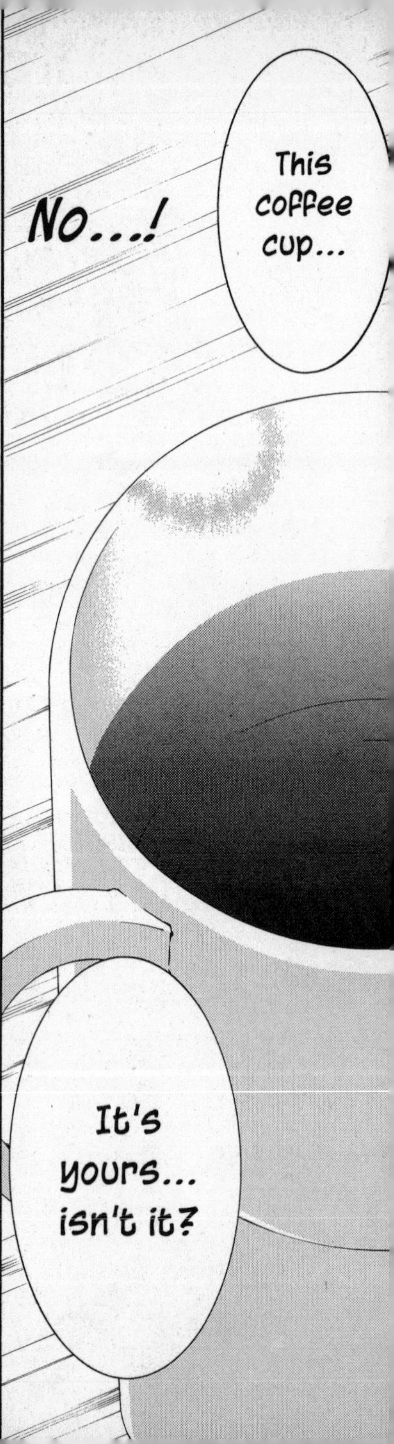
This coffee cup...
No...!
It's yours... isn't it?
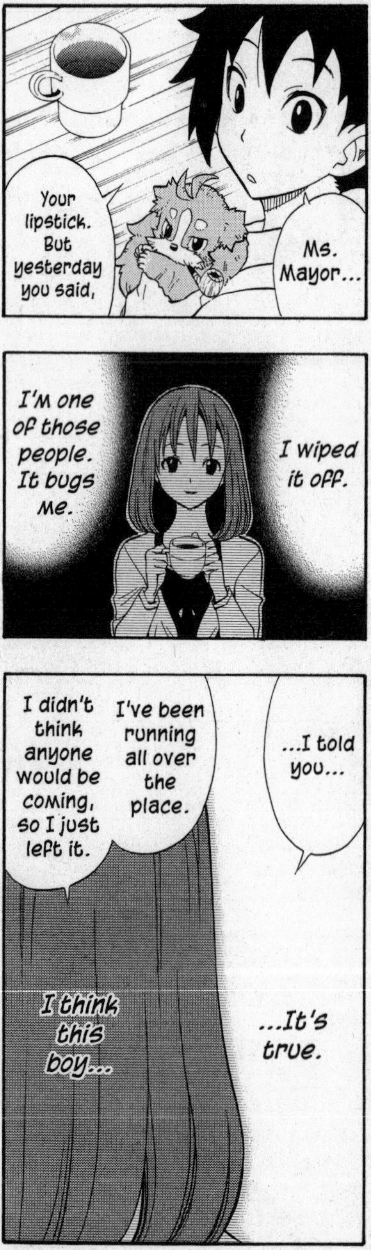
Ms. Mayor...
Your lipstick. But yesterday you said,
I wiped it off.
I'm one of those people. It bugs me.
...I told you...
I've been running all over the place.
I didn't think anyone would be coming, so I just left it.
...It's true.
I think this boy...

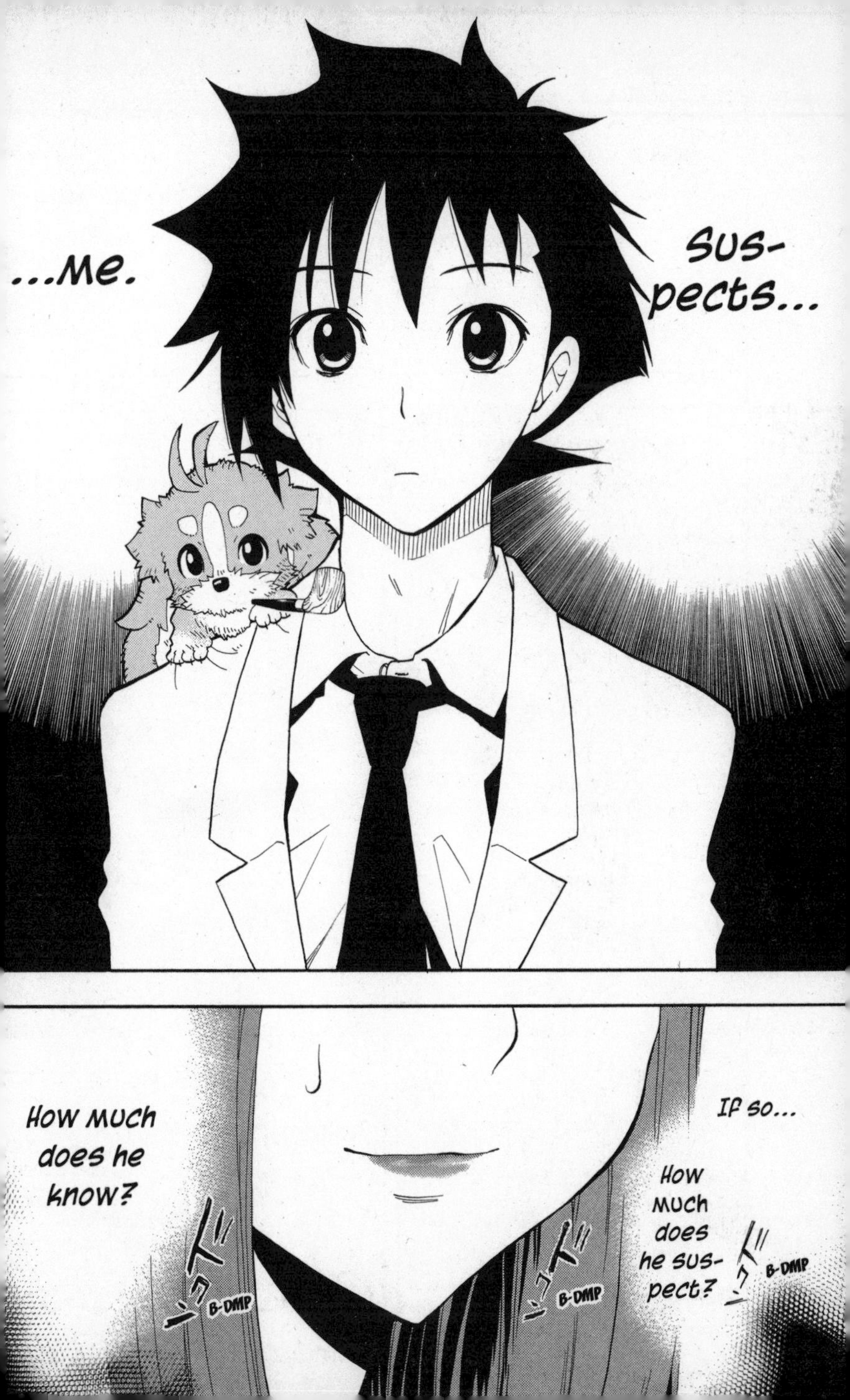
Sus-
pects...
...Me.
If so...
How much does he suspect?
B-DMP
How much does he know?
B-DMP
B-DMP

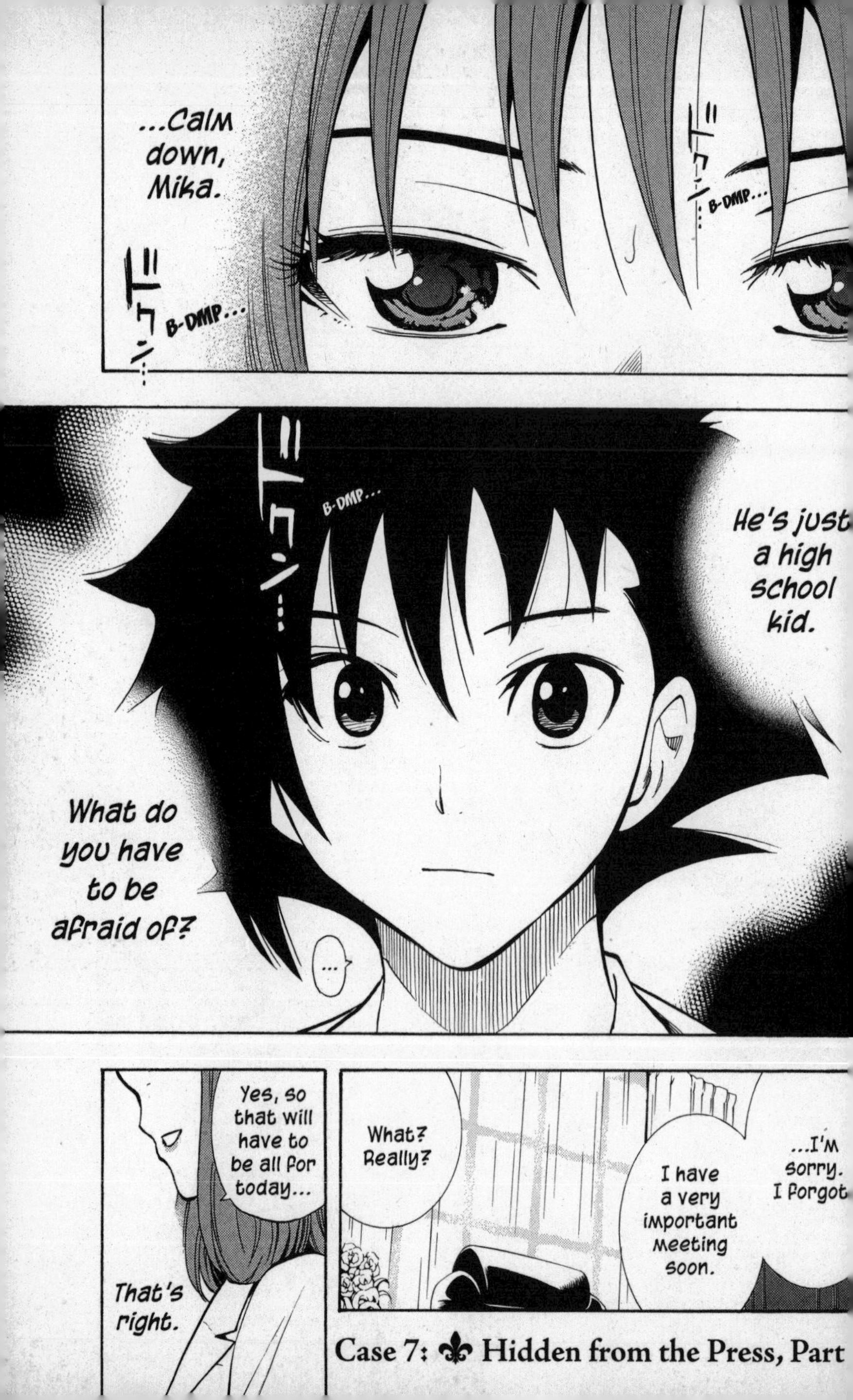
...Calm down, Mika.
ドクン…
B-DMP...
ドクン…
B-DMP...
ドクン…
B-DMP...
He's just a high school kid.
What do you have to be afraid of?
...
...I'm sorry. I forgot
I have a very important meeting soon.
What? Really?
Yes, so that will have to be all for today...
That's right.

Case 7: ⚜ Hidden from the Press, Part

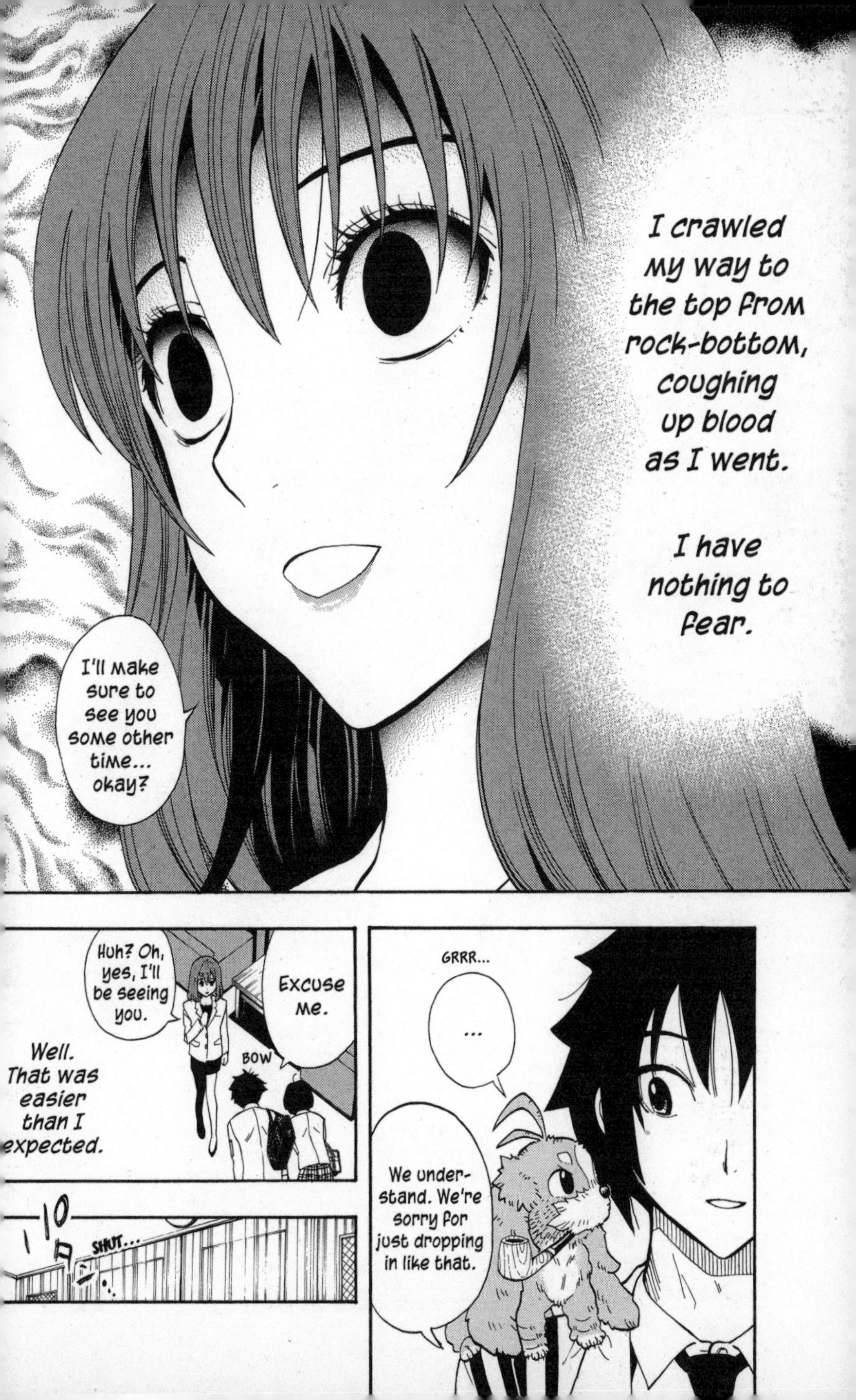
I crawled my way to the top from rock-bottom, coughing up blood as I went.
I have nothing to fear.
I'll make sure to see you some other time... okay?
GRRR...
...
We under-stand. We're sorry for just dropping in like that.
Excuse me.
BOW
Huh? Oh, yes, I'll be seeing you.
Well. That was easier than I expected.
SHUT...

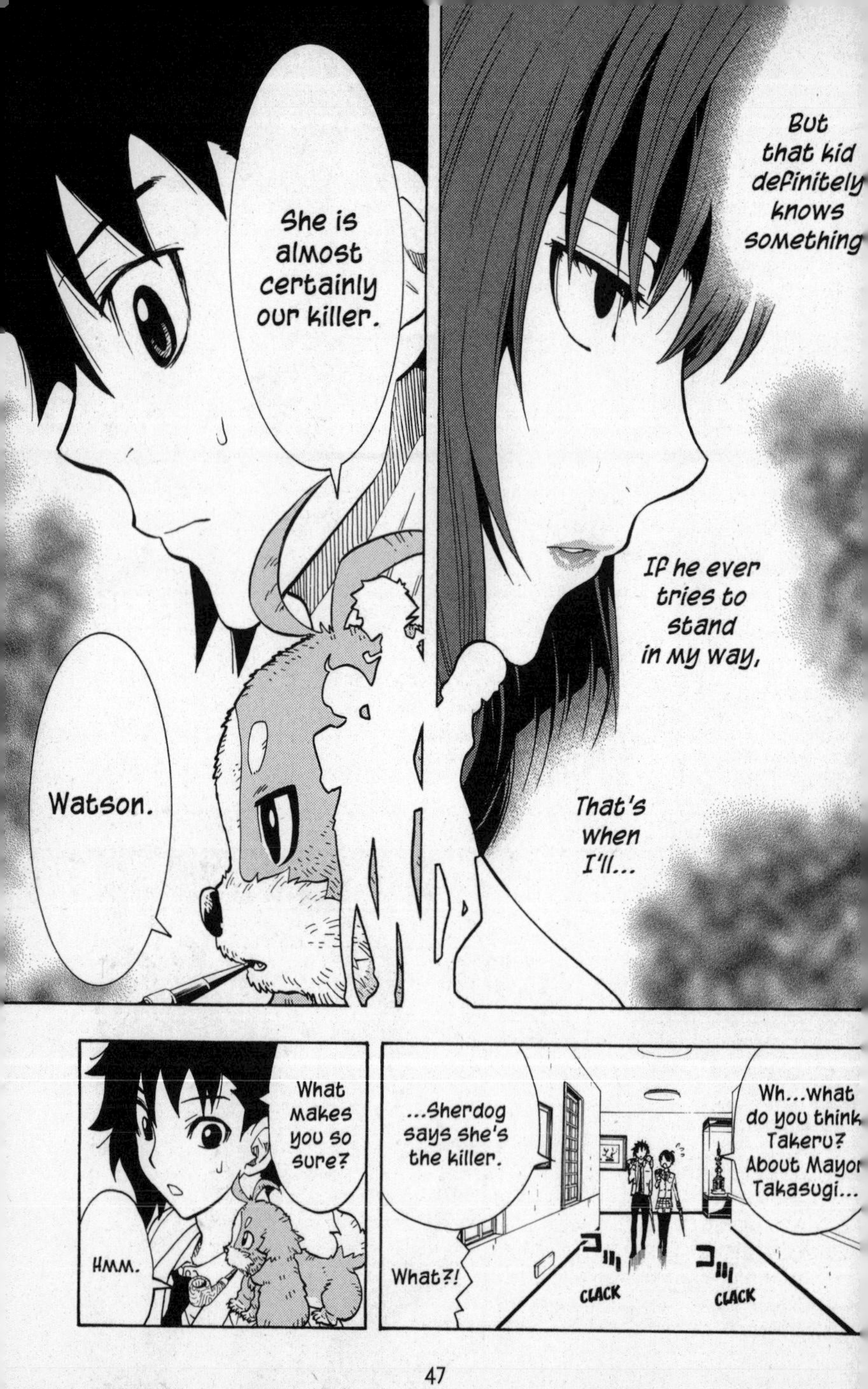
But that kid definitely knows something
If he ever tries to stand in my way,
That's when I'll...
She is almost certainly our killer.
Watson.
Wh...what do you think, Takeru? About Mayor Takasugi...
...Sherdog says she's the killer.
What?!
CLACK
CLACK
What makes you so sure?
Hmm.

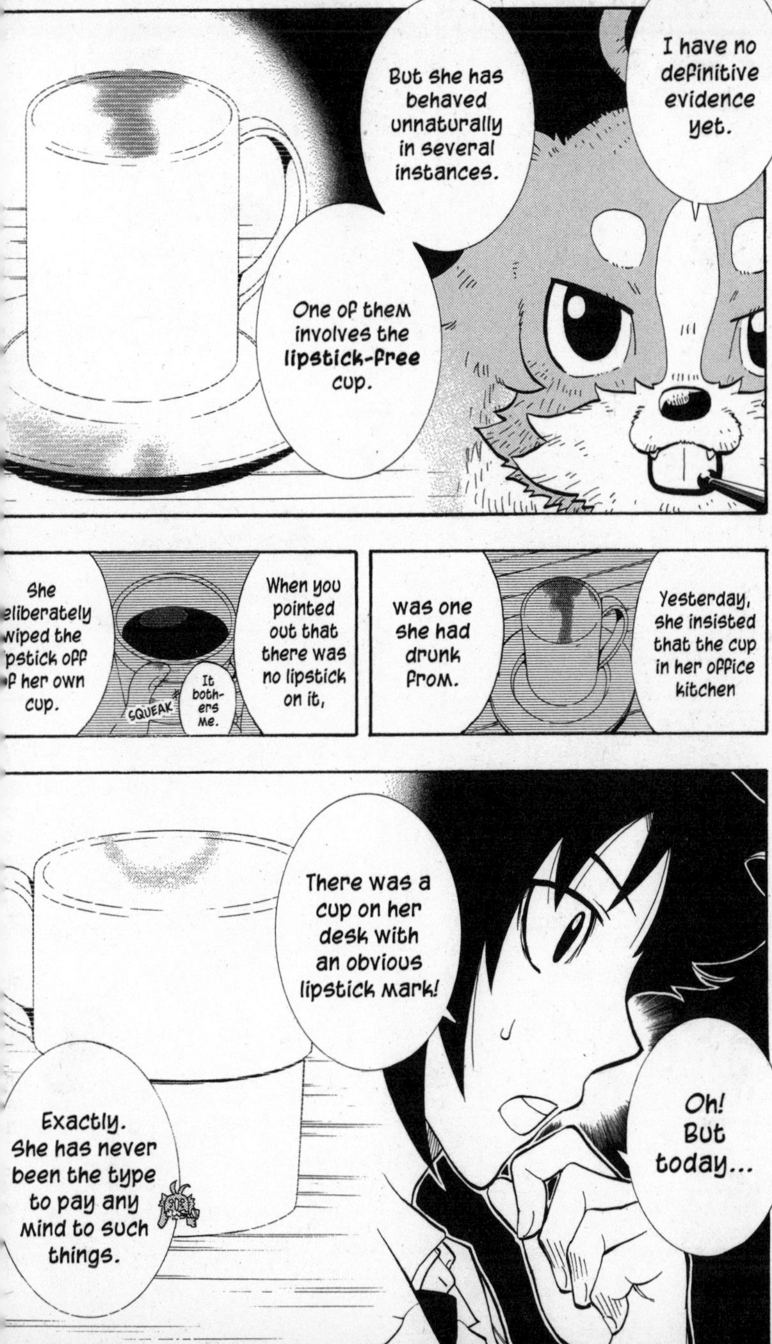
I have no definitive evidence yet.
But she has behaved unnaturally in several instances.
One of them involves the lipstick-free cup.
Yesterday, she insisted that the cup in her office kitchen
was one she had drunk from.
When you pointed out that there was no lipstick on it,
It bothers me.
SQUEAK
She eliberately wiped the pstick off f her own cup.
Oh! But today...
There was a cup on her desk with an obvious lipstick mark!
Exactly. She has never been the type to pay any mind to such things.

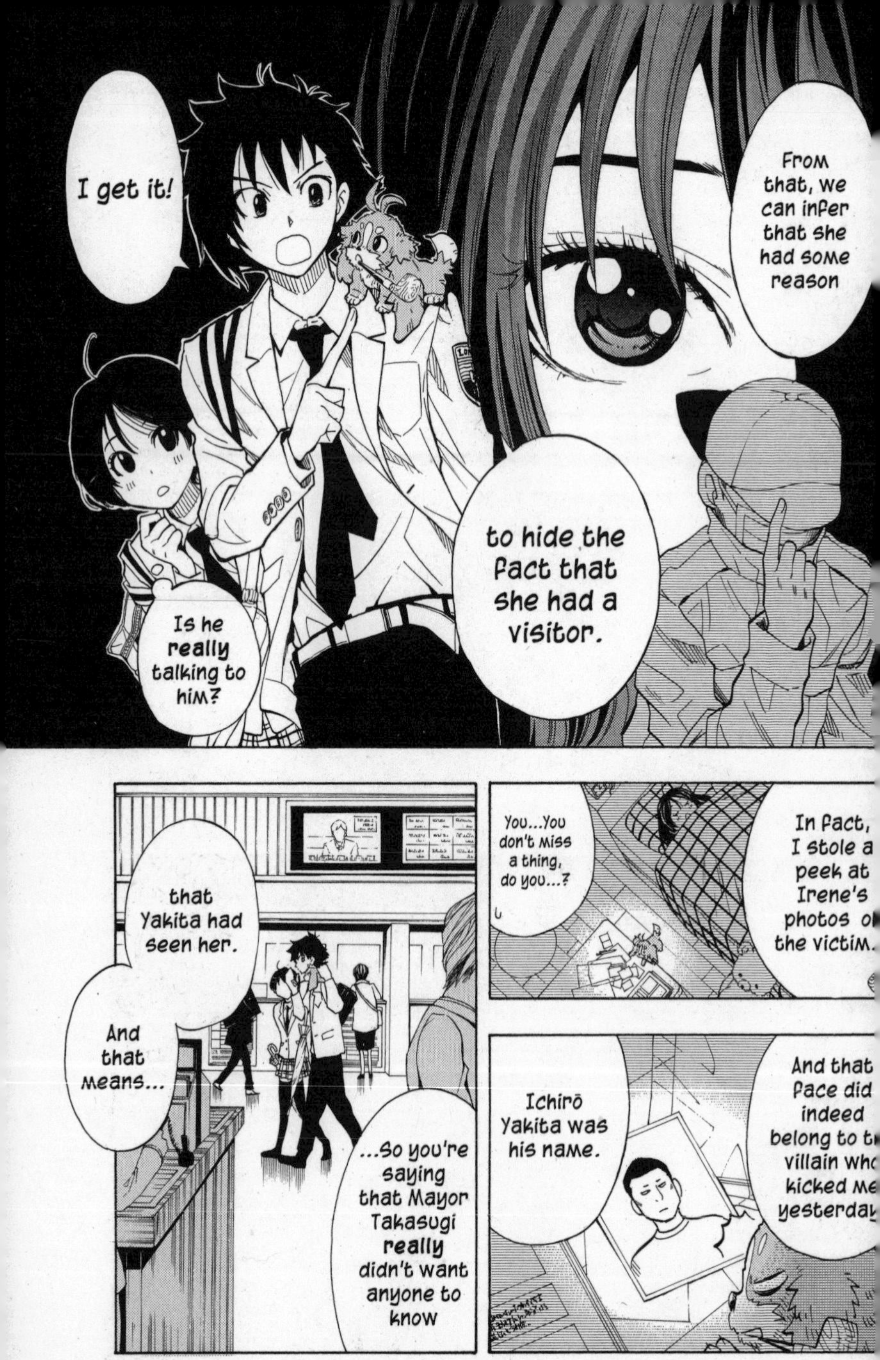

From that, we can infer that she had some reason
to hide the fact that she had a visitor.
I get it!
Is he really talking to him?
In fact, I stole a peek at Irene's photos o the victim.
You...You don't miss a thing, do you...?
And that face did indeed belong to t villain wh kicked me yesterda
Ichirō Yakita was his name.
...So you're saying that Mayor Takasugi really didn't want anyone to know
that Yakita had seen her.
And that means...

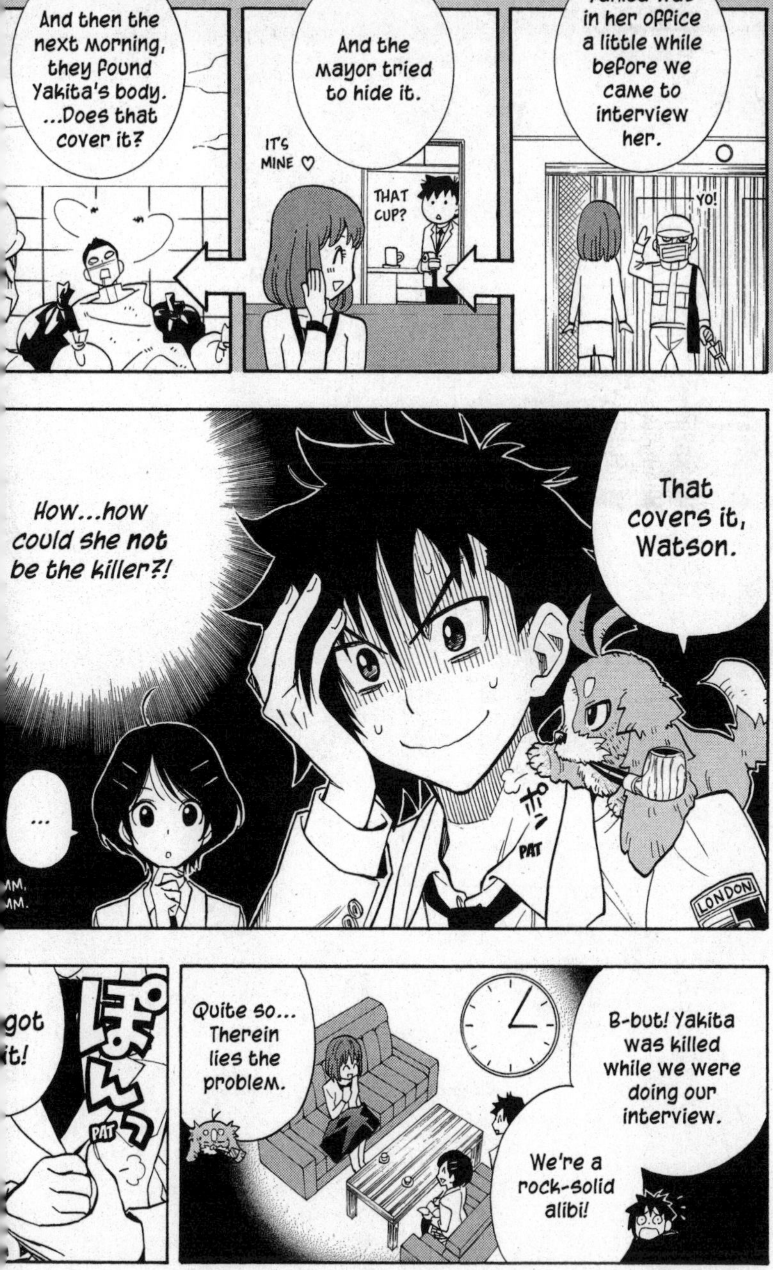

Yakita was in her office a little while before we came to interview her.
YO!
And the mayor tried to hide it.
IT'S MINE ♡
THAT CUP?
And then the next morning, they found Yakita's body. ...Does that cover it?
That covers it, Watson.
ポン
PAT
LONDON
How...how could she not be the killer?!
...
B-but! Yakita was killed while we were doing our interview.
We're a rock-solid alibi!
Quite so... Therein lies the problem.
ぽんっ
PAT

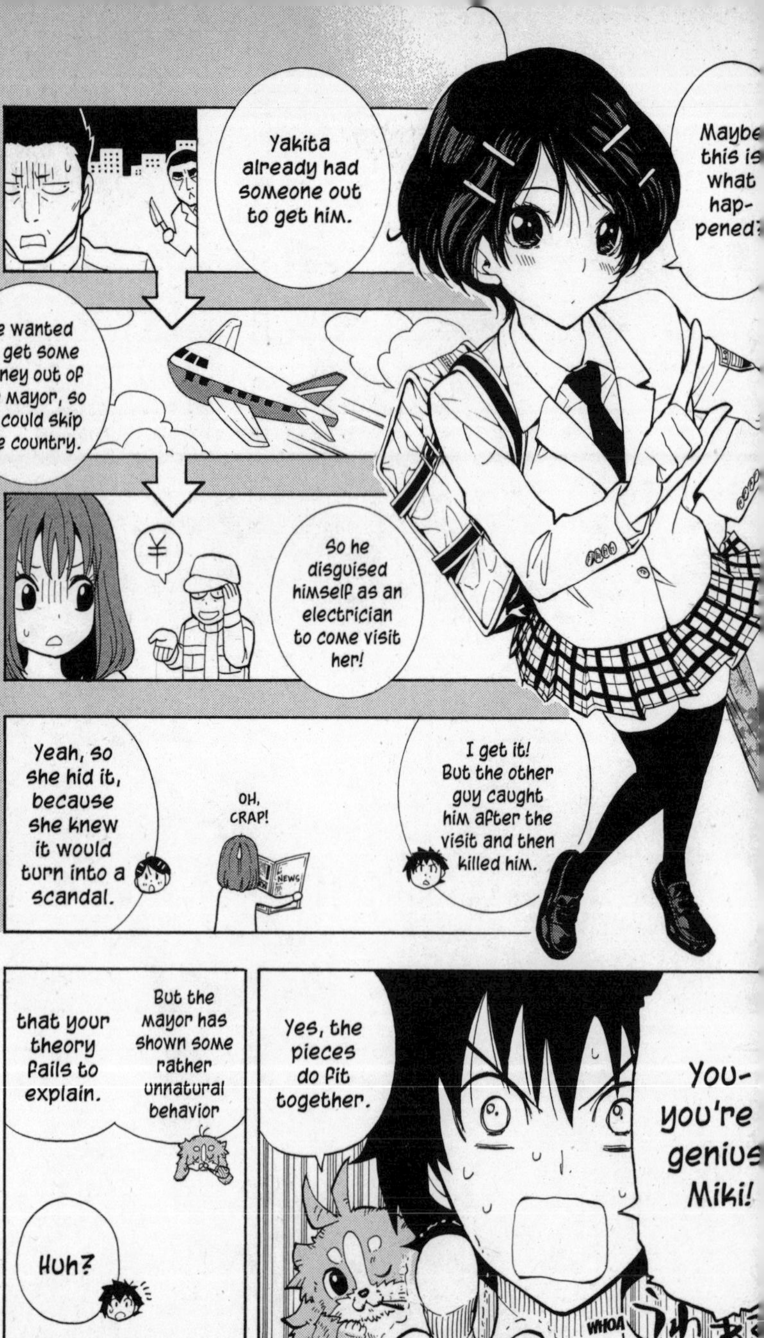
Maybe this is what hap- pened?
Yakita already had someone out to get him.
He wanted to get some money out of the mayor, so he could skip the country.
¥
So he disguised himself as an electrician to come visit her!
I get it! But the other guy caught him after the visit and then killed him.
OH, CRAP!
NEWS
Yeah, so she hid it, because she knew it would turn into a scandal.
You- you're genius Miki!
WHOA
Yes, the pieces do fit together.
But the mayor has shown some rather unnatural behavior
that your theory fails to explain.
Huh?

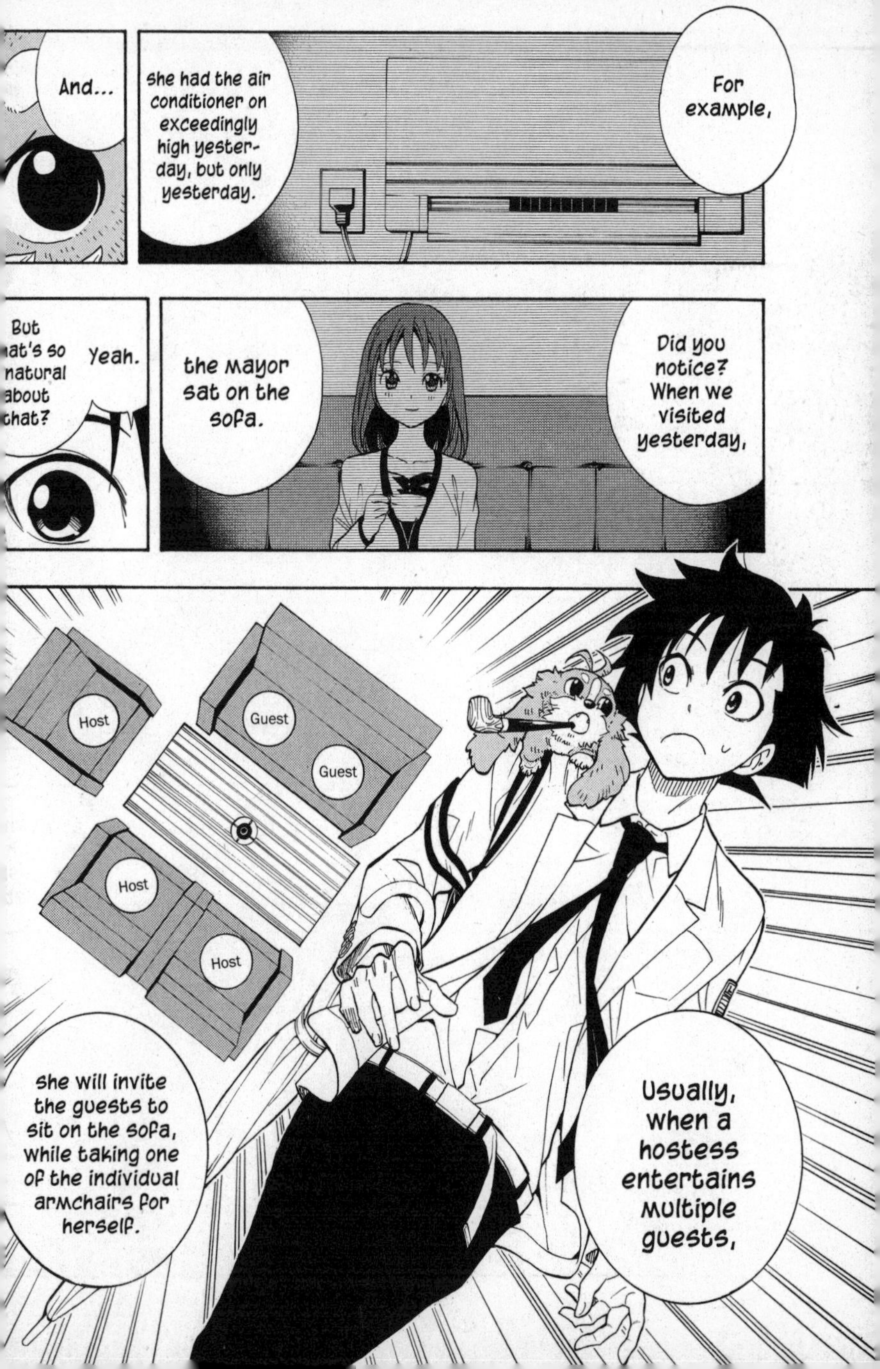

For example,
she had the air conditioner on exceedingly high yesterday, but only yesterday.
And...
Did you notice? When we visited yesterday,
the mayor sat on the sofa.
Yeah.
But at's so natural about hat?
Host
Guest
Guest
Host
Host
Usually, when a hostess entertains multiple guests,
she will invite the guests to sit on the sofa, while taking one of the individual armchairs for herself.

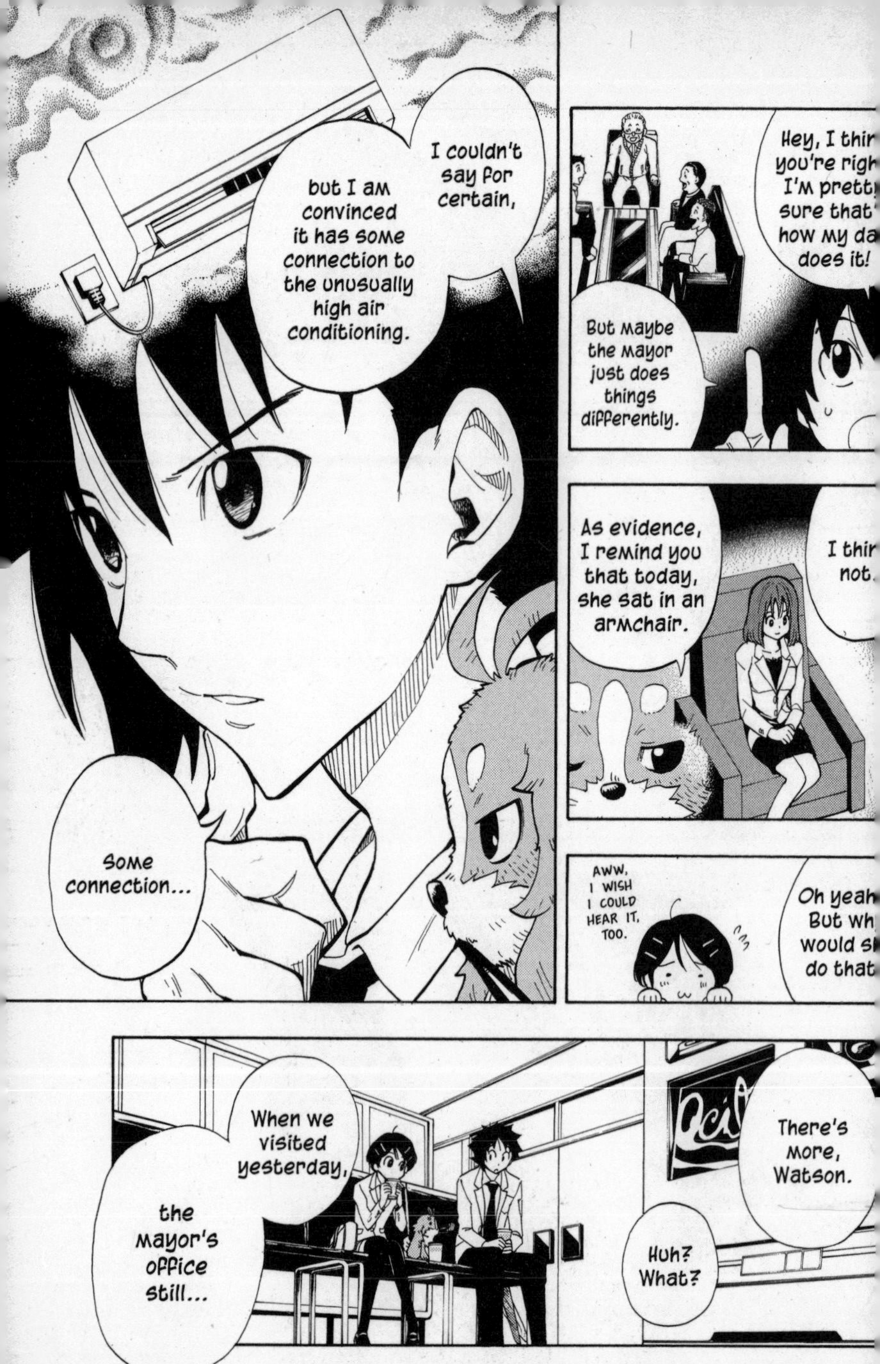
Hey, I thir you're righ I'm prett sure that how my da does it!
But maybe the mayor just does things differently.
I thir not.
As evidence, I remind you that today, she sat in an armchair.
Oh yeah But wh would s do that
AWW, I WISH I COULD HEAR IT, TOO.
I couldn't say for certain,
but I am convinced it has some connection to the unusually high air conditioning.
Some connection...
There's more, Watson.
Huh? What?
When we visited yesterday,
the mayor's office still...

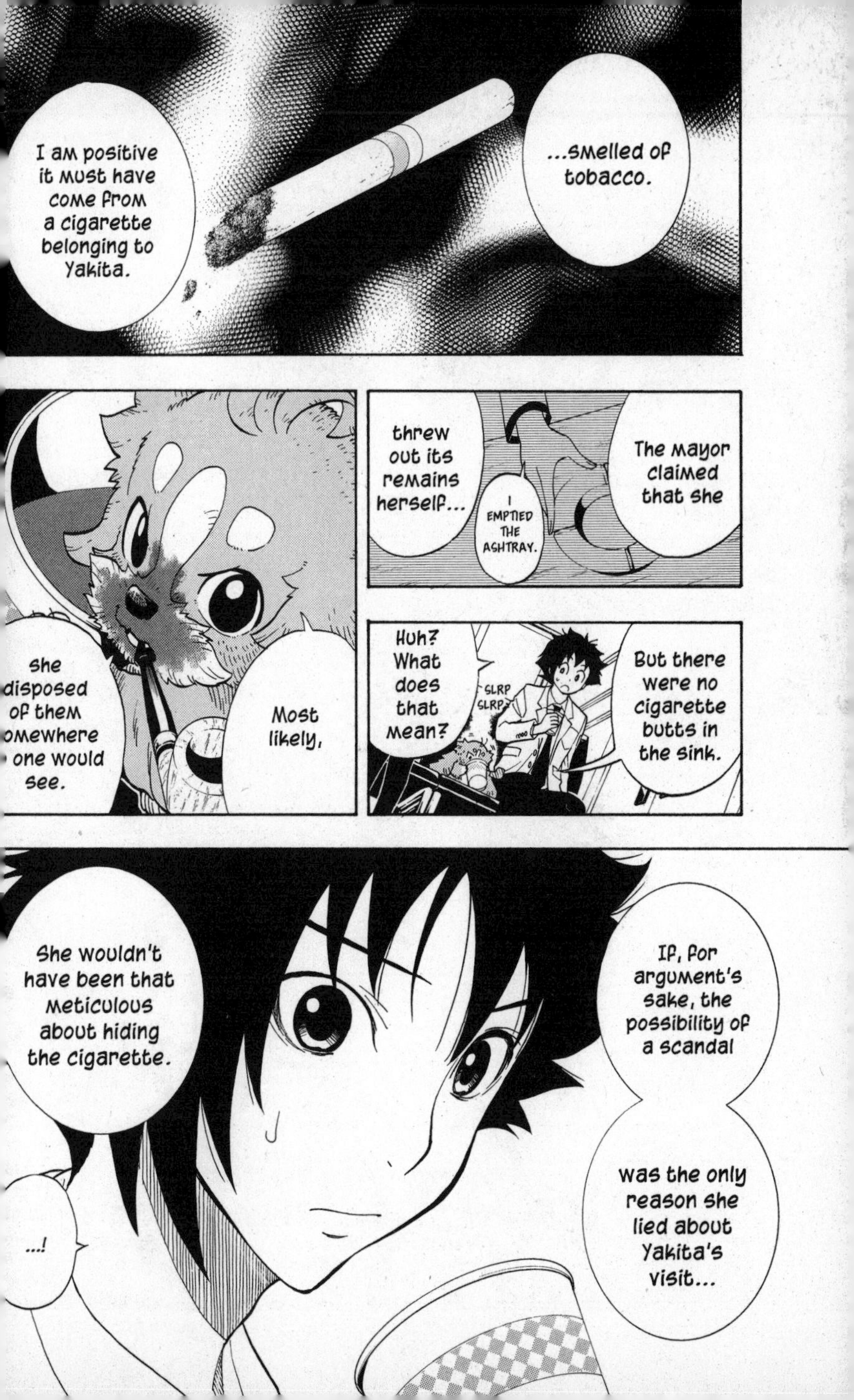
...smelled of tobacco.
I am positive it must have come from a cigarette belonging to Yakita.
The mayor claimed that she
I EMPTIED THE ASHTRAY.
threw out its remains herself...
But there were no cigarette butts in the sink.
SLRP SLRP
Huh? What does that mean?
Most likely,
she disposed of them omewhere one would see.
If, for argument's sake, the possibility of a scandal
was the only reason she lied about Yakita's visit...
She wouldn't have been that meticulous about hiding the cigarette.
...!

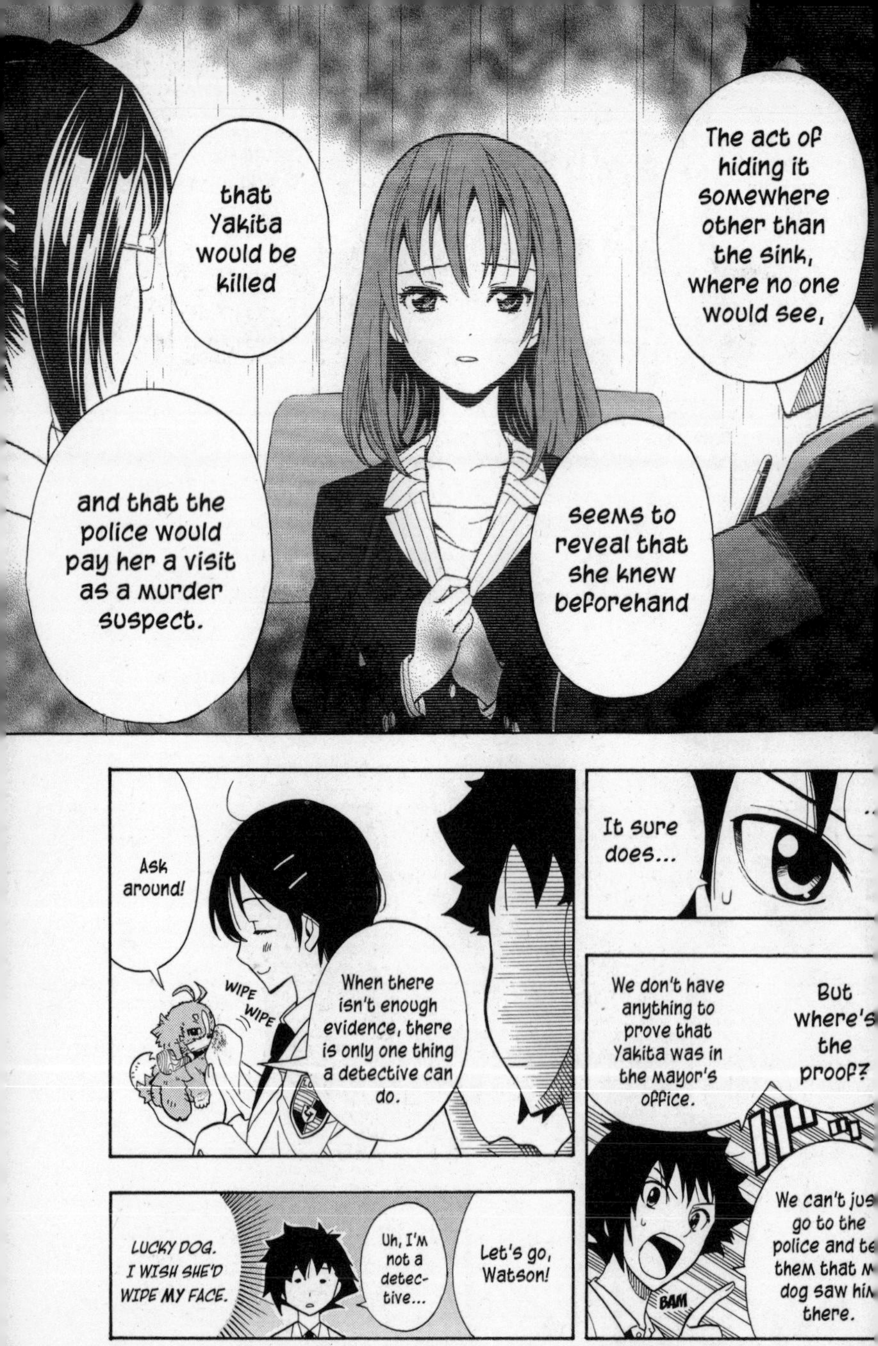
The act of hiding it somewhere other than the sink, where no one would see,
seems to reveal that she knew beforehand
that Yakita would be killed
and that the police would pay her a visit as a murder suspect.
It sure does...
...
But where's the proof?
We don't have anything to prove that Yakita was in the mayor's office.
We can't jus go to the police and te them that m dog saw hin there.
BAM
When there isn't enough evidence, there is only one thing a detective can do.
Ask around!
WIPE WIPE
Let's go, Watson!
Uh, I'm not a detec-tive...
LUCKY DOG. I WISH SHE'D WIPE MY FACE.

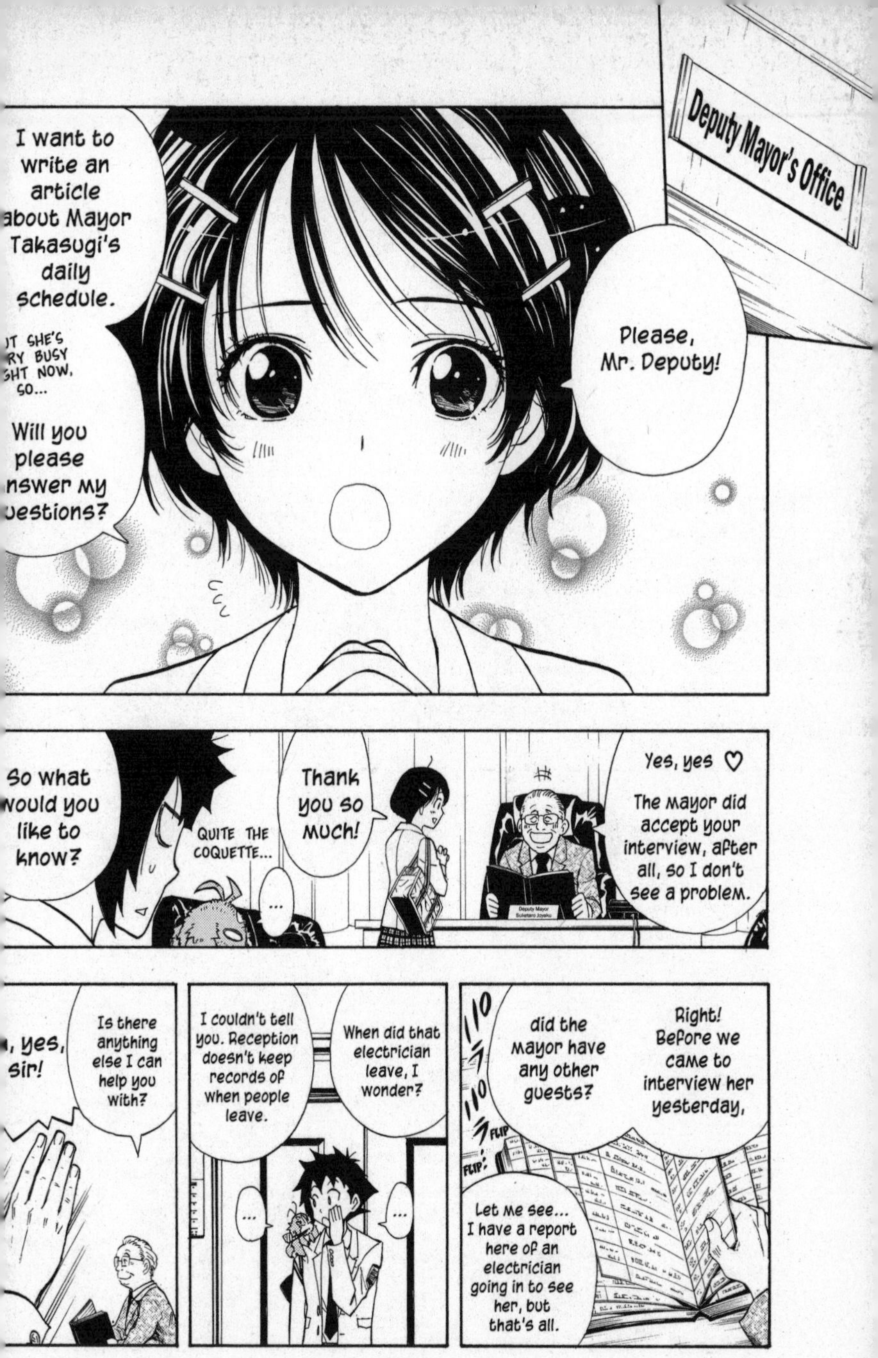
Deputy Mayor's Office
Please, Mr. Deputy!
I want to write an article about Mayor Takasugi's daily schedule.
JT SHE'S RY BUSY GHT NOW, SO...
Will you please nswer my uestions?
Yes, yes ♡
The mayor did accept your interview, after all, so I don't see a problem.
Thank you so MUCH!
QUITE THE COQUETTE...
...
So what vould you like to know?
Right! Before we came to interview her yesterday,
did the mayor have any other guests?
FLIP
FLIP
Let me see... I have a report here of an electrician going in to see her, but that's all.
When did that electrician leave, I wonder?
I couldn't tell you. Reception doesn't keep records of when people leave.
...
...
Is there anything else I can help you with?
, yes, sir!

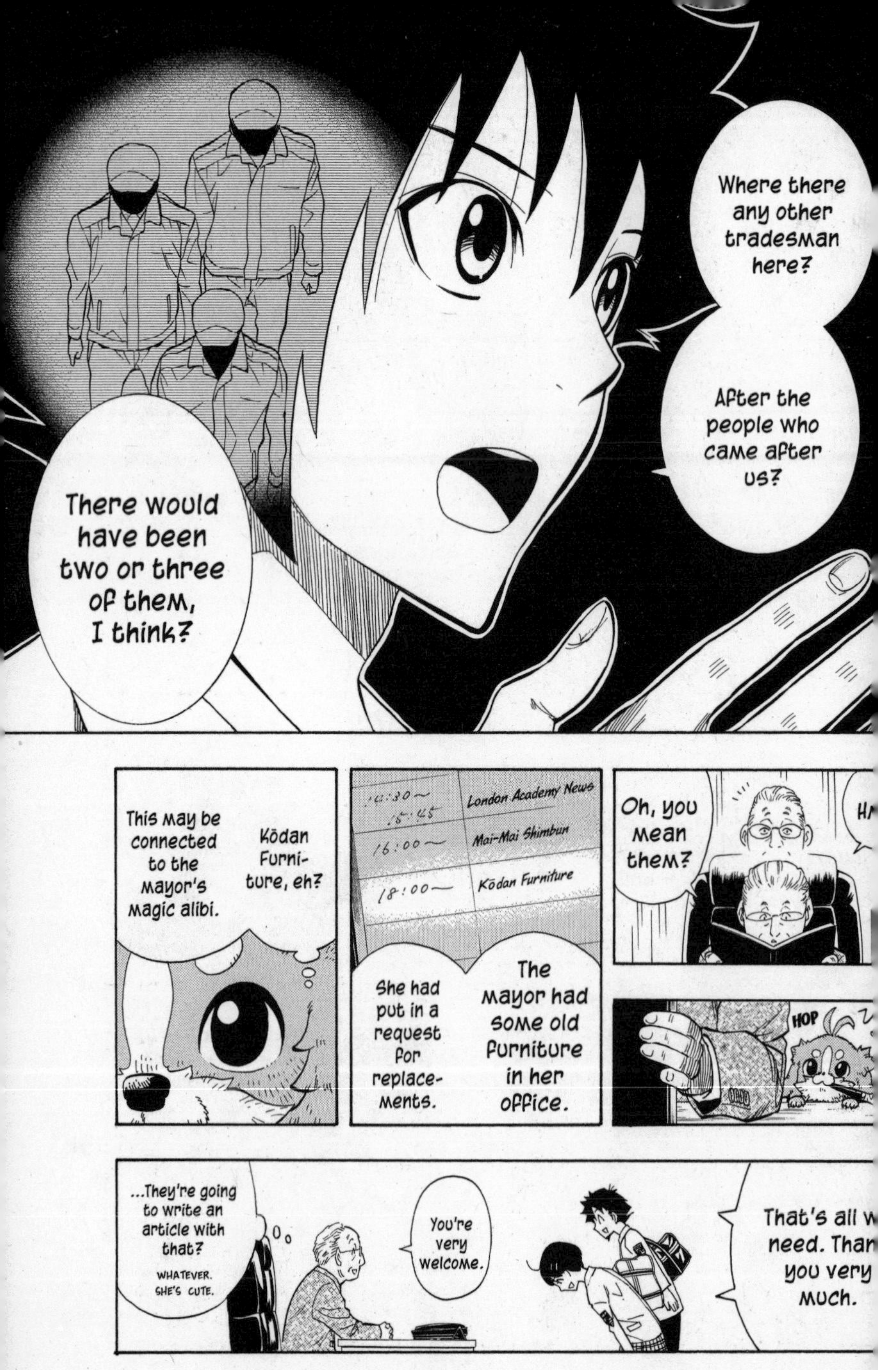
Where there any other tradesman here?
After the people who came after us?
There would have been two or three of them, I think?
HM
Oh, you mean them?
HOP
14:30~ 15:45 London Academy News
16:00~ Mai-Mai Shimbun
18:00~ Kōdan Furniture
The mayor had some old furniture in her office.
She had put in a request for replacements.
Kōdan Furniture, eh?
This may be connected to the mayor's magic alibi.
That's all w need. Than you very much.
You're very welcome.
...They're going to write an article with that?
WHATEVER. SHE'S CUTE.

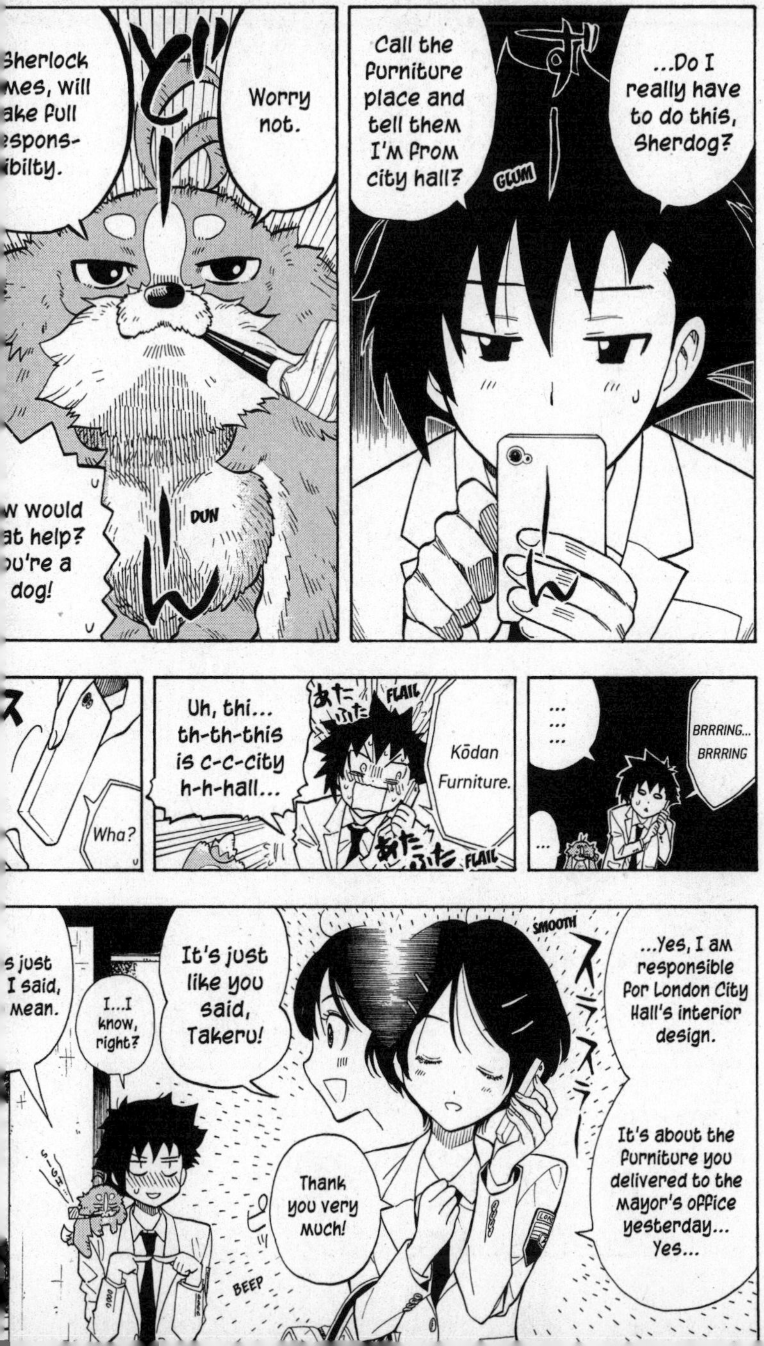

...Do I really have to do this, Sherdog?
Call the furniture place and tell them I'm from city hall?
GLUM
Worry not.
Sherlock
mes, will
ake full
espons-
ibilty.
DUN
w would
at help?
ou're a
dog!
BRRRING... BRRRING
...
...
...
...
Kōdan Furniture.
Uh, thi... th-th-this is c-c-city h-h-hall...
FLAIL
FLAIL
Wha?
SMOOTH
...Yes, I am responsible for London City Hall's interior design.
It's about the furniture you delivered to the mayor's office yesterday... Yes...
Thank you very much!
BEEP
It's just like you said, Takeru!
I...I know, right?
s just
I said,
mean.
SIGH

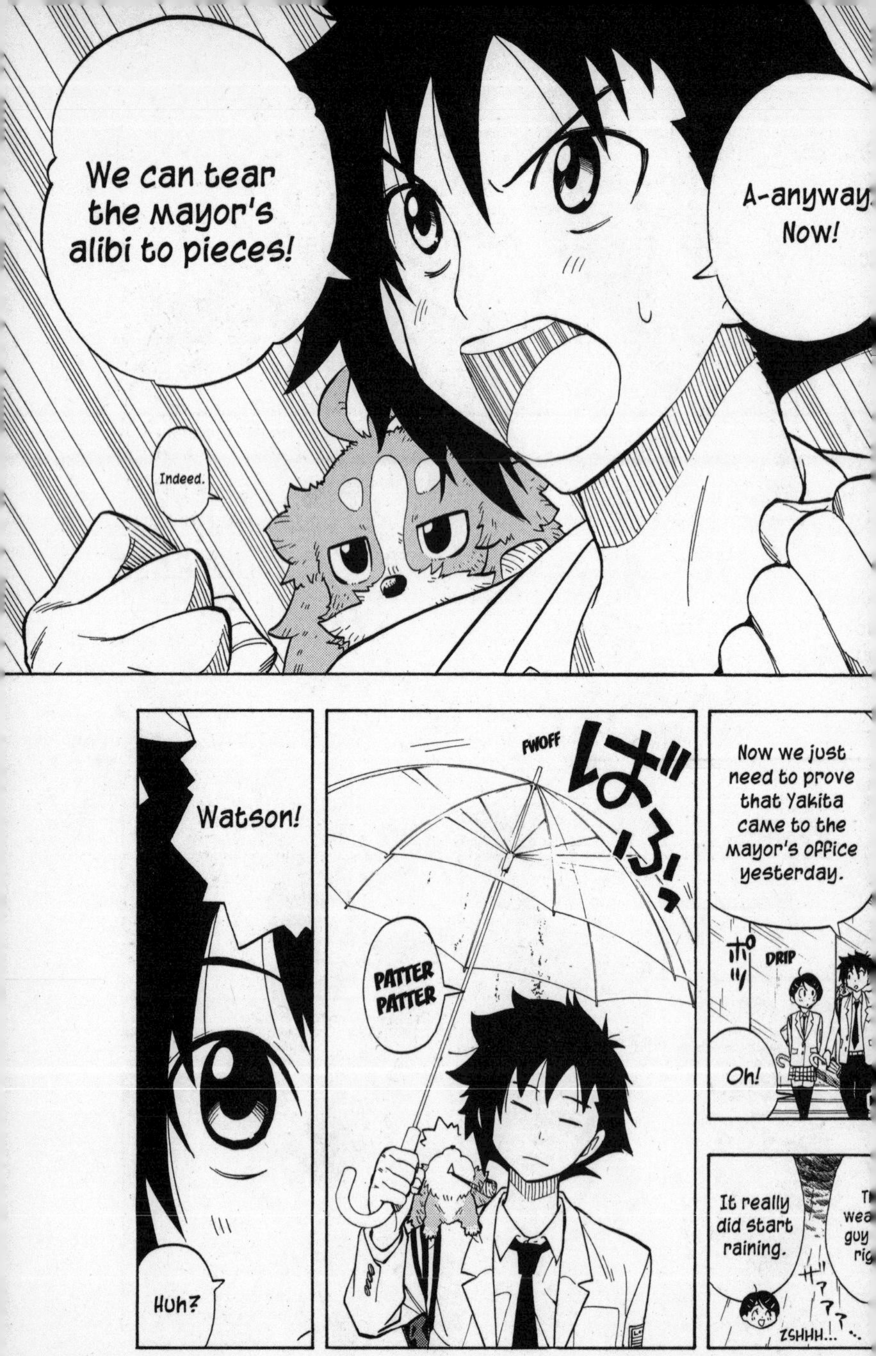
A-anyway. Now!
We can tear the mayor's alibi to pieces!
Indeed.
Now we just need to prove that Yakita came to the mayor's office yesterday.
ポツ
DRIP
Oh!
It really did start raining.
ザァァァ...
ZSHHH...
ばふっ
FWOFF
PATTER PATTER
Watson!
Huh?

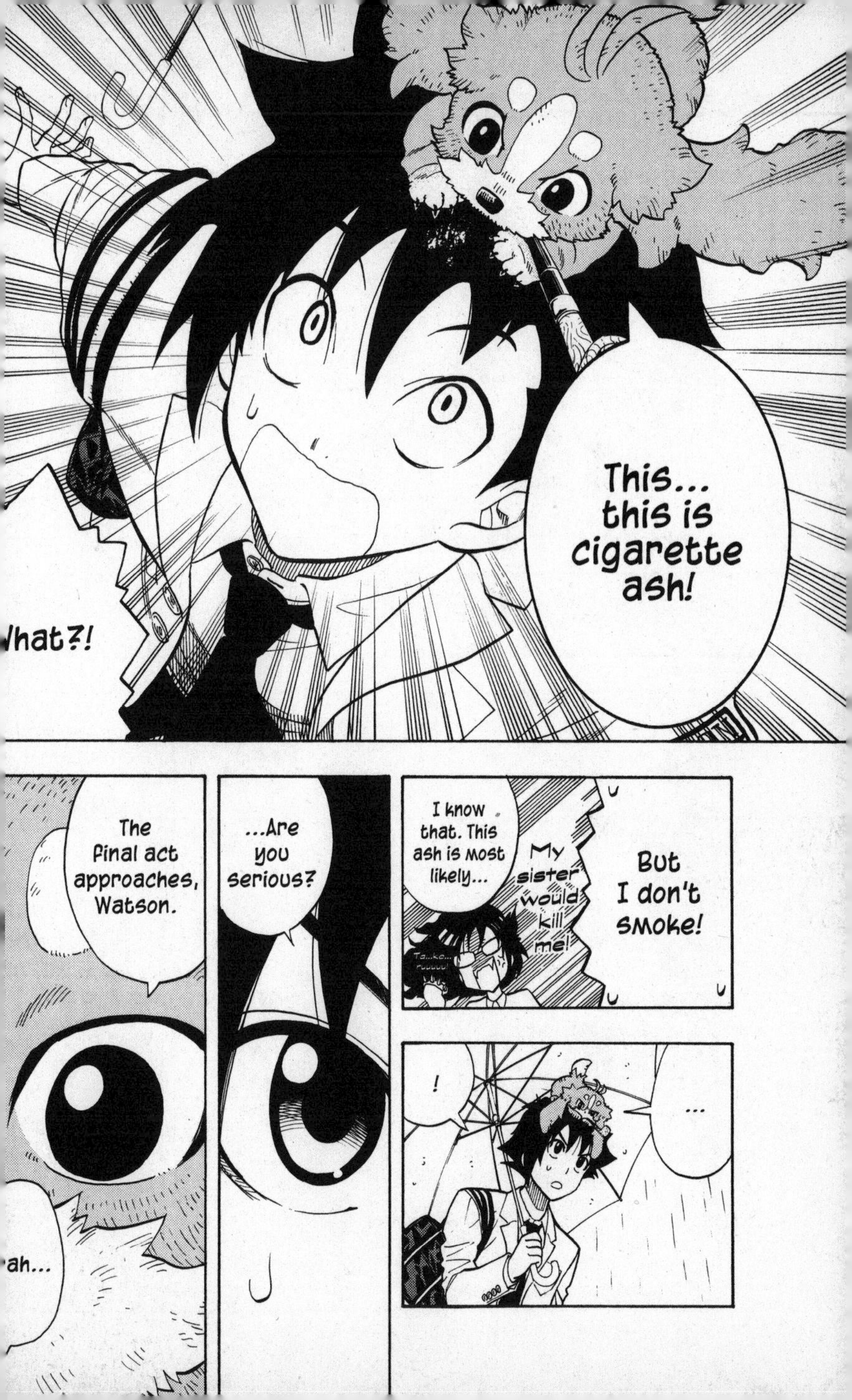

This... this is cigarette ash!
hat?!
But I don't smoke!
I know that. This ash is most likely...
My sister would kill me!
...
!
...Are you serious?
The final act approaches, Watson.
ah...

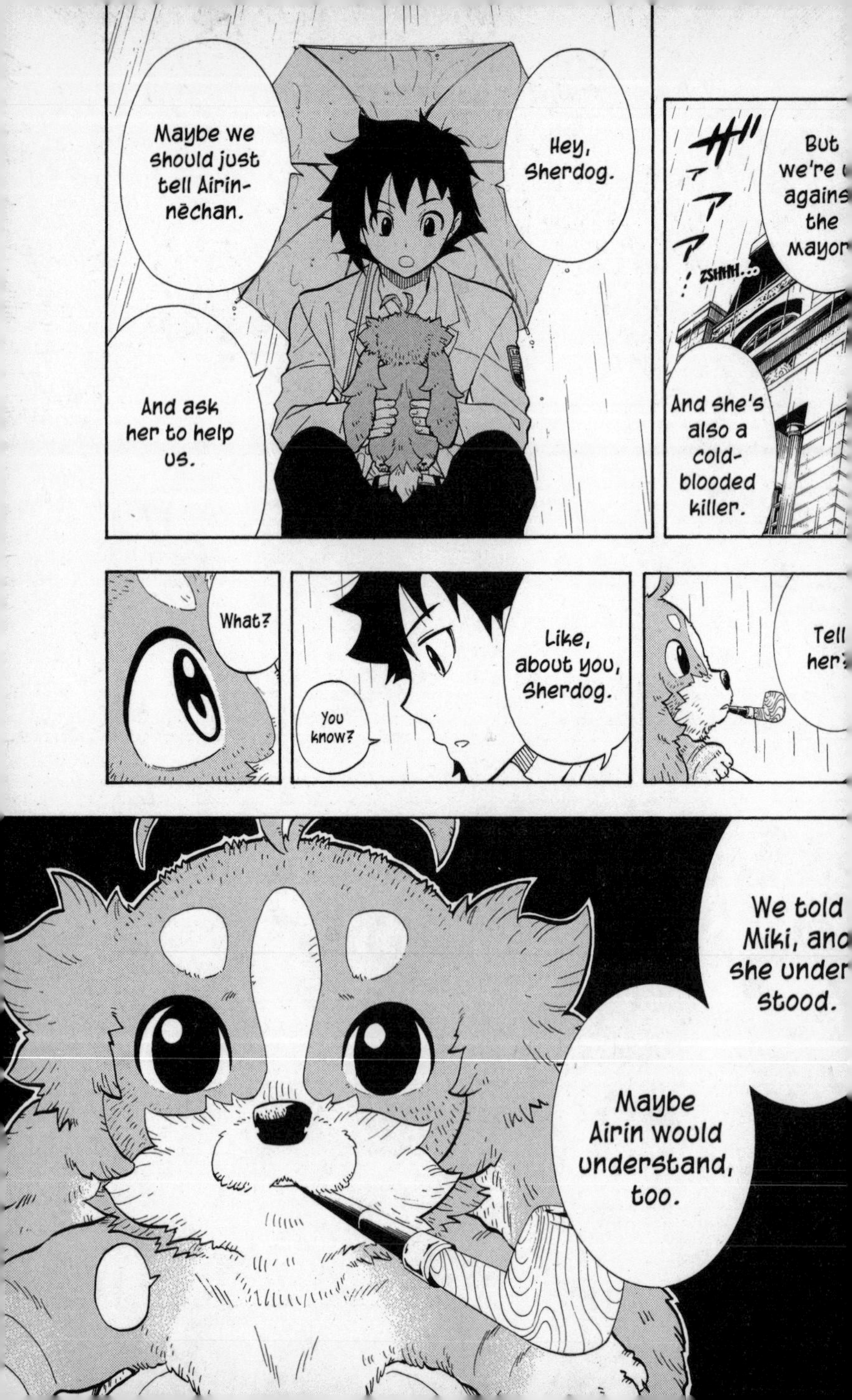
ザァァァ！
ZSHHH...
But we're agains the mayor
And she's also a cold-blooded killer.
Hey, Sherdog.
Maybe we should just tell Airin-nēchan.
And ask her to help us.
Tell her?
Like, about you, Sherdog.
You know?
What?
We told Miki, and she under stood.
Maybe Airin would understand, too.

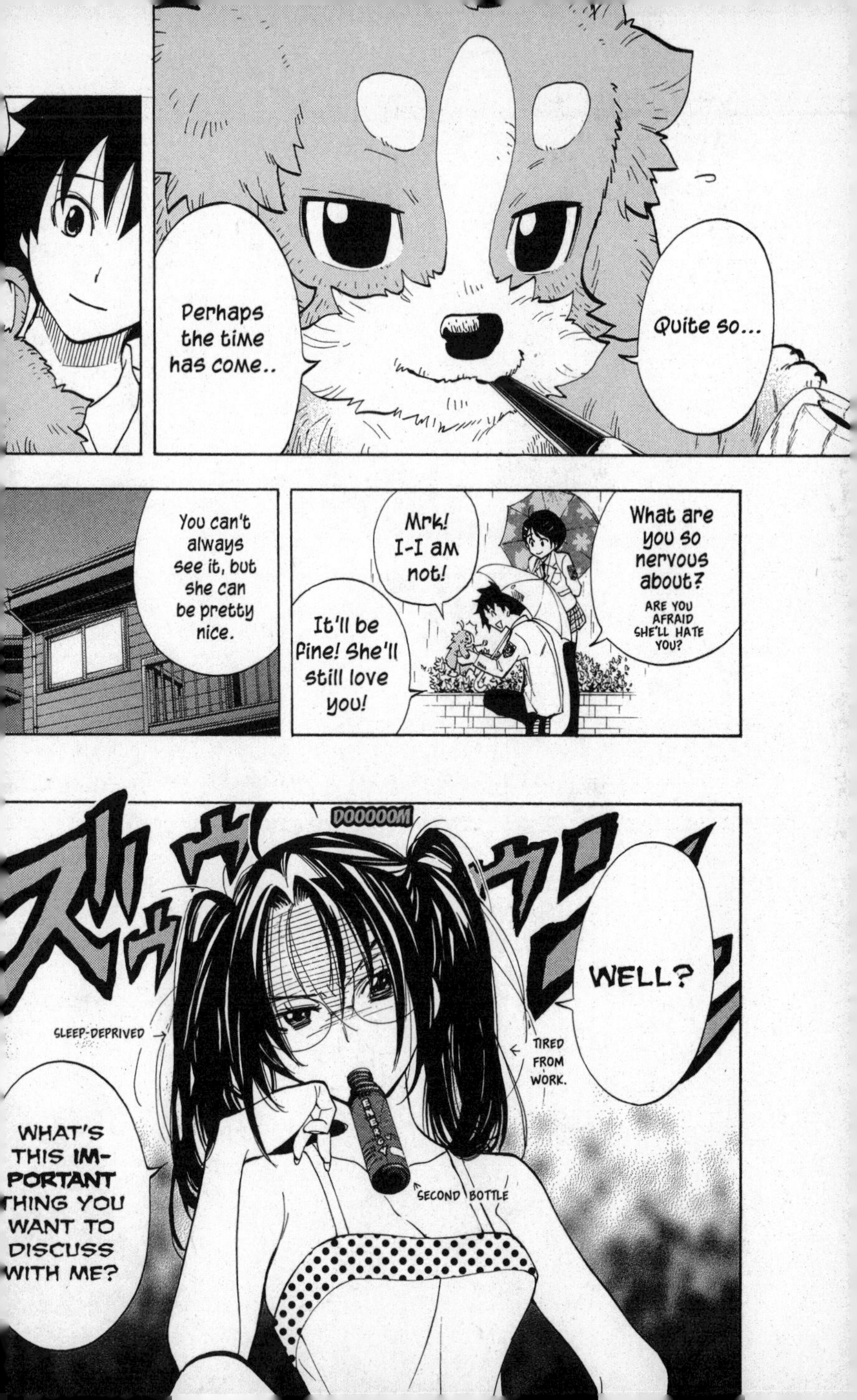
Quite so...
Perhaps the time has come..
What are you so nervous about?
ARE YOU AFRAID SHE'LL HATE YOU?
Mrk! I-I am not!
It'll be fine! She'll still love you!
You can't always see it, but she can be pretty nice.
DOOOOOM
WELL?
TIRED FROM WORK.
SLEEP-DEPRIVED
ENERGY
WHAT'S THIS IMPORTANT THING YOU WANT TO DISCUSS WITH ME?
SECOND BOTTLE

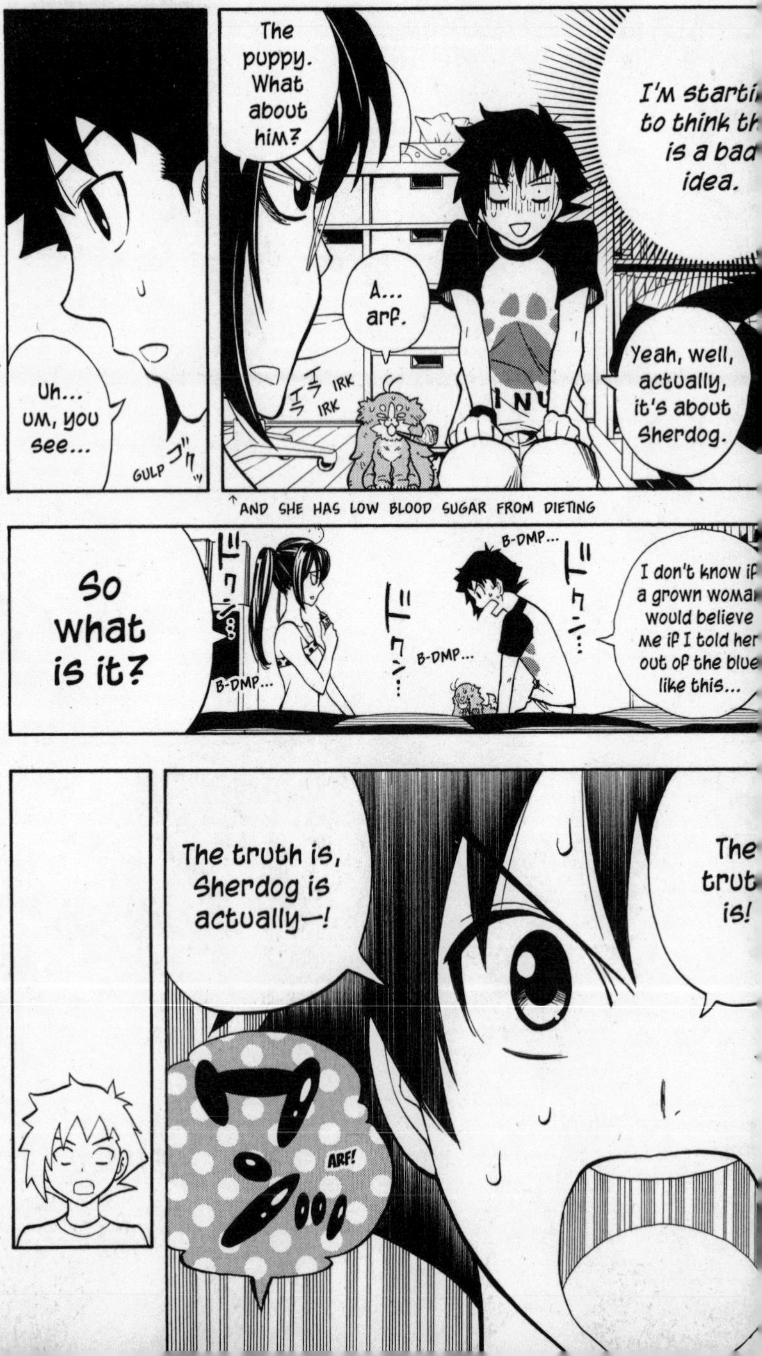

I'm starti
to think th
is a bad
idea.
Yeah, well, actually, it's about Sherdog.
The puppy. What about him?
A... arf.
IRK IRK
Uh... um, you see...
GULP
AND SHE HAS LOW BLOOD SUGAR FROM DIETING
I don't know if a grown woma would believe me if I told her out of the blue like this...
B-DMP...
B-DMP...
B-DMP...
So what is it?
The trut is!
The truth is, Sherdog is actually—!
ARF!

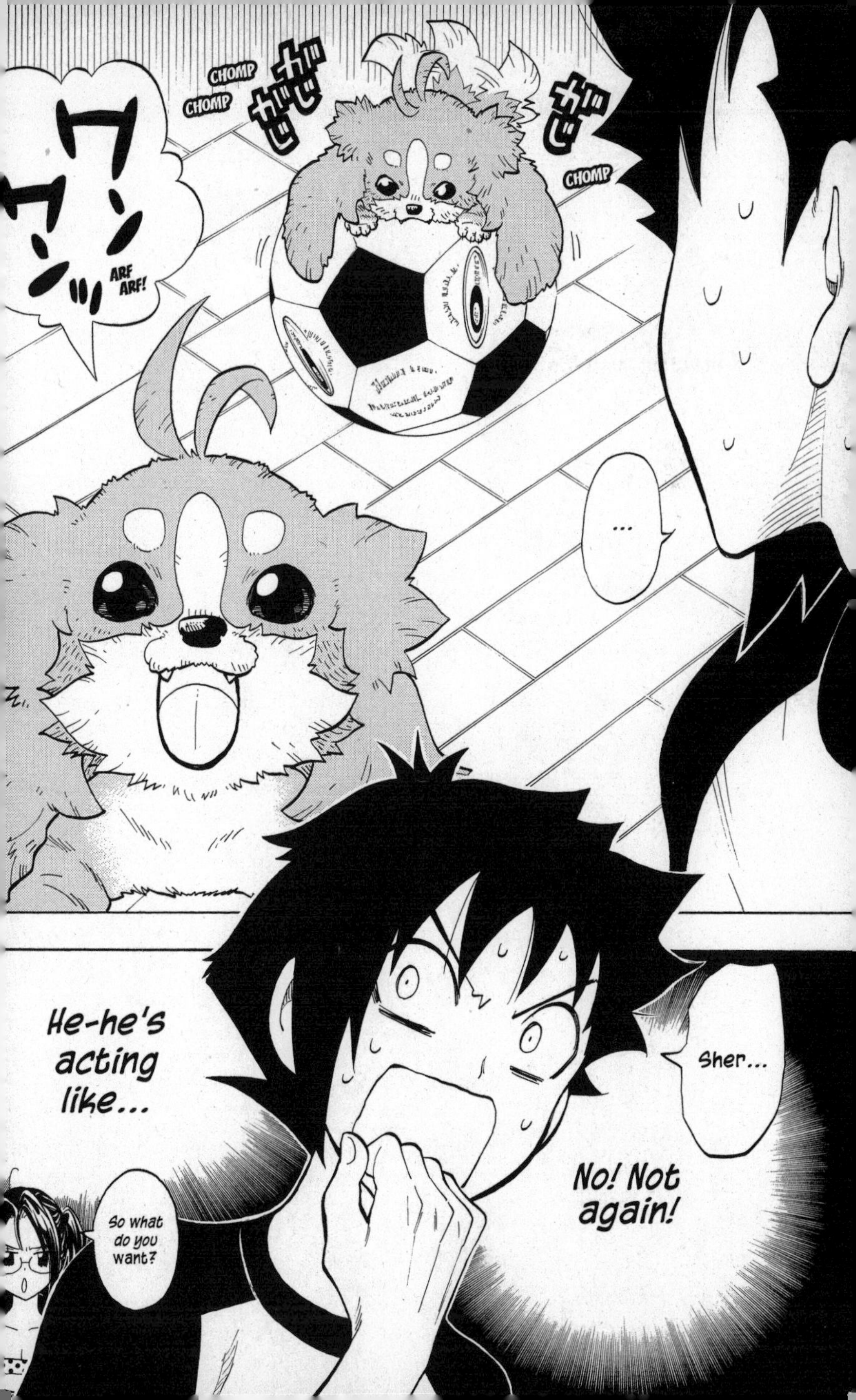
CHOMP
CHOMP
CHOMP
ARF ARF!
...
Sher...
No! Not again!
He-he's acting like...
So what do you want?

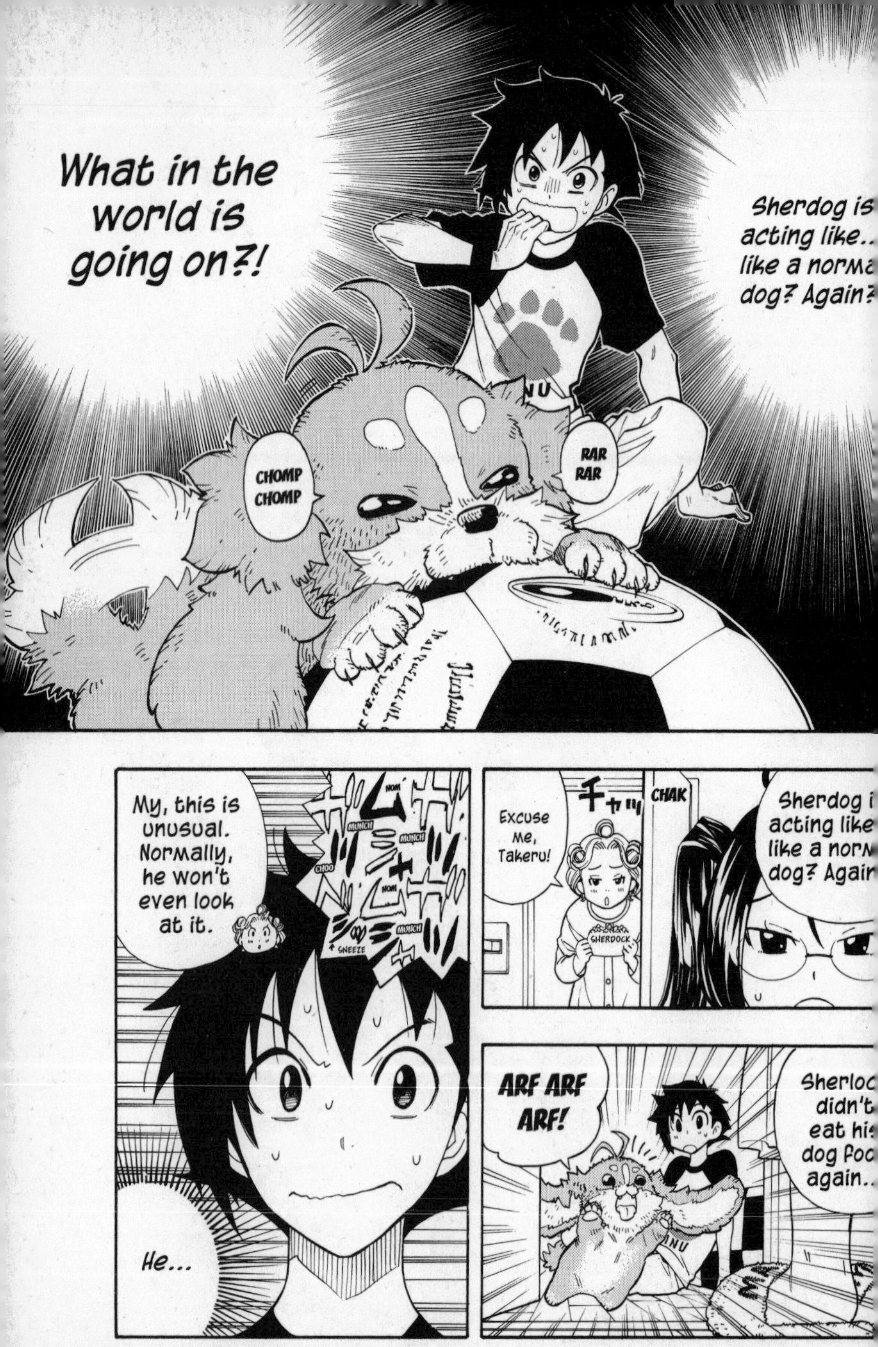
Sherdog is acting like... like a norma dog? Again?
RAR RAR
CHOMP CHOMP
What in the world is going on?!
Sherdog i acting like like a norm dog? Agair
CHAK
チャリ
Excuse me, Takeru!
SHERDOCK
Sherloc didn't eat his dog foo again...
ARF ARF ARF!
NOM
MUNCH
MUNCH
CHOO
NOM
MUNCH
SNEEZE
My, this is unusual. Normally, he won't even look at it.
He...

Case 7: ⚜ Hidden from the Press, Part 5

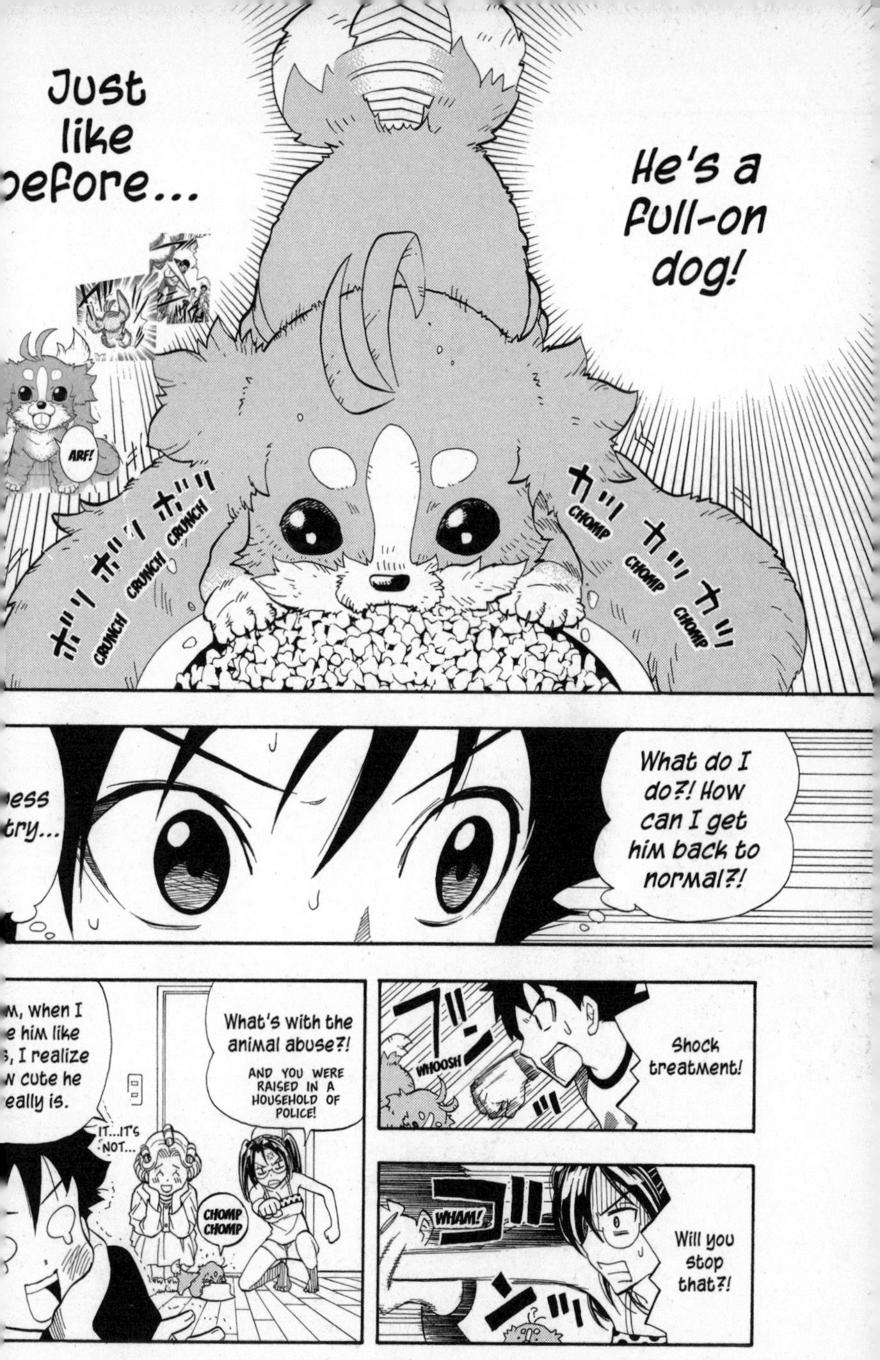

He's a full-on dog!
Just like before...
ARF!
CHOMP CHOMP CHOMP
CRUNCH CRUNCH CRUNCH
What do I do?! How can I get him back to normal?!
ess try...
WHOOSH
Shock treatment!
WHAM!
Will you stop that?!
What's with the animal abuse?!
AND YOU WERE RAISED IN A HOUSEHOLD OF POLICE!
m, when I e him like s, I realize w cute he eally is.
IT...IT'S NOT...
CHOMP CHOMP

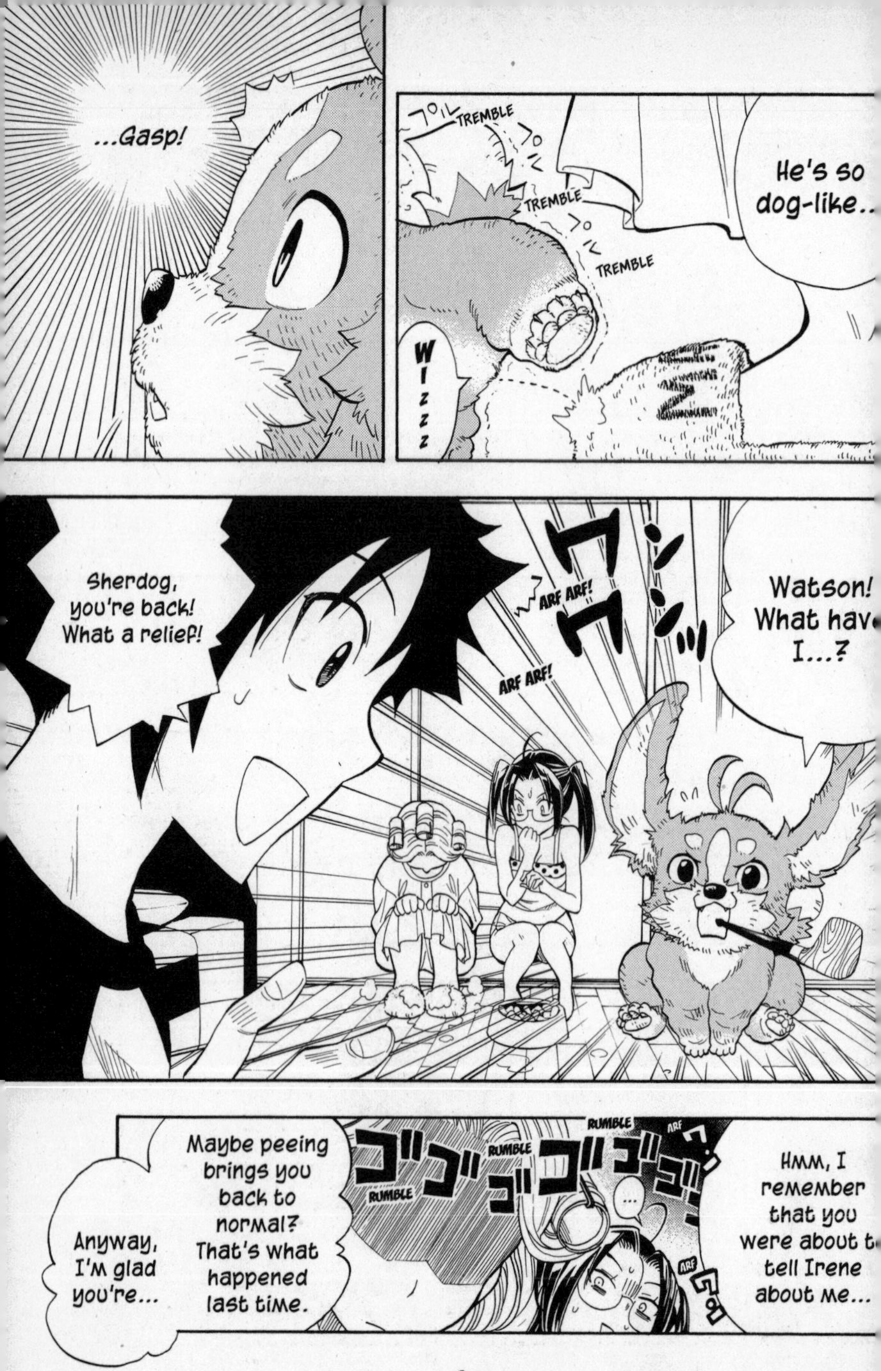
TREMBLE
TREMBLE
TREMBLE
He's so dog-like...
WIZZZ
...Gasp!
Watson! What hav I...?
ARF ARF!
ARF ARF!
Sherdog, you're back! What a relief!
Hmm, I remember that you were about t tell Irene about me...
ARF
ARF
RUMBLE
RUMBLE
RUMBLE
...
Maybe peeing brings you back to normal? That's what happened last time.
Anyway, I'm glad you're...

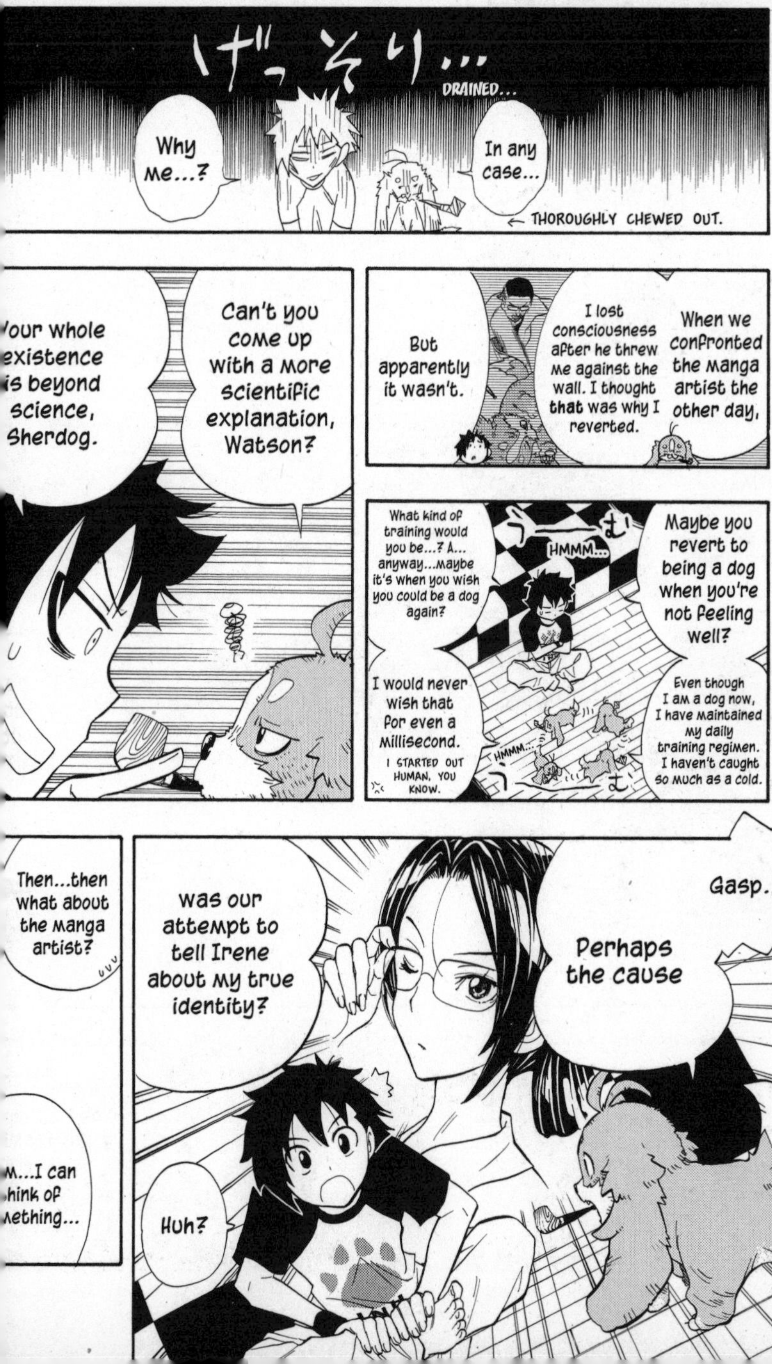
げっそり…
DRAINED...
In any case...
Why me...?
THOROUGHLY CHEWED OUT.
When we confronted the manga artist the other day,
I lost consciousness after he threw me against the wall. I thought that was why I reverted.
But apparently it wasn't.
Maybe you revert to being a dog when you're not feeling well?
HMMM...
Even though I am a dog now, I have maintained my daily training regimen. I haven't caught so much as a cold.
What kind of training would you be...? A... anyway...maybe it's when you wish you could be a dog again?
I would never wish that for even a millisecond.
I STARTED OUT HUMAN, YOU KNOW.
HMMM...
Can't you come up with a more scientific explanation, Watson?
our whole existence is beyond science, Sherdog.
Gasp...!
Perhaps the cause
was our attempt to tell Irene about my true identity?
Huh?
Then...then what about the manga artist?
m...I can hink of ething...

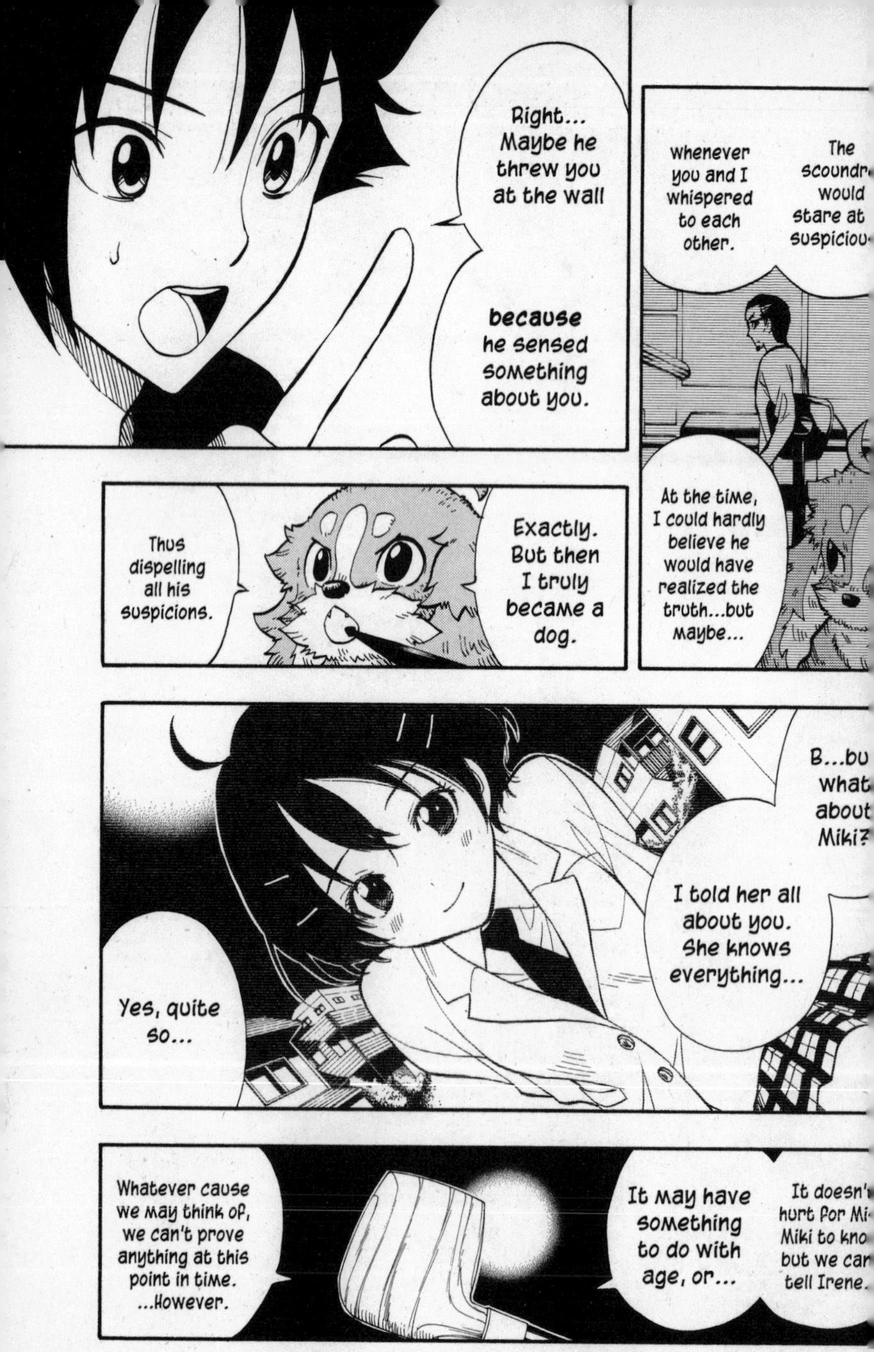
The scoundr would stare at suspiciou
whenever you and I whispered to each other.
At the time, I could hardly believe he would have realized the truth...but maybe...
Right... Maybe he threw you at the wall
because he sensed something about you.
Exactly. But then I truly became a dog.
Thus dispelling all his suspicions.
B...bu what about Miki?
I told her all about you. She knows everything...
Yes, quite so...
It doesn't hurt for Mi Miki to kno but we car tell Irene.
It may have something to do with age, or...
Whatever cause we may think of, we can't prove anything at this point in time. ...However.

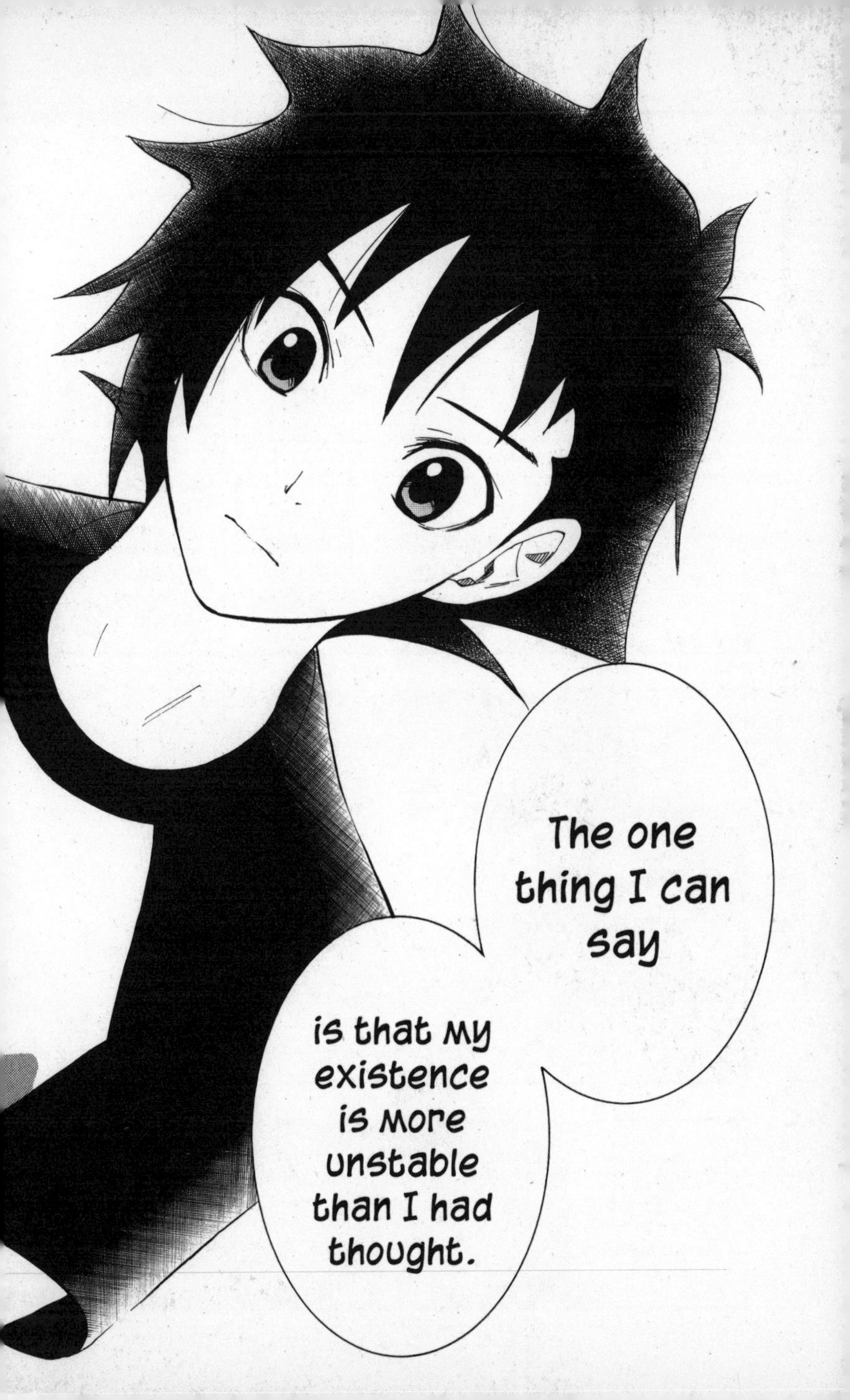
The one thing I can say
is that my existence is more unstable than I had thought.

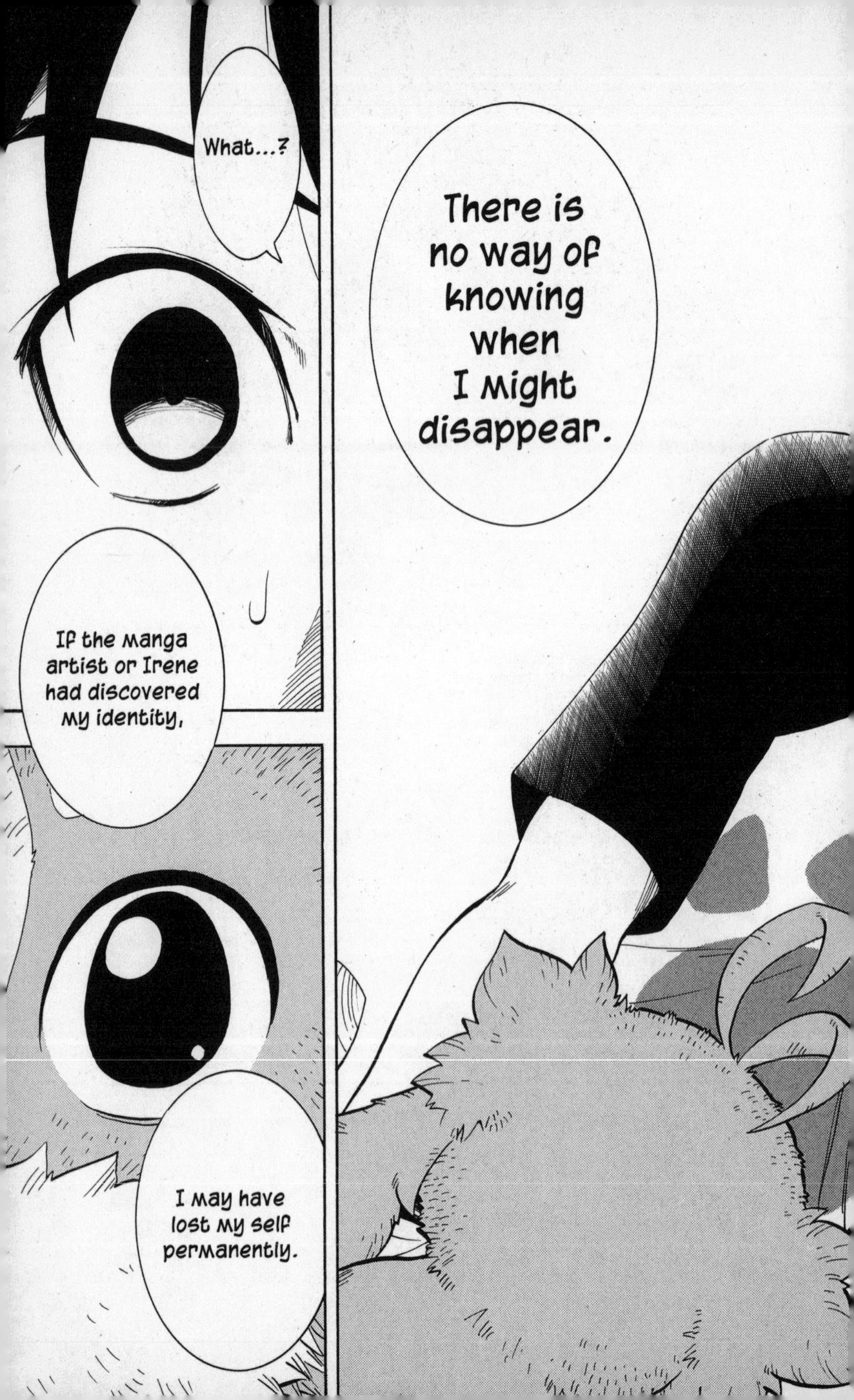
There is no way of knowing when I might disappear.
What...?
If the manga artist or Irene had discovered my identity,
I may have lost my self permanently.

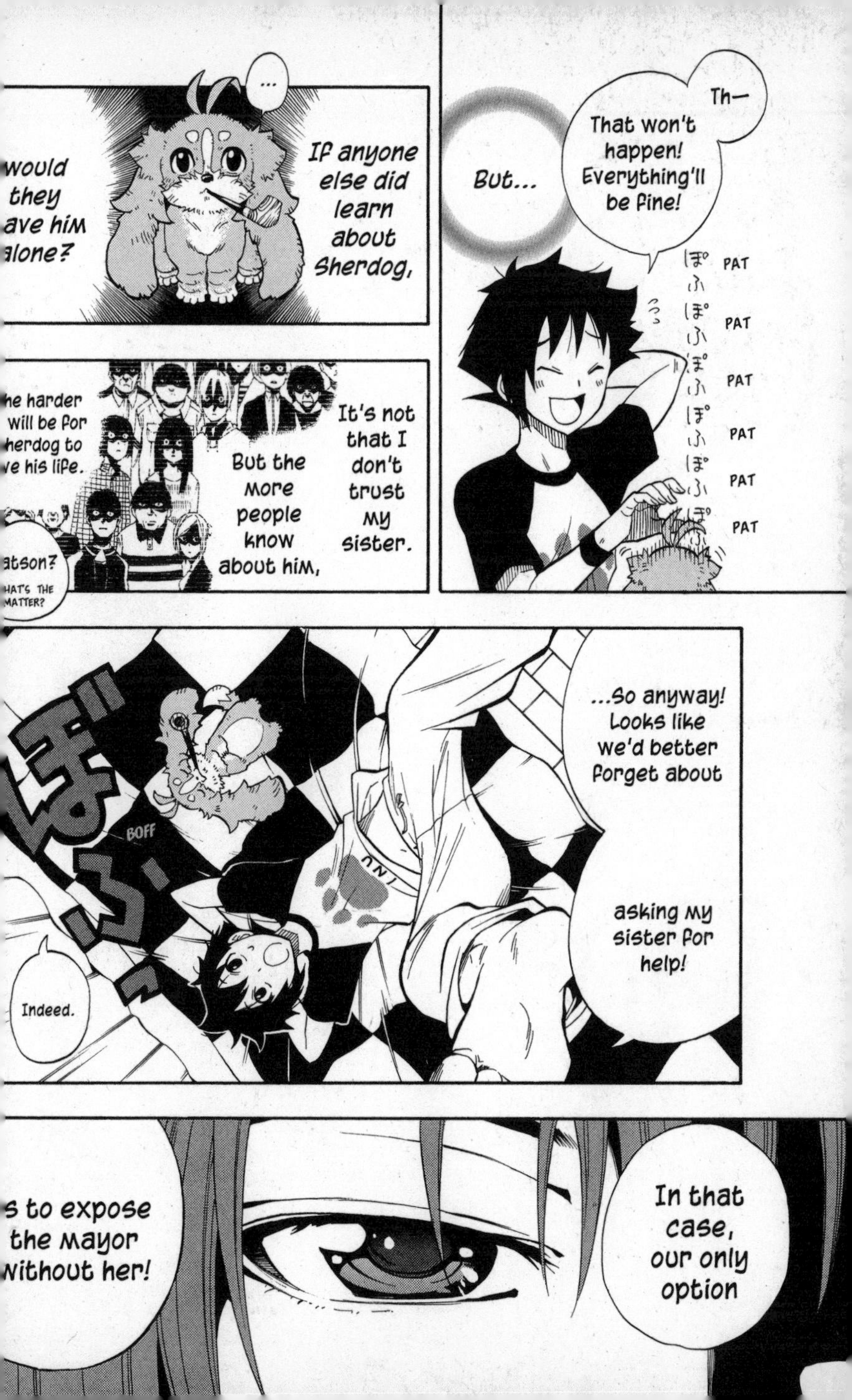
Th—
That won't happen! Everything'll be fine!
But...
PAT
PAT
PAT
PAT
PAT
PAT
...
If anyone else did learn about Sherdog,
would they ave him alone?
It's not that I don't trust my sister.
But the more people know about him,
he harder will be for herdog to ve his life.
atson?
HAT'S THE MATTER?
...So anyway! Looks like we'd better forget about
asking my sister for help!
ぼふ
BOFF
Indeed.
In that case, our only option
s to expose the mayor without her!

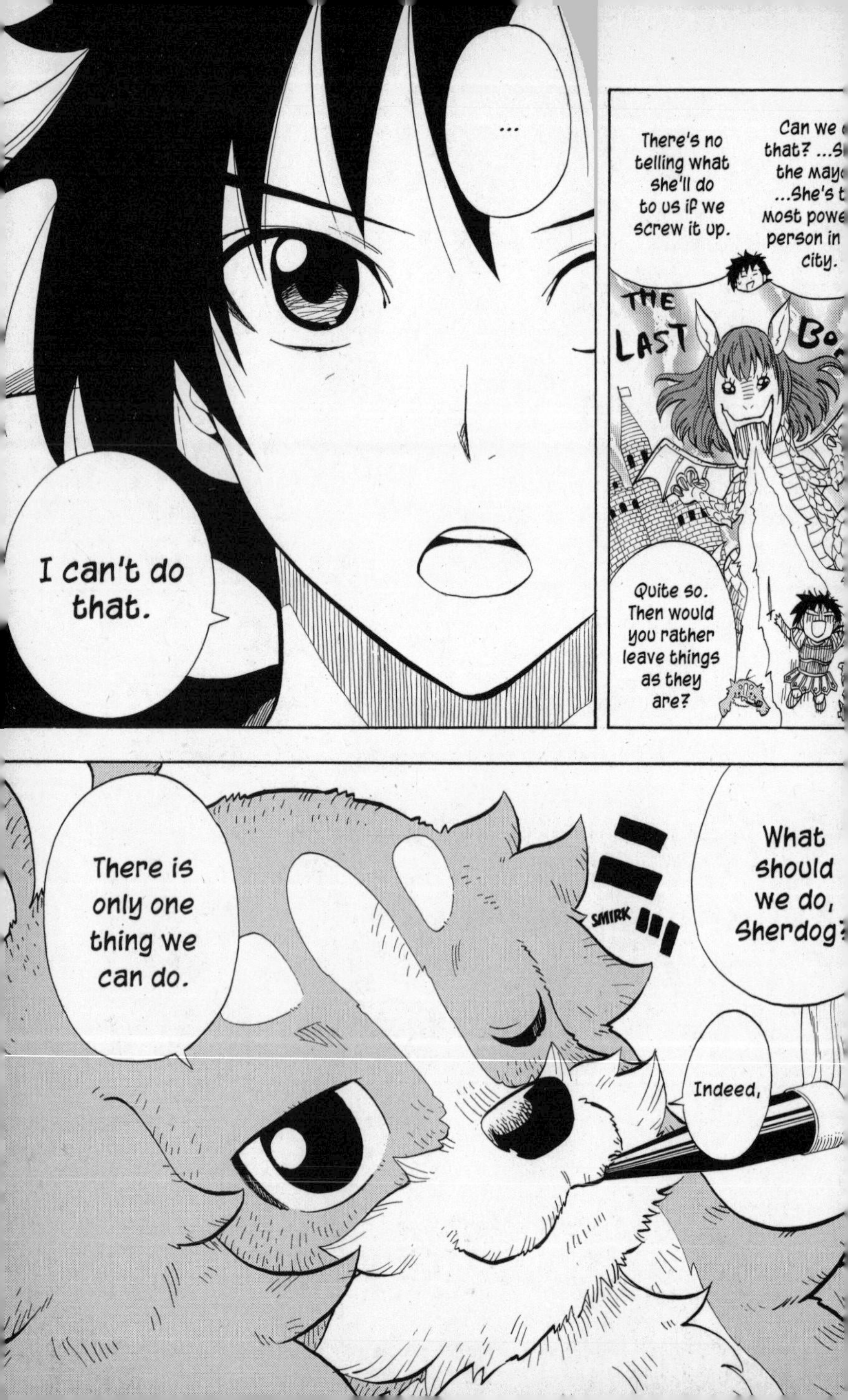

Can we
that? ...S
the may
...She's t
most powe
person in
city.
There's no telling what she'll do to us if we screw it up.
THE LAST Bo
Quite so. Then would you rather leave things as they are?
...
I can't do that.
What should we do, Sherdog?
Indeed,
SMIRK
There is only one thing we can do.

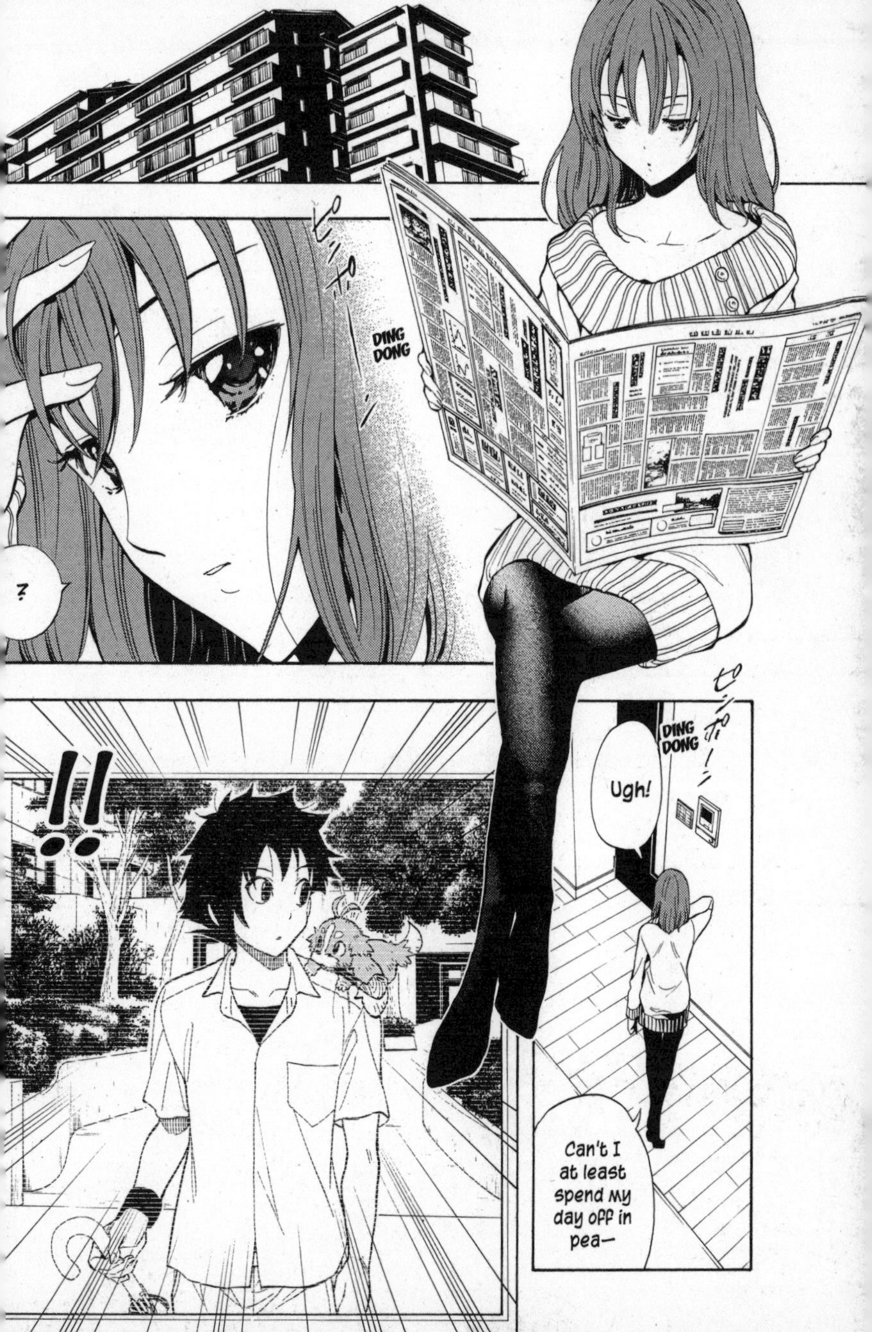
DING DONG
?
DING DONG
Ugh!
Can't I at least spend my day off in pea—
!!

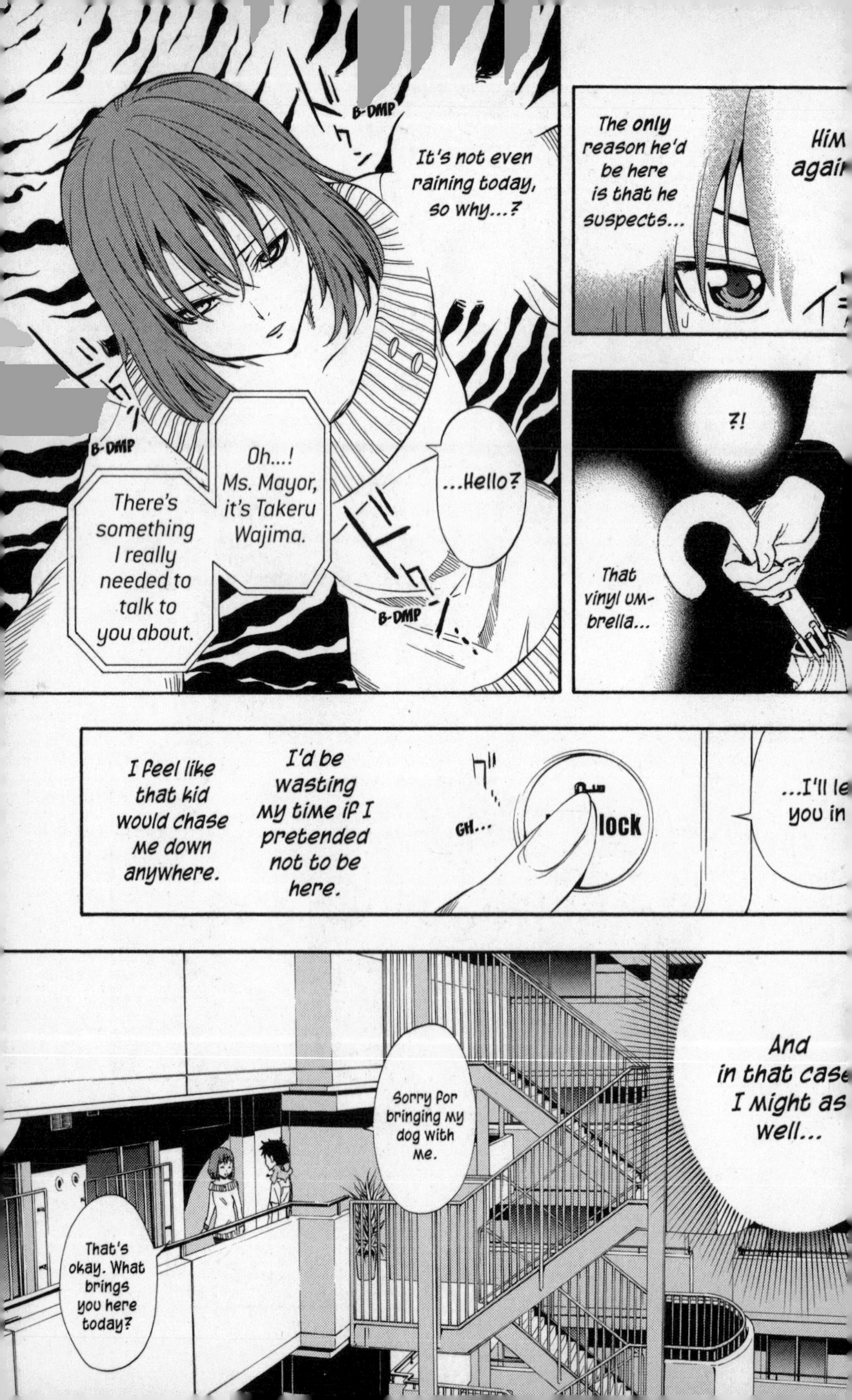

HIM agai
The only reason he'd be here is that he suspects...
?!
That vinyl umbrella...
B-DMP
It's not even raining today, so why...?
B-DMP
...Hello?
Oh...! Ms. Mayor, it's Takeru Wajima.
There's something I really needed to talk to you about.
B-DMP
...I'll le you in
lock
GH...
I'd be wasting my time if I pretended not to be here.
I feel like that kid would chase me down anywhere.
And in that cas I might as well...
Sorry for bringing my dog with me.
That's okay. What brings you here today?

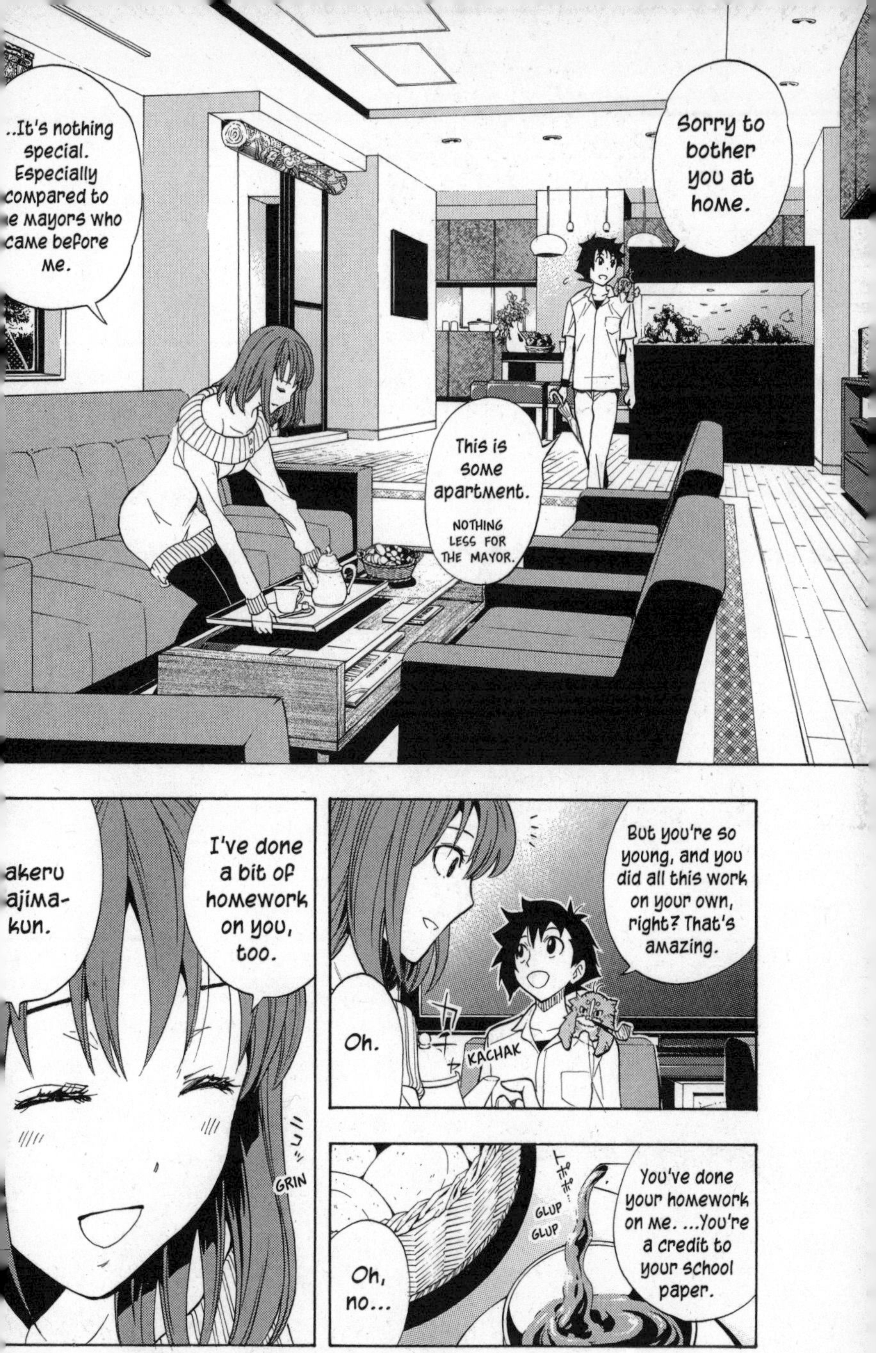
Sorry to bother you at home.
This is some apartment.
NOTHING LESS FOR THE MAYOR.
..It's nothing special. Especially compared to e mayors who came before me.
But you're so young, and you did all this work on your own, right? That's amazing.
KACHAK
Oh.
You've done your homework on me. ...You're a credit to your school paper.
GLUP GLUP
Oh, no...
I've done a bit of homework on you, too.
akeru ajima-kun.
GRIN

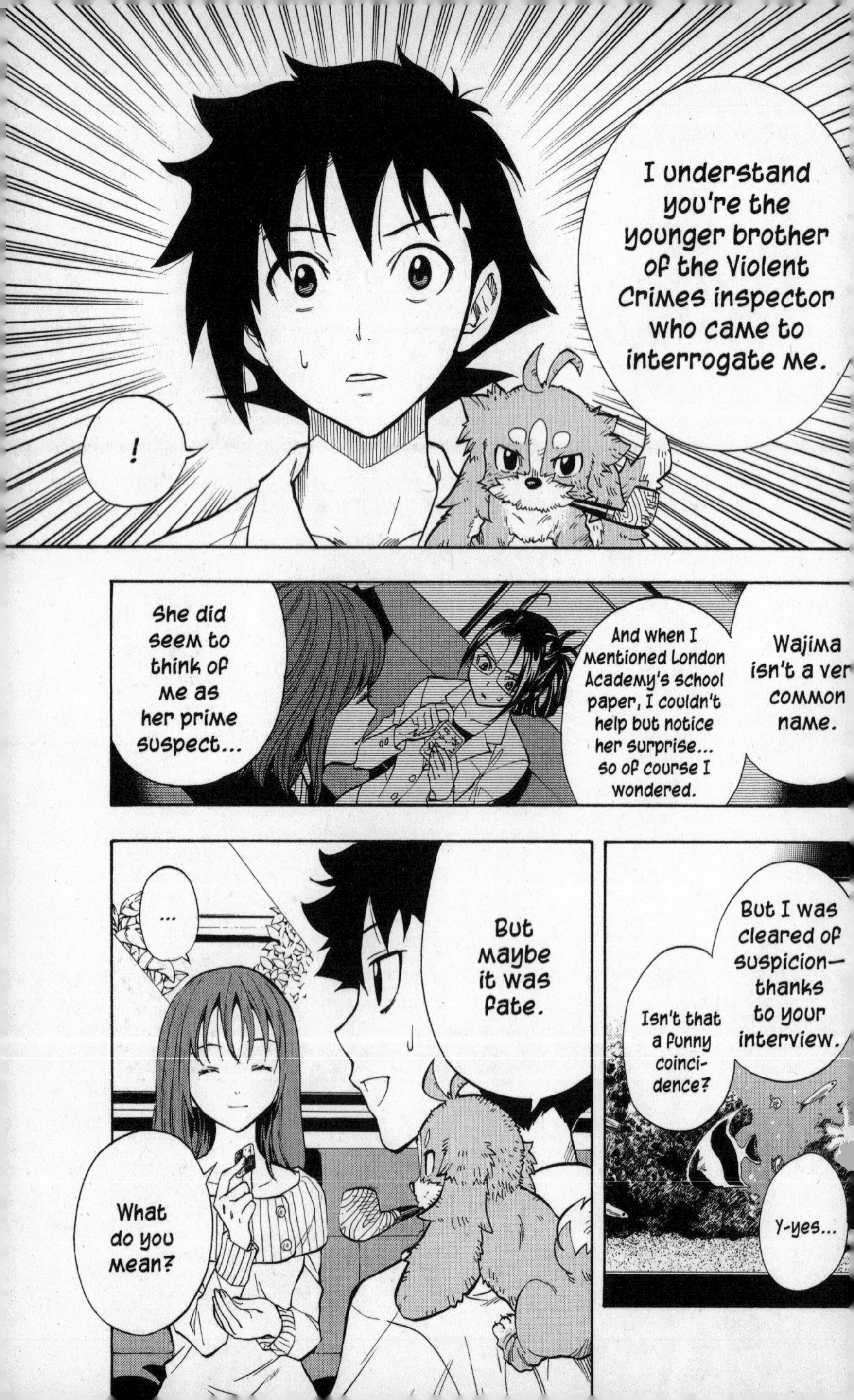
I understand you're the younger brother of the Violent Crimes inspector who came to interrogate me.
!
Wajima isn't a ver common name.
And when I mentioned London Academy's school paper, I couldn't help but notice her surprise... so of course I wondered.
She did seem to think of me as her prime suspect...
But I was cleared of suspicion—thanks to your interview.
Isn't that a funny coincidence?
Y-yes...
But maybe it was fate.
...
What do you mean?

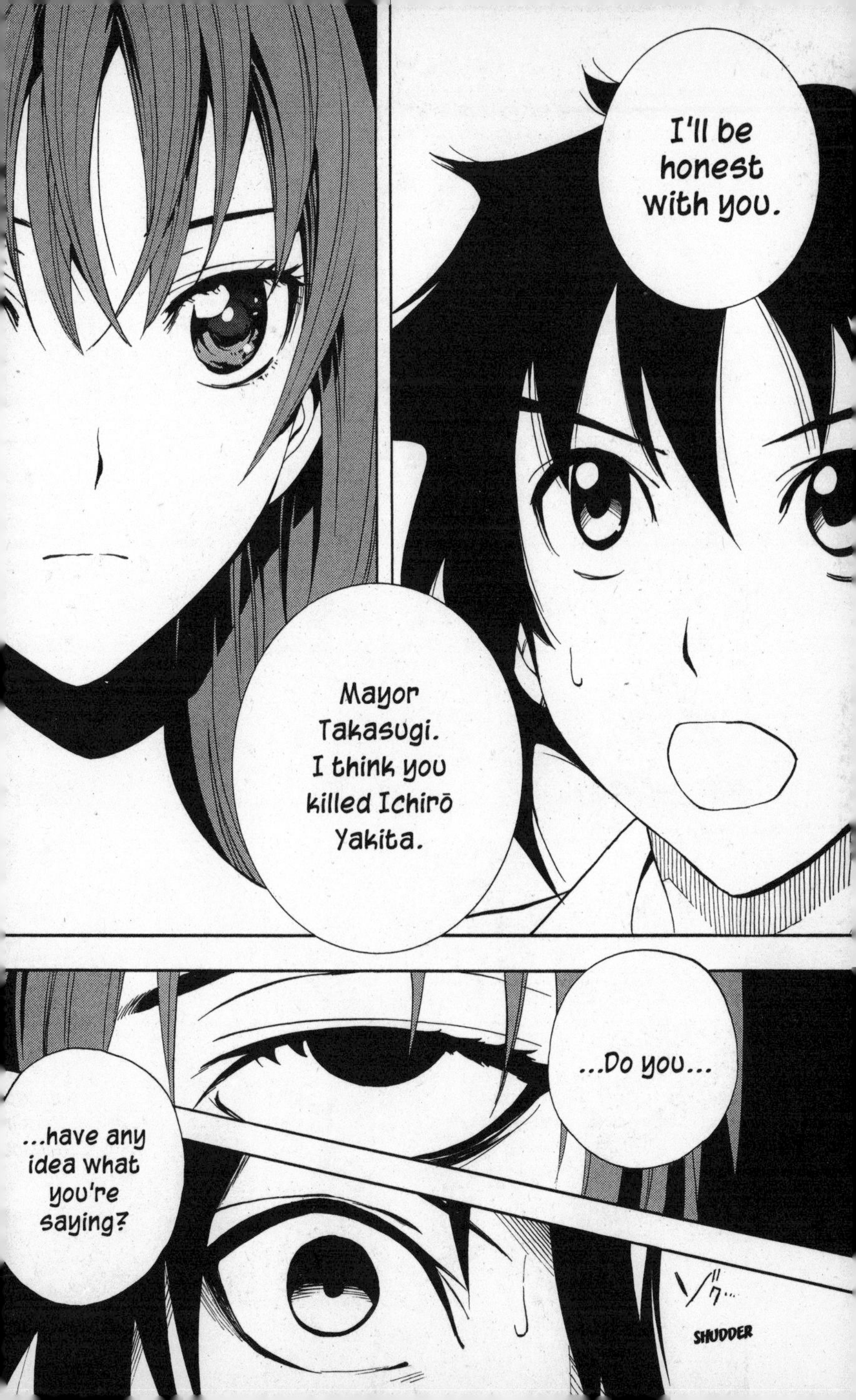
I'll be honest with you.
Mayor Takasugi. I think you killed Ichirō Yakita.
...Do you...
...have any idea what you're saying?
ゾワ...
SHUDDER

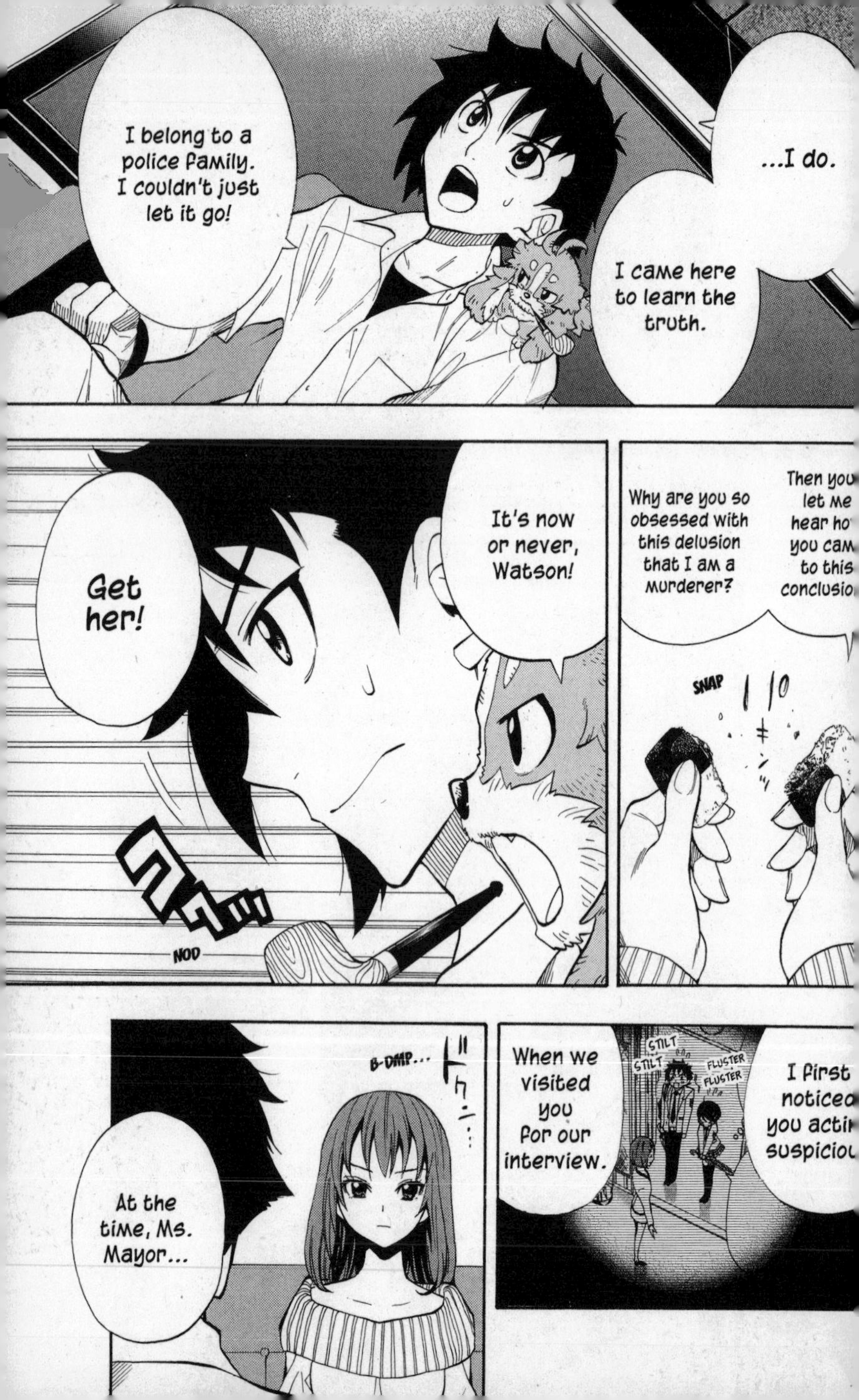
...I do.
I came here to learn the truth.
I belong to a police family. I couldn't just let it go!
Then you let me hear ho you cam to this conclusio
Why are you so obsessed with this delusion that I am a murderer?
SNAP
It's now or never, Watson!
Get her!
NOD
I first noticed you actin suspiciou
When we visited you for our interview.
STILT
STILT
FLUSTER
FLUSTER
B-DMP...
At the time, Ms. Mayor...

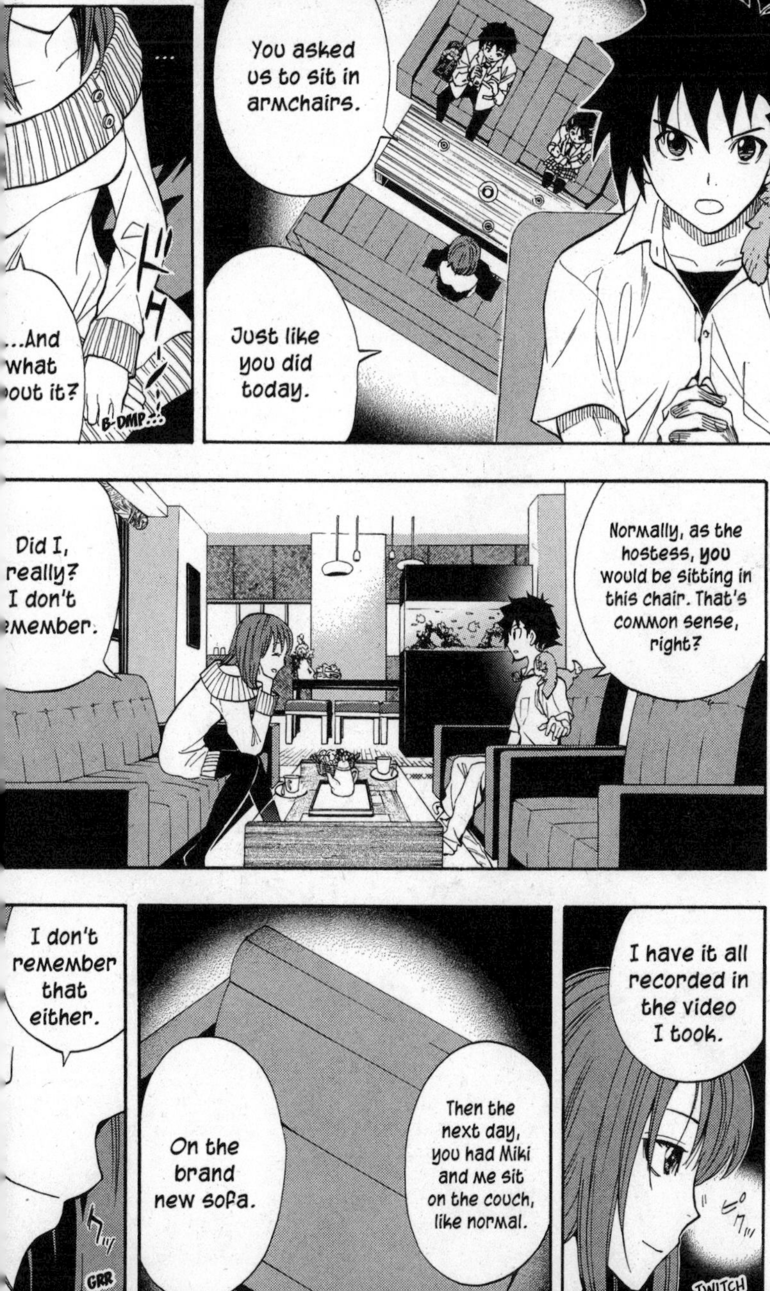
You asked us to sit in armchairs.
Just like you did today.
...
...And what bout it?
B-DMP...
Normally, as the hostess, you would be sitting in this chair. That's common sense, right?
Did I, really? I don't emember.
I have it all recorded in the video I took.
TWITCH
Then the next day, you had Miki and me sit on the couch, like normal.
On the brand new sofa.
I don't remember that either.
GRR

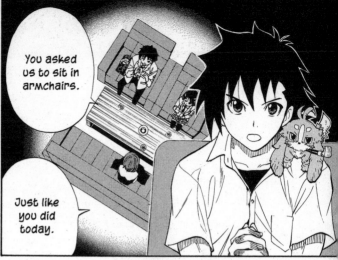

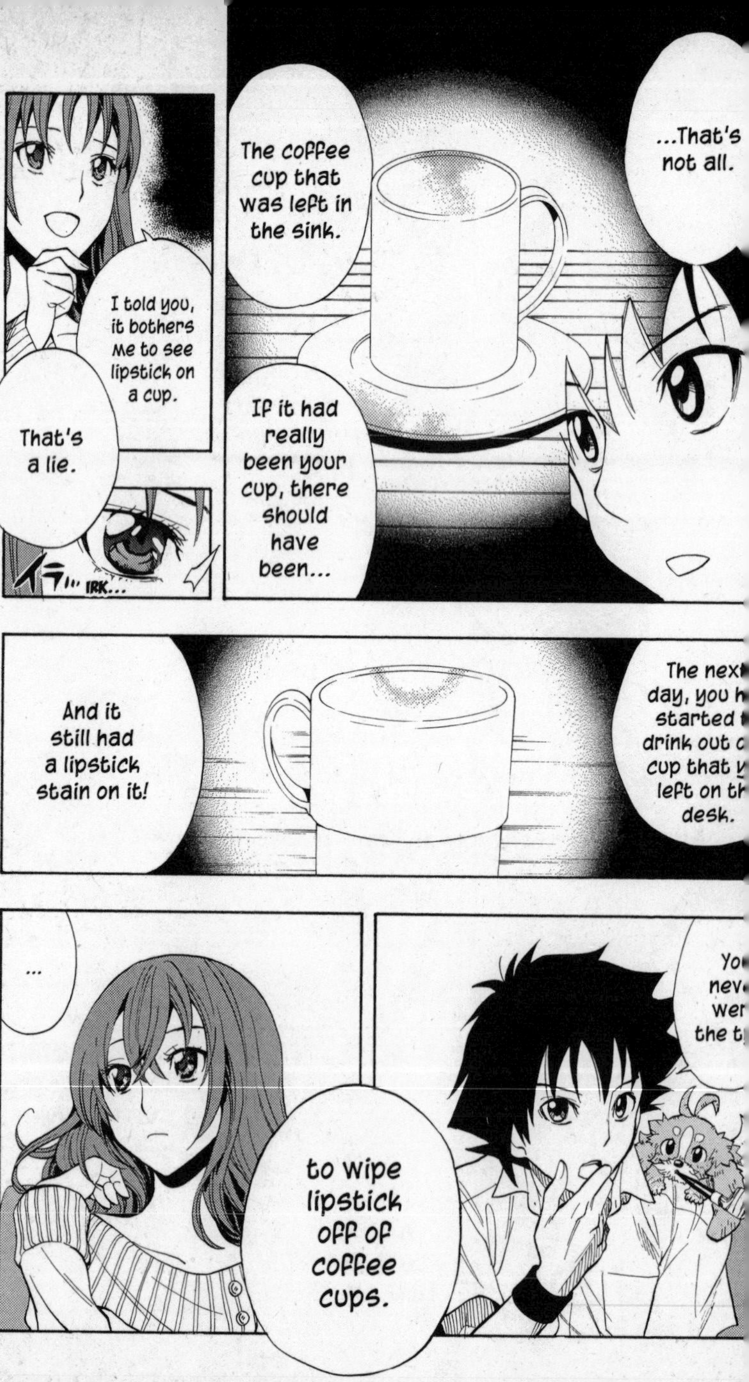
...That's not all.
The coffee cup that was left in the sink.
If it had really been your cup, there should have been...
I told you, it bothers me to see lipstick on a cup.
That's a lie.
IRK...
The nex day, you h started drink out o cup that y left on th desk.
And it still had a lipstick stain on it!
Yo nev wer the t
to wipe lipstick off of coffee cups.
...

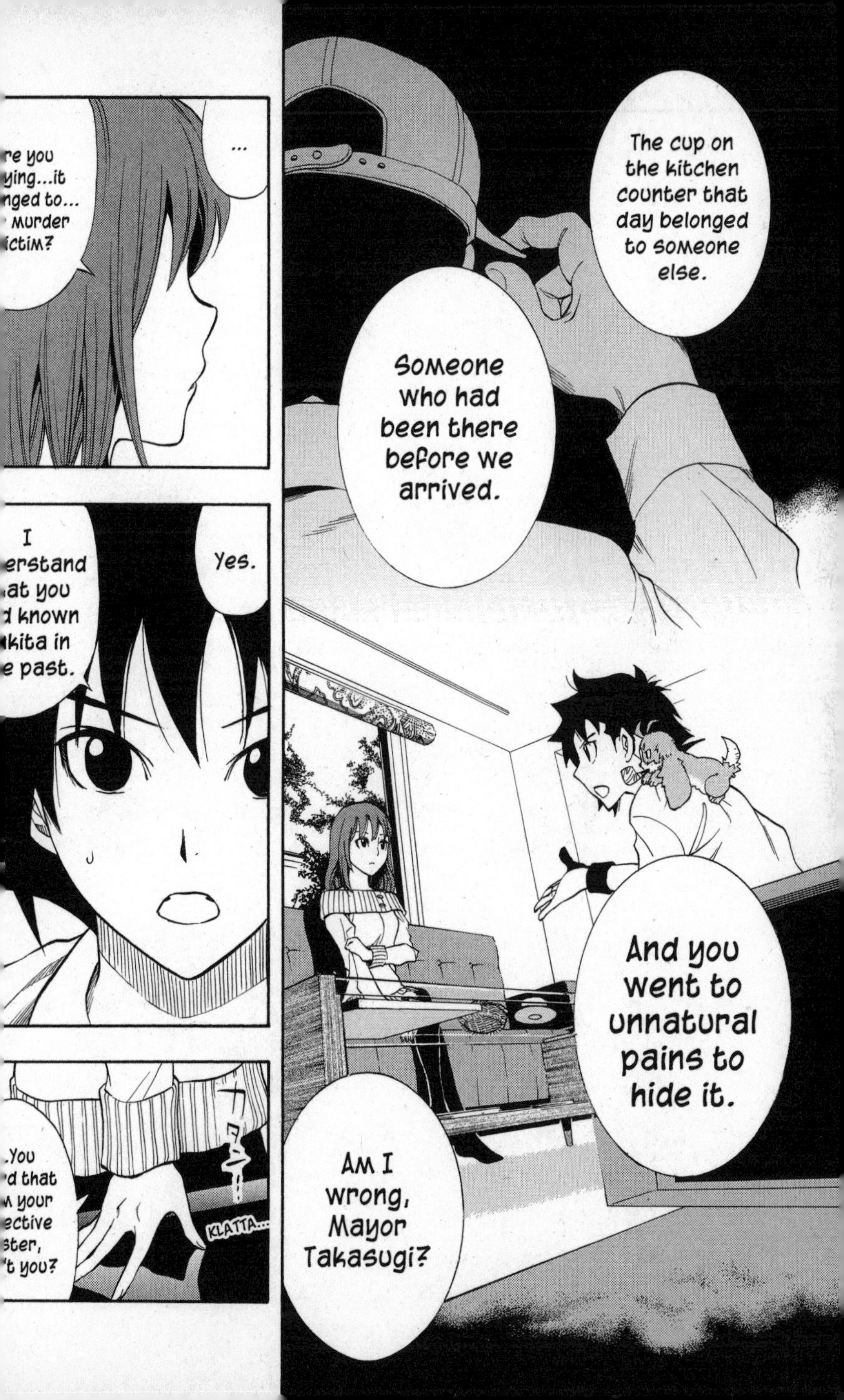

The cup on the kitchen counter that day belonged to someone else.
Someone who had been there before we arrived.
And you went to unnatural pains to hide it.
Am I wrong, Mayor Takasugi?
...
re you ying...it nged to... murder ictim?
Yes.
I erstand at you d known kita in e past.
KLATTA...
.You d that n your ective ster, 't you?

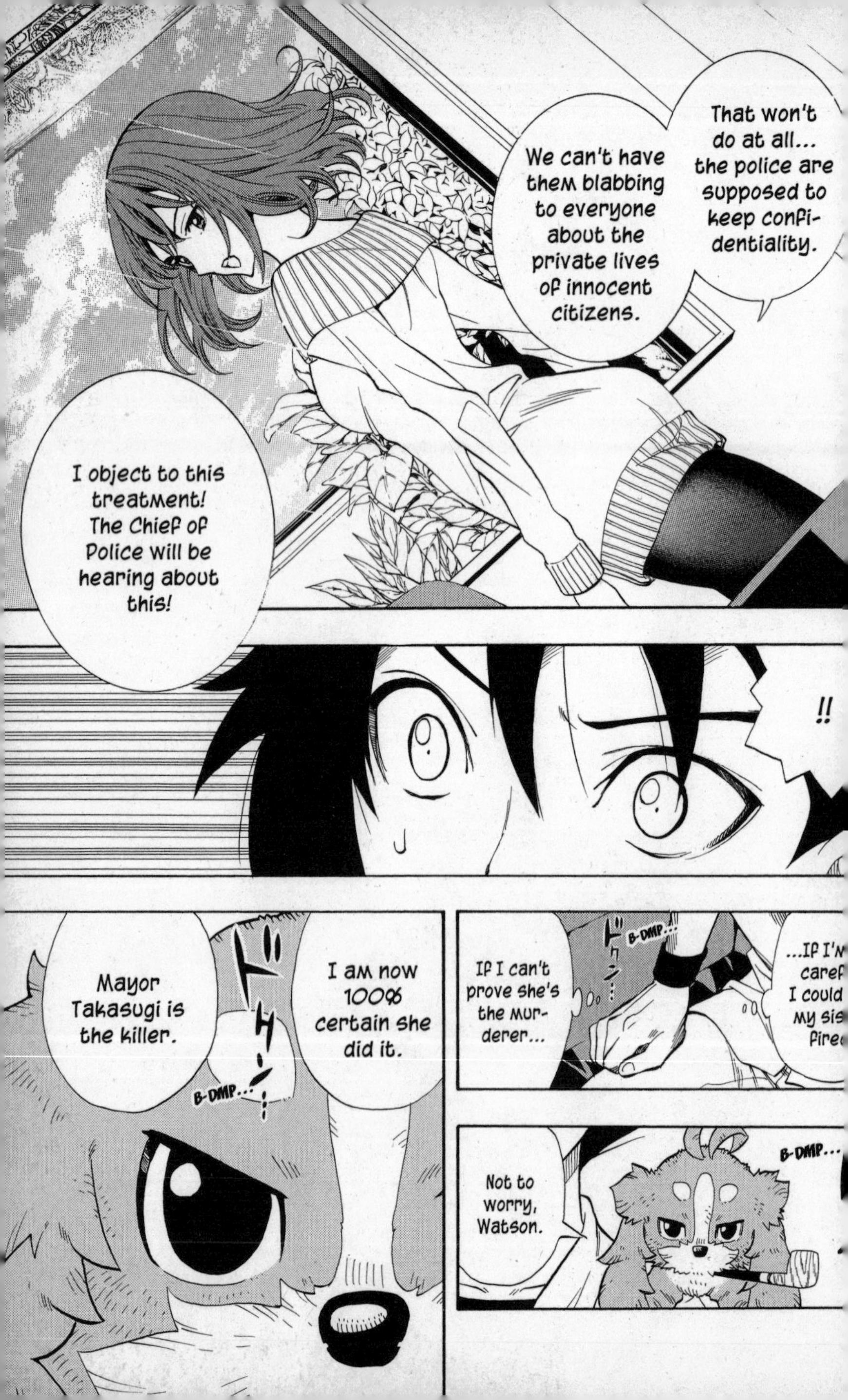
That won't do at all... the police are supposed to keep confi-dentiality.
We can't have them blabbing to everyone about the private lives of innocent citizens.
I object to this treatment! The Chief of Police will be hearing about this!
!!
...If I'M caref I could my sis fire
B-DMP...
If I can't prove she's the mur-derer...
B-DMP...
Not to worry, Watson.
I am now 100% certain she did it.
Mayor Takasugi is the killer.
B-DMP...

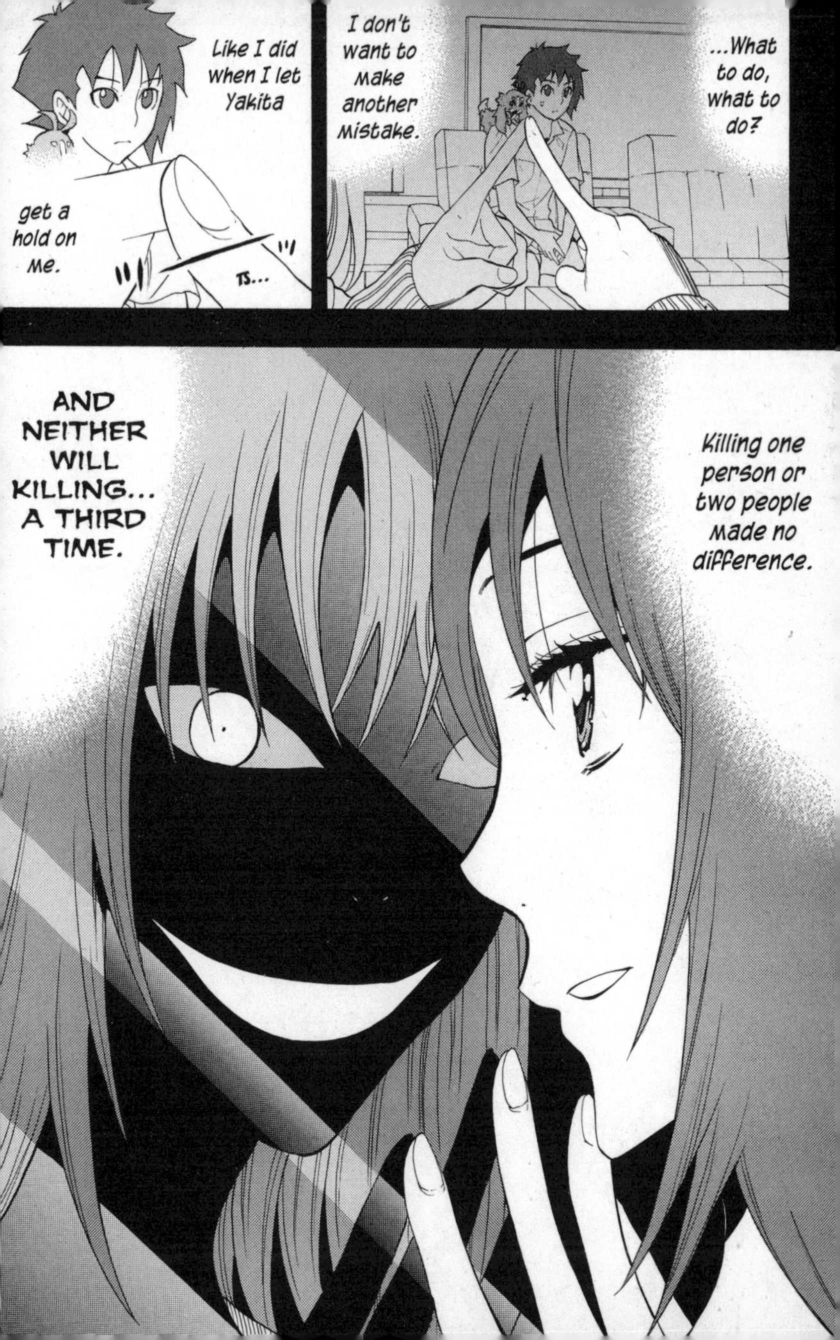
...What to do, what to do?
I don't want to make another mistake.
Like I did when I let Yakita
get a hold on me.
TS...
Killing one person or two people made no difference.
AND NEITHER WILL KILLING... A THIRD TIME.

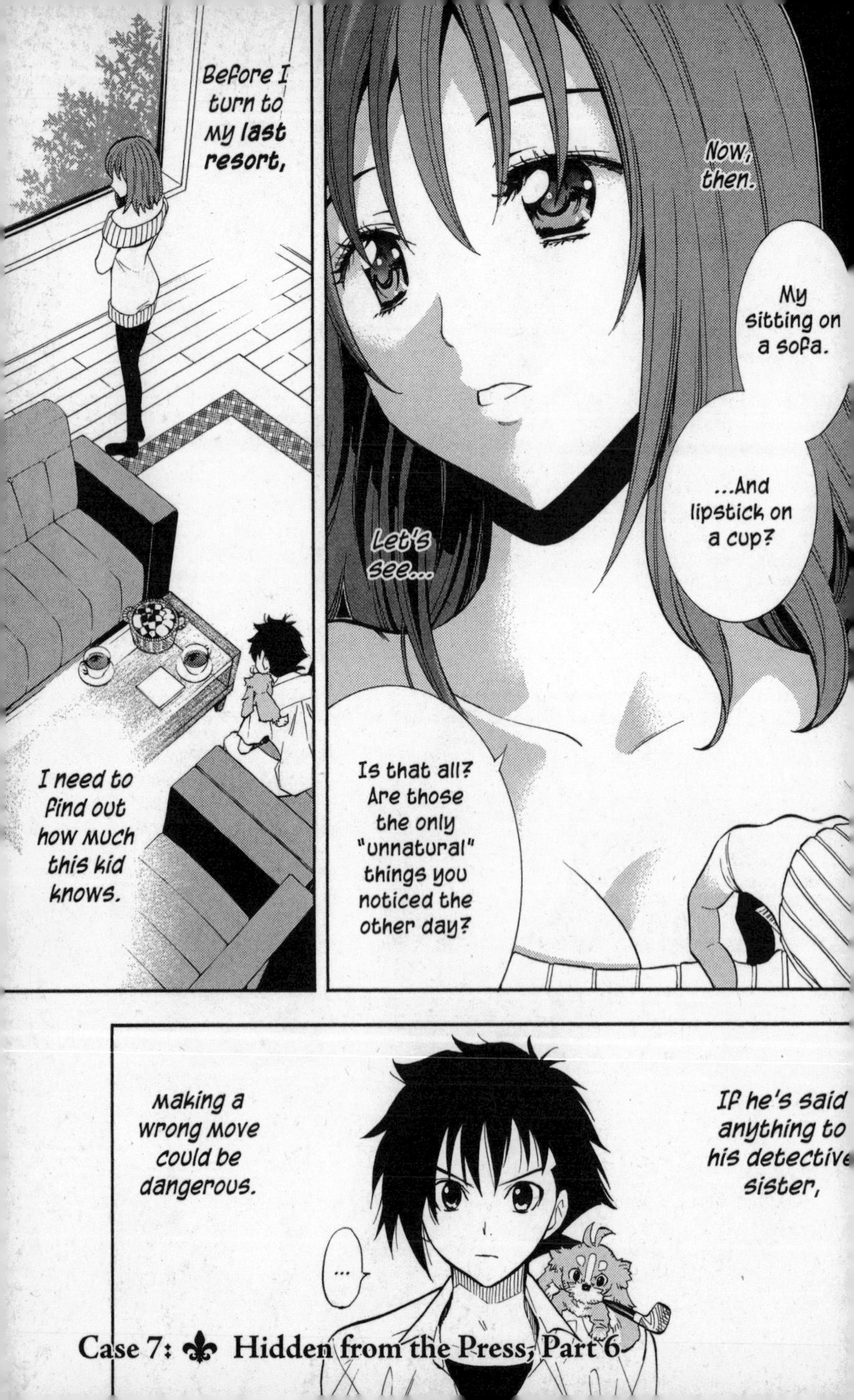
Now, then.
My sitting on a sofa.
...And lipstick on a cup?
Let's see...
Is that all? Are those the only "unnatural" things you noticed the other day?
Before I turn to my last resort,
I need to find out how much this kid knows.
If he's said anything to his detective sister,
Making a wrong move could be dangerous.
...

Case 7: ⚜ Hidden from the Press, Part 6

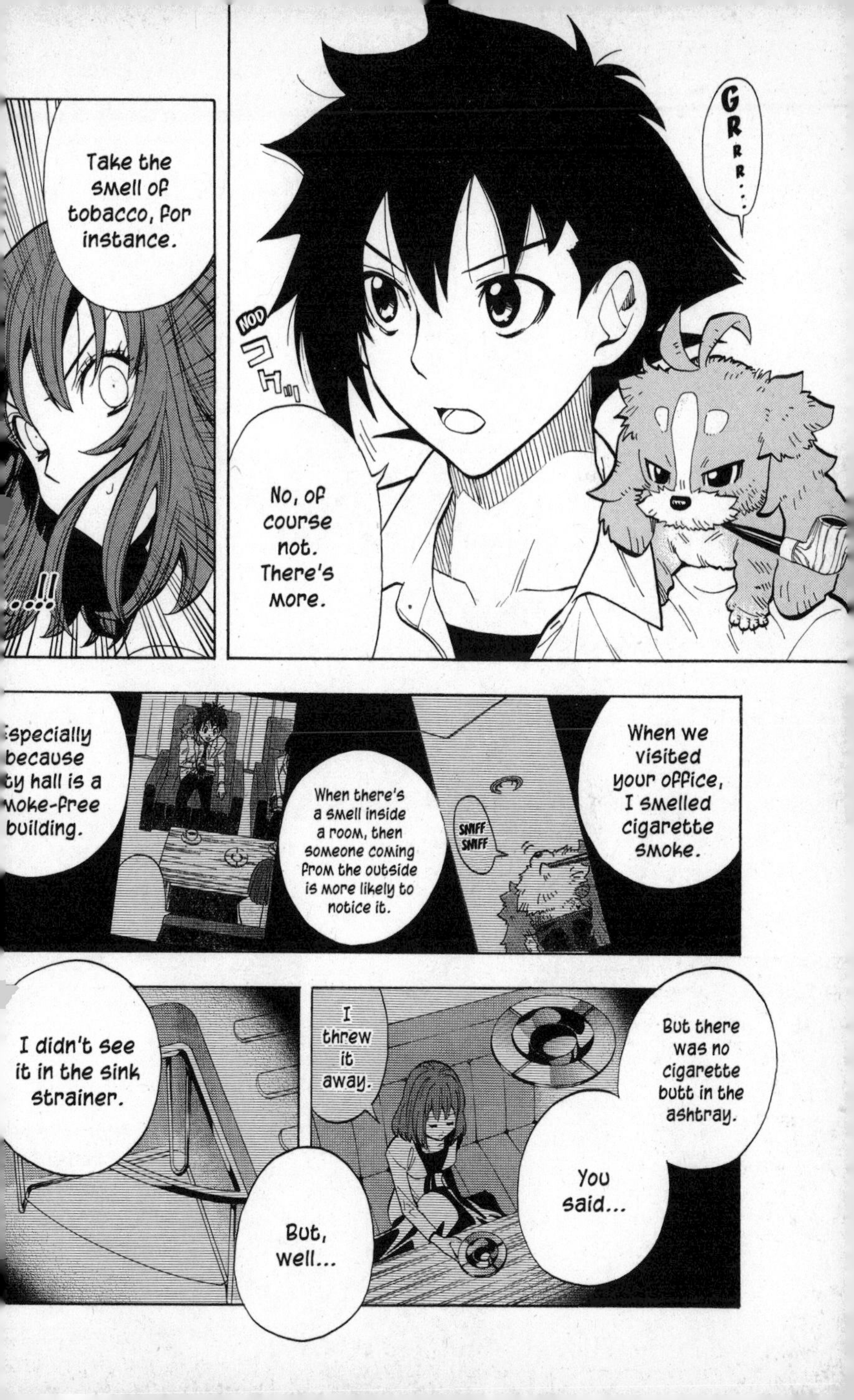
GRrr...
NOD
No, of course not. There's more.
Take the smell of tobacco, for instance.
...!!
When we visited your office, I smelled cigarette smoke.
SNIFF SNIFF
When there's a smell inside a room, then someone coming from the outside is more likely to notice it.
specially because ty hall is a moke-free building.
But there was no cigarette butt in the ashtray.
You said...
I threw it away.
But, well...
I didn't see it in the sink strainer.

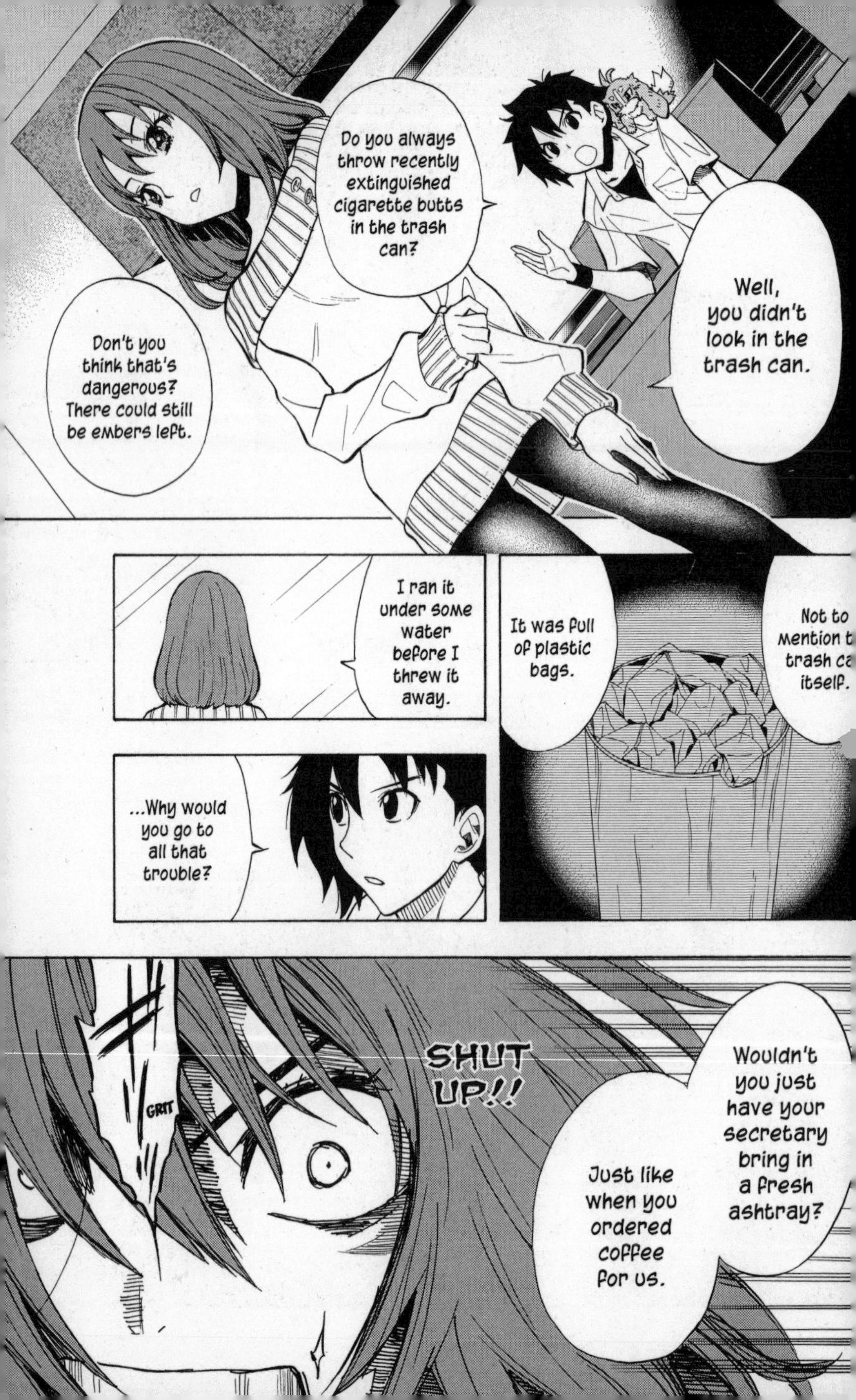
Well, you didn't look in the trash can.
Do you always throw recently extinguished cigarette butts in the trash can?
Don't you think that's dangerous? There could still be embers left.
Not to mention t trash ca itself.
It was full of plastic bags.
I ran it under some water before I threw it away.
...Why would you go to all that trouble?
Wouldn't you just have your secretary bring in a fresh ashtray?
Just like when you ordered coffee for us.
SHUT UP!!
GRIT

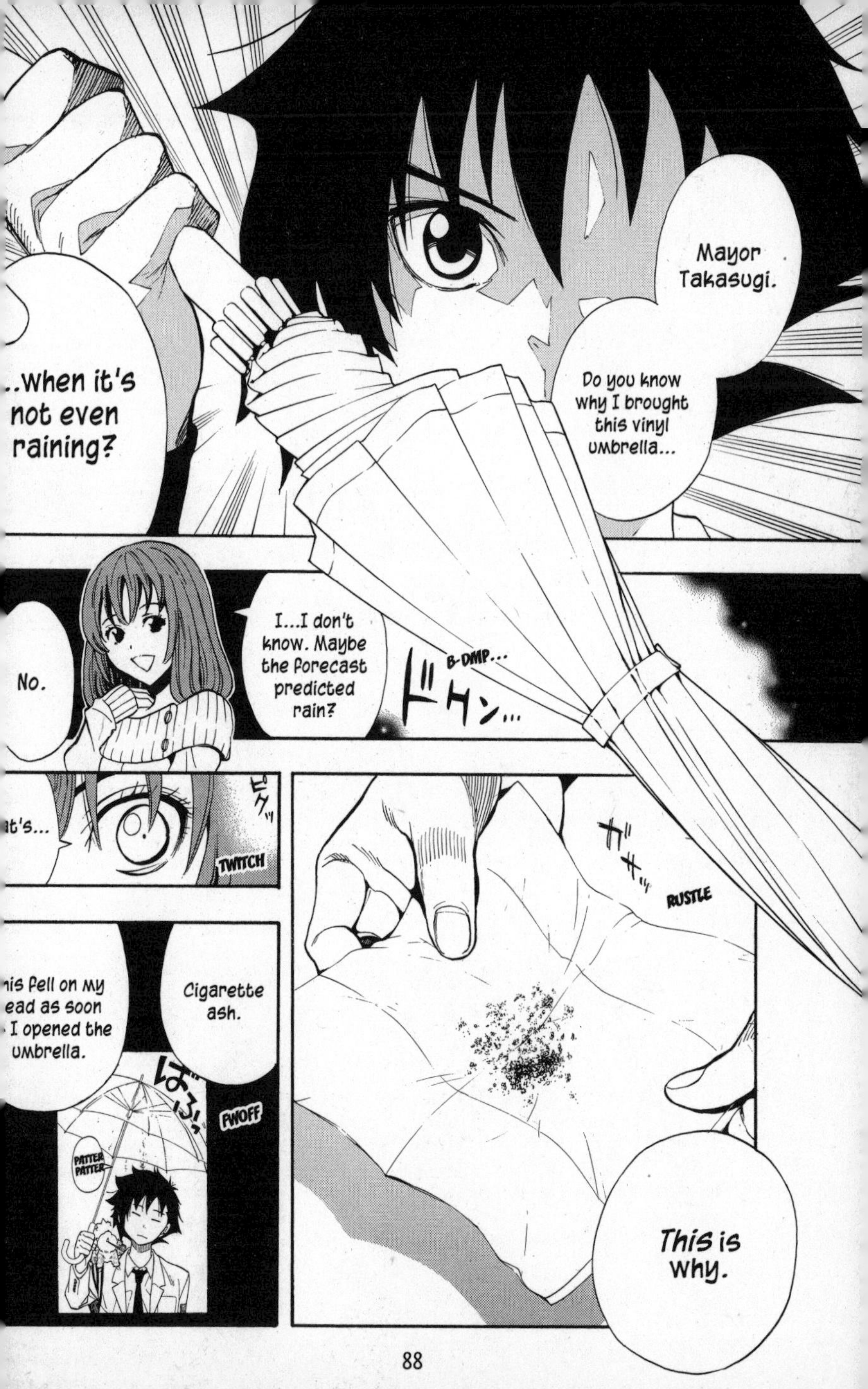
Mayor Takasugi.
Do you know why I brought this vinyl umbrella...
..when it's not even raining?
ドクン...
B-DMP...
I...I don't know. Maybe the forecast predicted rain?
No.
ガサッ
RUSTLE
This is why.
at's...
ピクッ
TWITCH
Cigarette ash.
nis fell on my
ead as soon
I opened the
umbrella.
ぼふっ
PWOFF
PATTER PATTER

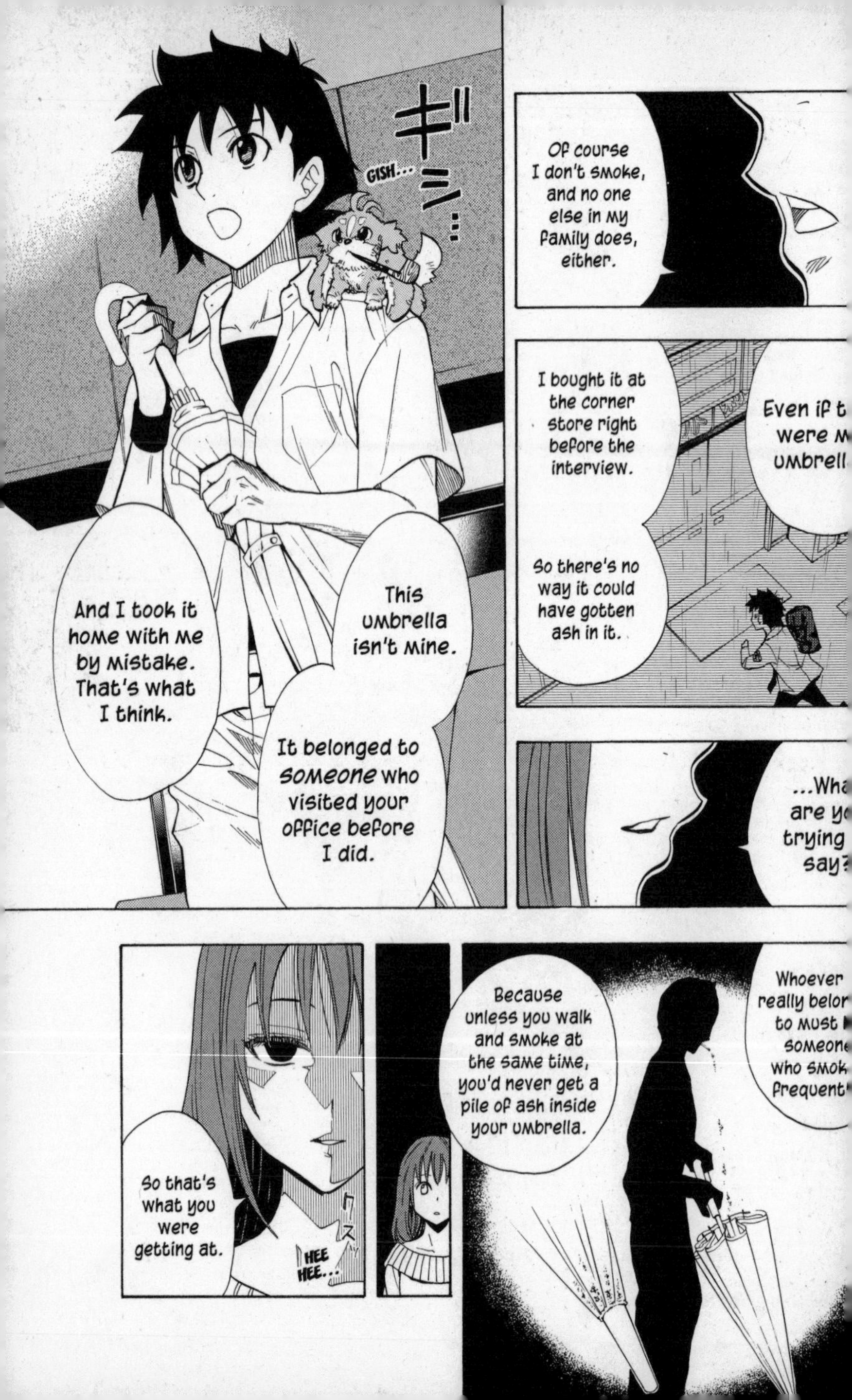

Of course I don't smoke, and no one else in my family does, either.
Even if t were m umbrell
I bought it at the corner store right before the interview.
So there's no way it could have gotten ash in it.
...Wha are y trying say?
GISH...
This umbrella isn't mine.
It belonged to *someone* who visited your office before I did.
And I took it home with me by mistake. That's what I think.
Whoever really belor to must someone who smok frequent
Because unless you walk and smoke at the same time, you'd never get a pile of ash inside your umbrella.
HEE HEE...
So that's what you were getting at.

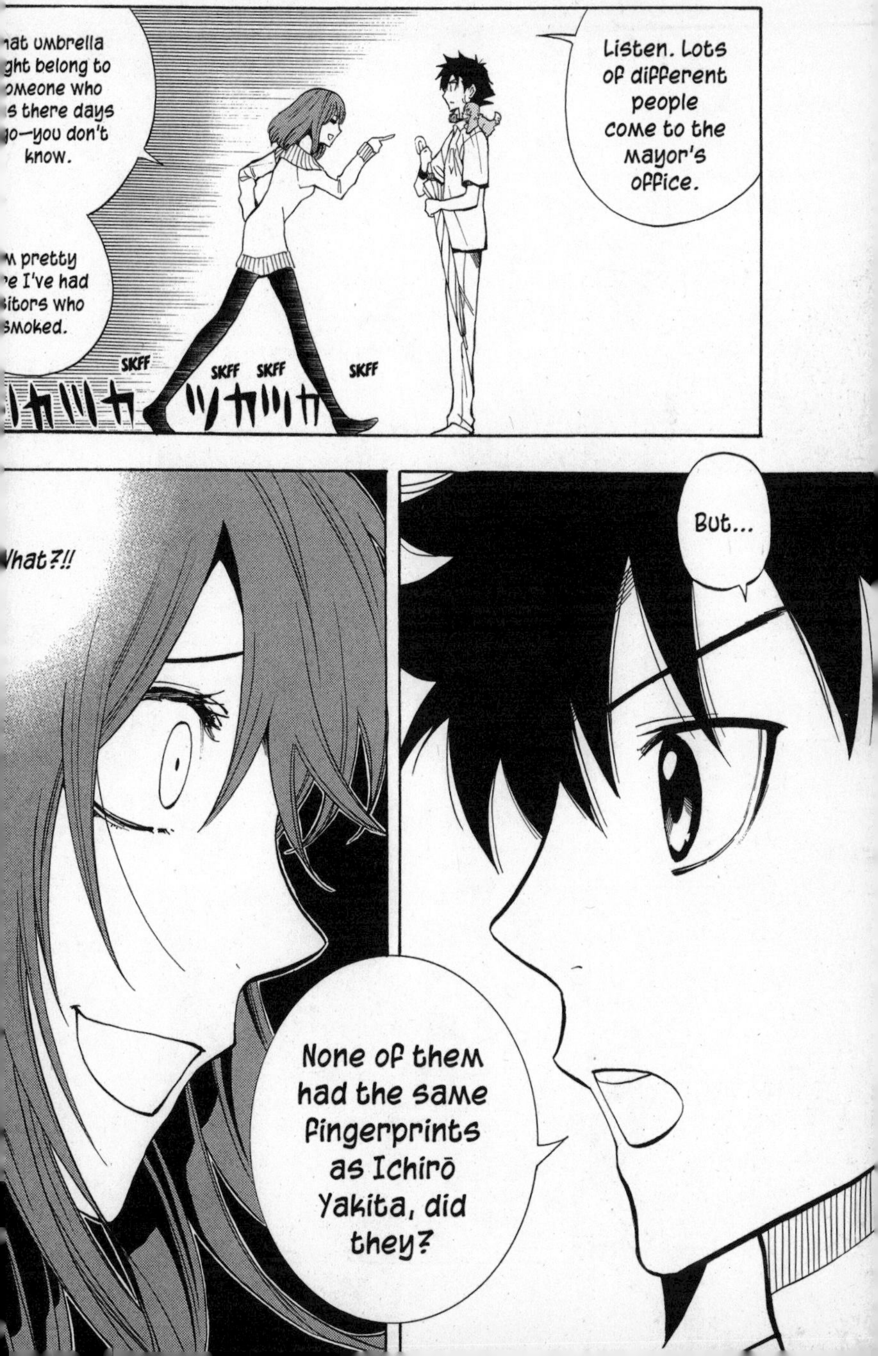
Listen. Lots of different people come to the mayor's office.
nat umbrella ght belong to omeone who s there days o—you don't know.
m pretty e I've had sitors who smoked.
SKFF
SKFF
SKFF
SKFF
But...
None of them had the same fingerprints as Ichirō Yakita, did they?
What?!!

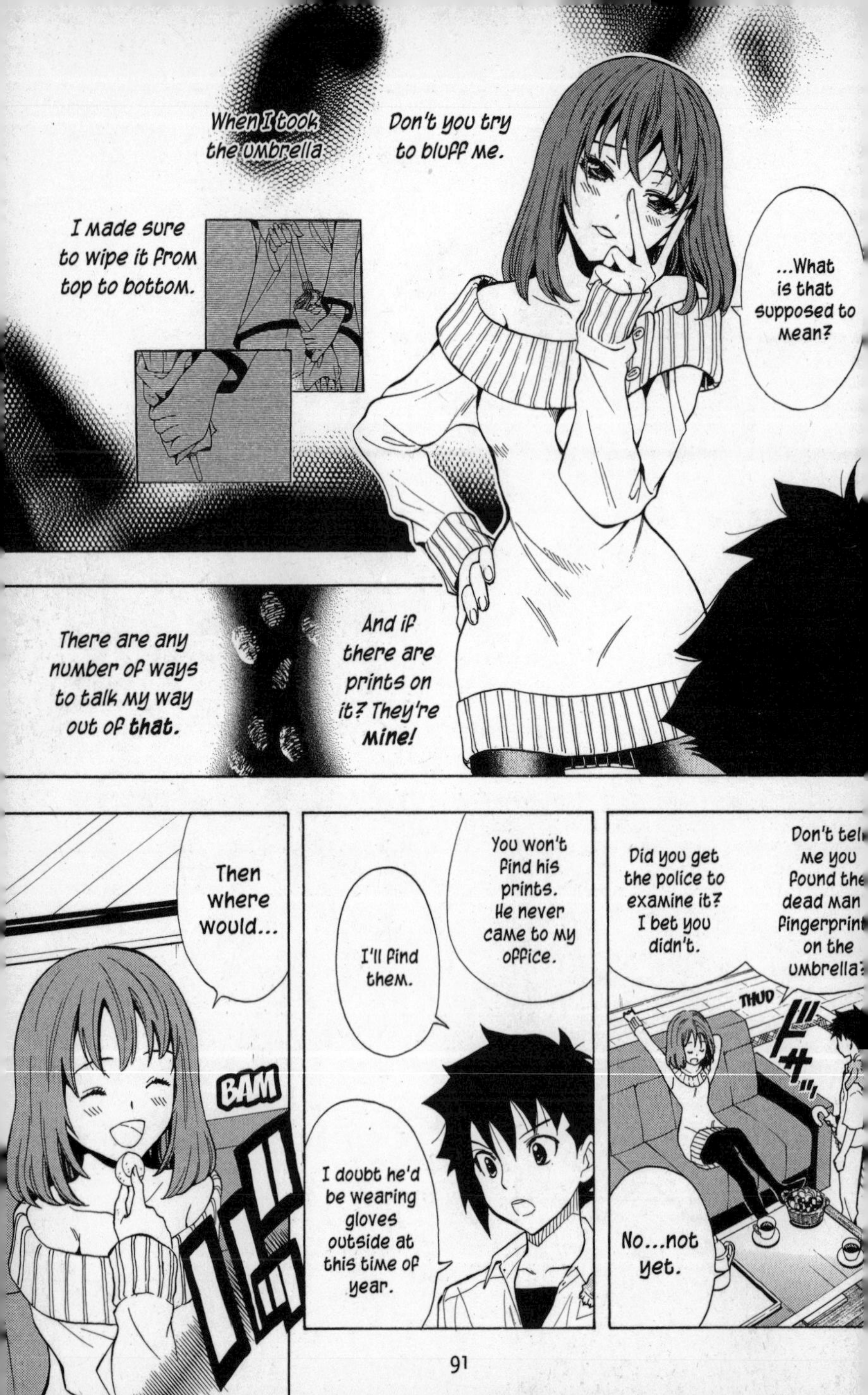
...What is that supposed to mean?
Don't you try to bluff me.
When I took the umbrella
I made sure to wipe it from top to bottom.
And if there are prints on it? They're **mine!**
There are any number of ways to talk my way out of **that.**
Don't tel me you found the dead man fingerprin on the umbrella?
Did you get the police to examine it? I bet you didn't.
THUD
No...not yet.
You won't find his prints. He never came to my office.
I'll find them.
I doubt he'd be wearing gloves outside at this time of year.
Then where would...
BAM

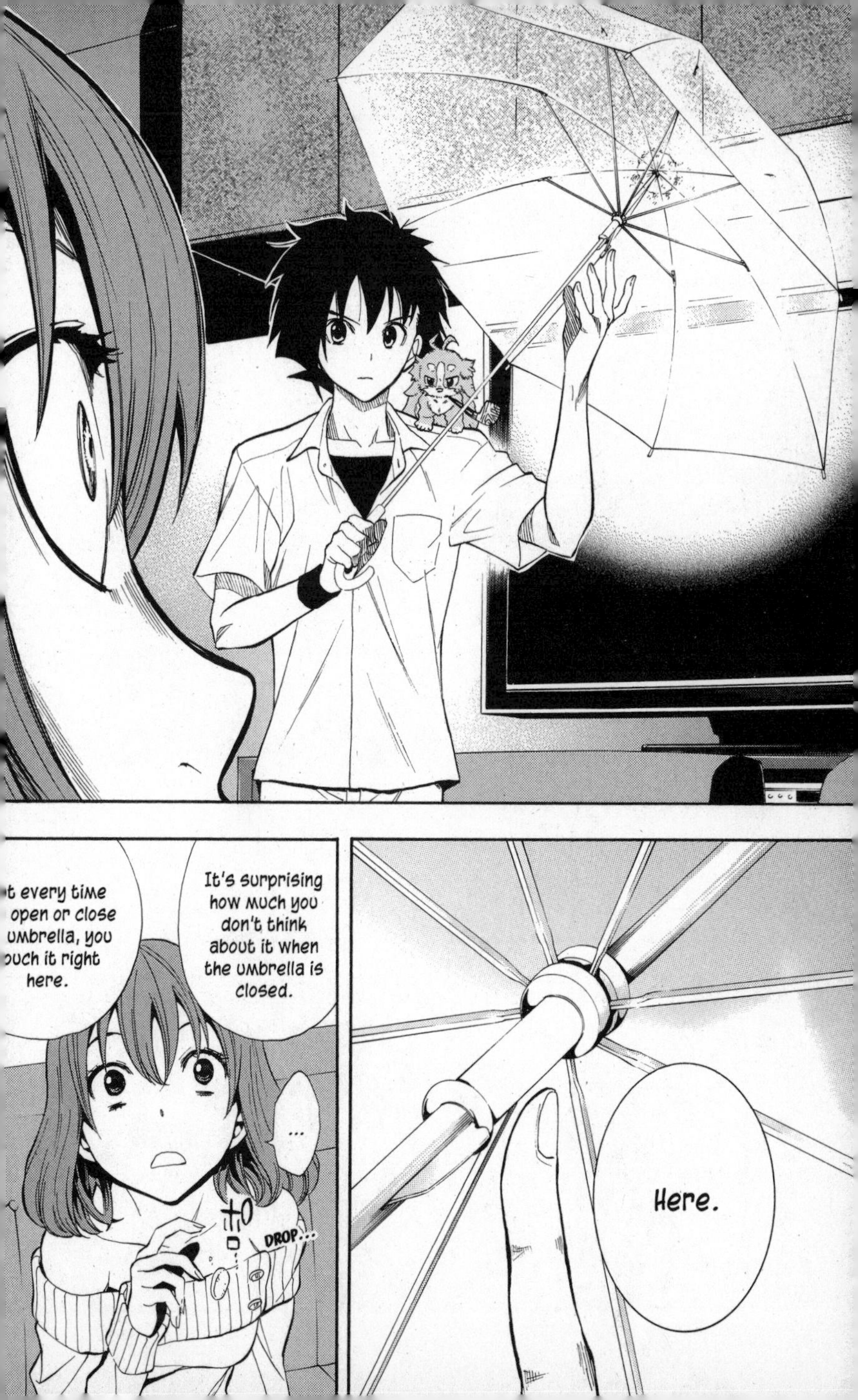
Here.
It's surprising how much you don't think about it when the umbrella is closed.
t every time open or close umbrella, you ouch it right here.
...
DROP...

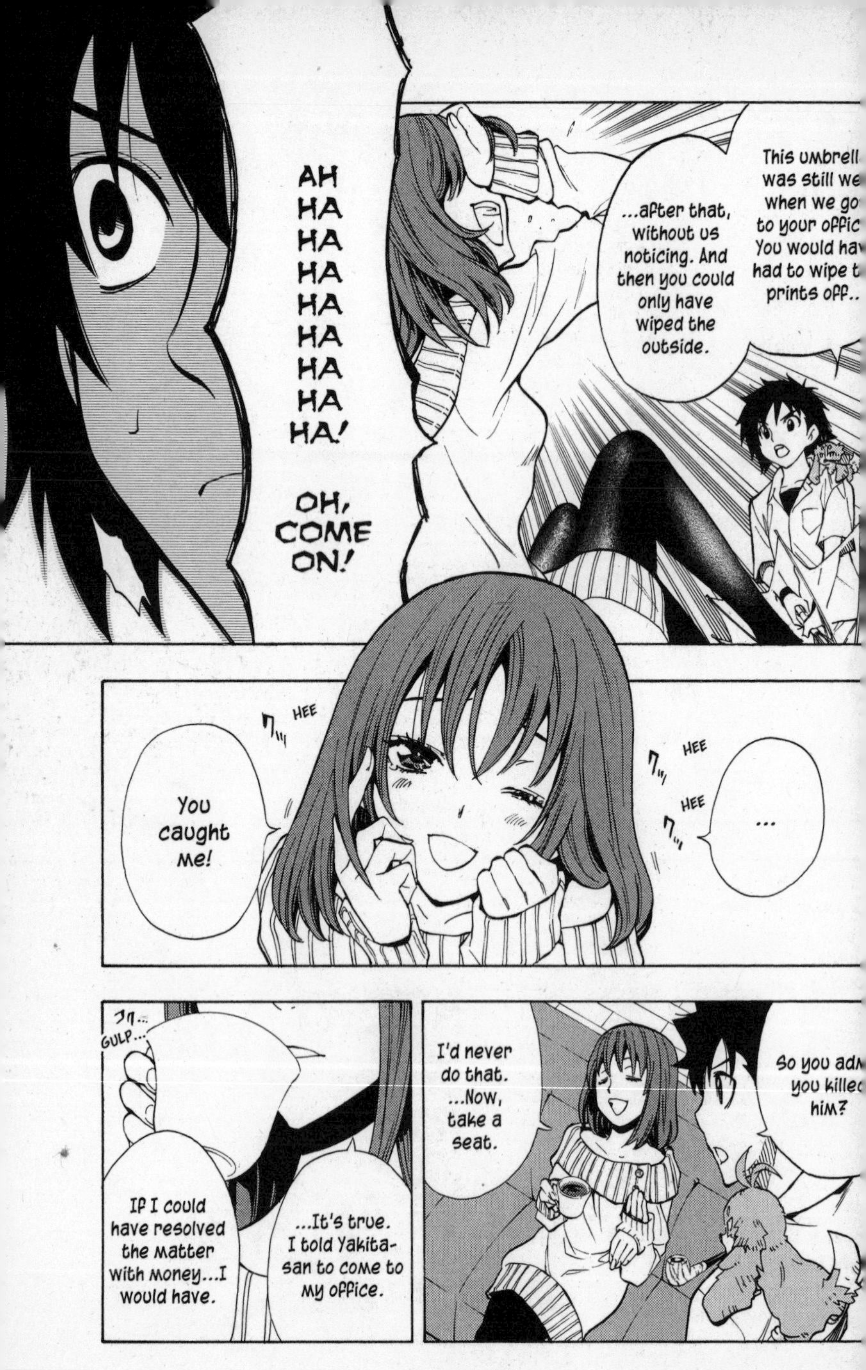
This umbrell was still we when we go to your offic You would hav had to wipe t prints off..
...after that, without us noticing. And then you could only have wiped the outside.
AH HA HA HA HA HA HA HA HA!
OH, COME ON!
HEE
HEE
...
HEE
You caught me!
So you adm you killed him?
I'd never do that. ...Now, take a seat.
GULP...
...It's true. I told Yakita-san to come to my office.
If I could have resolved the matter with money...I would have.

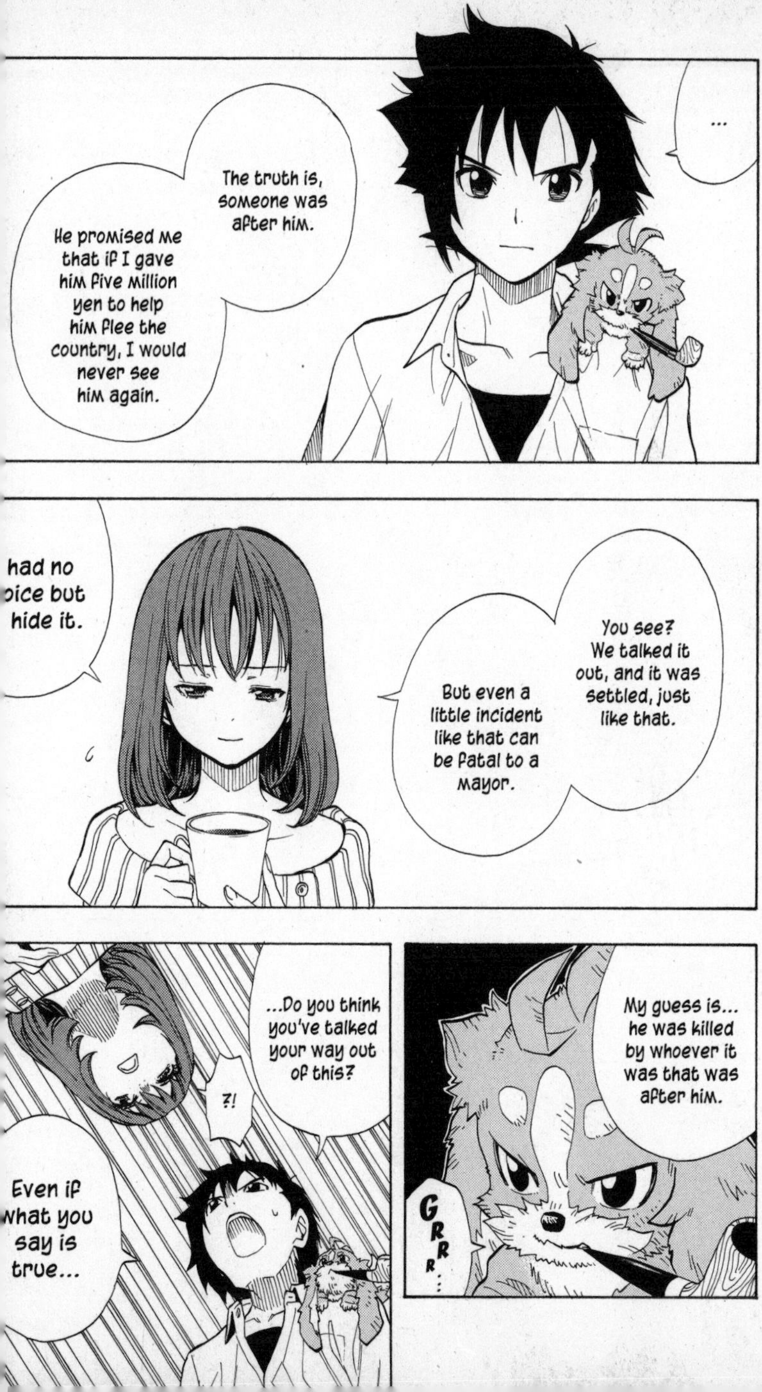
...
The truth is, someone was after him.
He promised me that if I gave him five million yen to help him flee the country, I would never see him again.
You see? We talked it out, and it was settled, just like that.
But even a little incident like that can be fatal to a mayor.
had no oice but hide it.
My guess is... he was killed by whoever it was that was after him.
GRRR...
...Do you think you've talked your way out of this?
?!
Even if what you say is true...

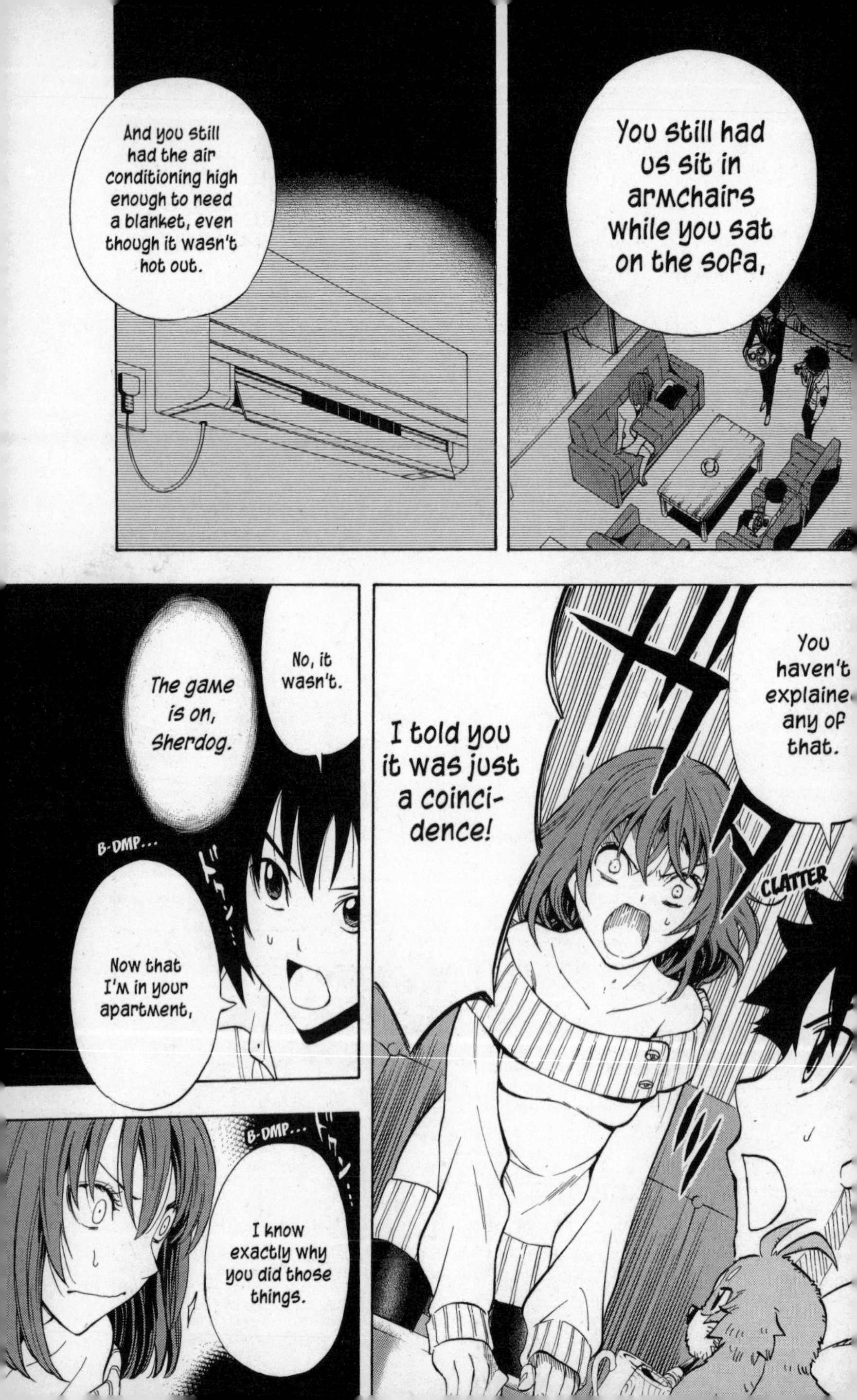
You still had us sit in armchairs while you sat on the sofa,
And you still had the air conditioning high enough to need a blanket, even though it wasn't hot out.
You haven't explaine any of that.
I told you it was just a coinci-dence!
CLATTER
No, it wasn't.
The game is on, Sherdog.
B-DMP...
Now that I'm in your apartment,
B-DMP...
I know exactly why you did those things.

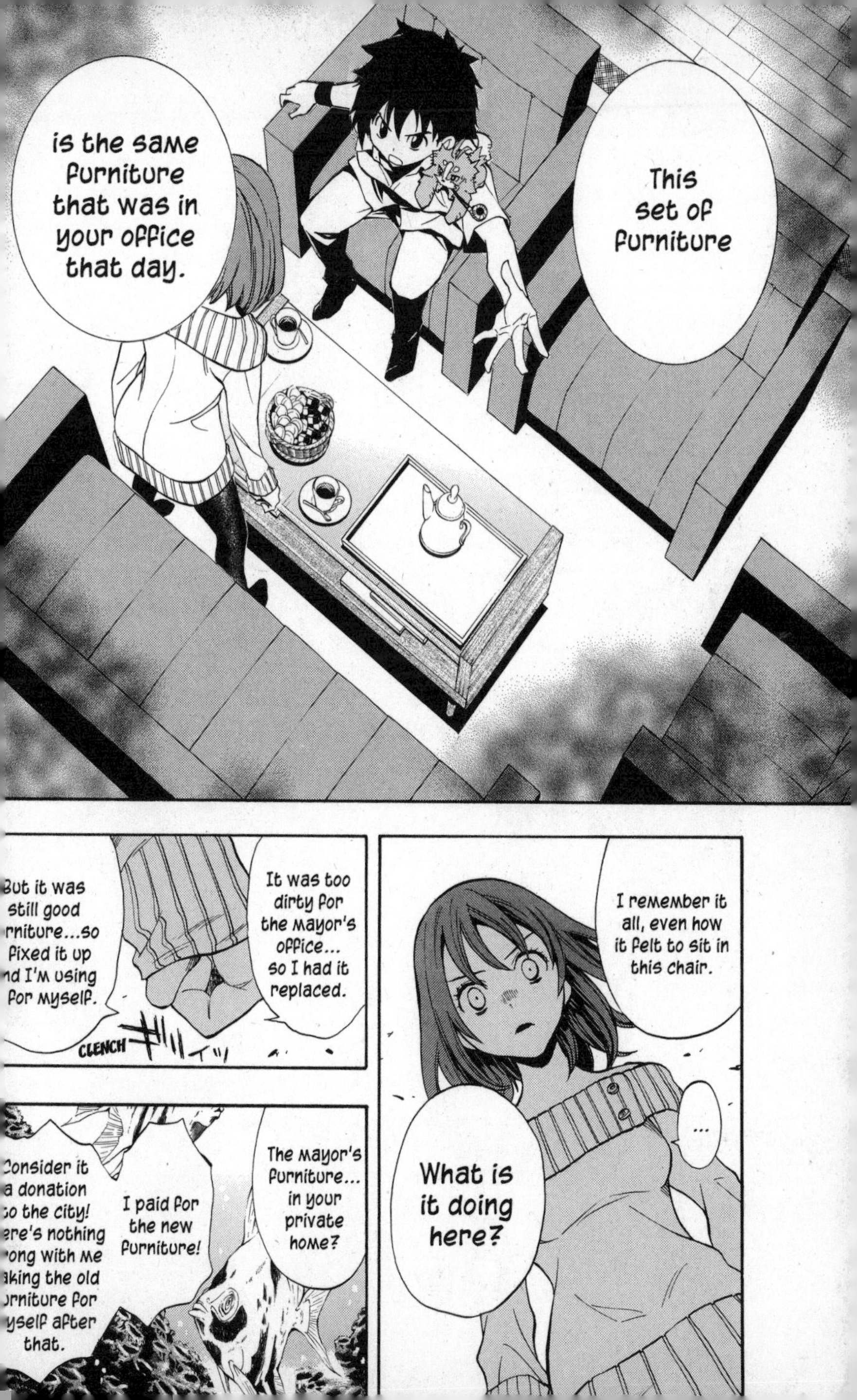

This set of furniture
is the same furniture that was in your office that day.
I remember it all, even how it felt to sit in this chair.
...
What is it doing here?
It was too dirty for the mayor's office... so I had it replaced.
But it was still good rniture...so fixed it up nd I'm using for myself.
CLENCH
The mayor's furniture... in your private home?
I paid for the new furniture!
Consider it a donation o the city! ere's nothing rong with me aking the old rniture for yself after that.

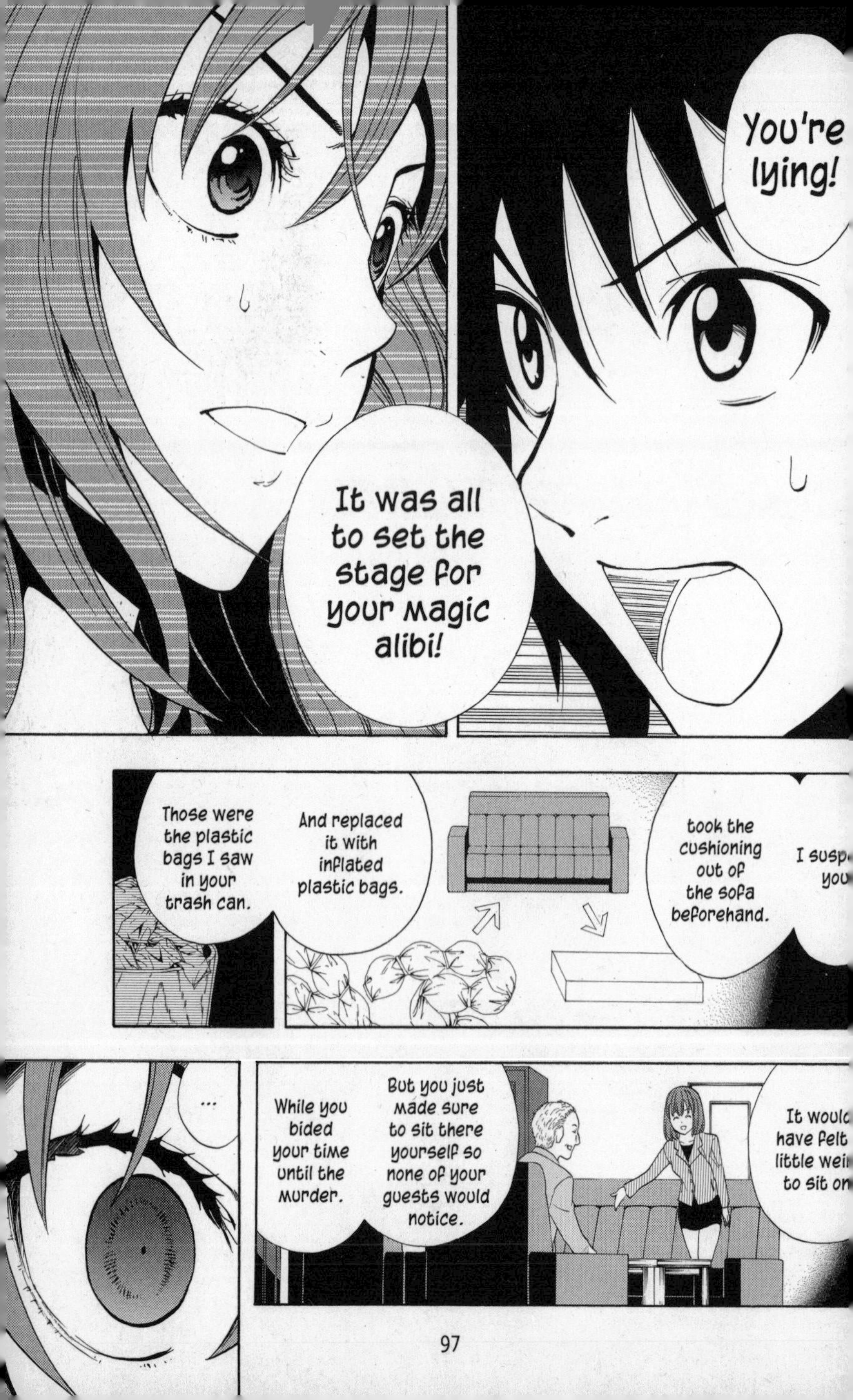
You're lying!
It was all to set the stage for your magic alibi!
I susp you
took the cushioning out of the sofa beforehand.
And replaced it with inflated plastic bags.
Those were the plastic bags I saw in your trash can.
It woul have felt little wei to sit on
But you just made sure to sit there yourself so none of your guests would notice.
While you bided your time until the murder.
...

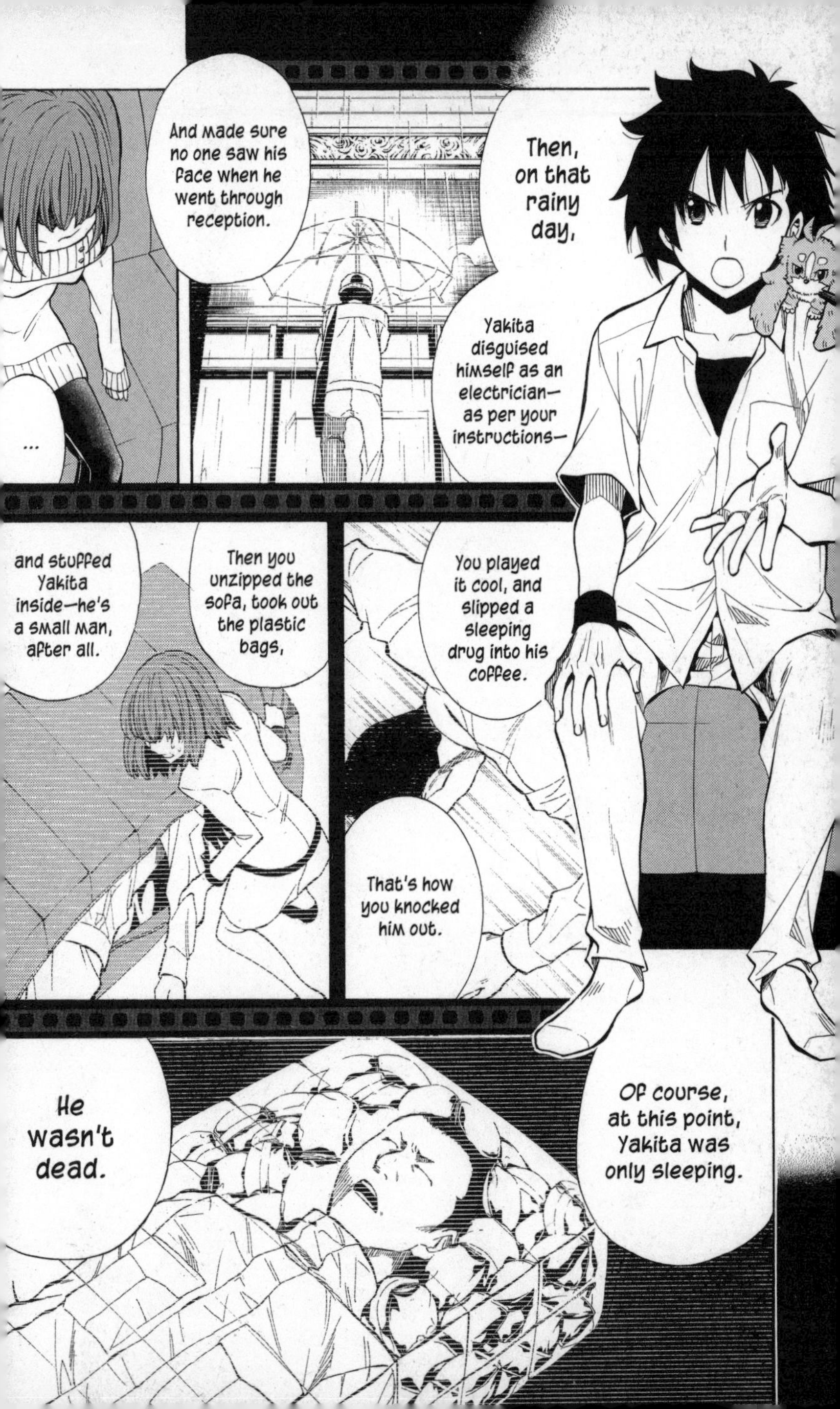
Then, on that rainy day,
Yakita disguised himself as an electrician—as per your instructions—
And made sure no one saw his face when he went through reception.
...
You played it cool, and slipped a sleeping drug into his coffee.
That's how you knocked him out.
Then you unzipped the sofa, took out the plastic bags,
and stuffed Yakita inside—he's a small man, after all.
Of course, at this point, Yakita was only sleeping.
He wasn't dead.

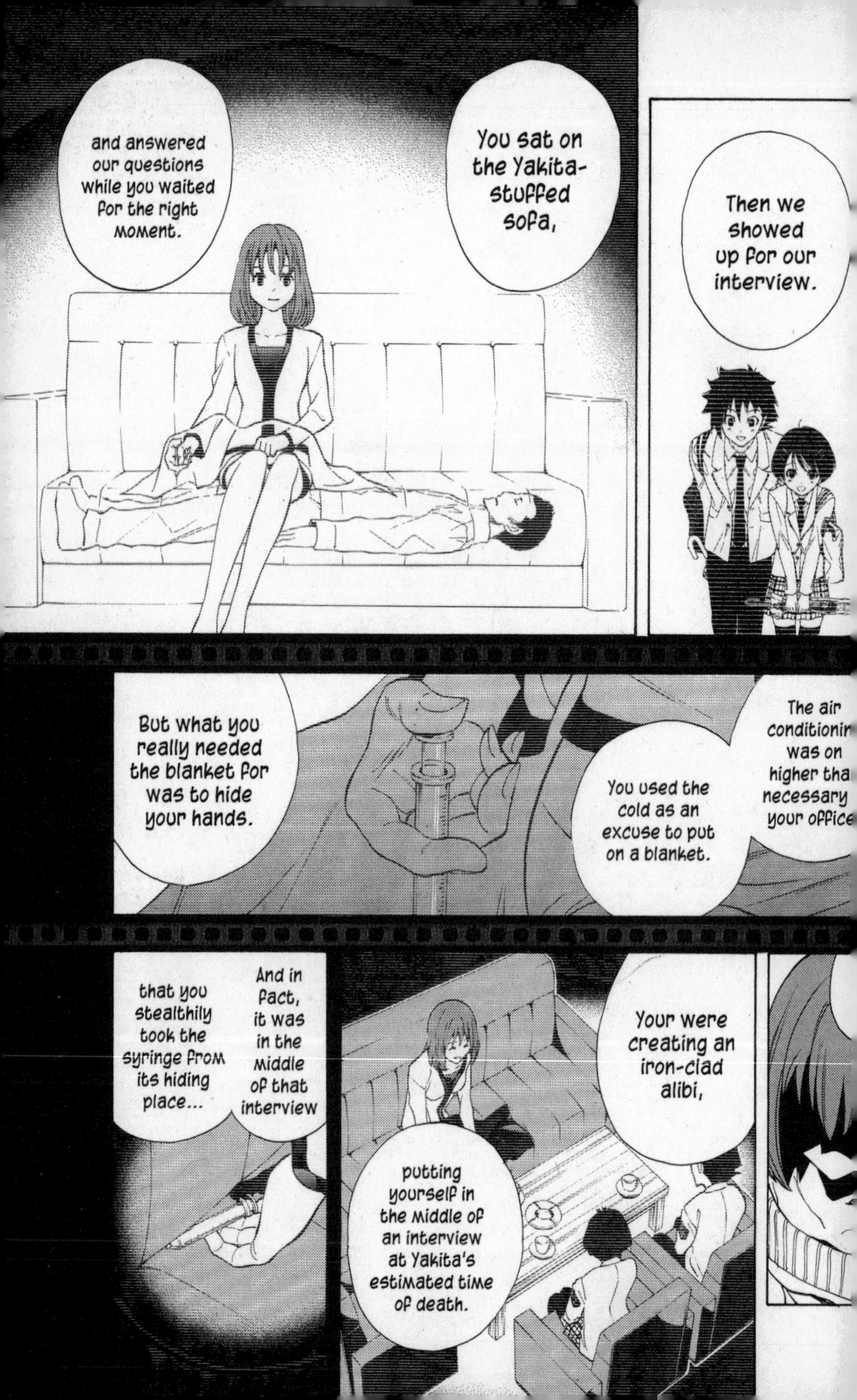
Then we showed up for our interview.
You sat on the Yakita-stuffed sofa,
and answered our questions while you waited for the right moment.
The air conditionin was on higher tha necessary your office
You used the cold as an excuse to put on a blanket.
But what you really needed the blanket for was to hide your hands.
Your were creating an iron-clad alibi,
putting yourself in the middle of an interview at Yakita's estimated time of death.
And in fact, it was in the middle of that interview
that you stealthily took the syringe from its hiding place...

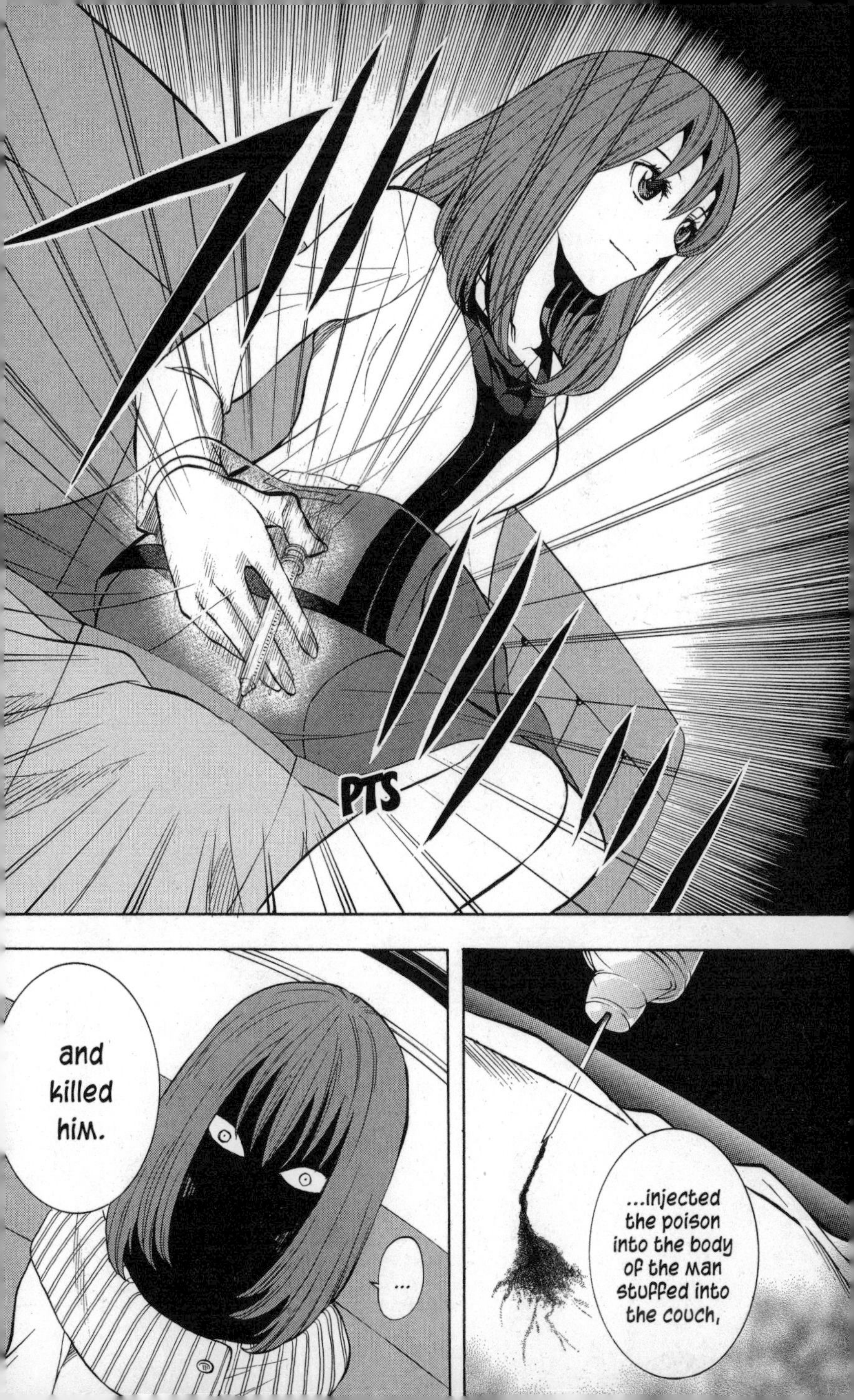
PTS
...injected the poison into the body of the man stuffed into the couch,
and killed him.
...

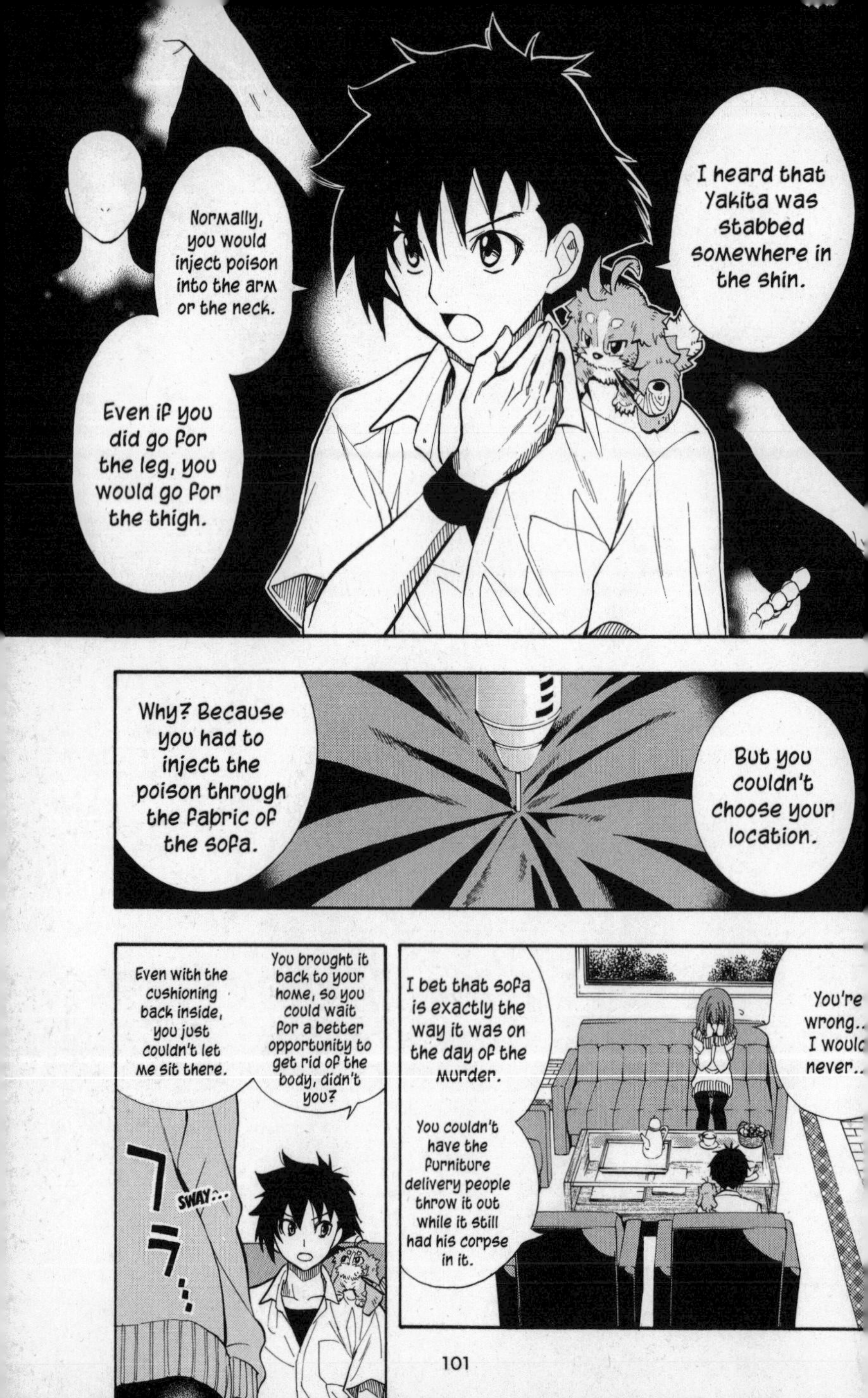
I heard that Yakita was stabbed somewhere in the shin.
Normally, you would inject poison into the arm or the neck.
Even if you did go for the leg, you would go for the thigh.
But you couldn't choose your location.
Why? Because you had to inject the poison through the fabric of the sofa.
You're wrong... I would never...
I bet that sofa is exactly the way it was on the day of the murder.
You couldn't have the furniture delivery people throw it out while it still had his corpse in it.
You brought it back to your home, so you could wait for a better opportunity to get rid of the body, didn't you?
Even with the cushioning back inside, you just couldn't let me sit there.
SWAY...

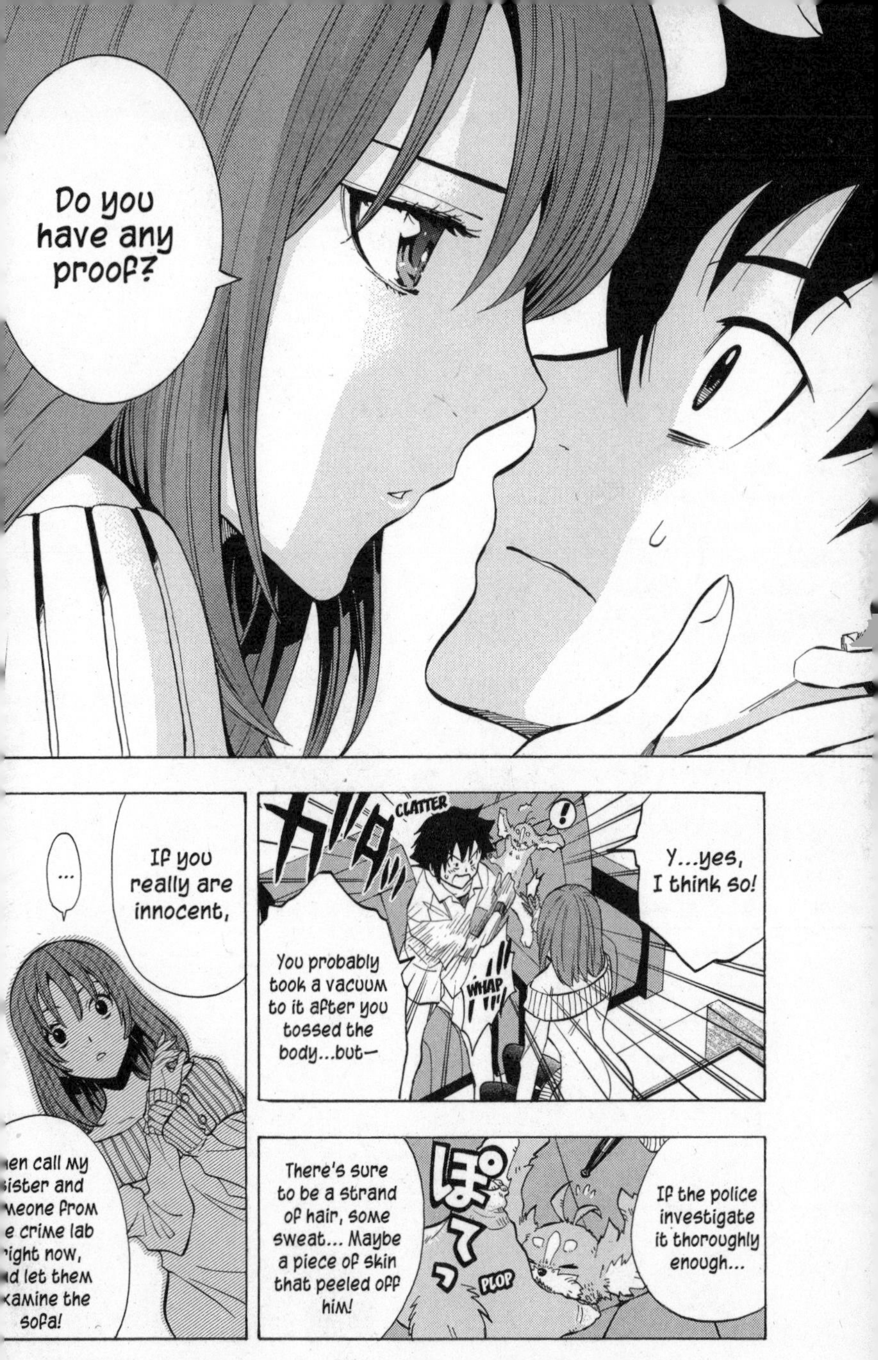
Do you have any proof?
Y...yes, I think so!
CLATTER
!
WHAP
You probably took a vacuum to it after you tossed the body...but—
If the police investigate it thoroughly enough...
There's sure to be a strand of hair, some sweat... Maybe a piece of skin that peeled off him!
ぽてっ
PLOP
If you really are innocent,
...
en call my sister and meone from e crime lab right now, d let them xamine the sofa!

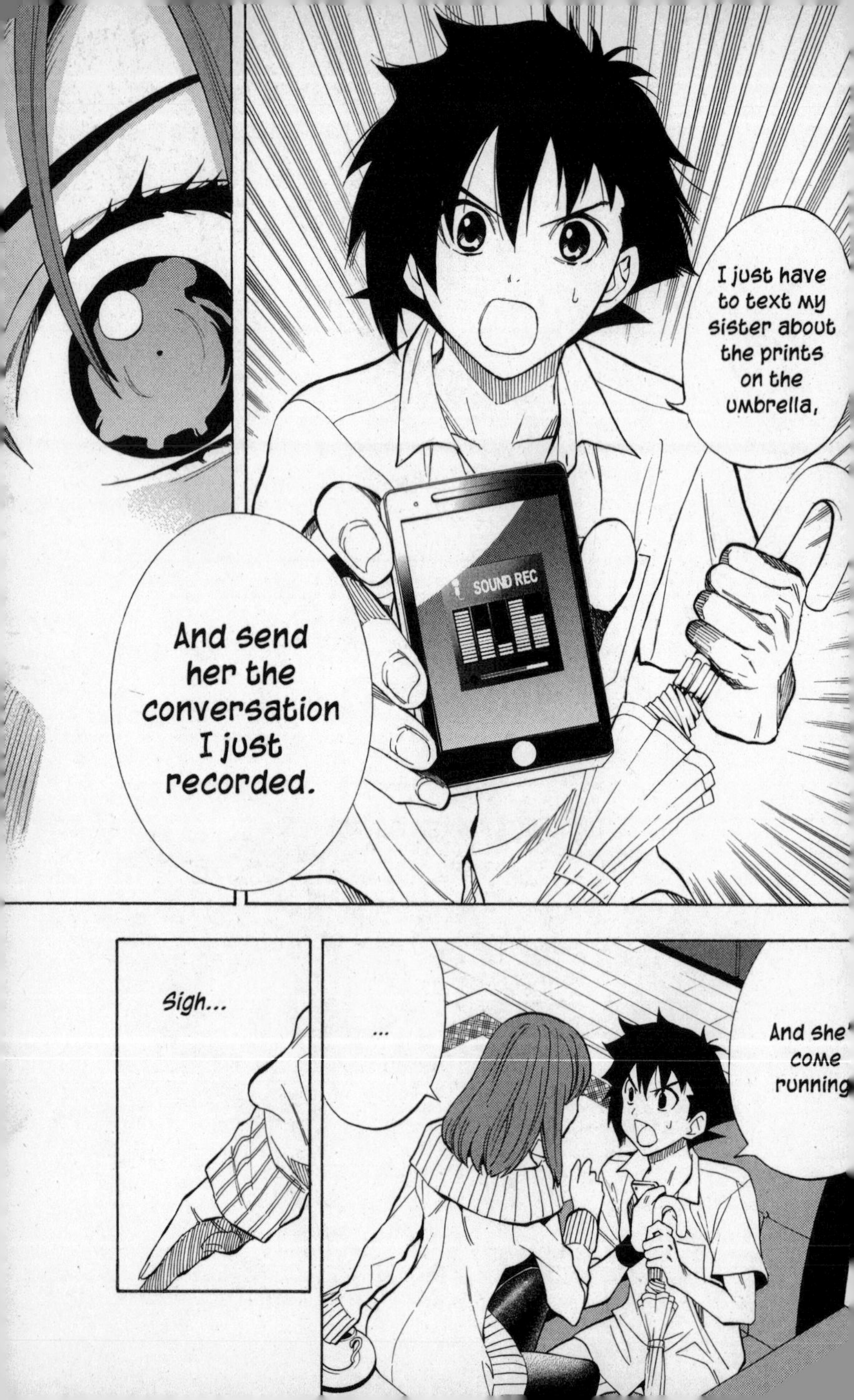
I just have to text my sister about the prints on the umbrella,
SOUND REC
And send her the conversation I just recorded.
And she' come running
...
Sigh...

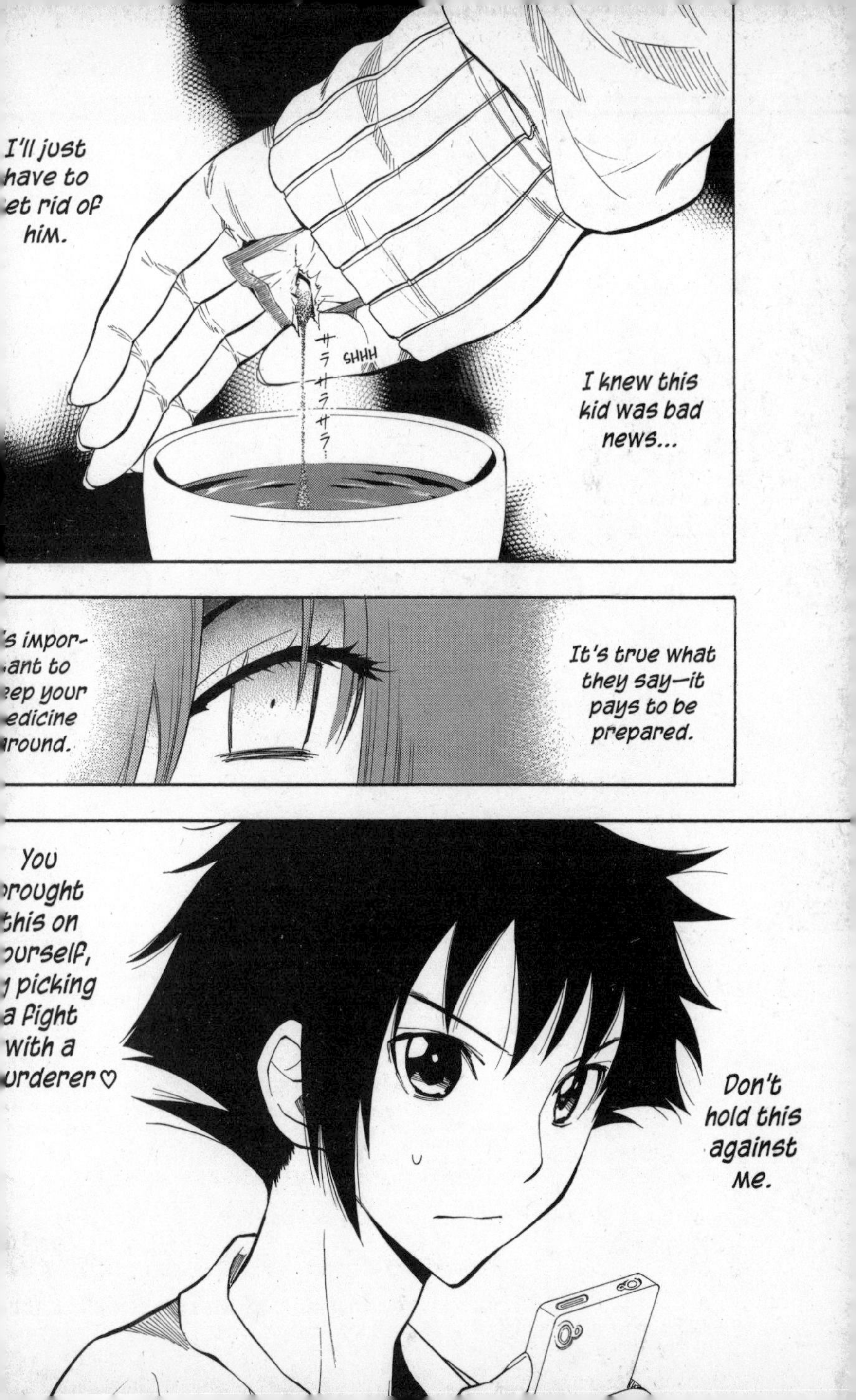
I knew this kid was bad news...
サラサラサラ
SHHH
I'll just have to et rid of him.
It's true what they say—it pays to be prepared.
's impor-ant to ep your edicine round.
Don't hold this against me.
You rought this on ourself, picking a fight with a urderer♡

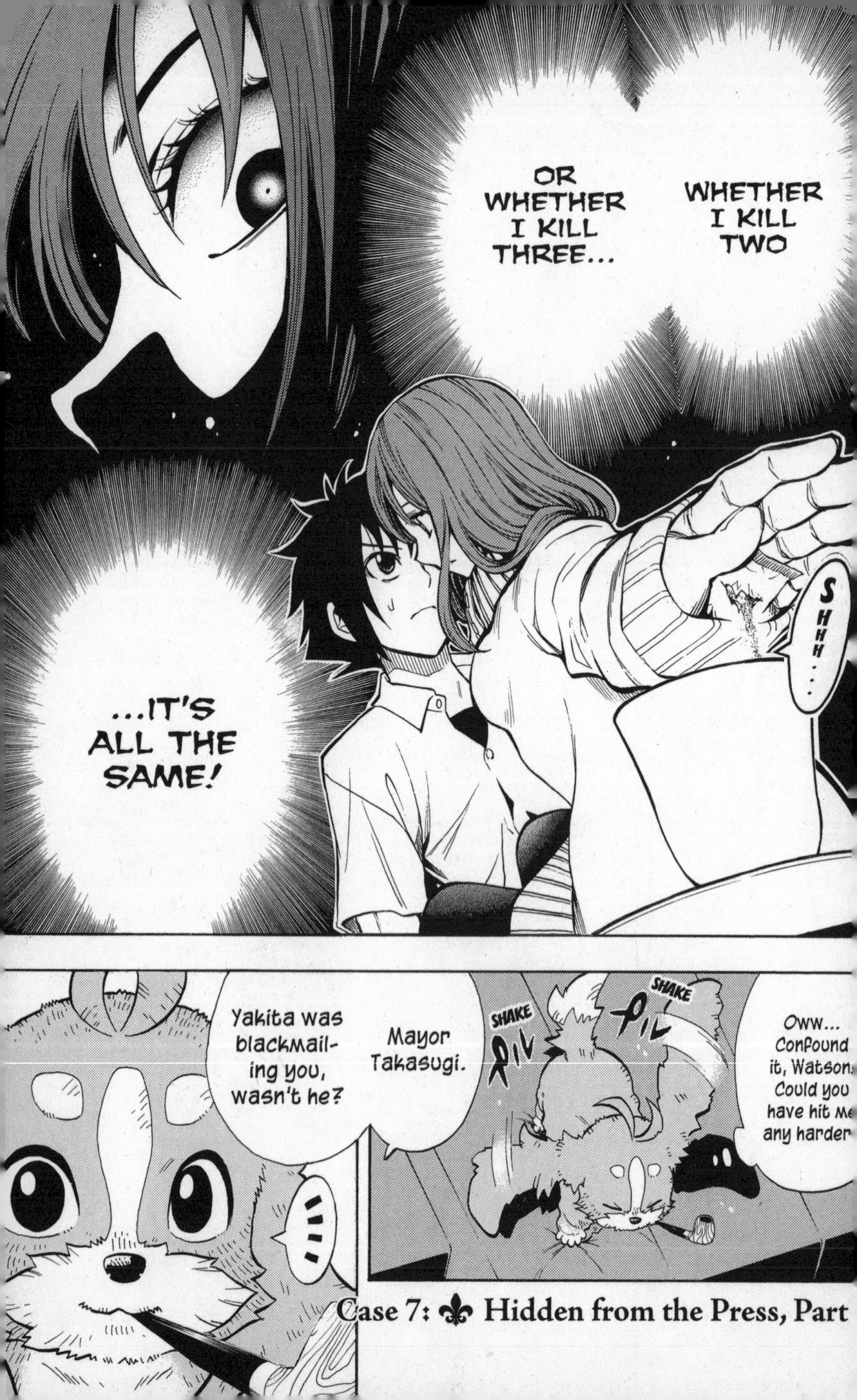
WHETHER I KILL TWO
OR WHETHER I KILL THREE...
...IT'S ALL THE SAME!
SHHH...
SHAKE
SHAKE
Oww... Confound it, Watson. Could you have hit me any harder
Mayor Takasugi.
Yakita was blackmailing you, wasn't he?
!!!

Case 7: ⚜ Hidden from the Press, Part

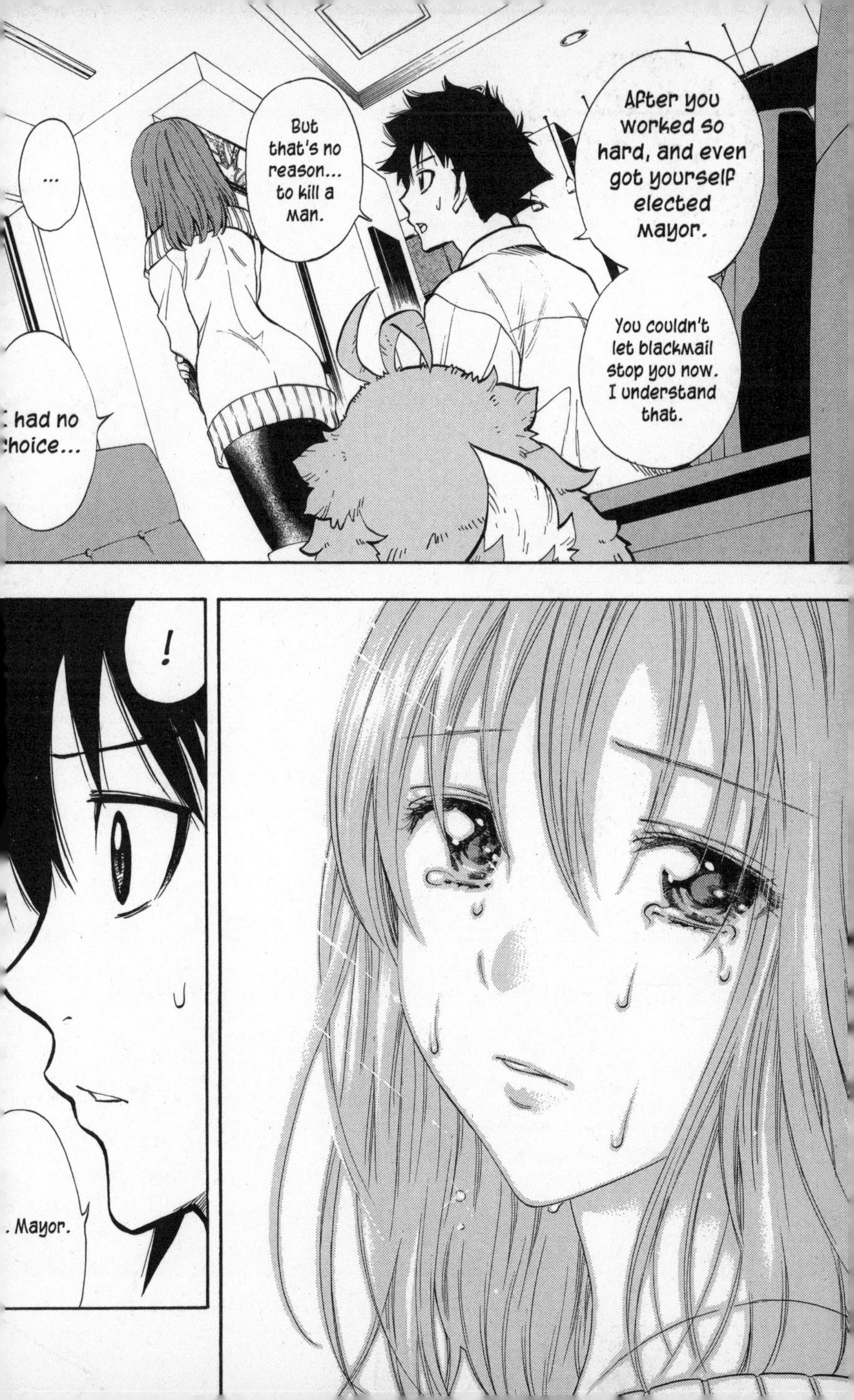
After you worked so hard, and even got yourself elected mayor.
You couldn't let blackmail stop you now. I understand that.
But that's no reason... to kill a man.
...
had no
hoice...
!
. Mayor.

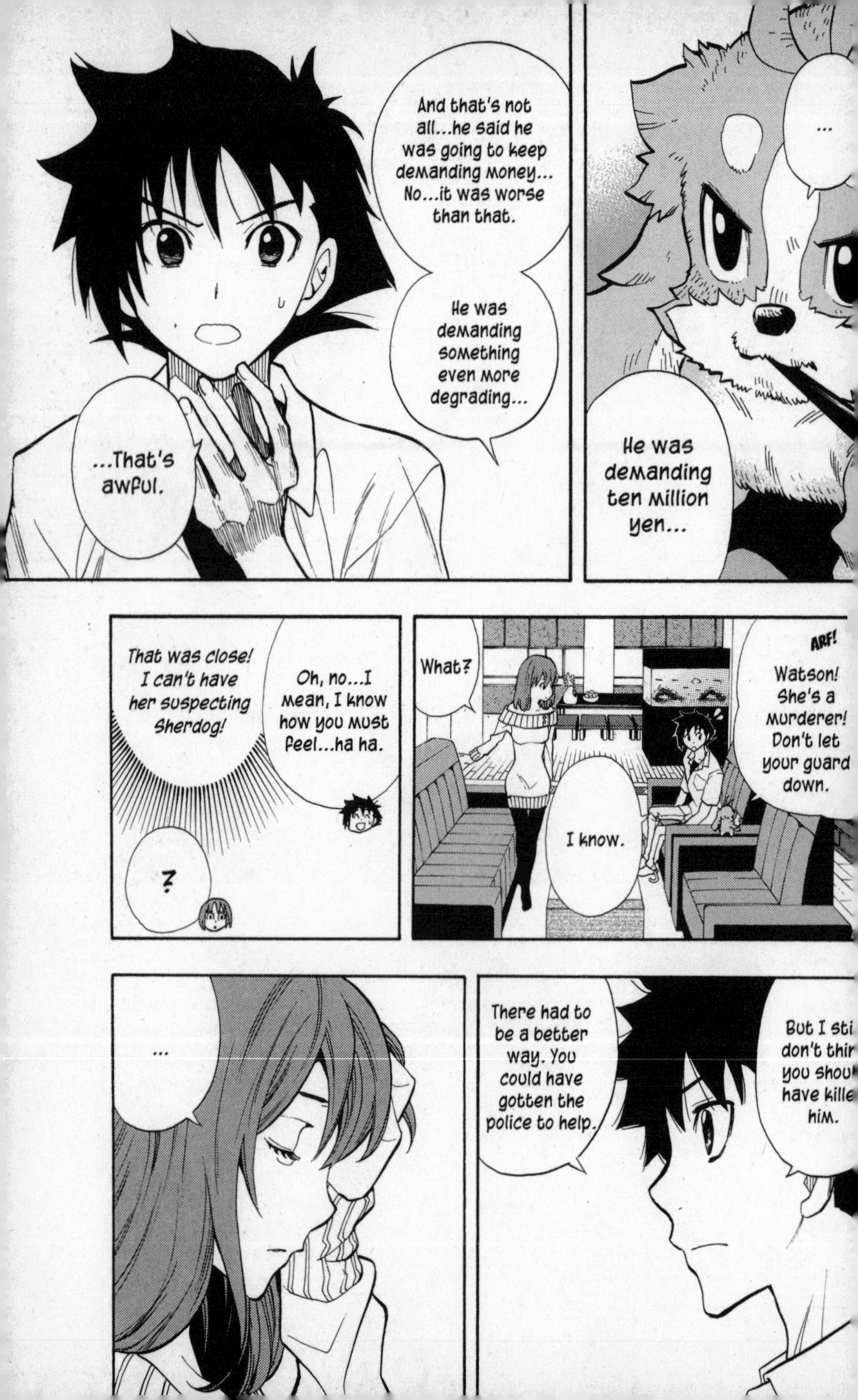
...
He was demanding ten million yen...
And that's not all...he said he was going to keep demanding money... No...it was worse than that.
He was demanding something even more degrading...
...That's awful.
ARF!
Watson! She's a murderer! Don't let your guard down.
I know.
What?
Oh, no...I mean, I know how you must feel...ha ha.
That was close! I can't have her suspecting Sherdog!
?
But I sti don't thir you shou have kille him.
There had to be a better way. You could have gotten the police to help.
...

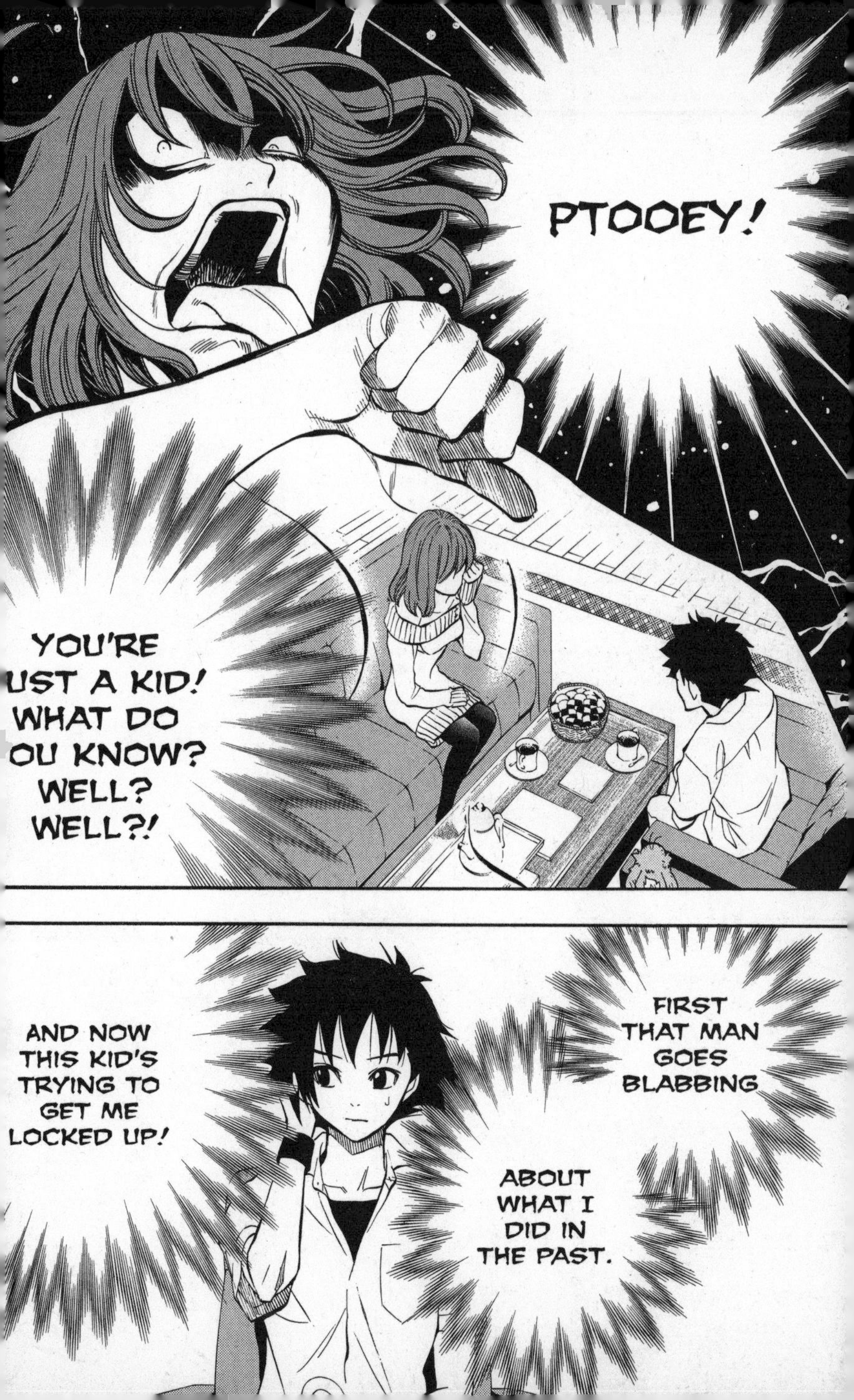
PTOOEY!
YOU'RE UST A KID! WHAT DO OU KNOW? WELL? WELL?!
FIRST THAT MAN GOES BLABBING
ABOUT WHAT I DID IN THE PAST.
AND NOW THIS KID'S TRYING TO GET ME LOCKED UP!

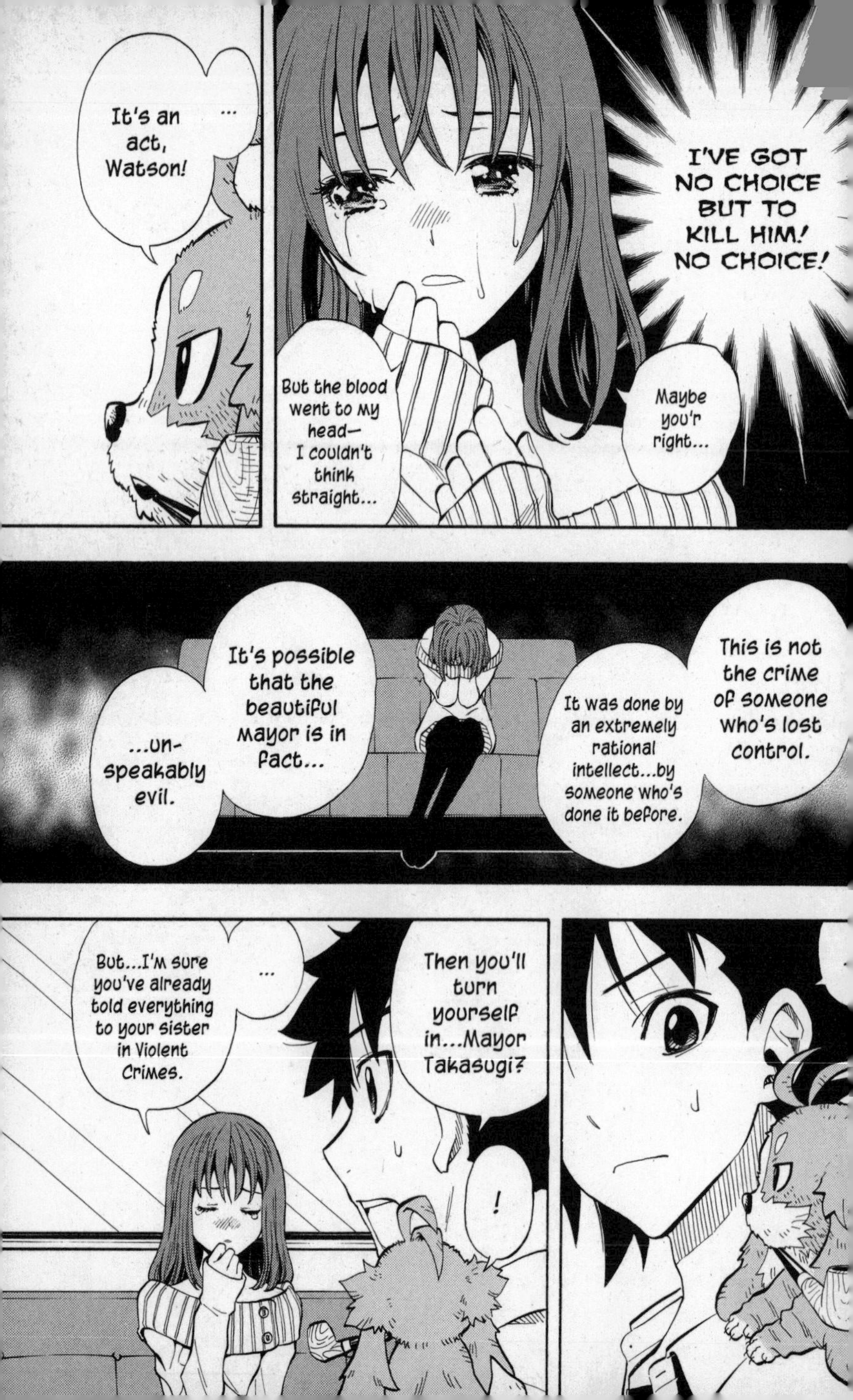
I'VE GOT NO CHOICE BUT TO KILL HIM! NO CHOICE!
Maybe you'r right...
But the blood went to my head— I couldn't think straight...
...
It's an act, Watson!
This is not the crime of someone who's lost control.
It was done by an extremely rational intellect...by someone who's done it before.
It's possible that the beautiful mayor is in fact...
...un-speakably evil.
Then you'll turn yourself in...Mayor Takasugi?
...
But...I'm sure you've already told everything to your sister in Violent Crimes.
!

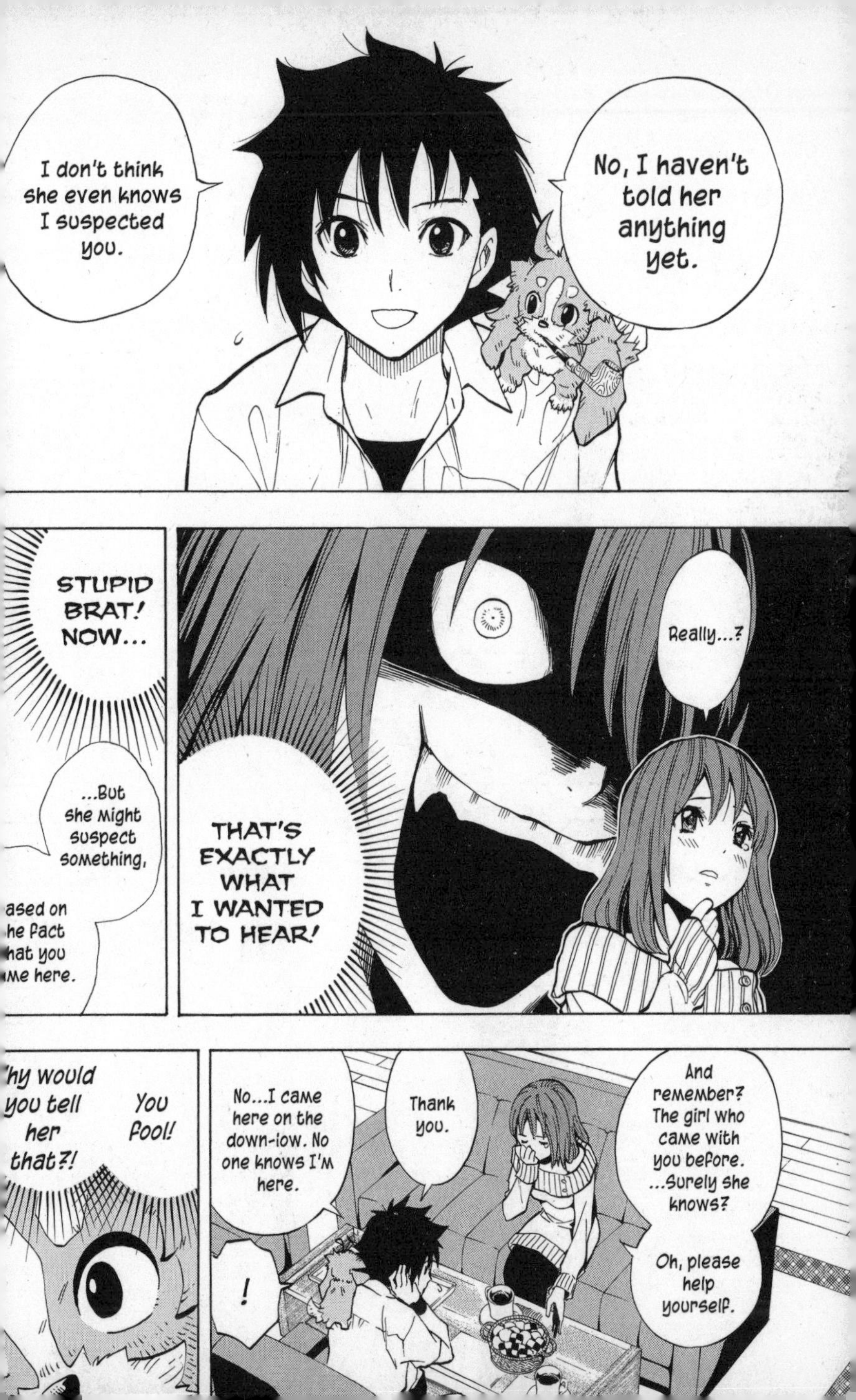
No, I haven't told her anything yet.
I don't think she even knows I suspected you.
Really...?
THAT'S EXACTLY WHAT I WANTED TO HEAR!
STUPID BRAT! NOW...
...But she might suspect something,
ased on he fact hat you me here.
And remember? The girl who came with you before. ...Surely she knows?
Oh, please help yourself.
Thank you.
No...I came here on the down-low. No one knows I'm here.
!
You fool!
hy would you tell her that?!

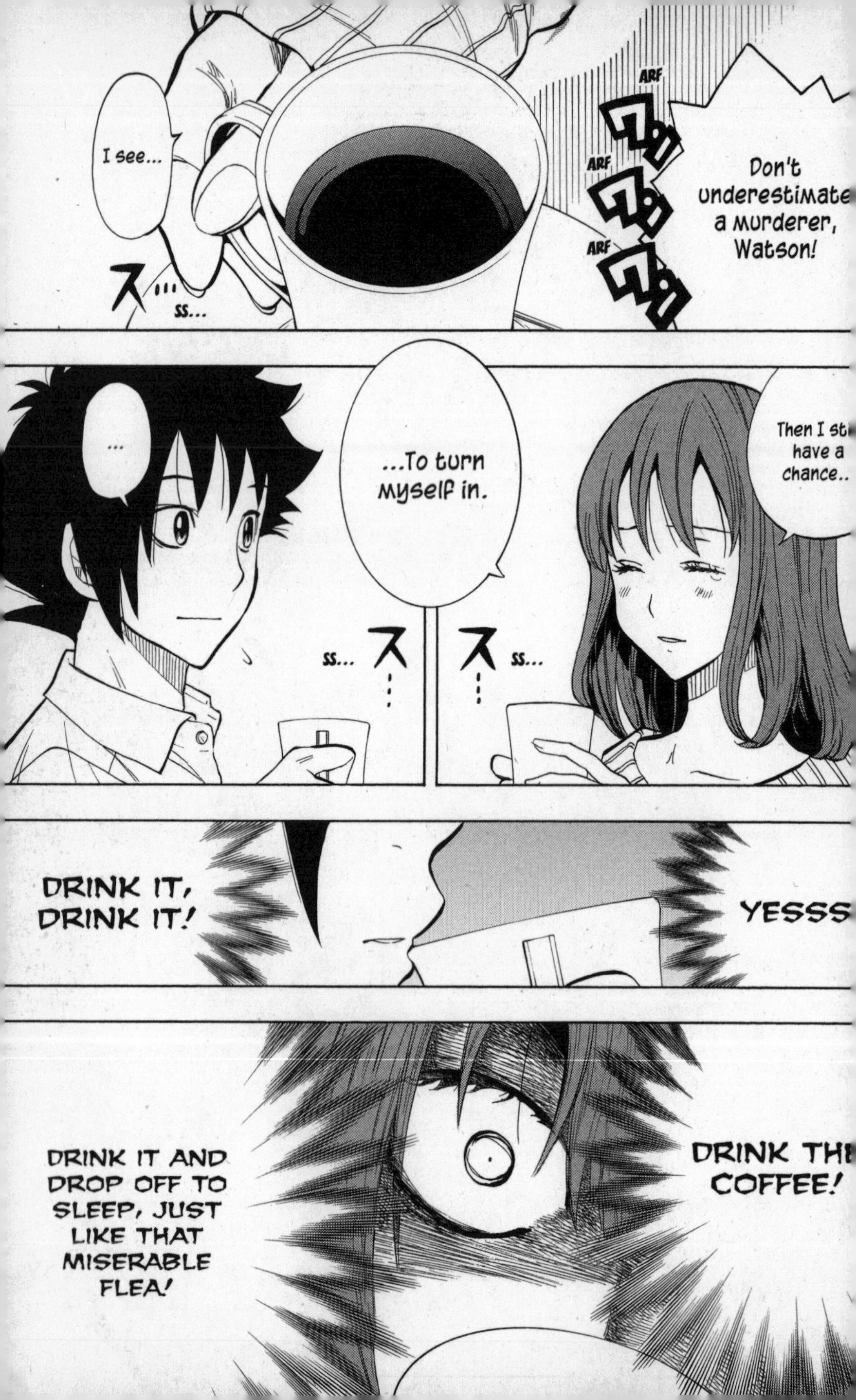
ARF
ARF
ARF
Don't underestimate a murderer, Watson!
I see...
ス... ss...
Then I sti have a chance..
ス... ss...
...To turn myself in.
ss... ス...
...
YESSS
DRINK IT, DRINK IT!
DRINK TH COFFEE!
DRINK IT AND DROP OFF TO SLEEP, JUST LIKE THAT MISERABLE FLEA!

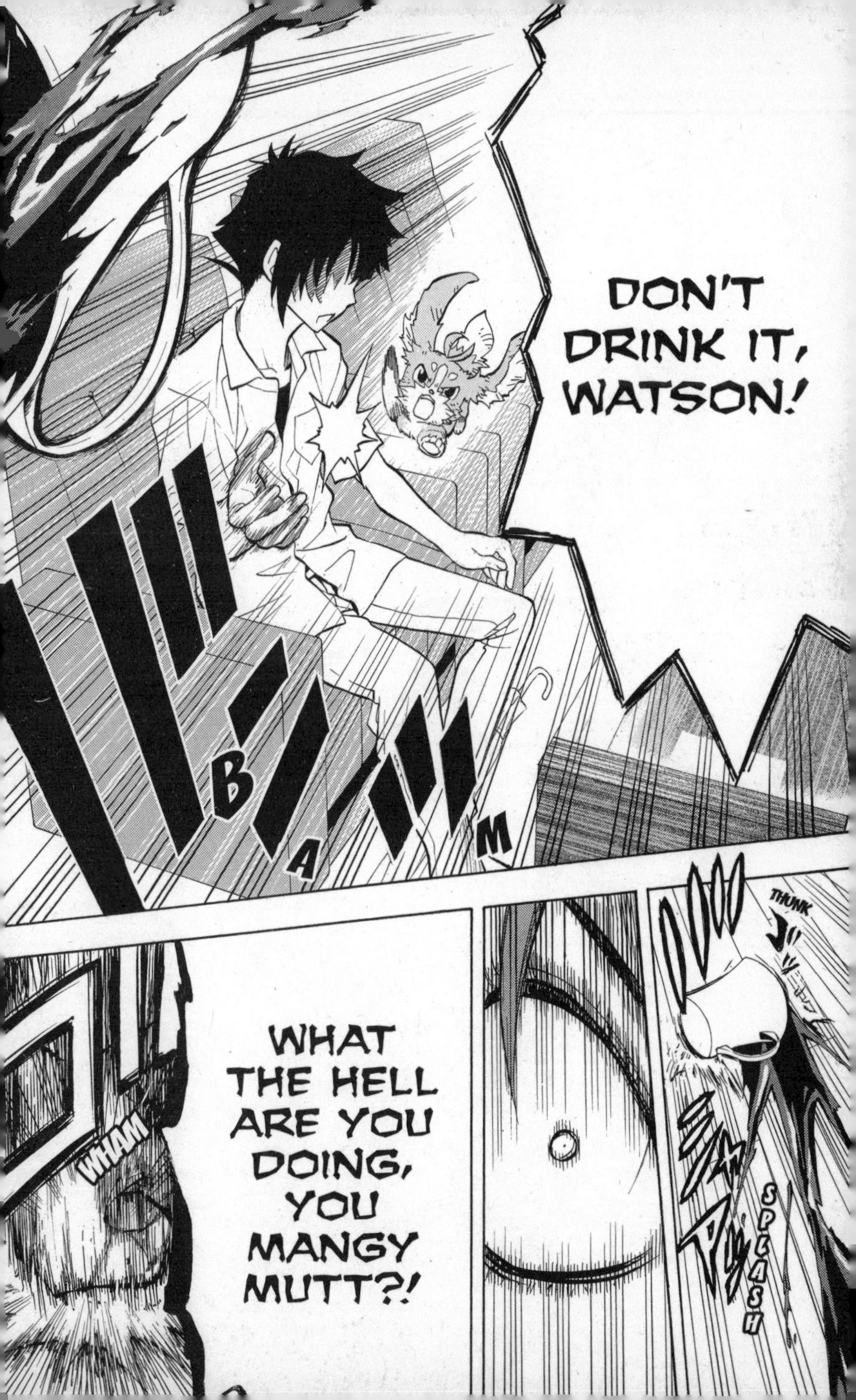
DON'T DRINK IT, WATSON!
BAM
THUNK
SPLASH
WHAT THE HELL ARE YOU DOING, YOU MANGY MUTT?!
WHAM

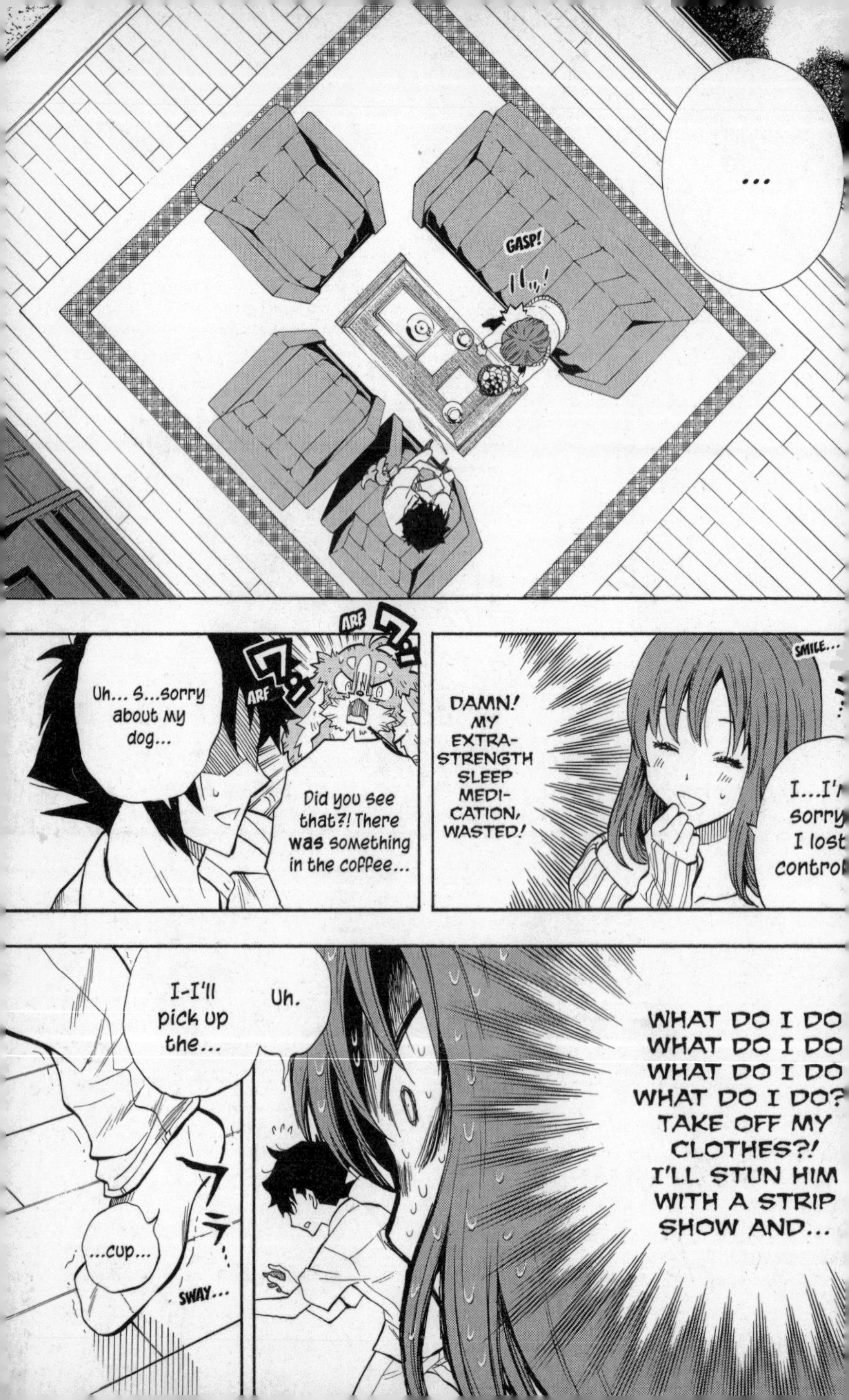
...
GASP!
SMILE...
I...I' sorry I lost contro
DAMN! MY EXTRA-STRENGTH SLEEP MEDI-CATION, WASTED!
ARF
ARF
Did you see that?! There was something in the coffee...
Uh... S...sorry about my dog...
WHAT DO I DO WHAT DO I DO WHAT DO I DO WHAT DO I DO? TAKE OFF MY CLOTHES?! I'LL STUN HIM WITH A STRIP SHOW AND...
Uh.
I-I'll pick up the...
...cup...
SWAY...

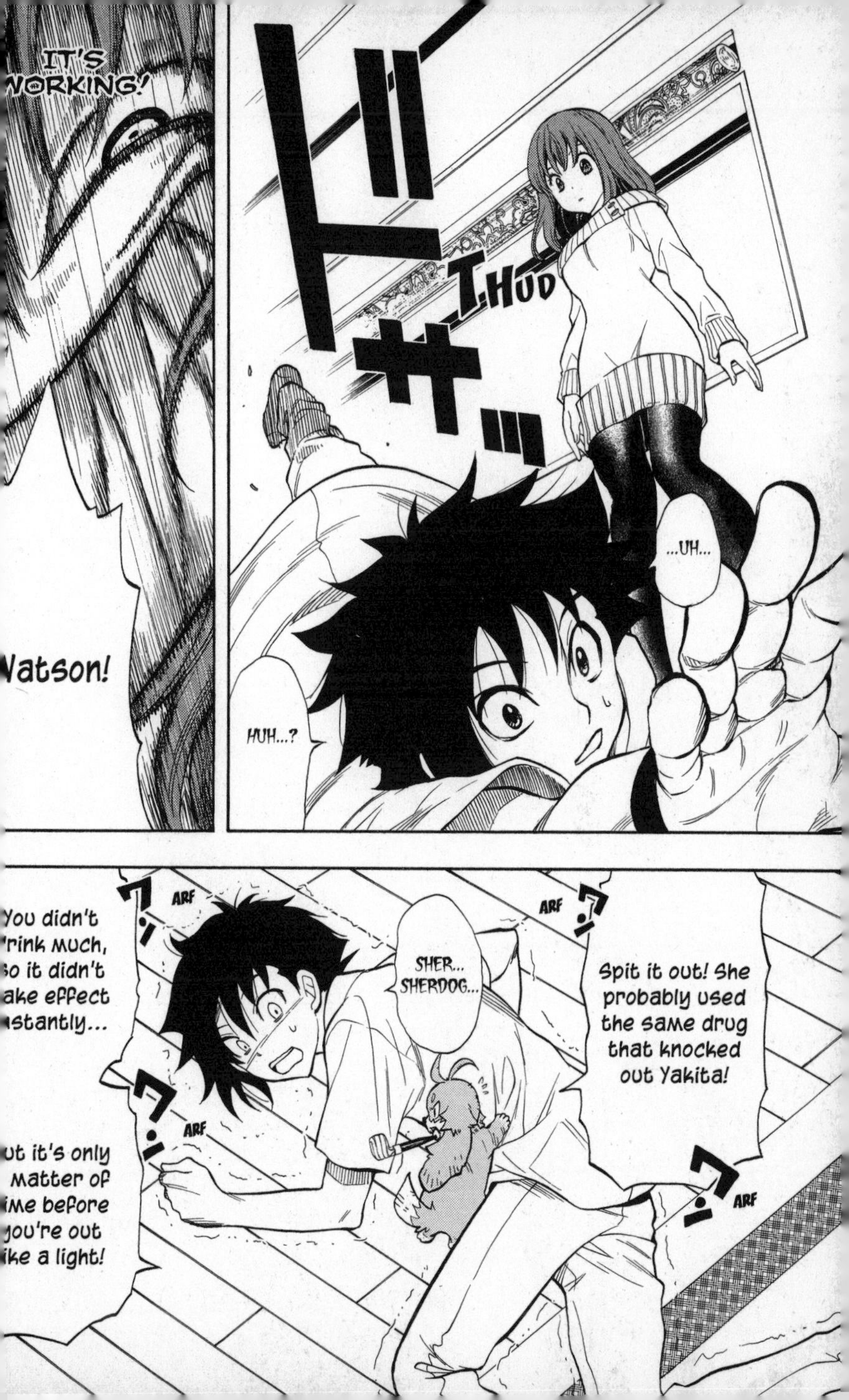
THUD
...UH...
HUH...?
IT'S
VORKING!
Vatson!
Spit it out! She probably used the same drug that knocked out Yakita!
ARF
SHER... SHERDOG...
ARF
You didn't 'rink much, so it didn't ake effect astantly...
ARF
ut it's only matter of ime before you're out ike a light!
ARF

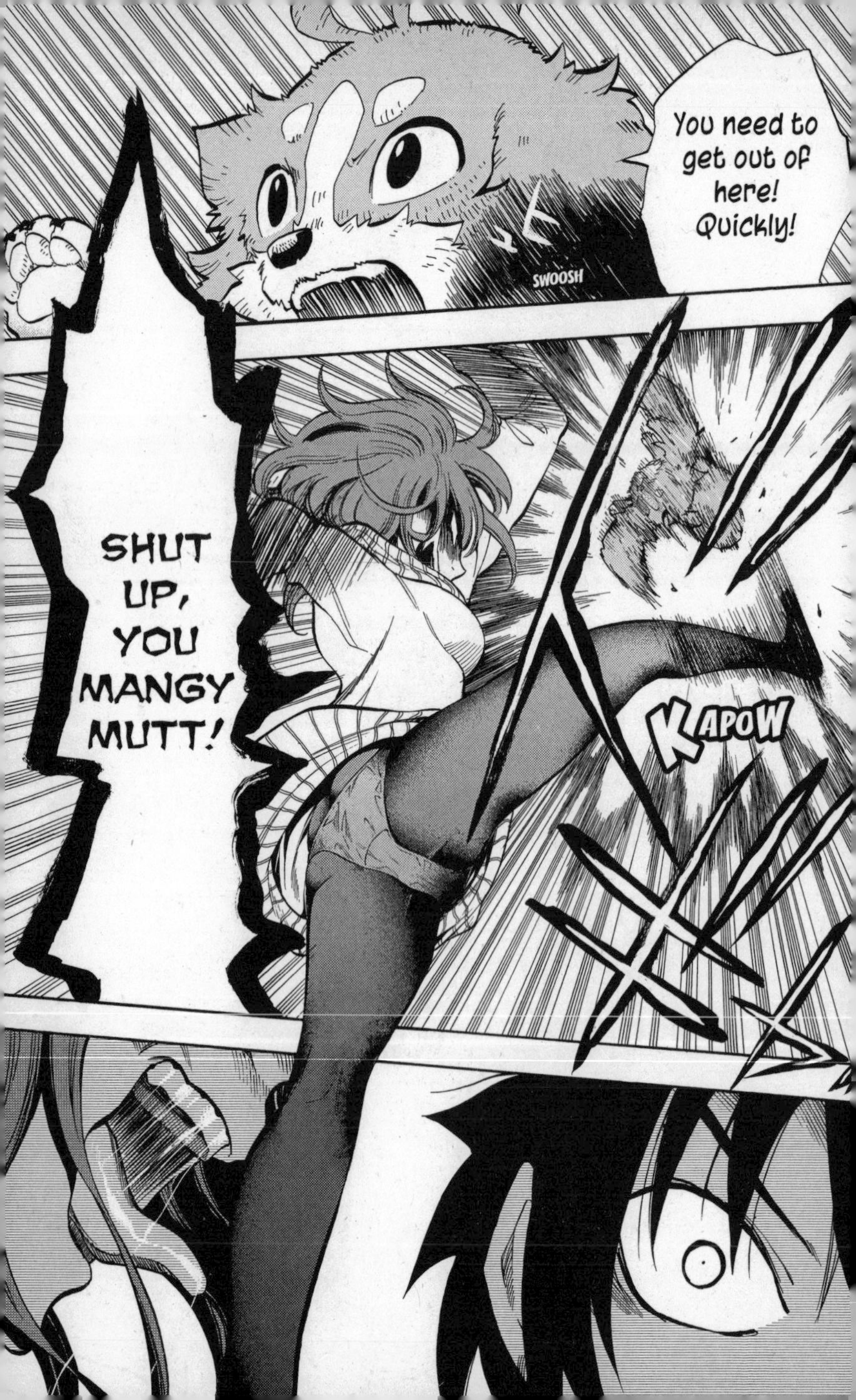
You need to get out of here! Quickly!
SWOOSH
SHUT UP, YOU MANGY MUTT!
KAPOW

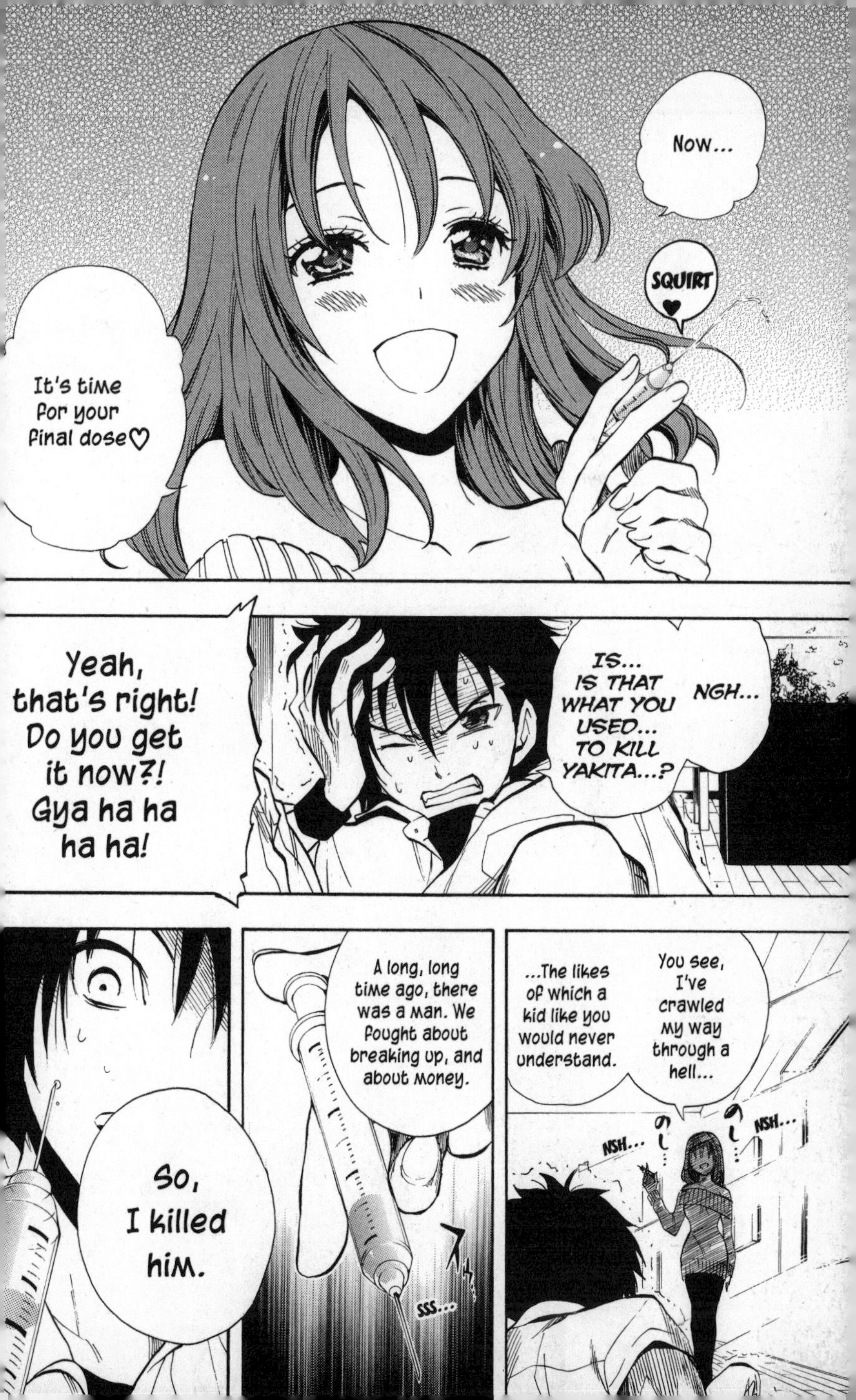
Now...
SQUIRT ♥
It's time for your final dose♡
NGH...
IS... IS THAT WHAT YOU USED... TO KILL YAKITA...?
Yeah, that's right! Do you get it now?! Gya ha ha ha ha!
You see, I've crawled my way through a hell...
...The likes of which a kid like you would never understand.
NSH...
NSH...
A long, long time ago, there was a man. We fought about breaking up, and about money.
SSS...
So, I killed him.

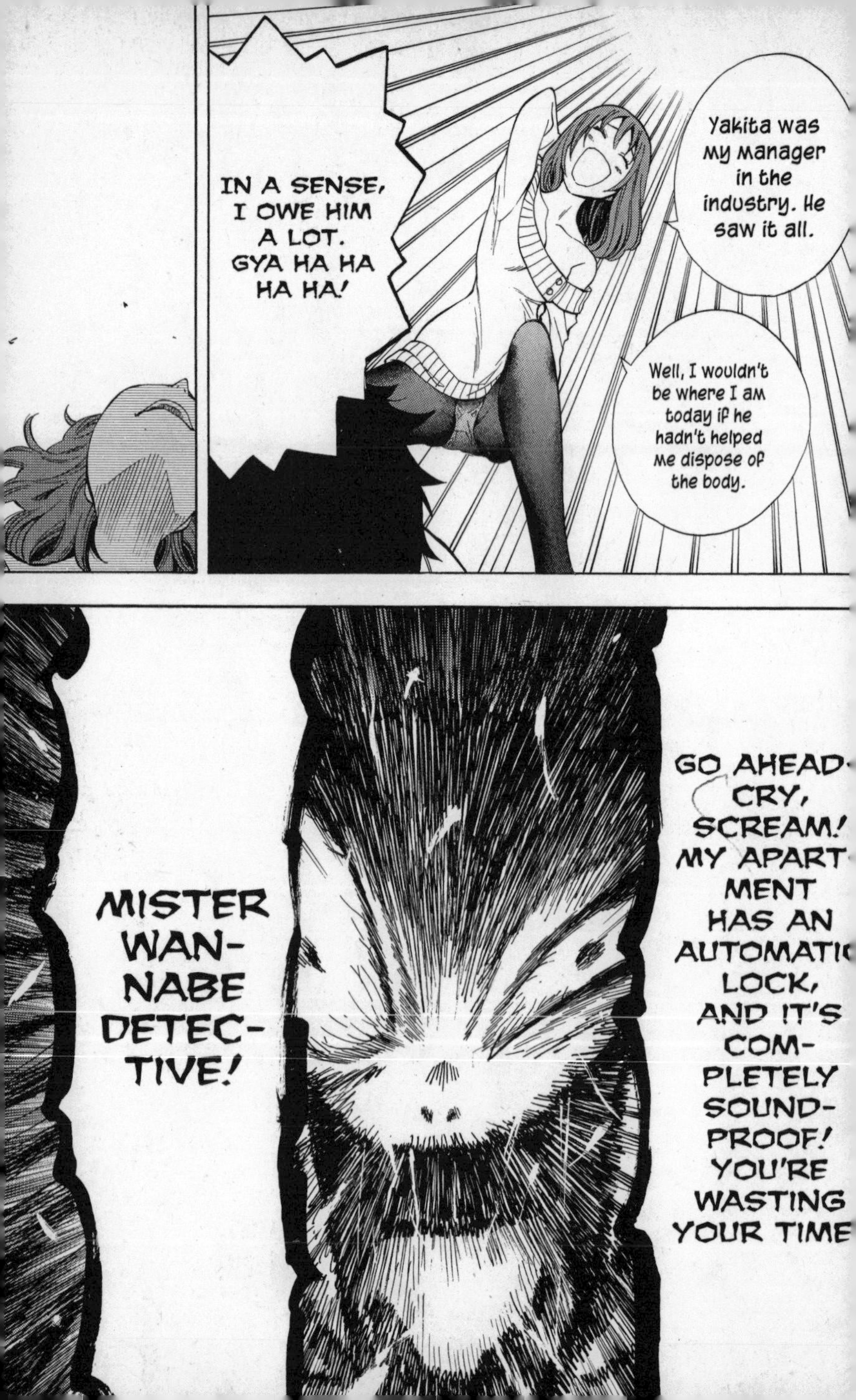
Yakita was my manager in the industry. He saw it all.
Well, I wouldn't be where I am today if he hadn't helped me dispose of the body.
IN A SENSE, I OWE HIM A LOT. GYA HA HA HA HA!
GO AHEAD- CRY, SCREAM! MY APART- MENT HAS AN AUTOMATIC LOCK, AND IT'S COM- PLETELY SOUND- PROOF! YOU'RE WASTING YOUR TIME
MISTER WAN- NABE DETEC- TIVE!

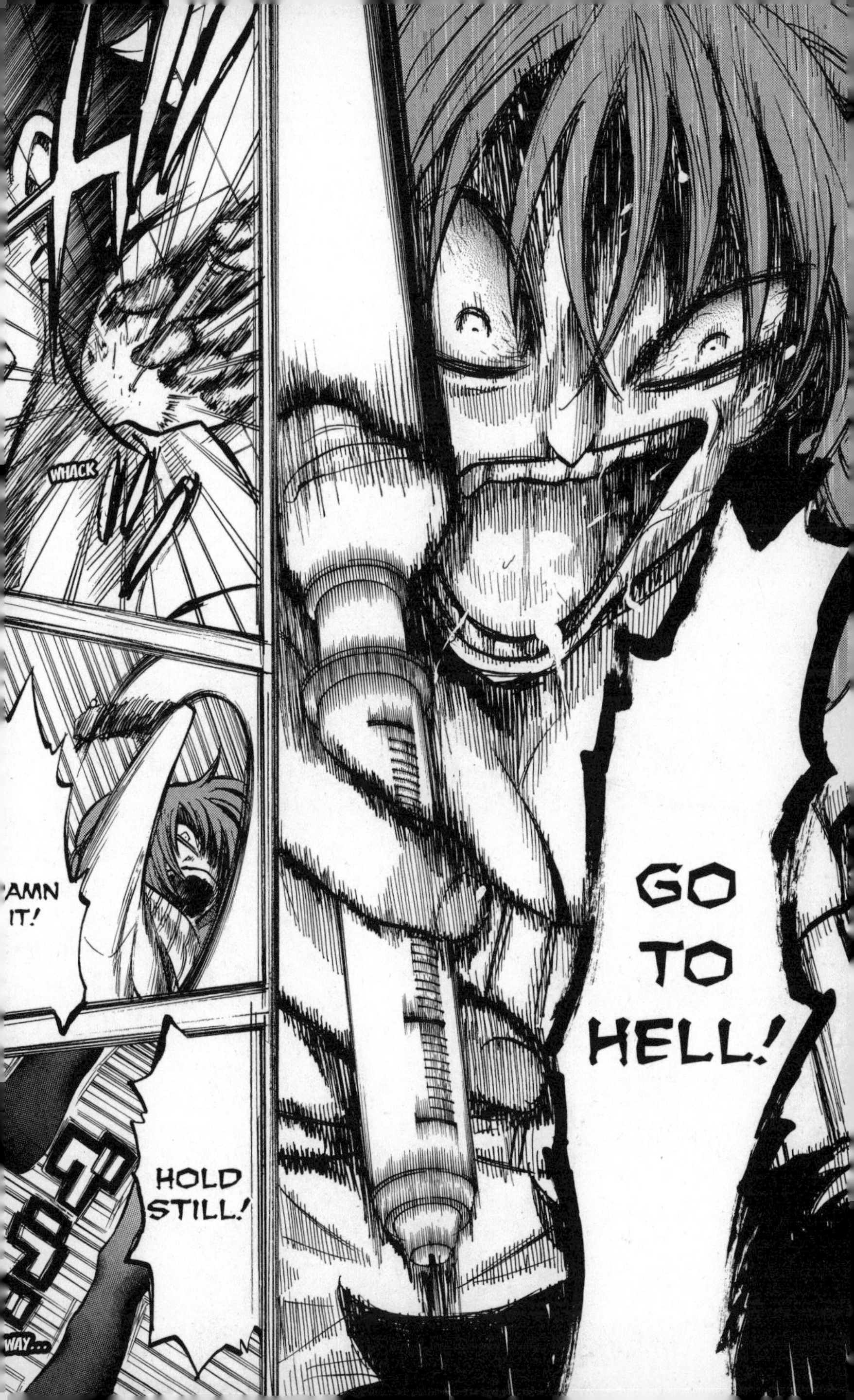
GO TO HELL!
WHACK
AMN IT!
HOLD STILL!
WAY...

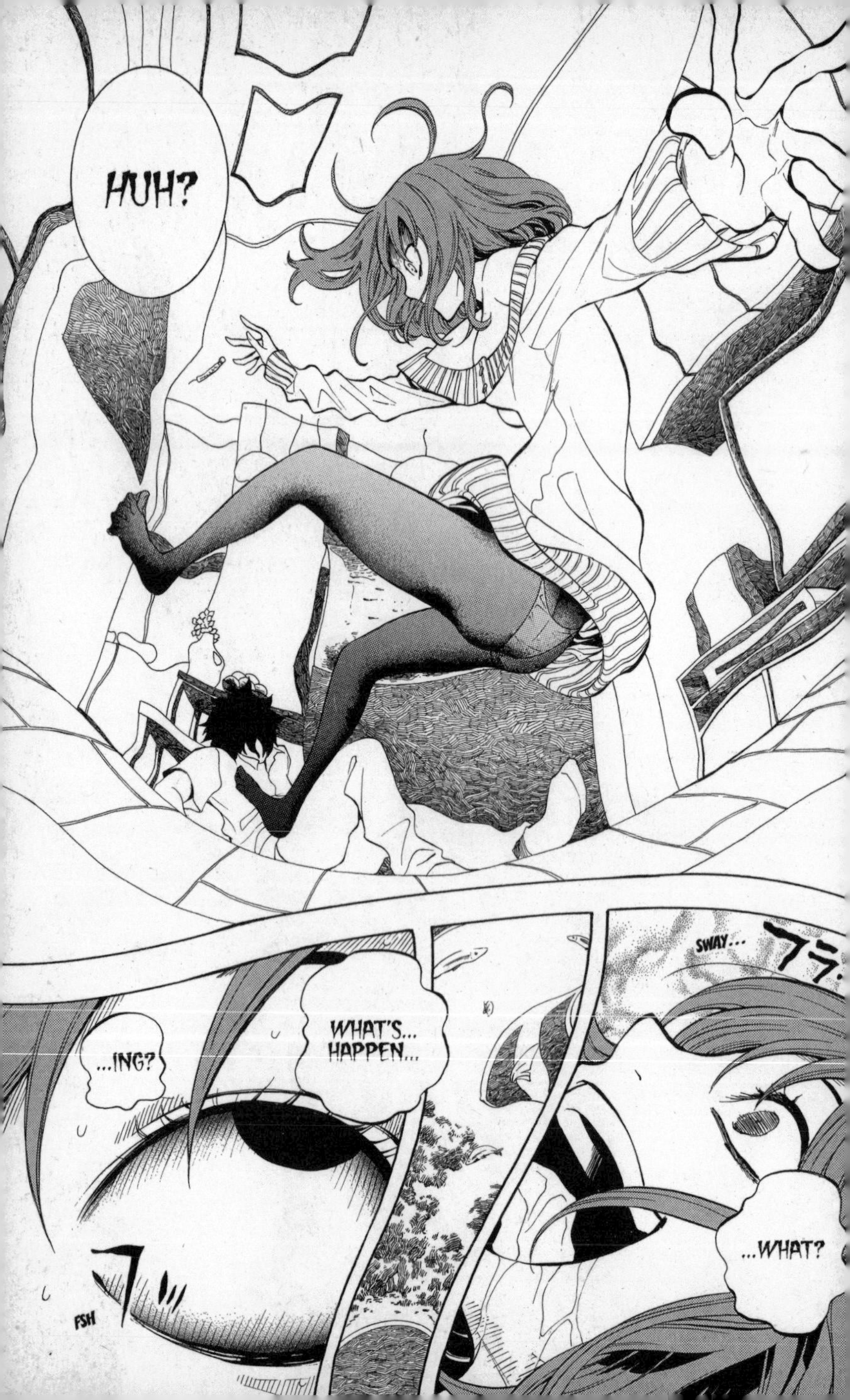
HUH?
SWAY...
フラ
...WHAT?
WHAT'S... HAPPEN...
...ING?
FSH
フッ

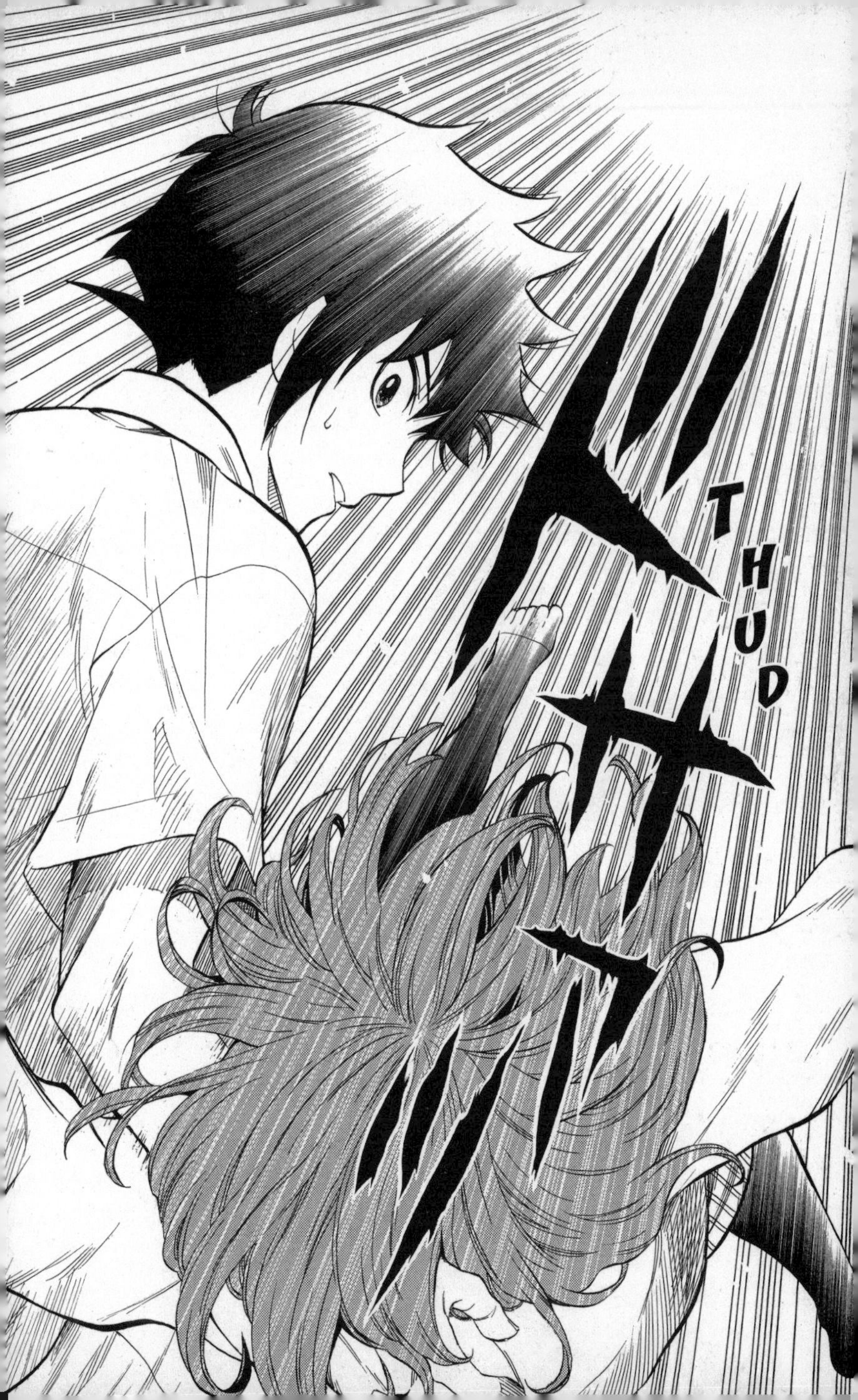
THUD

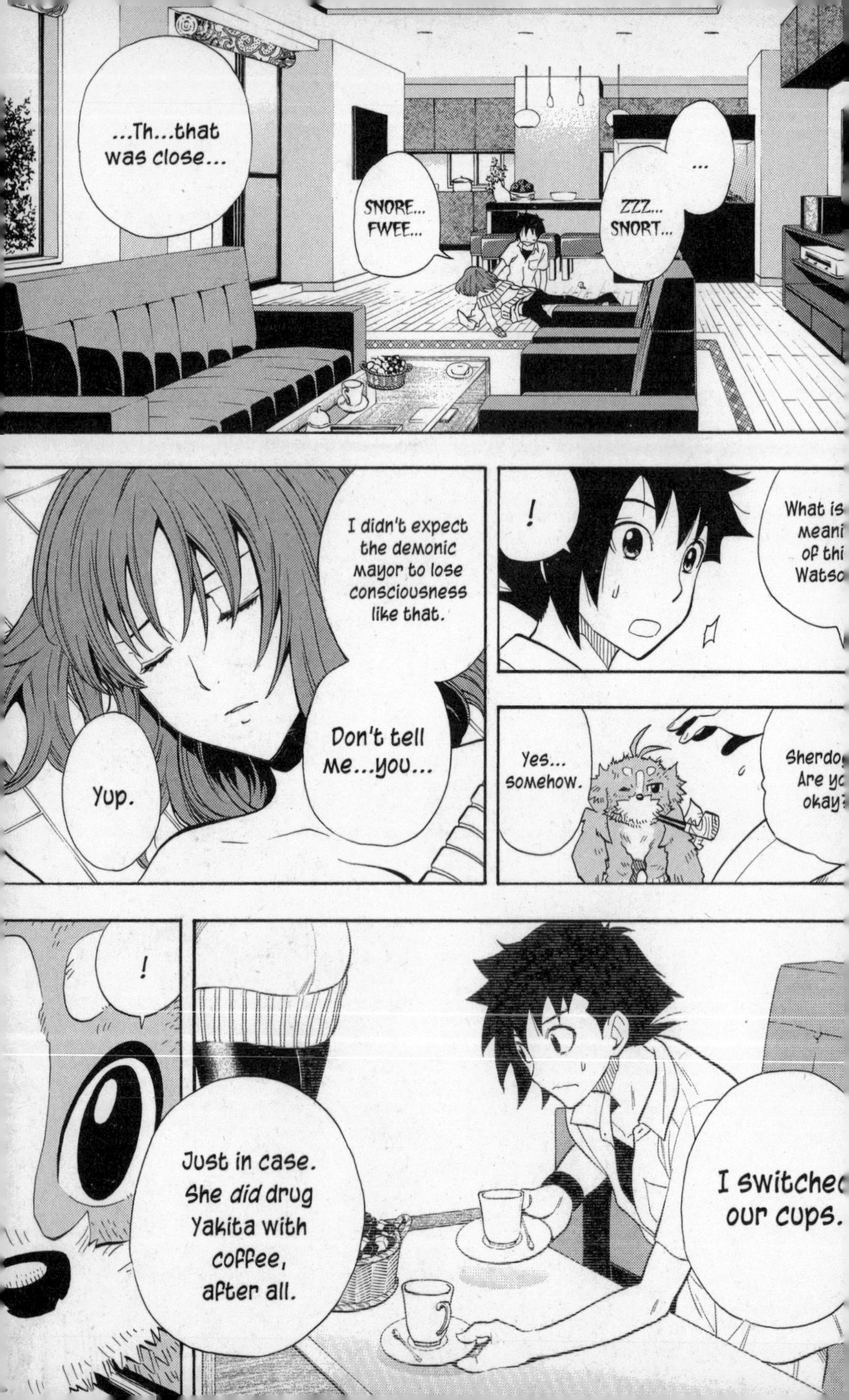
...
ZZZ... SNORT...
SNORE... FWEE...
...Th...that was close...
What is
meani
of thi
Watso
!
Sherdo
Are yo
okay?
Yes... somehow.
I didn't expect the demonic mayor to lose consciousness like that.
Don't tell me...you...
Yup.
I switche
our cups.
Just in case. She *did* drug Yakita with coffee, after all.
!

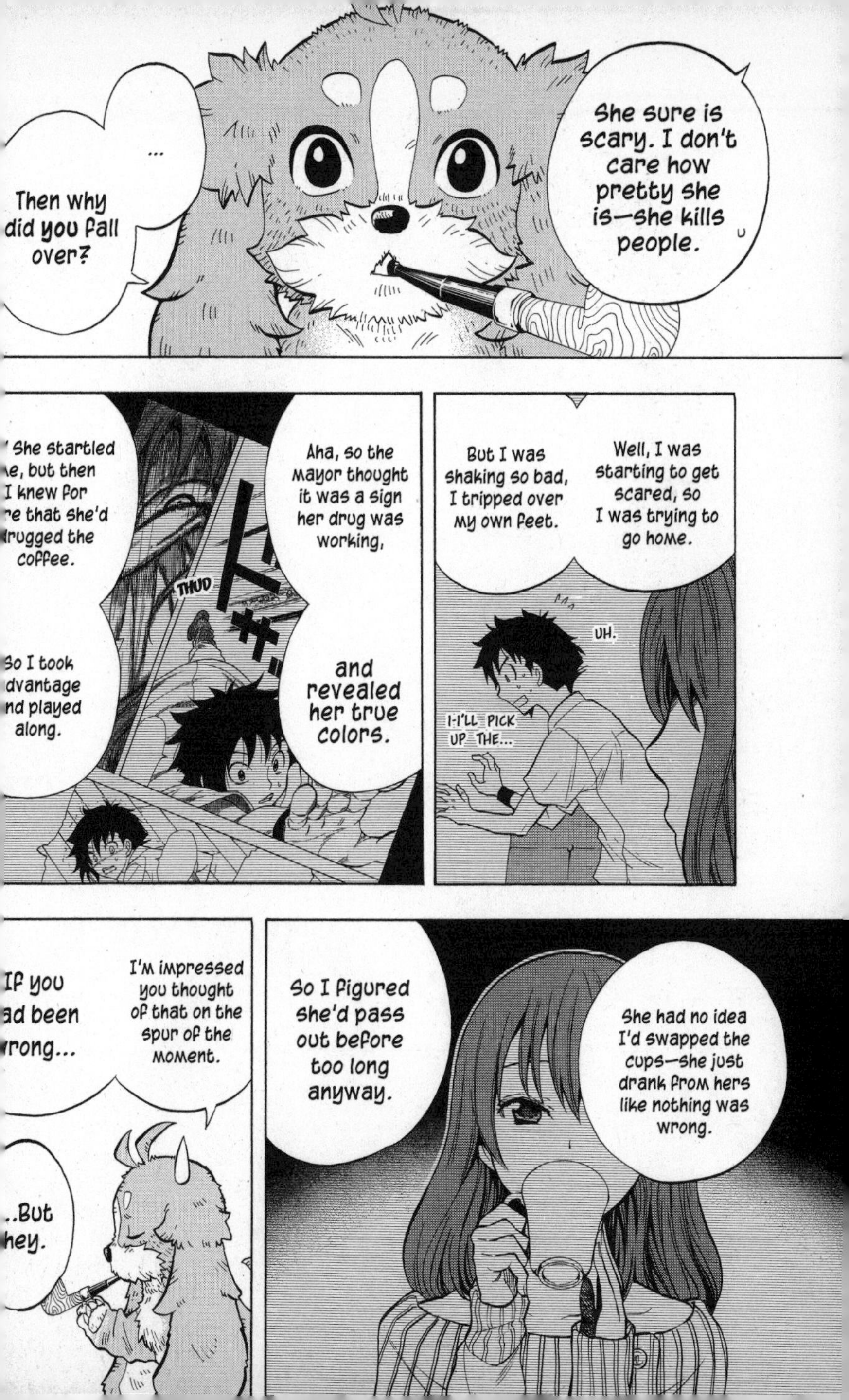

She sure is scary. I don't care how pretty she is—she kills people.
...
Then why did you fall over?
Well, I was starting to get scared, so I was trying to go home.
But I was shaking so bad, I tripped over my own feet.
UH.
I-I'LL PICK UP THE...
Aha, so the mayor thought it was a sign her drug was working,
She startled e, but then I knew for re that she'd rugged the coffee.
THUD
and revealed her true colors.
So I took dvantage nd played along.
She had no idea I'd swapped the cups—she just drank from hers like nothing was wrong.
So I figured she'd pass out before too long anyway.
I'm impressed you thought of that on the spur of the moment.
If you ad been rong...
..But hey.

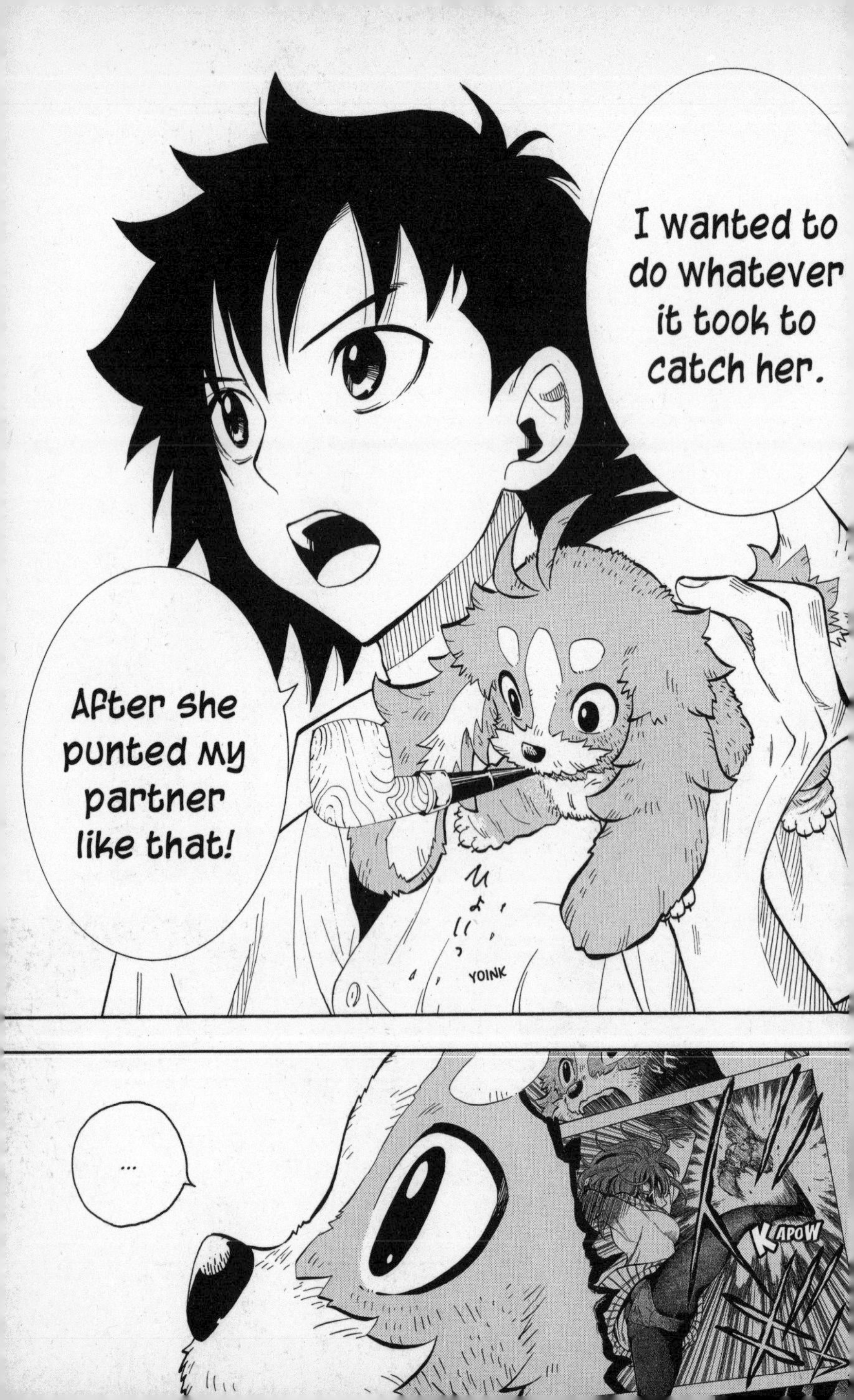

I wanted to do whatever it took to catch her.
After she punted my partner like that!
YOINK
KAPOW
...

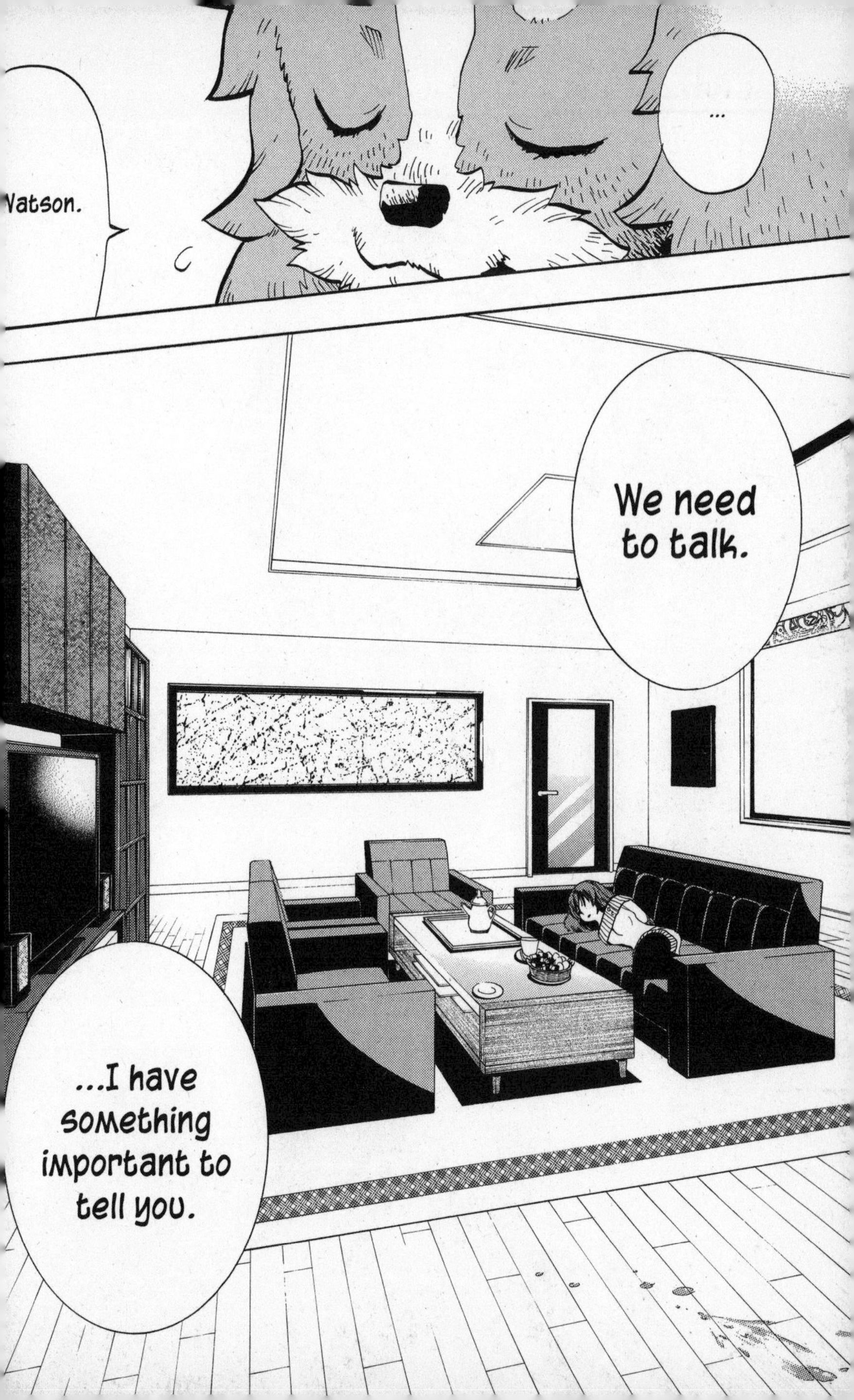
...
Vatson.
We need to talk.
...I have something important to tell you.

Coffee Time 3: The best Assistant

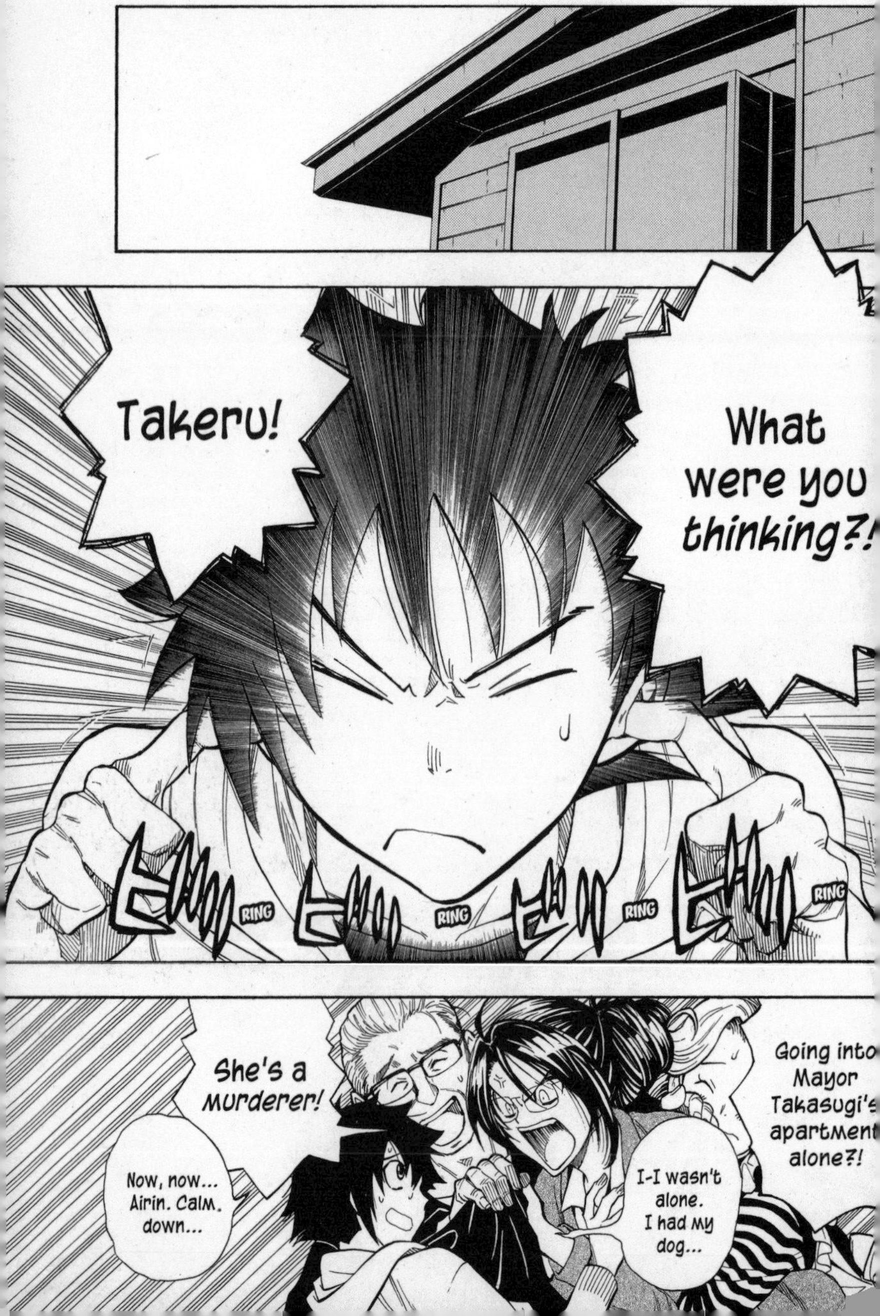
What were you thinking?!
Takeru!
RING
RING
RING
RING
Going into Mayor Takasugi's apartment alone?!
She's a murderer!
I-I wasn't alone. I had my dog...
Now, now... Airin. Calm down...

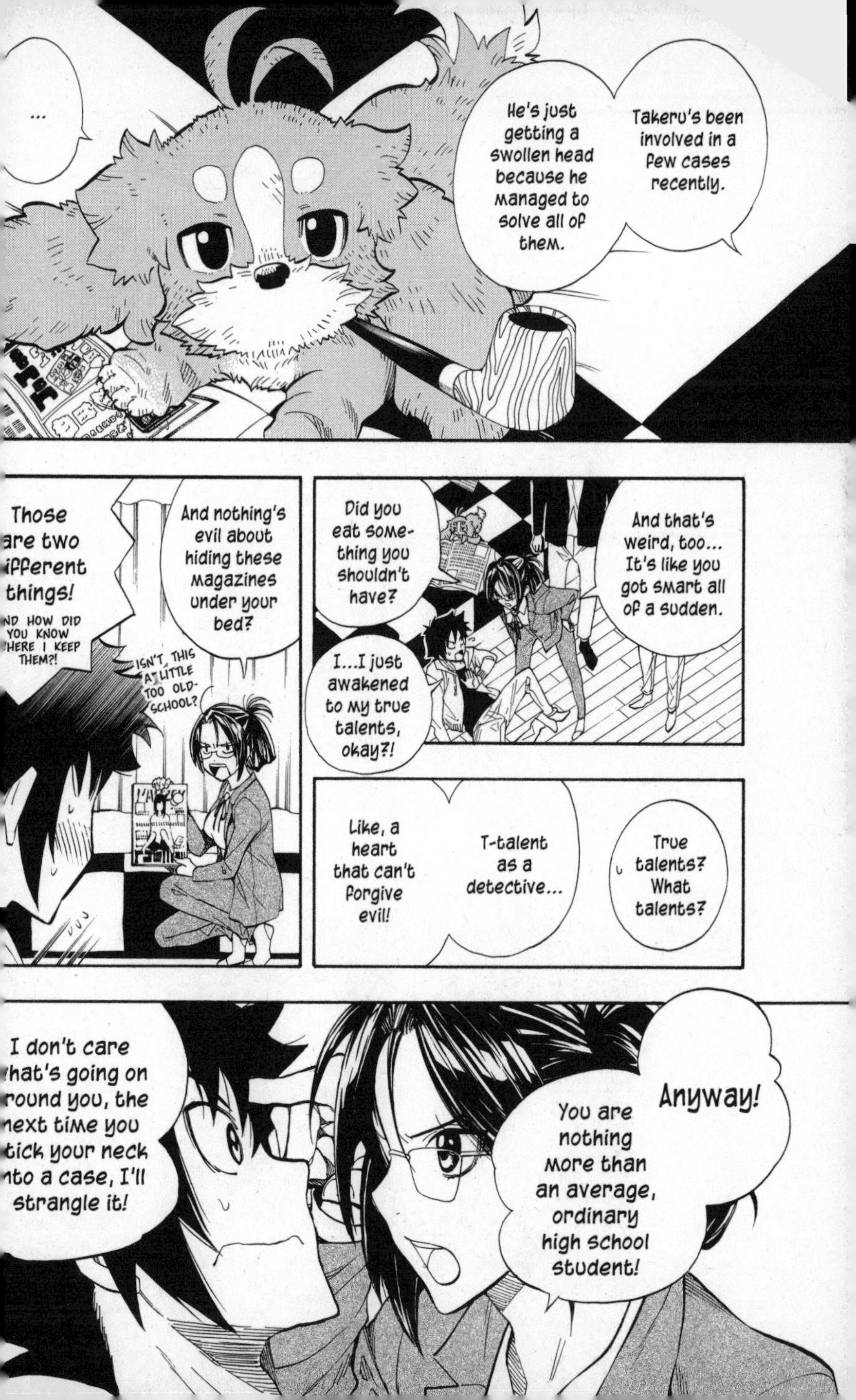
Takeru's been involved in a few cases recently.
He's just getting a swollen head because he managed to solve all of them.
...
And that's weird, too... It's like you got smart all of a sudden.
Did you eat something you shouldn't have?
I...I just awakened to my true talents, okay?!
True talents? What talents?
T-talent as a detective...
Like, a heart that can't forgive evil!
And nothing's evil about hiding these magazines under your bed?
ISN'T THIS A LITTLE TOO OLD-SCHOOL?
Those are two ifferent things!
ND HOW DID YOU KNOW HERE I KEEP THEM?!
Anyway!
You are nothing more than an average, ordinary high school student!
I don't care hat's going on round you, the ext time you tick your neck nto a case, I'll strangle it!

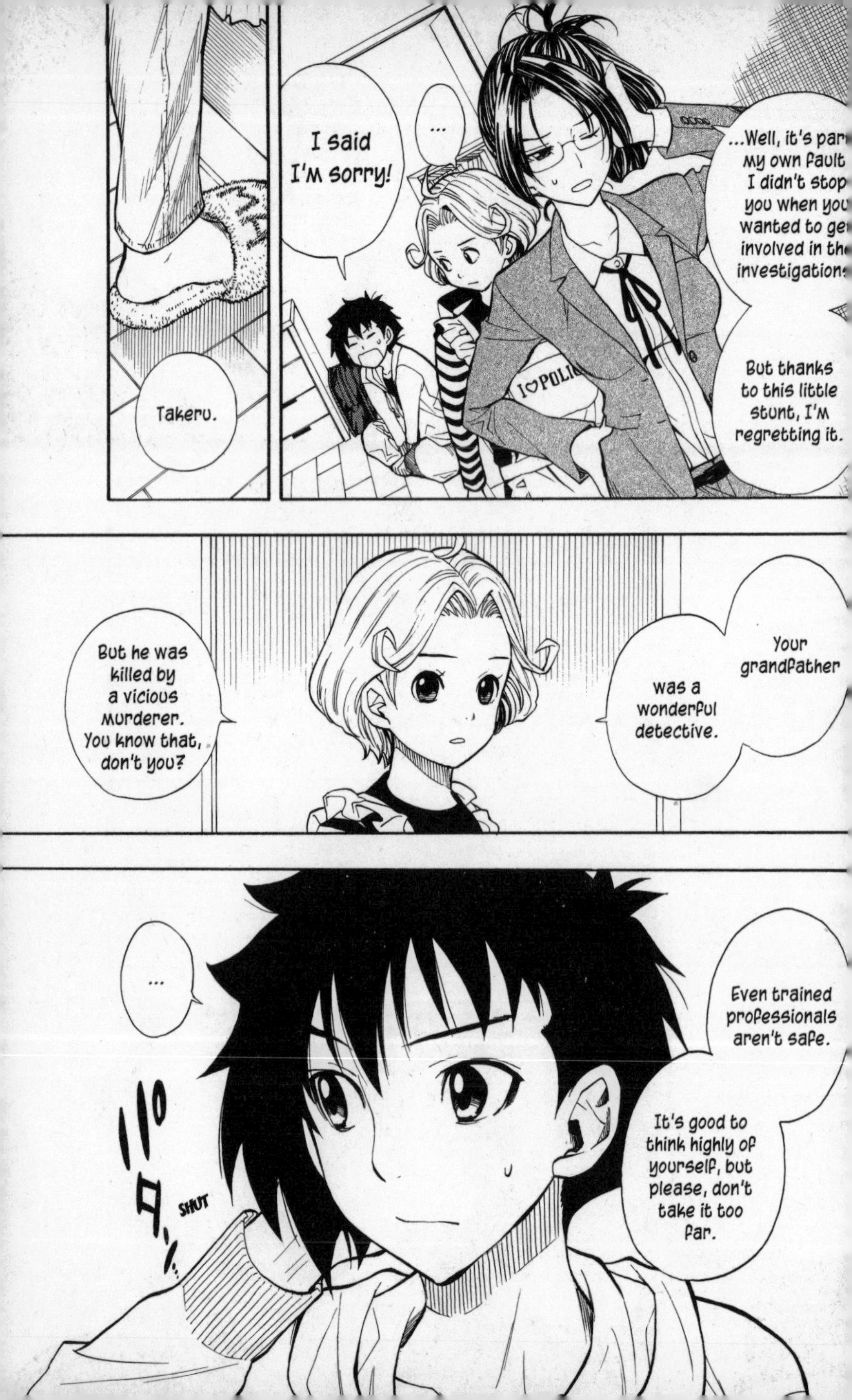
...Well, it's par my own fault I didn't stop you when you wanted to ge involved in the investigation
But thanks to this little stunt, I'm regretting it.
...
I said I'm sorry!
Takeru.
Your grandfather was a wonderful detective.
But he was killed by a vicious murderer. You know that, don't you?
Even trained professionals aren't safe.
It's good to think highly of yourself, but please, don't take it too far.
...
SHUT

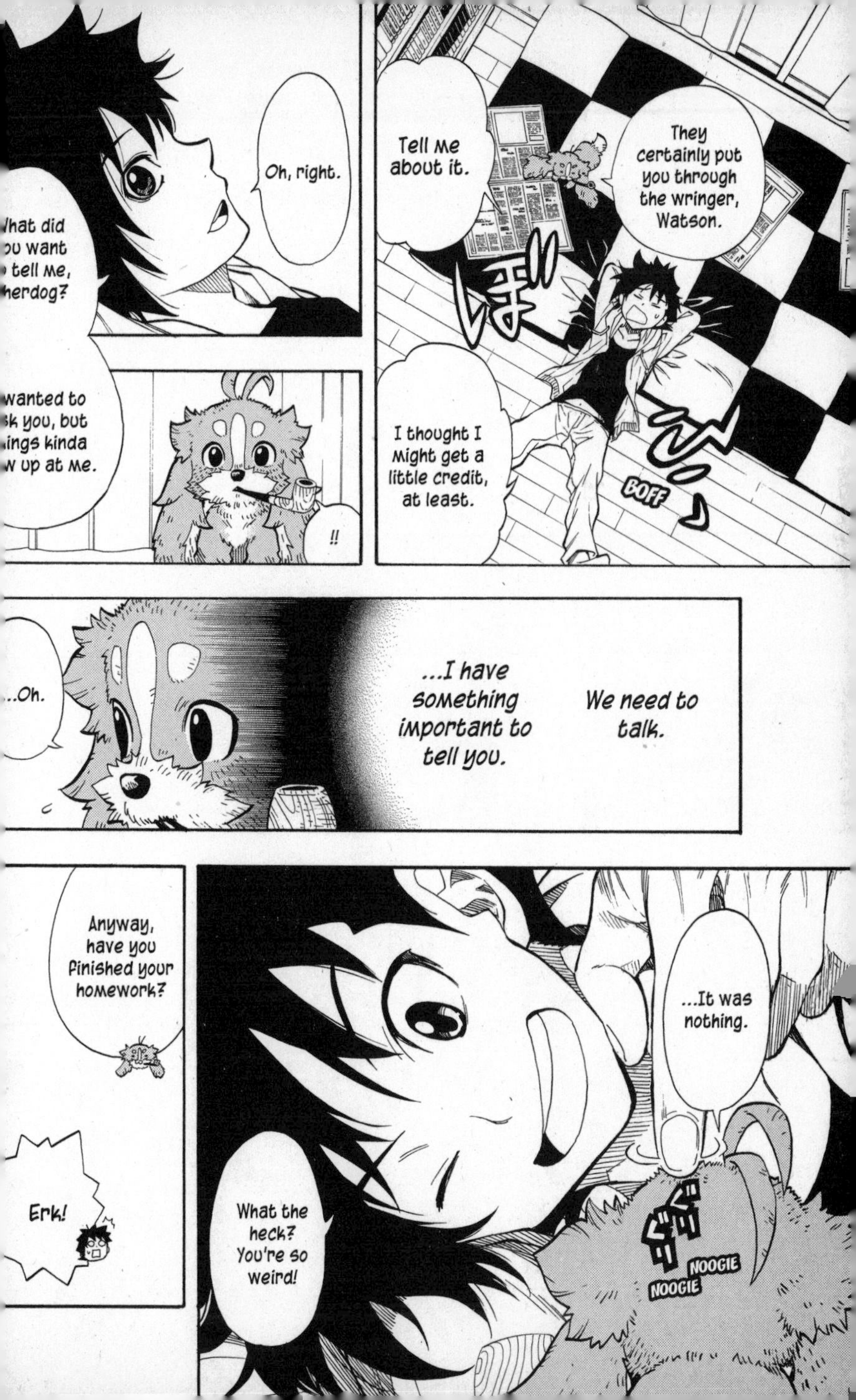
They certainly put you through the wringer, Watson.
Tell me about it.
BOFF
I thought I might get a little credit, at least.
Oh, right.
hat did ou want tell me, herdog?
wanted to sk you, but ings kinda w up at me.
!!
We need to talk.
...I have something important to tell you.
...Oh.
...It was nothing.
NOOGIE
NOOGIE
What the heck? You're so weird!
Anyway, have you finished your homework?
Erk!

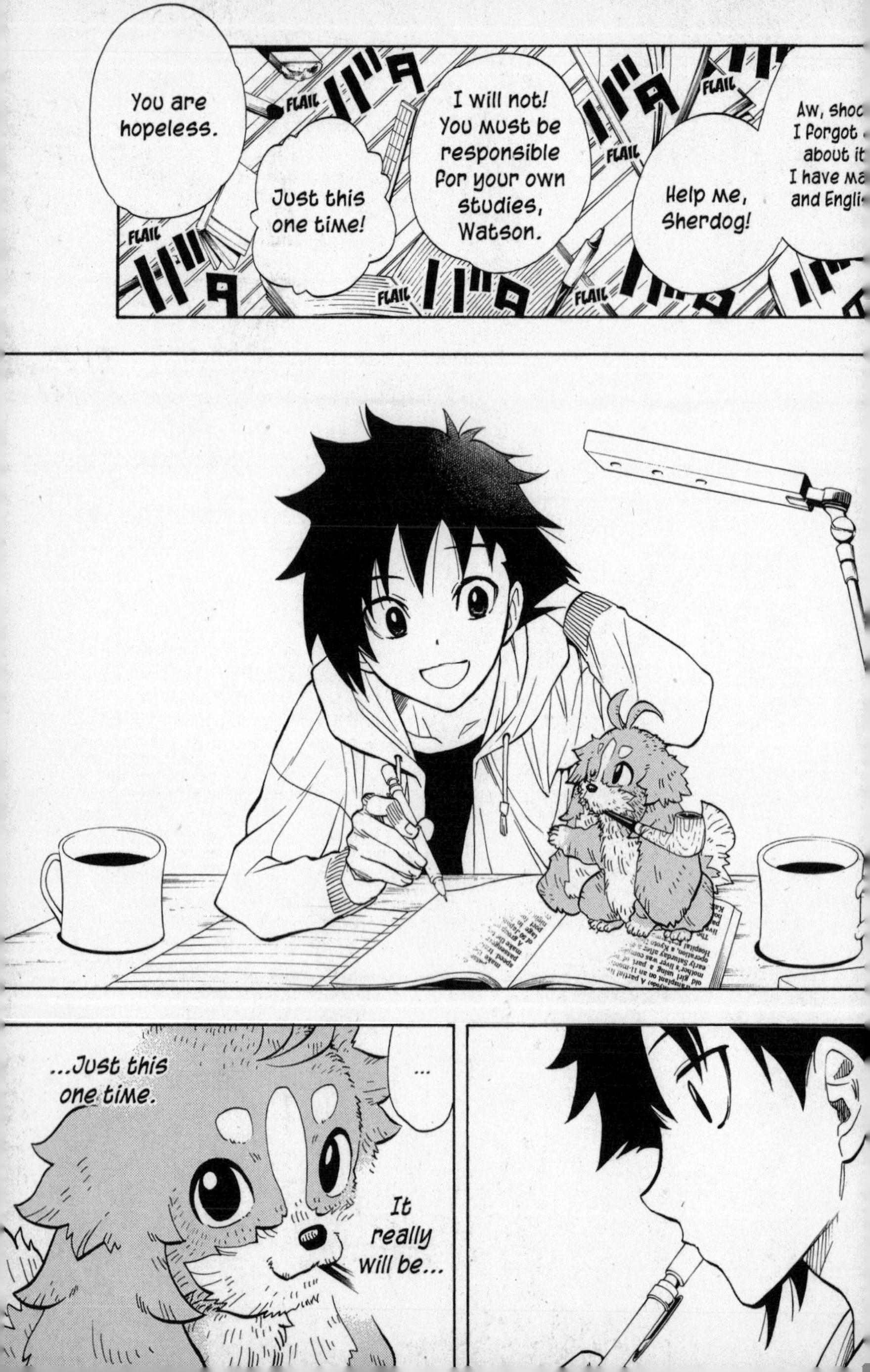
Aw, shoc
I forgot
about it
I have Ma
and Engli
FLAIL
Help me, Sherdog!
FLAIL
I will not! You must be responsible for your own studies, Watson.
FLAIL
Just this one time!
FLAIL
You are hopeless.
FLAIL
...
...Just this one time.
It really will be...

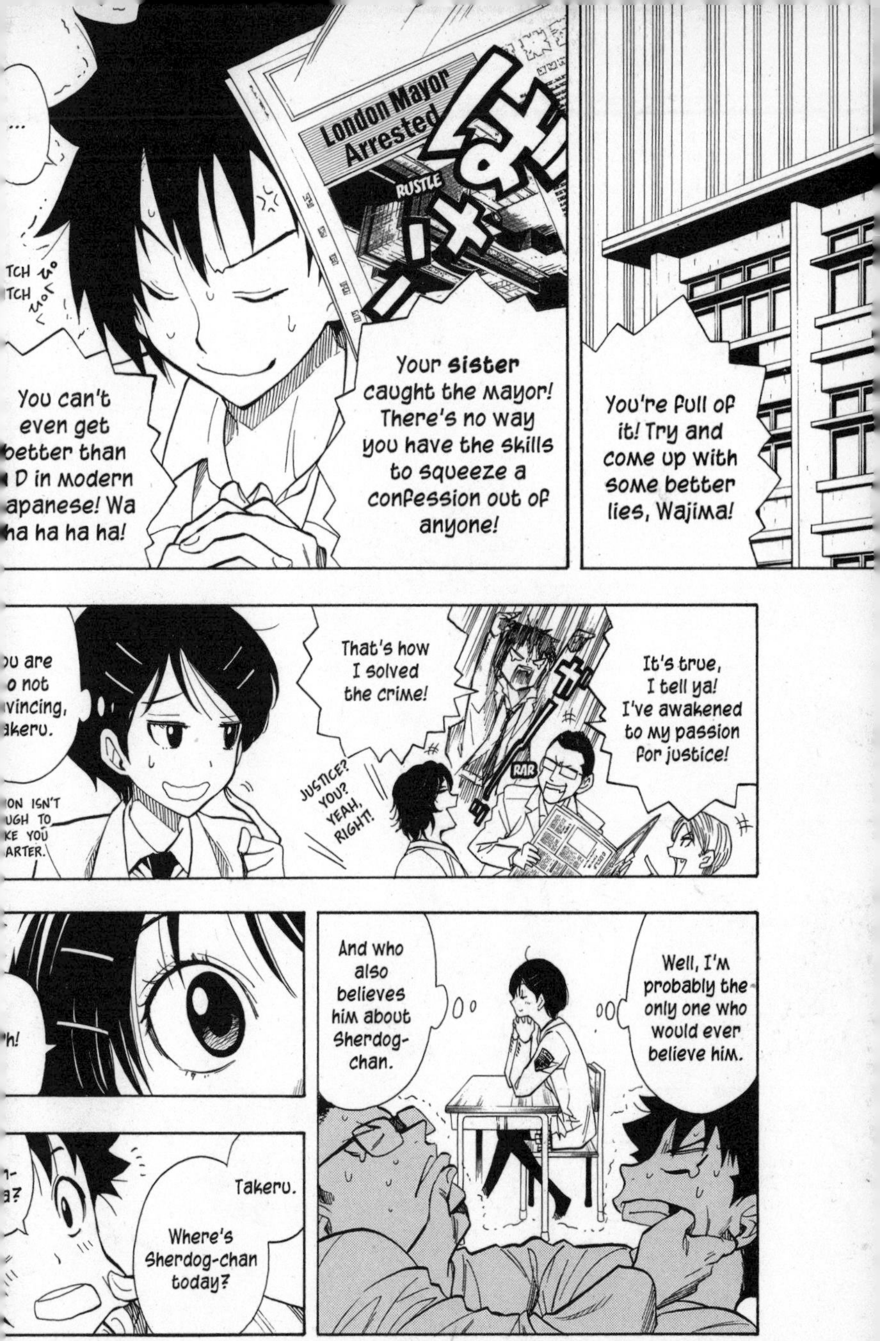
You're full of it! Try and come up with some better lies, Wajima!
London Mayor Arrested
RUSTLE
Your sister caught the mayor! There's no way you have the skills to squeeze a confession out of anyone!
TCH TCH
...
You can't even get etter than D in modern apanese! Wa ha ha ha ha!
It's true, I tell ya! I've awakened to my passion for justice!
RAR
That's how I solved the crime!
JUSTICE? YOU? YEAH, RIGHT!
ou are o not vincing, akeru.
ON ISN'T UGH TO KE YOU ARTER.
Well, I'm probably the only one who would ever believe him.
And who also believes him about Sherdog-chan.
h!
Takeru.
Where's Sherdog-chan today?

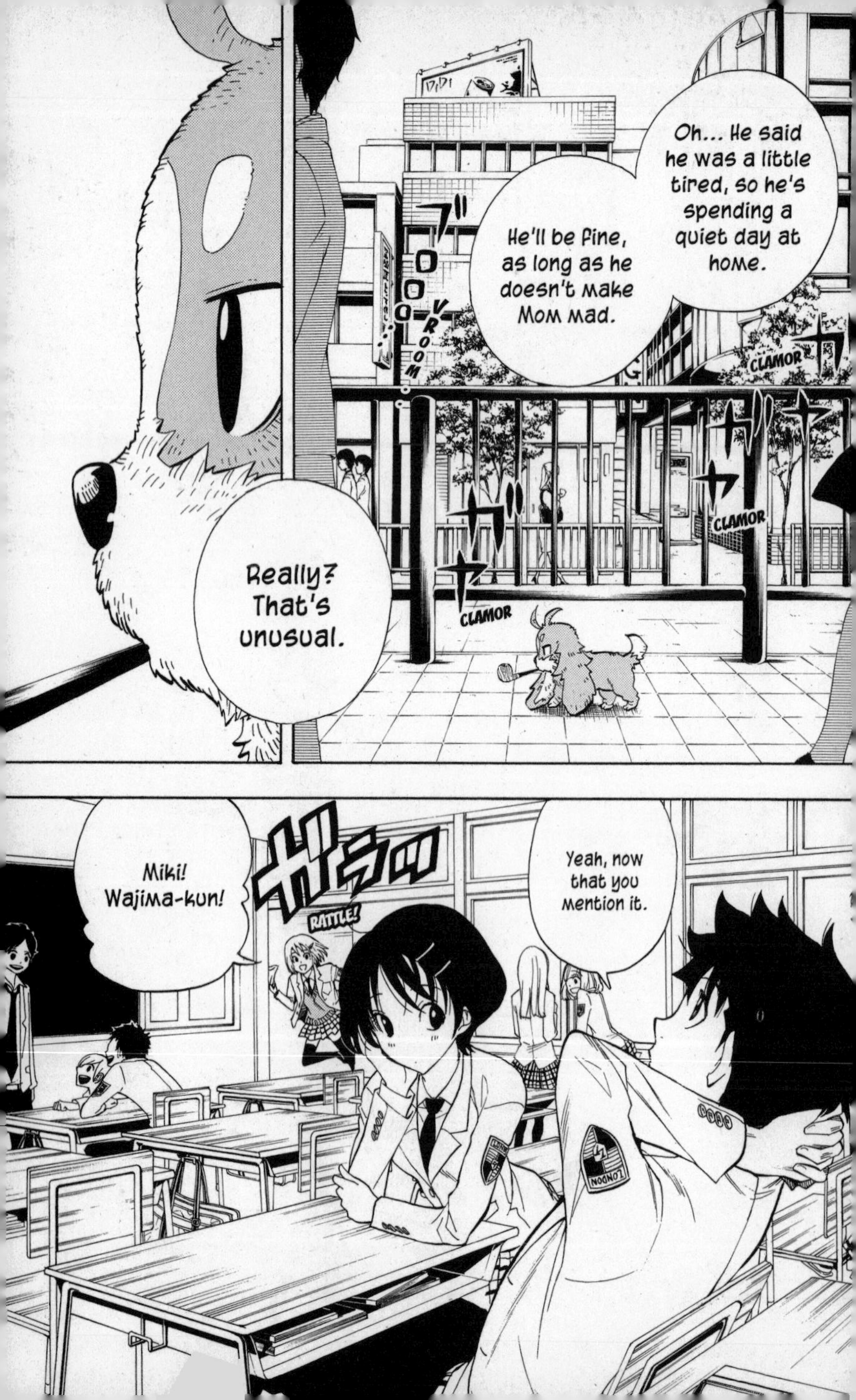
Oh... He said he was a little tired, so he's spending a quiet day at home.
He'll be fine, as long as he doesn't make Mom mad.
CLAMOR
CLAMOR
VROOOM
CLAMOR
Really? That's unusual.
Yeah, now that you mention it.
RATTLE!
Miki! Wajima-kun!

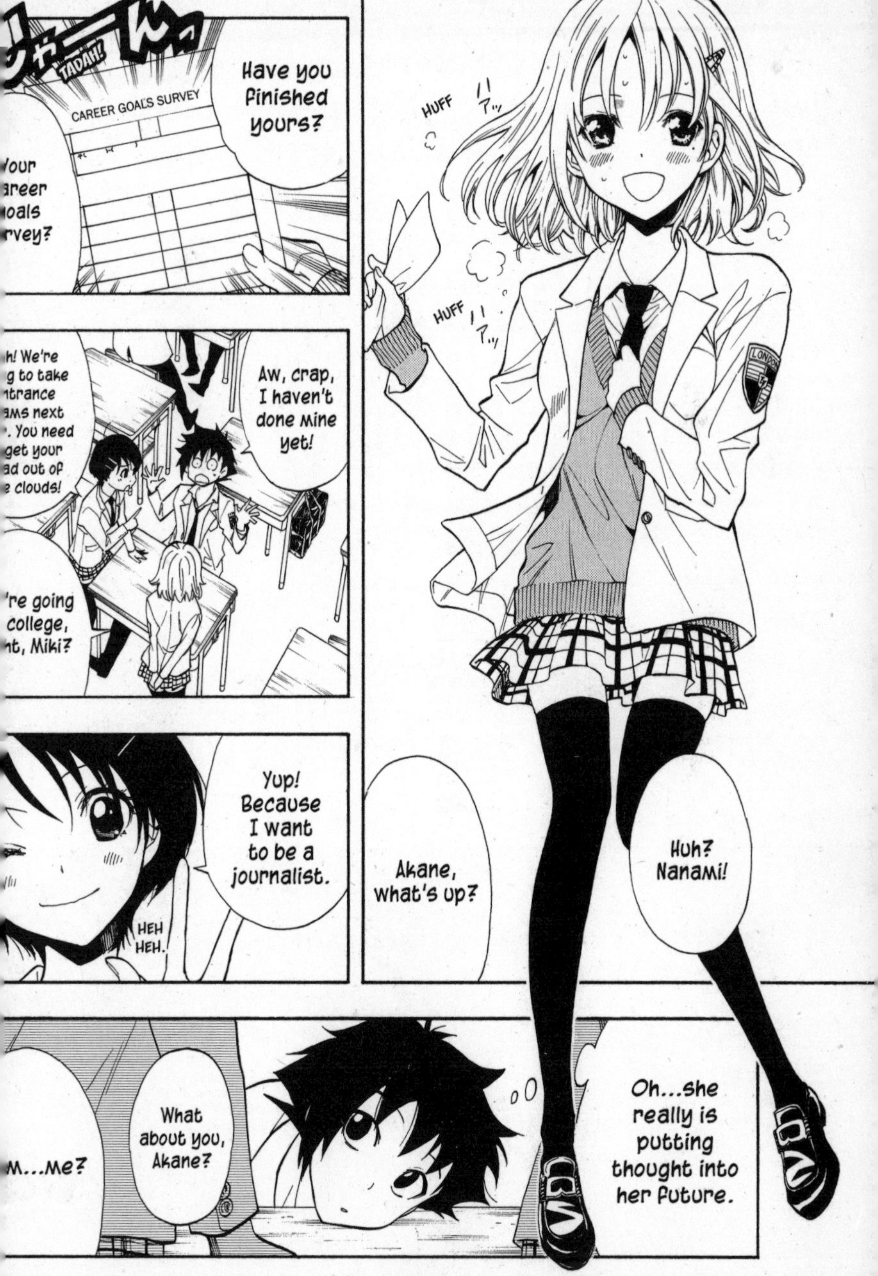
HUFF
HUFF
Huh? Nanami!
Akane, what's up?
TADAH!
Have you finished yours?
CAREER GOALS SURVEY
/our areer ioals rvey?
Aw, crap, I haven't done mine yet!
h! We're g to take ntrance ams next . You need get your ad out of e clouds!
're going college, nt, Miki?
Yup! Because I want to be a journalist.
HEH HEH.
Oh...she really is putting thought into her future.
What about you, Akane?
M...Me?

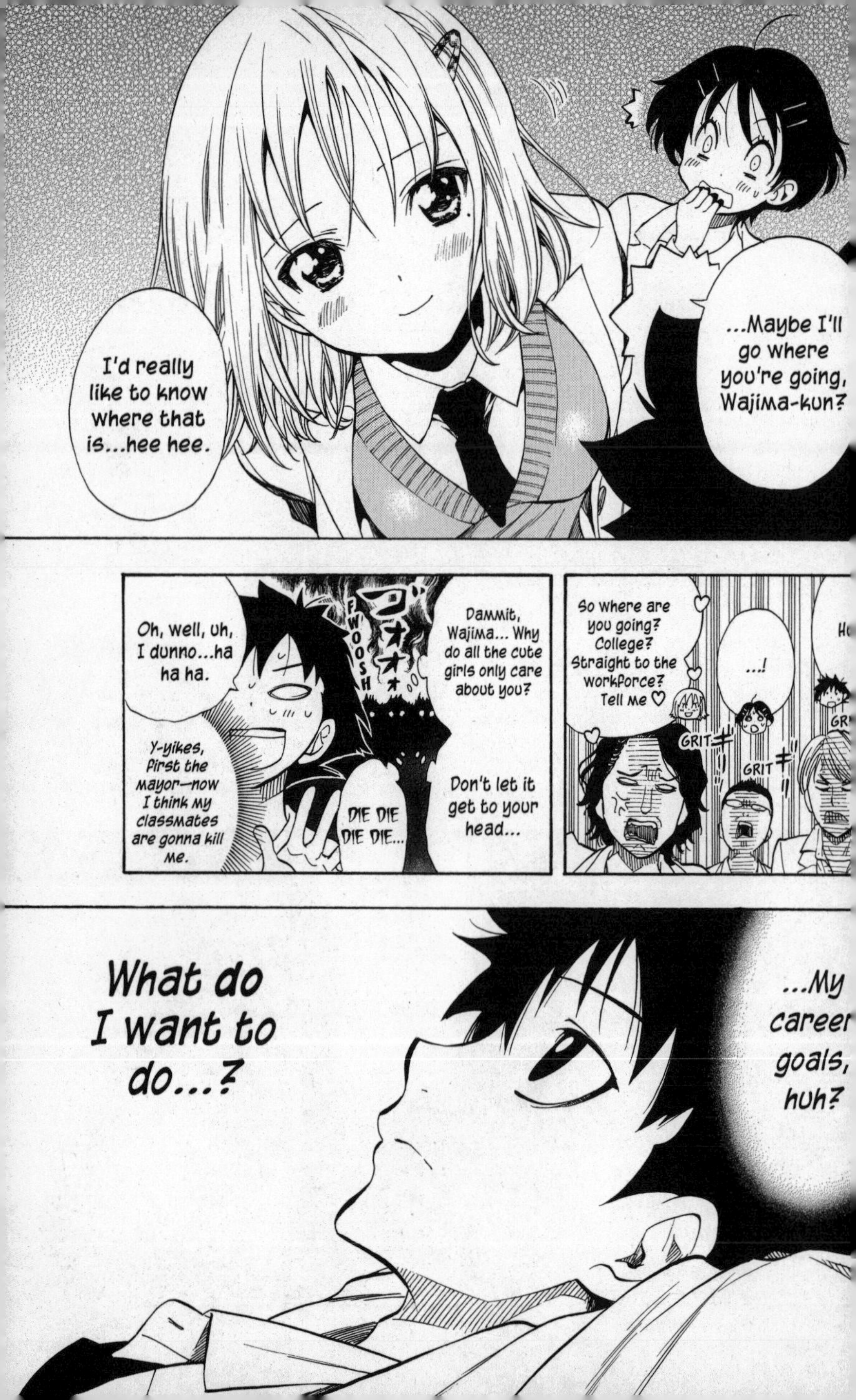
...Maybe I'll go where you're going, Wajima-kun?
I'd really like to know where that is...hee hee.
So where are you going? College? Straight to the workforce? Tell me ♡
...!
GRIT
GRIT
Dammit, Wajima... Why do all the cute girls only care about you?
FWOOSH
Don't let it get to your head...
DIE DIE DIE DIE...
Oh, well, uh, I dunno...ha ha ha.
Y-yikes, first the mayor—now I think my classmates are gonna kill me.
...My career goals, huh?
What do I want to do...?

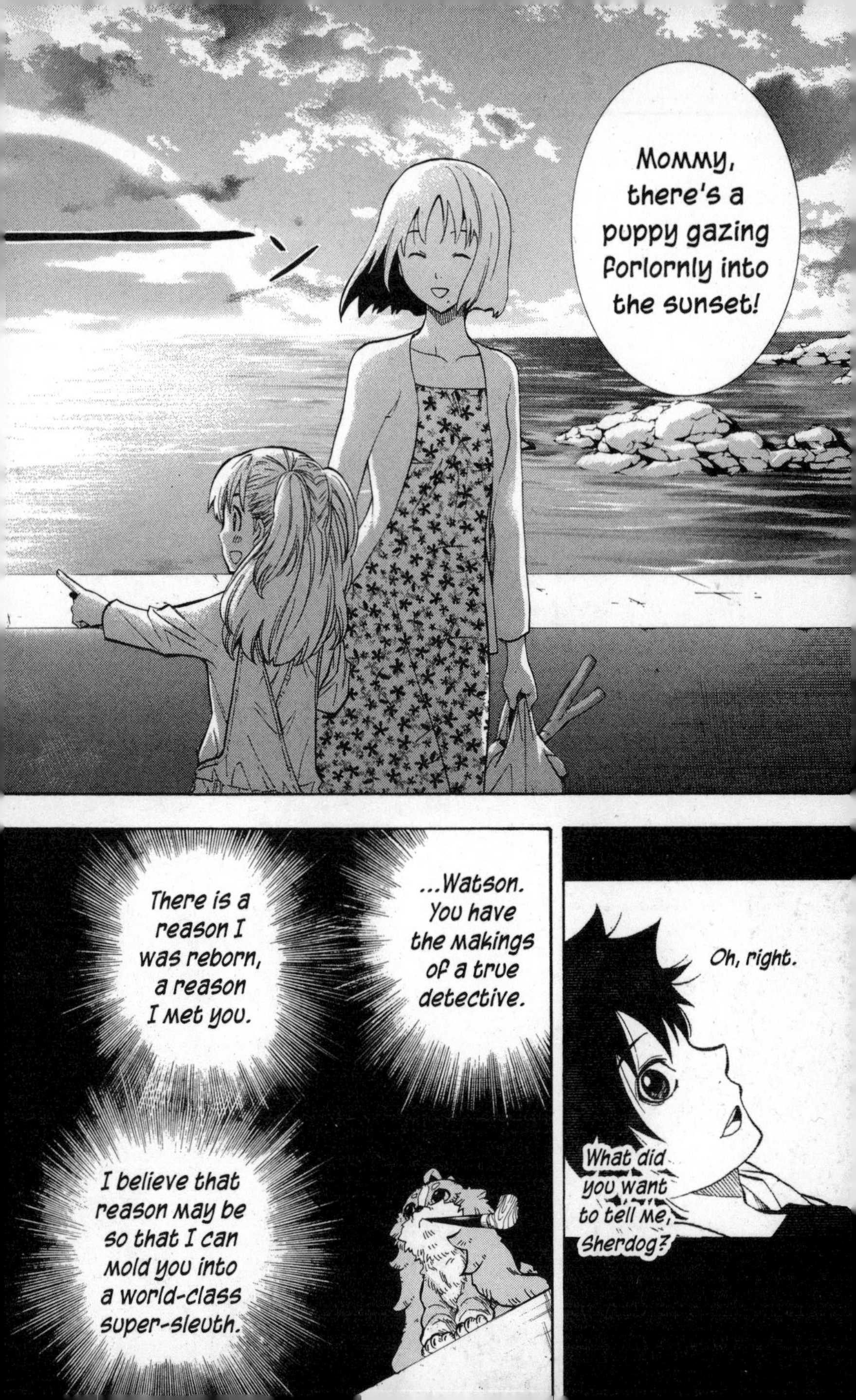
Mommy, there's a puppy gazing forlornly into the sunset!
Oh, right.
What did you want to tell me, Sherdog?
...Watson. You have the makings of a true detective.
There is a reason I was reborn, a reason I met you.
I believe that reason may be so that I can mold you into a world-class super-sleuth.

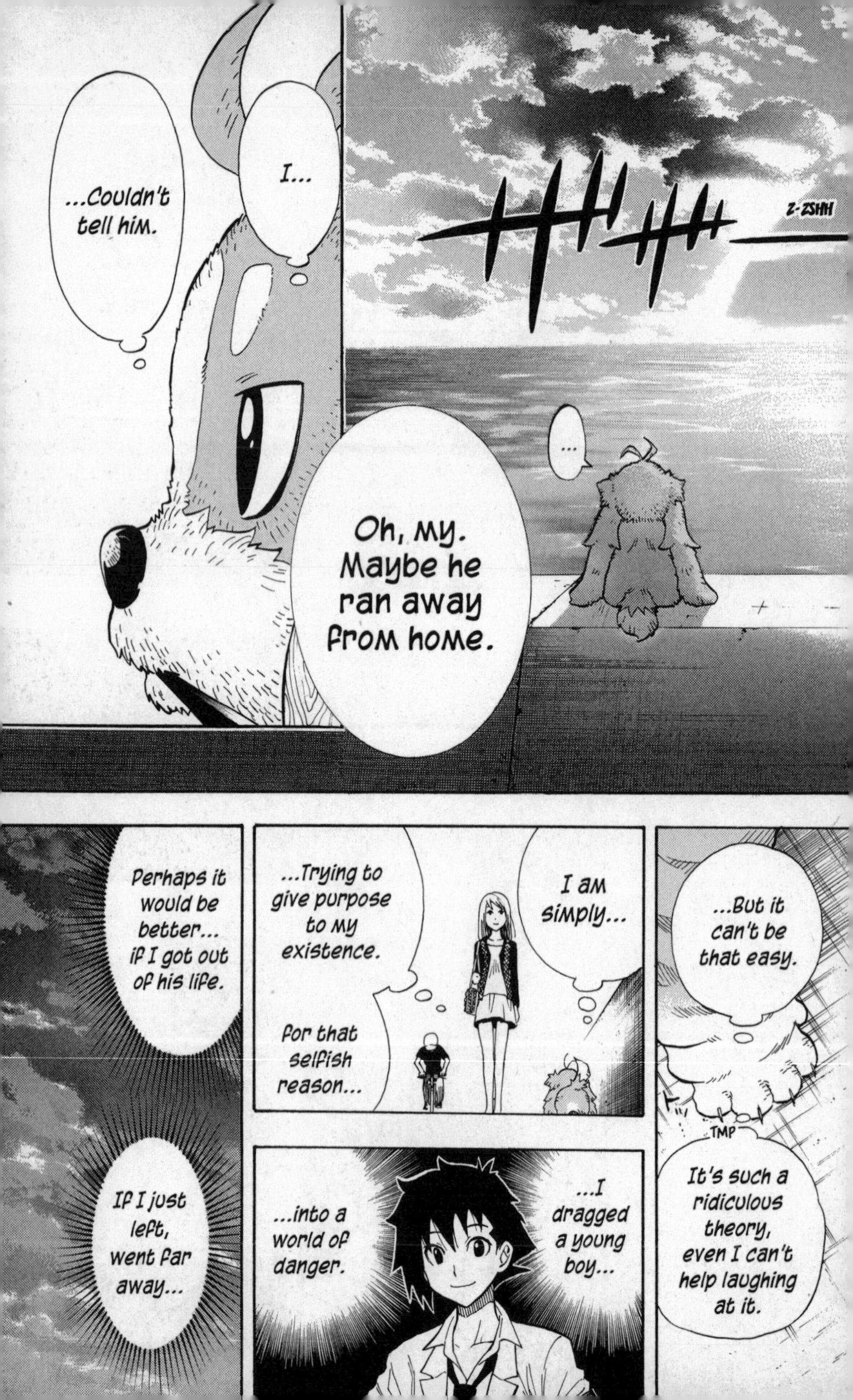
Z-ZSHH
...
Oh, my. Maybe he ran away from home.
I...
...Couldn't tell him.
...But it can't be that easy.
TMP
It's such a ridiculous theory, even I can't help laughing at it.
I am simply...
...Trying to give purpose to my existence.
For that selfish reason...
...I dragged a young boy...
...into a world of danger.
Perhaps it would be better... if I got out of his life.
If I just left, went far away...

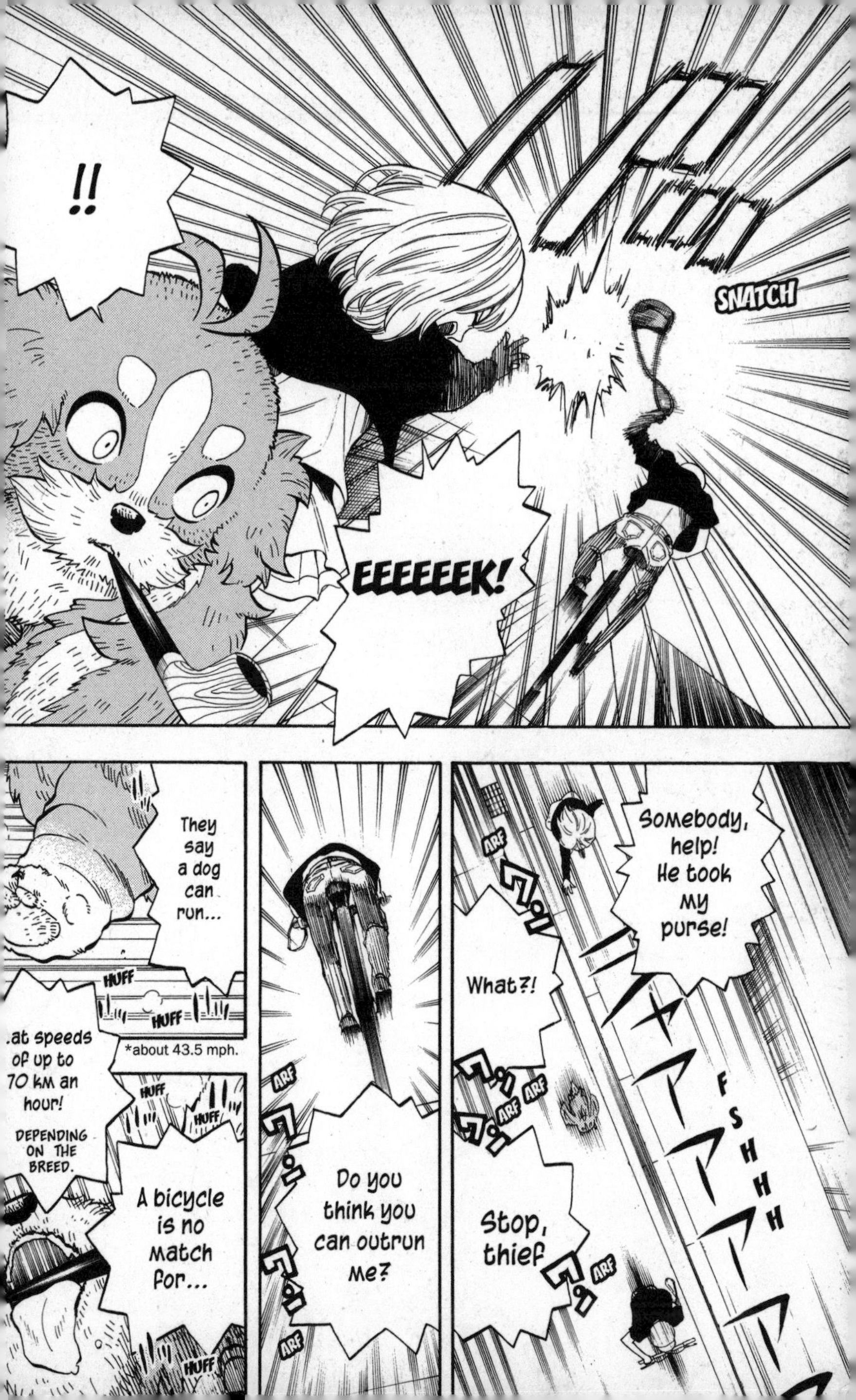
SNATCH
!!
EEEEEEK!
Somebody, help! He took my purse!
ARF
What?!
FSHHHH
ARF ARF
Stop, thief
ARF
ARF
Do you think you can outrun me?
ARF
They say a dog can run...
HUFF
HUFF
.at speeds of up to 70 km an hour!
*about 43.5 mph.
DEPENDING ON THE BREED.
HUFF
HUFF
A bicycle is no match for...
HUFF

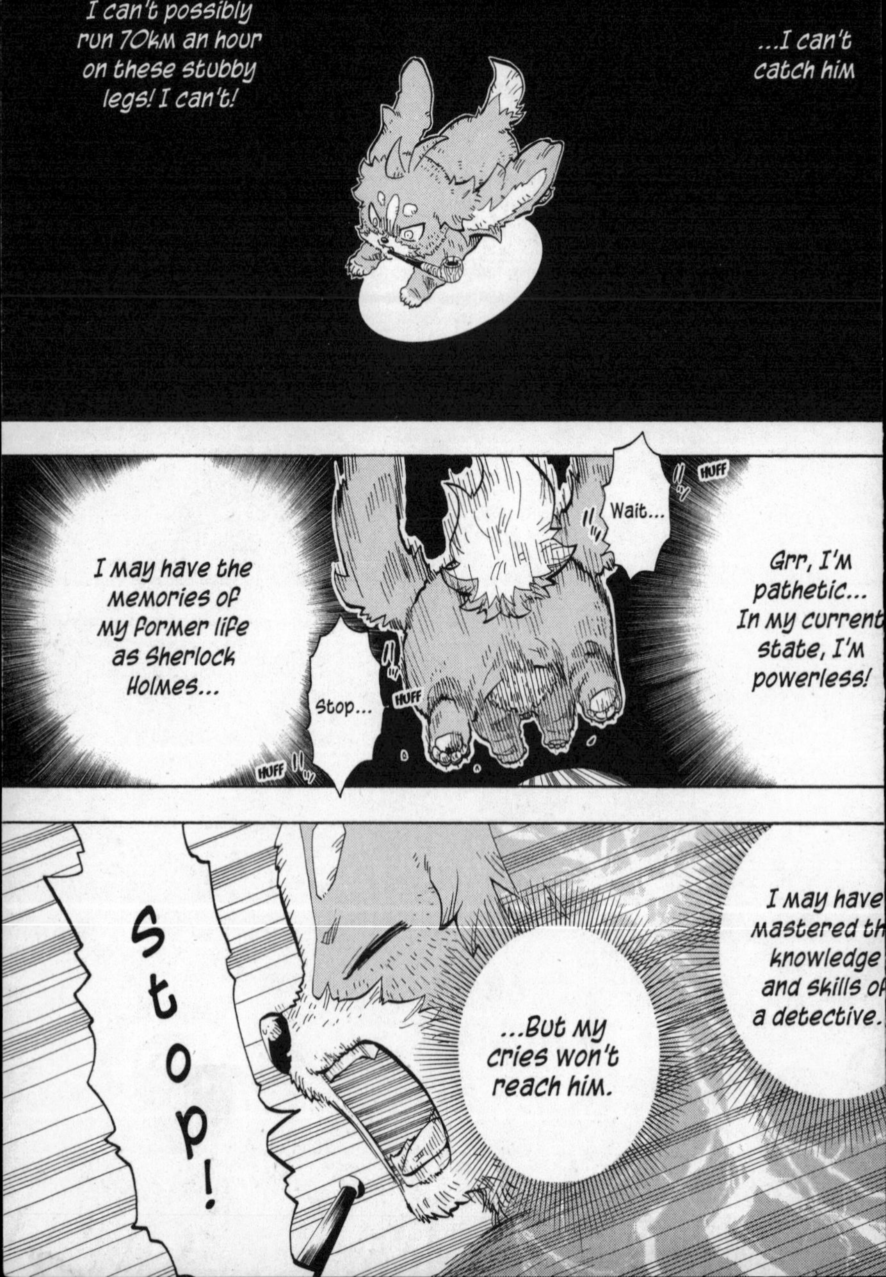
...I can't catch him
I can't possibly run 70km an hour on these stubby legs! I can't!
Grr, I'm pathetic... In my current state, I'm powerless!
HUFF
Wait...
Stop...
HUFF
I may have the memories of my former life as Sherlock Holmes...
HUFF
I may have mastered th knowledge and skills of a detective.
...But my cries won't reach him.
Stop!

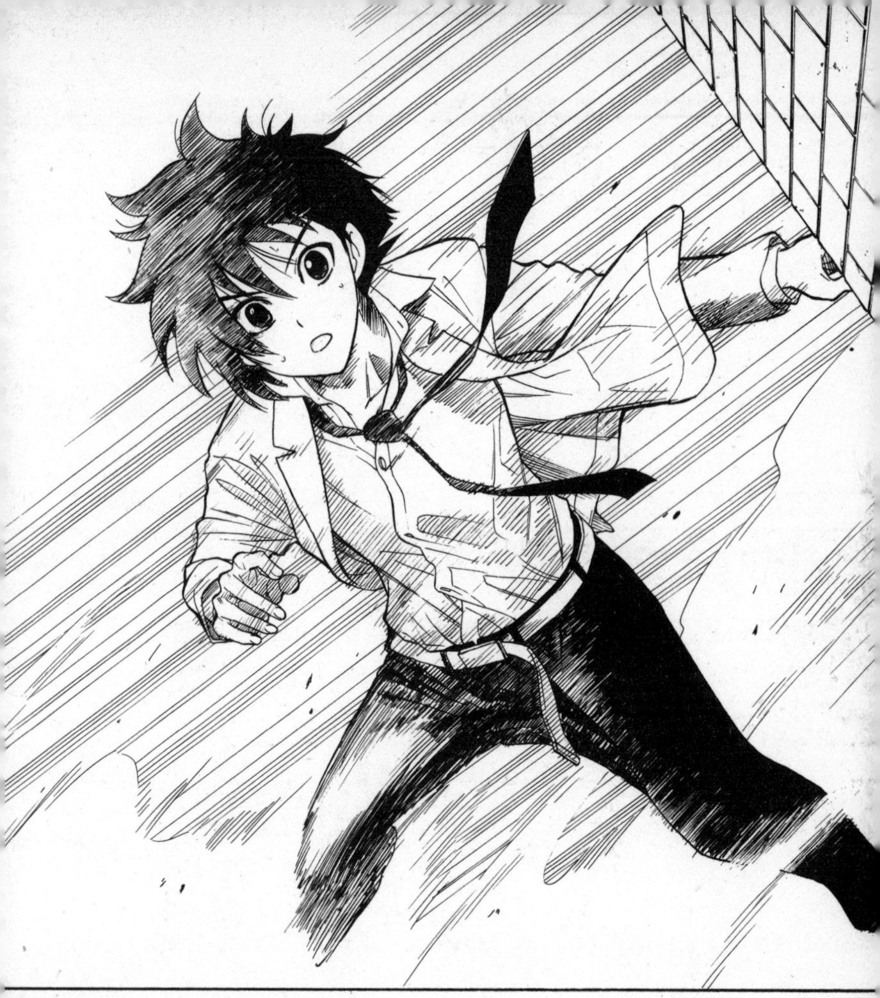

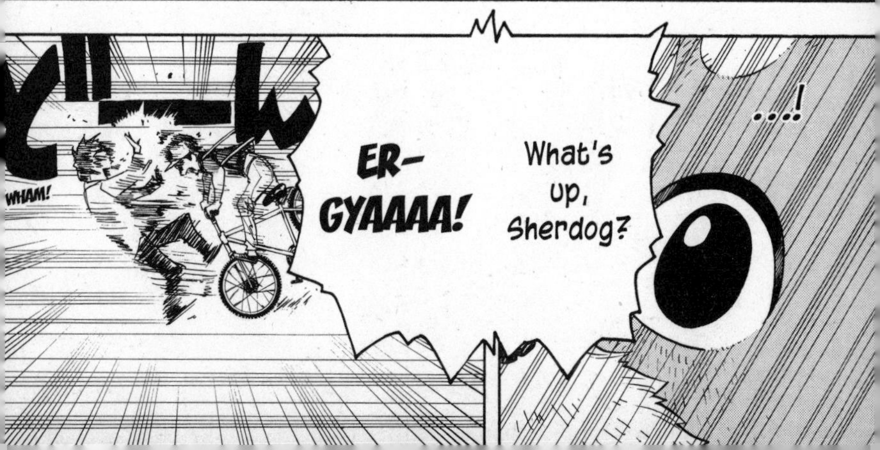
...!
What's up, Sherdog?
ER-GYAAAA!
WHAM!

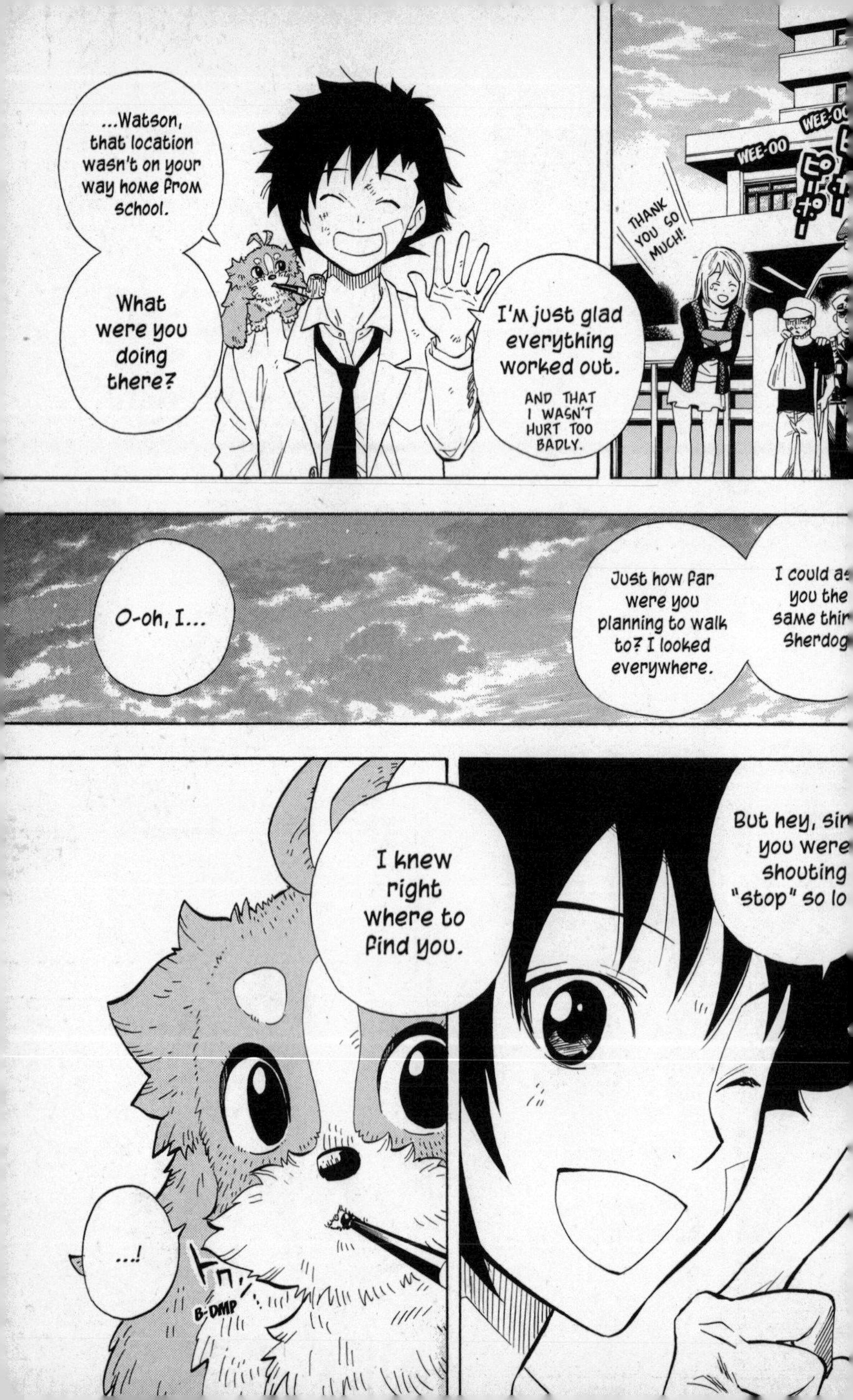
WEE-OO
WEE-OO
THANK YOU SO MUCH!
I'm just glad everything worked out.
AND THAT I WASN'T HURT TOO BADLY.
...Watson, that location wasn't on your way home from school.
What were you doing there?
I could as you the same thir Sherdog
Just how far were you planning to walk to? I looked everywhere.
O-oh, I...
But hey, sir you were shouting "stop" so lo
I knew right where to find you.
...!
B-DMP

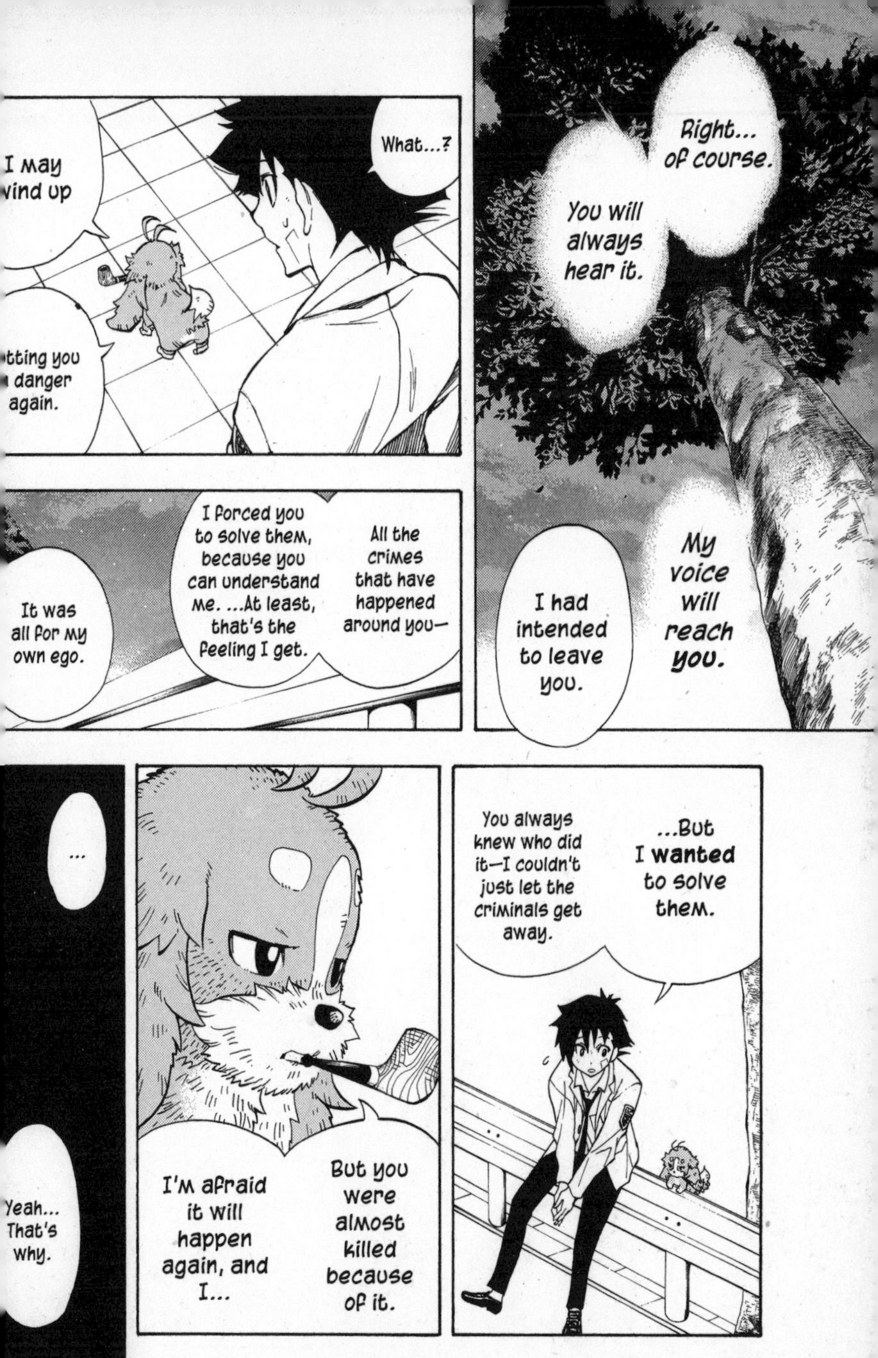
Right... of course.
You will always hear it.
My voice will reach you.
I had intended to leave you.
What...?
I may wind up
tting you danger again.
All the crimes that have happened around you—
I forced you to solve them, because you can understand me. ...At least, that's the feeling I get.
It was all for my own ego.
...But I wanted to solve them.
You always knew who did it—I couldn't just let the criminals get away.
But you were almost killed because of it.
I'm afraid it will happen again, and I...
...
Yeah... That's why.

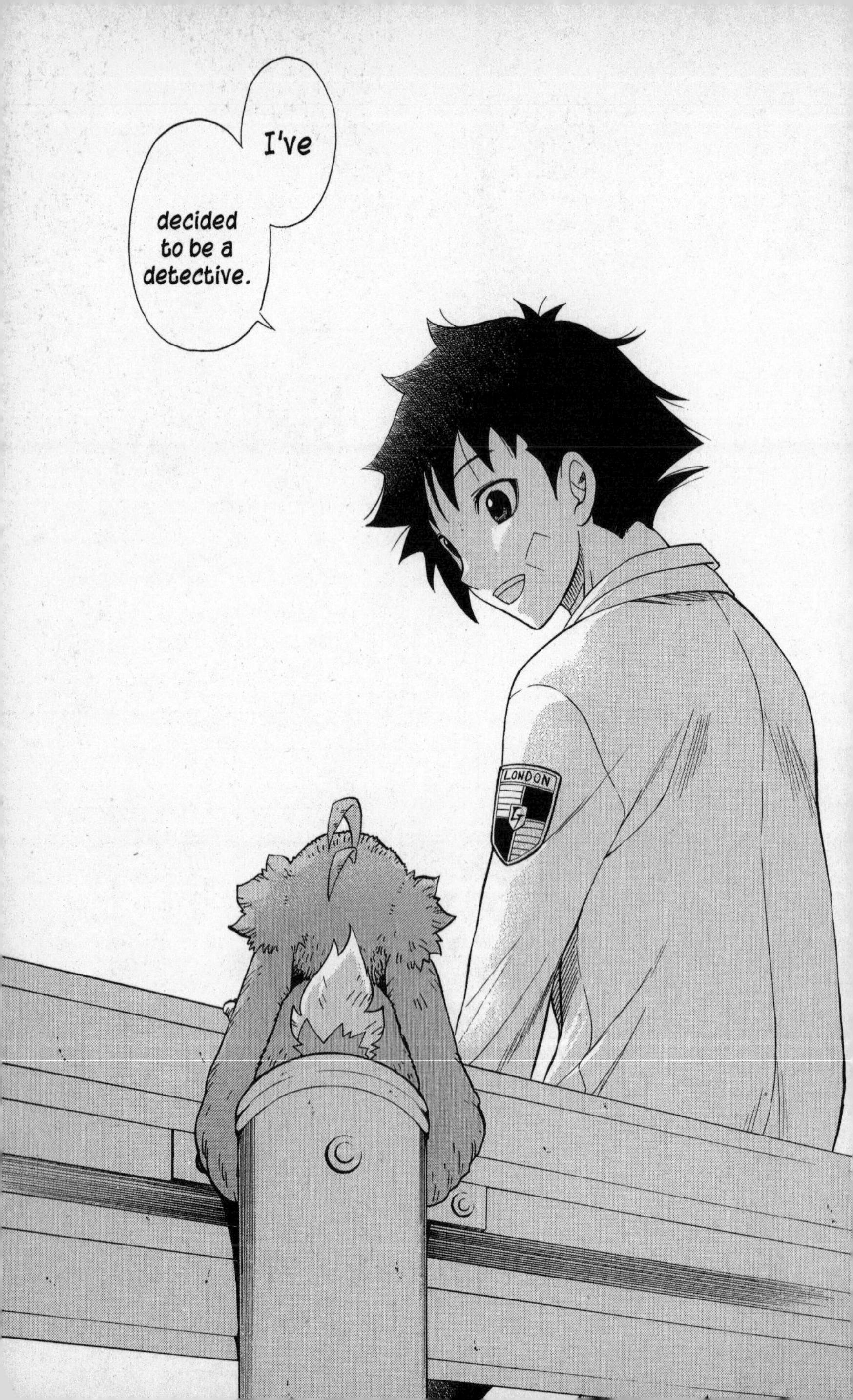
I've
decided to be a detective.
LONDON

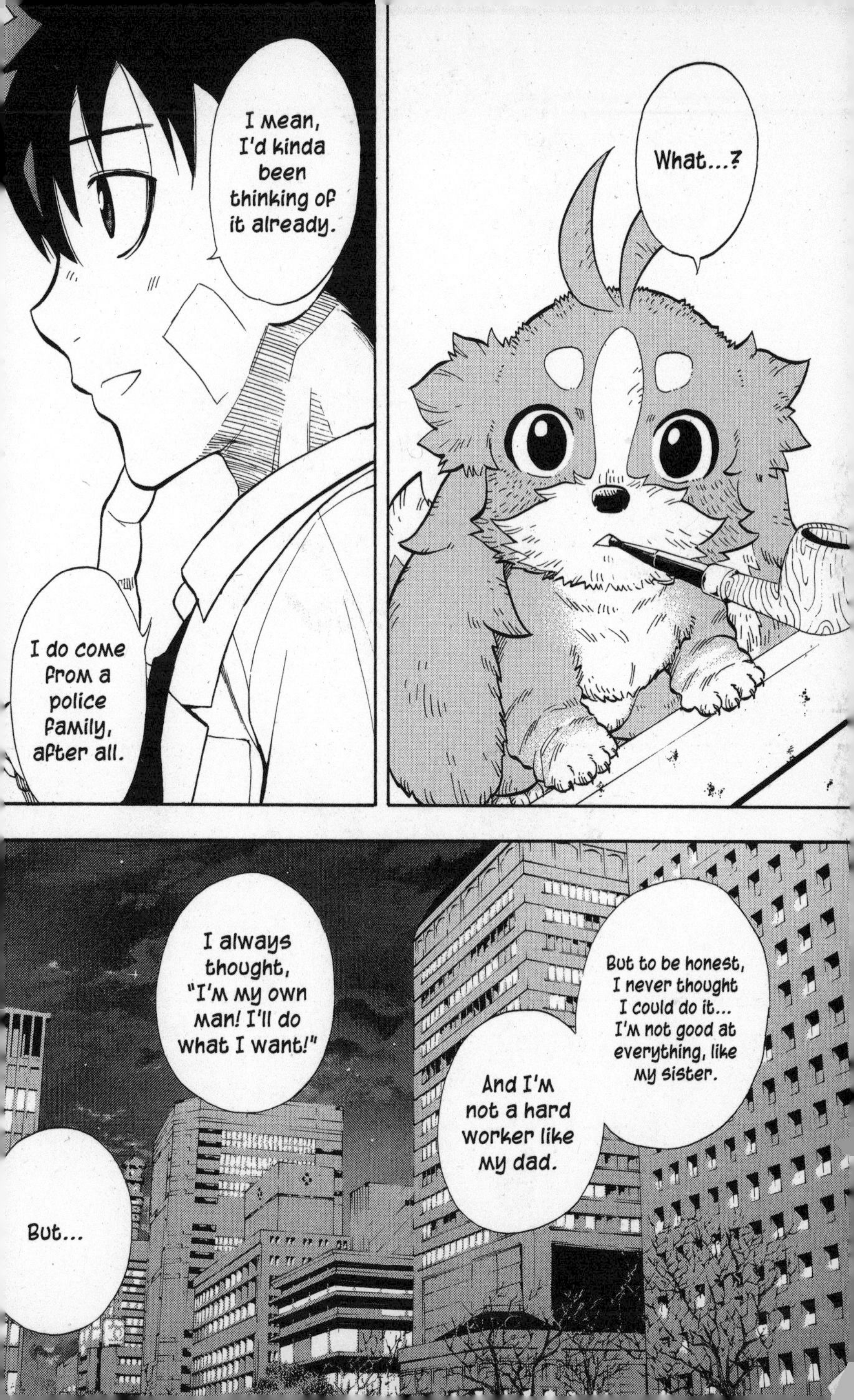
What...?
I mean, I'd kinda been thinking of it already.
I do come from a police family, after all.
But to be honest, I never thought I could do it... I'm not good at everything, like my sister.
And I'm not a hard worker like my dad.
I always thought, "I'm my own man! I'll do what I want!"
But...

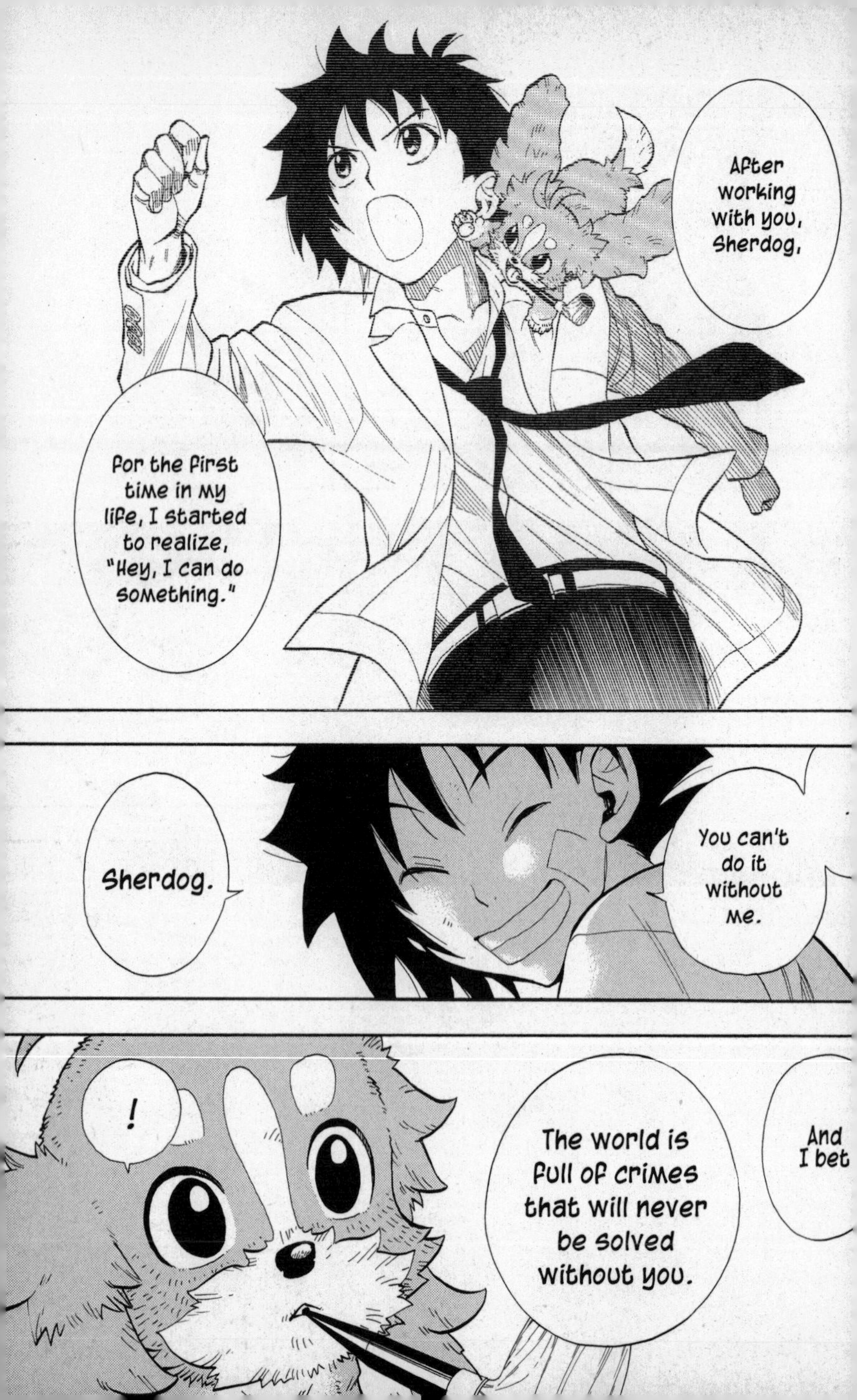
After working with you, Sherdog,
For the first time in my life, I started to realize, "Hey, I can do something."
You can't do it without me.
Sherdog.
And I bet
The world is full of crimes that will never be solved without you.
!

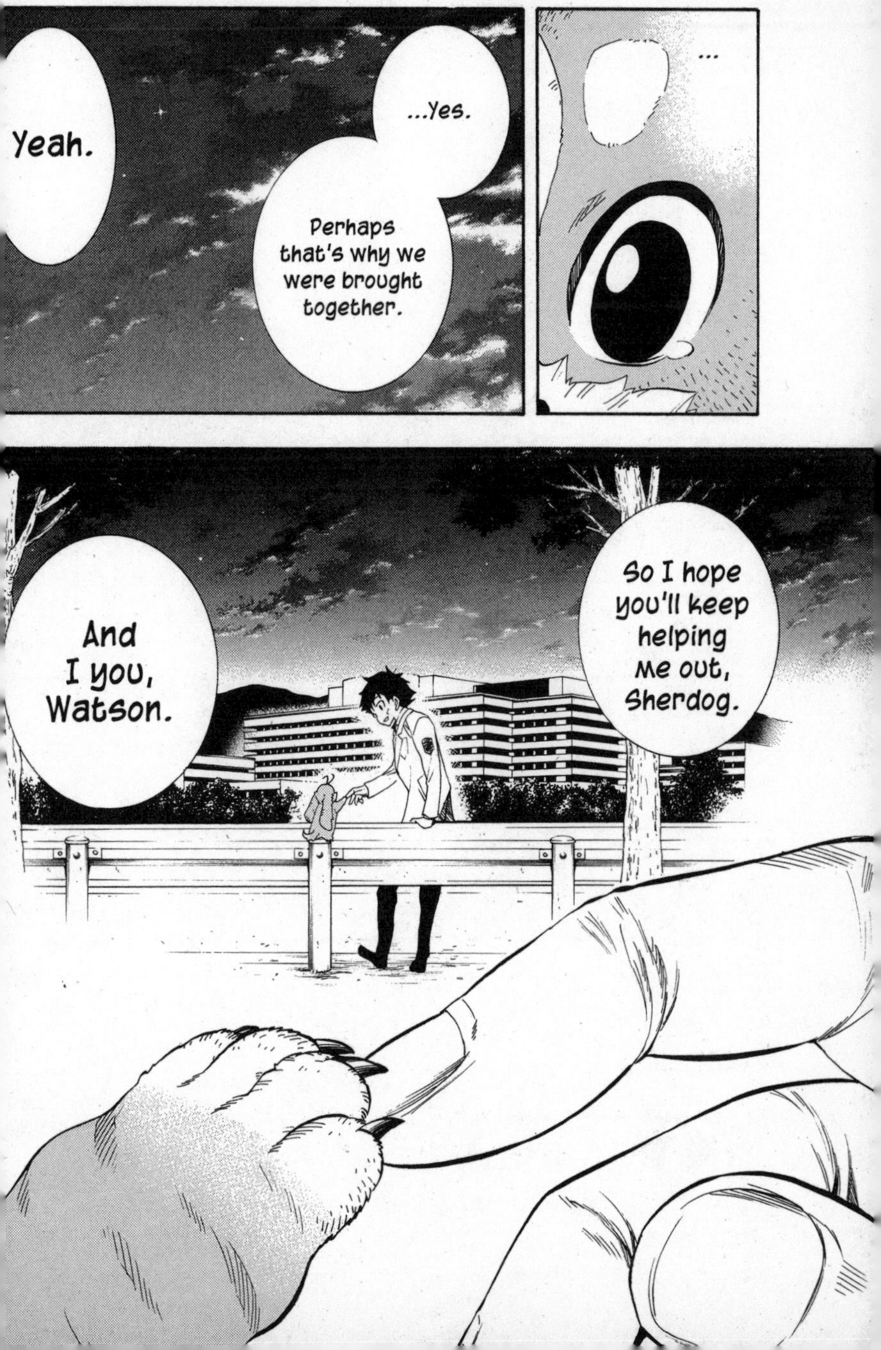
...
...Yes.
Perhaps that's why we were brought together.
Yeah.
So I hope you'll keep helping me out, Sherdog.
And I you, Watson.

Case 8: ⚜ Requiem for a New Beginning, Part 1

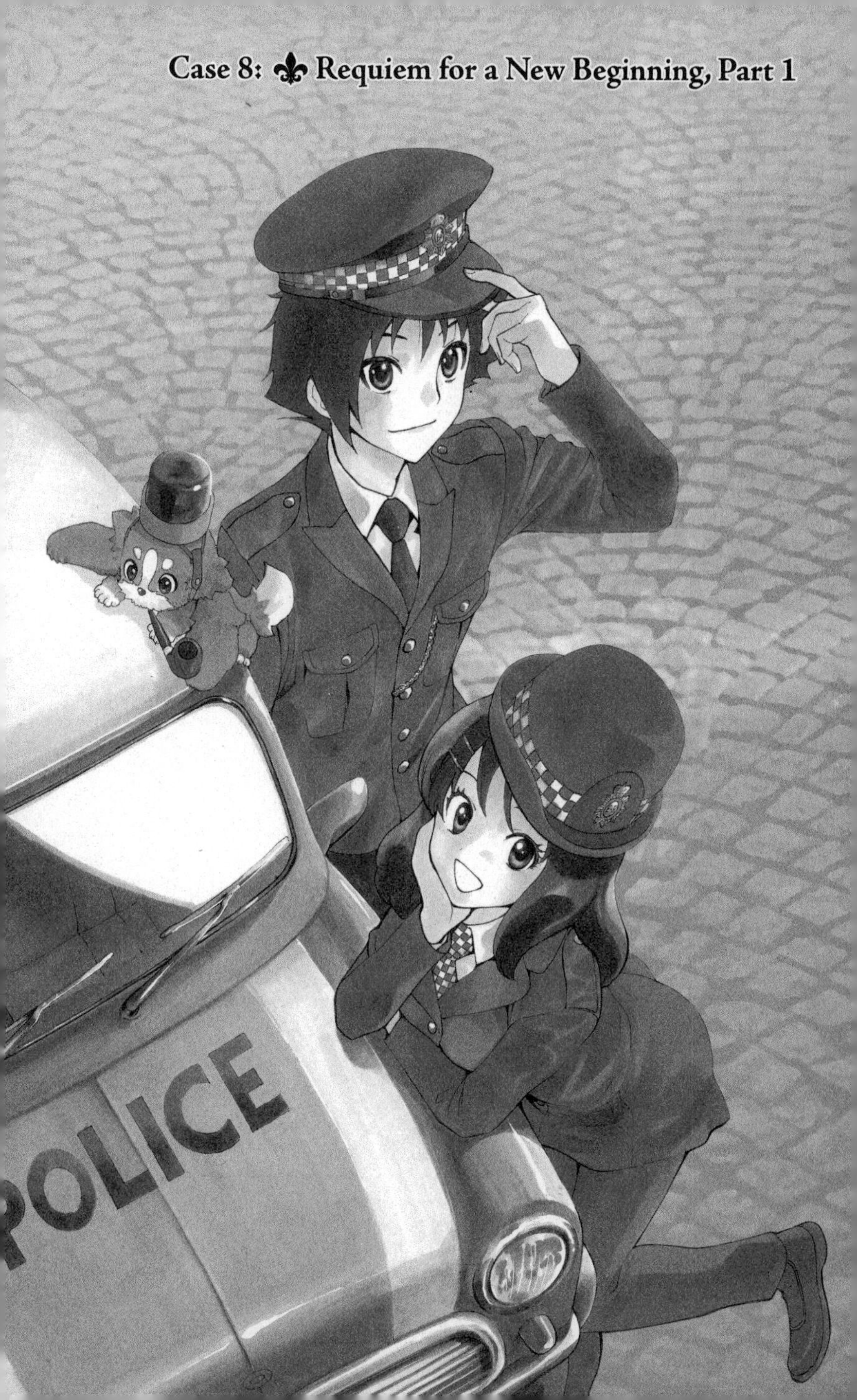
POLICE

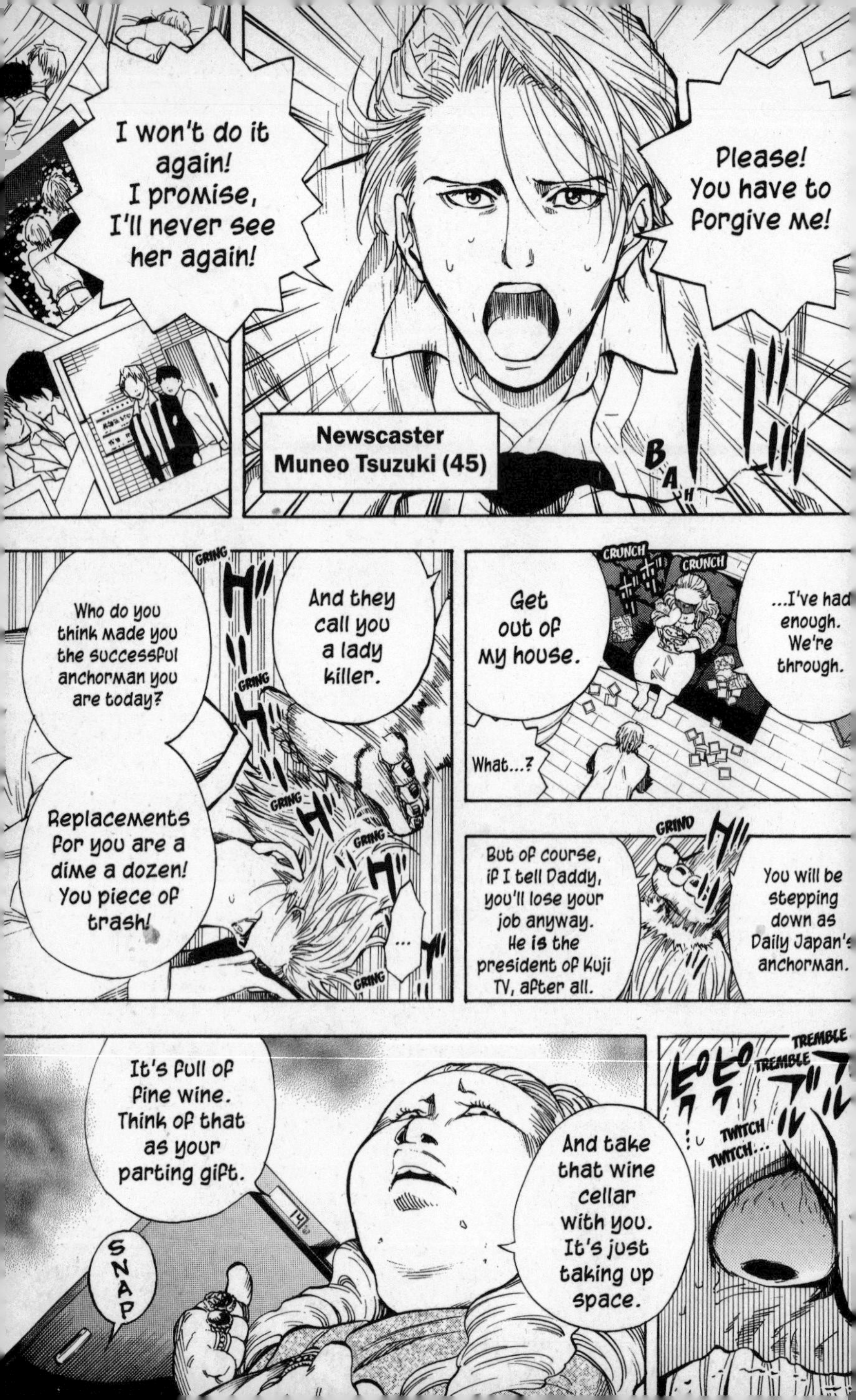
Please! You have to forgive me!
BAH
Newscaster Muneo Tsuzuki (45)
I won't do it again! I promise, I'll never see her again!
CRUNCH
CRUNCH
...I've had enough. We're through.
Get out of my house.
What...?
GRIND
You will be stepping down as Daily Japan's anchorman.
But of course, if I tell Daddy, you'll lose your job anyway. He is the president of Kuji TV, after all.
GRING
And they call you a lady killer.
Who do you think made you the successful anchorman you are today?
GRING
GRING
GRING
Replacements for you are a dime a dozen! You piece of trash!
...
GRING
TREMBLE
TREMBLE
TWITCH
TWITCH...
And take that wine cellar with you. It's just taking up space.
It's full of fine wine. Think of that as your parting gift.
SNAP

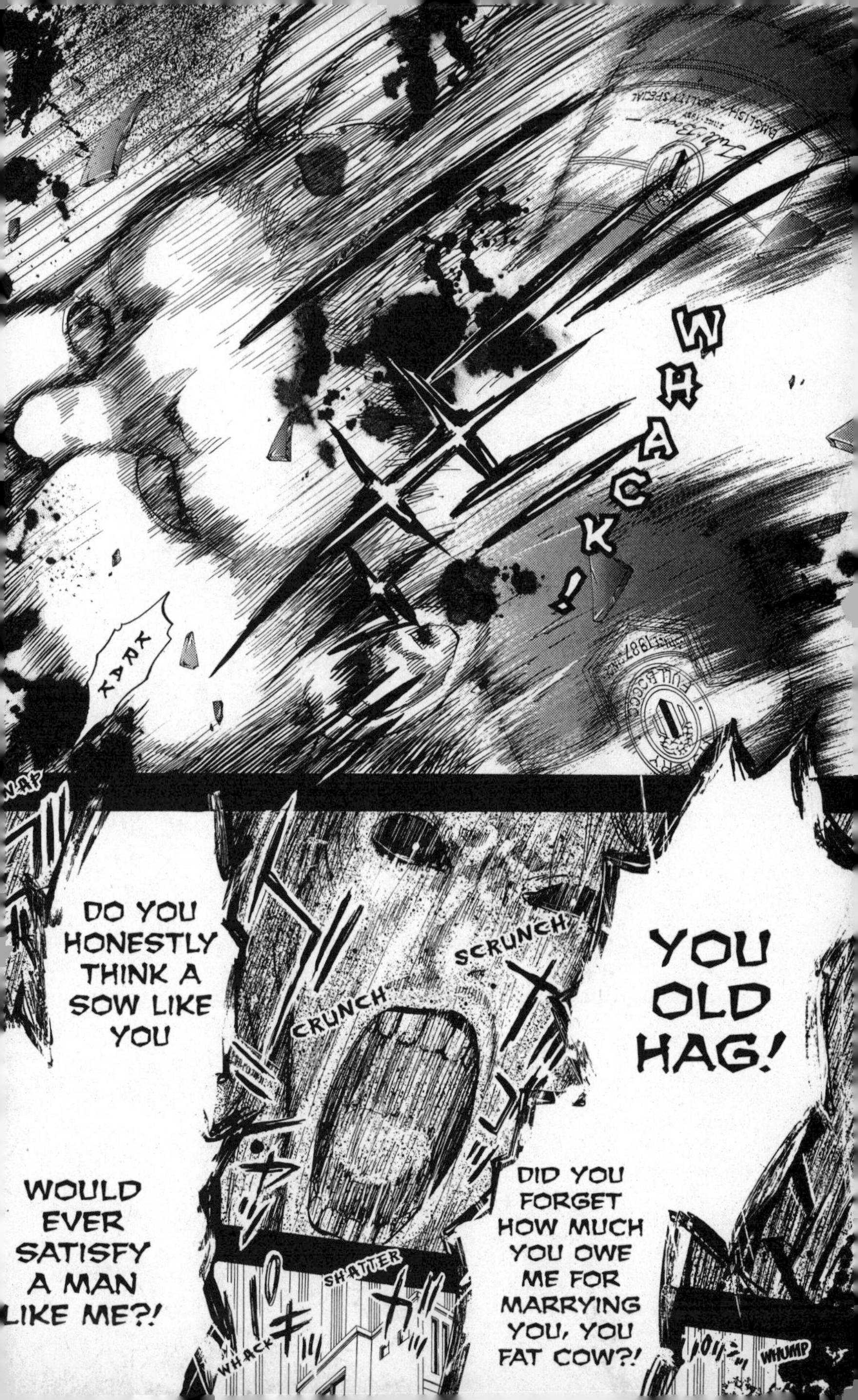
WHACK!
KRAK
YOU OLD HAG!
SCRUNCH
CRUNCH
DO YOU HONESTLY THINK A SOW LIKE YOU
WOULD EVER SATISFY A MAN LIKE ME?!
DID YOU FORGET HOW MUCH YOU OWE ME FOR MARRYING YOU, YOU FAT COW?!
WHUMP
SHATTER
WHACK

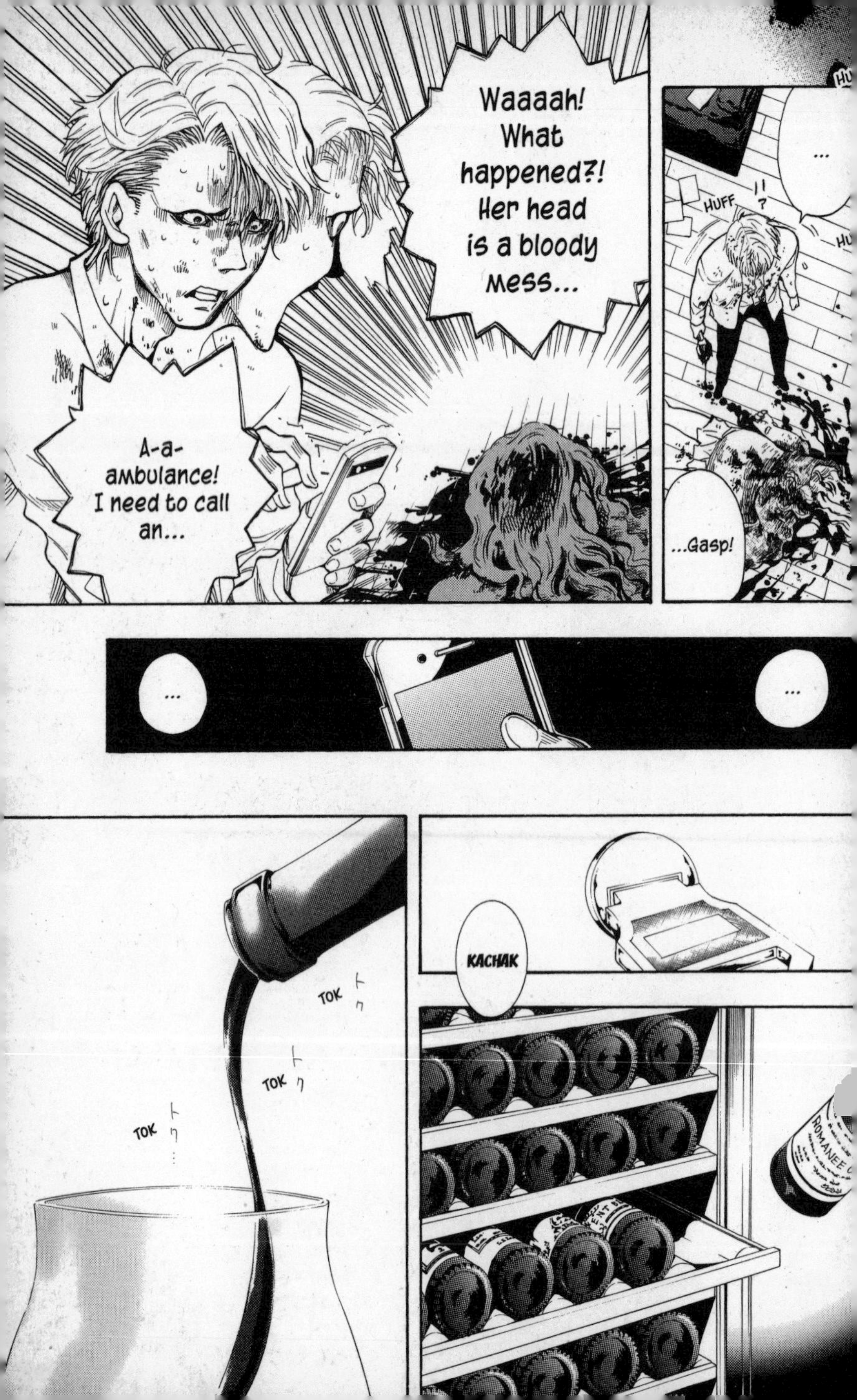

HUFF
...
...Gasp!
Waaaah! What happened?! Her head is a bloody mess...
A-a-ambulance! I need to call an...
...
...
KACHAK
TOK
TOK
TOK

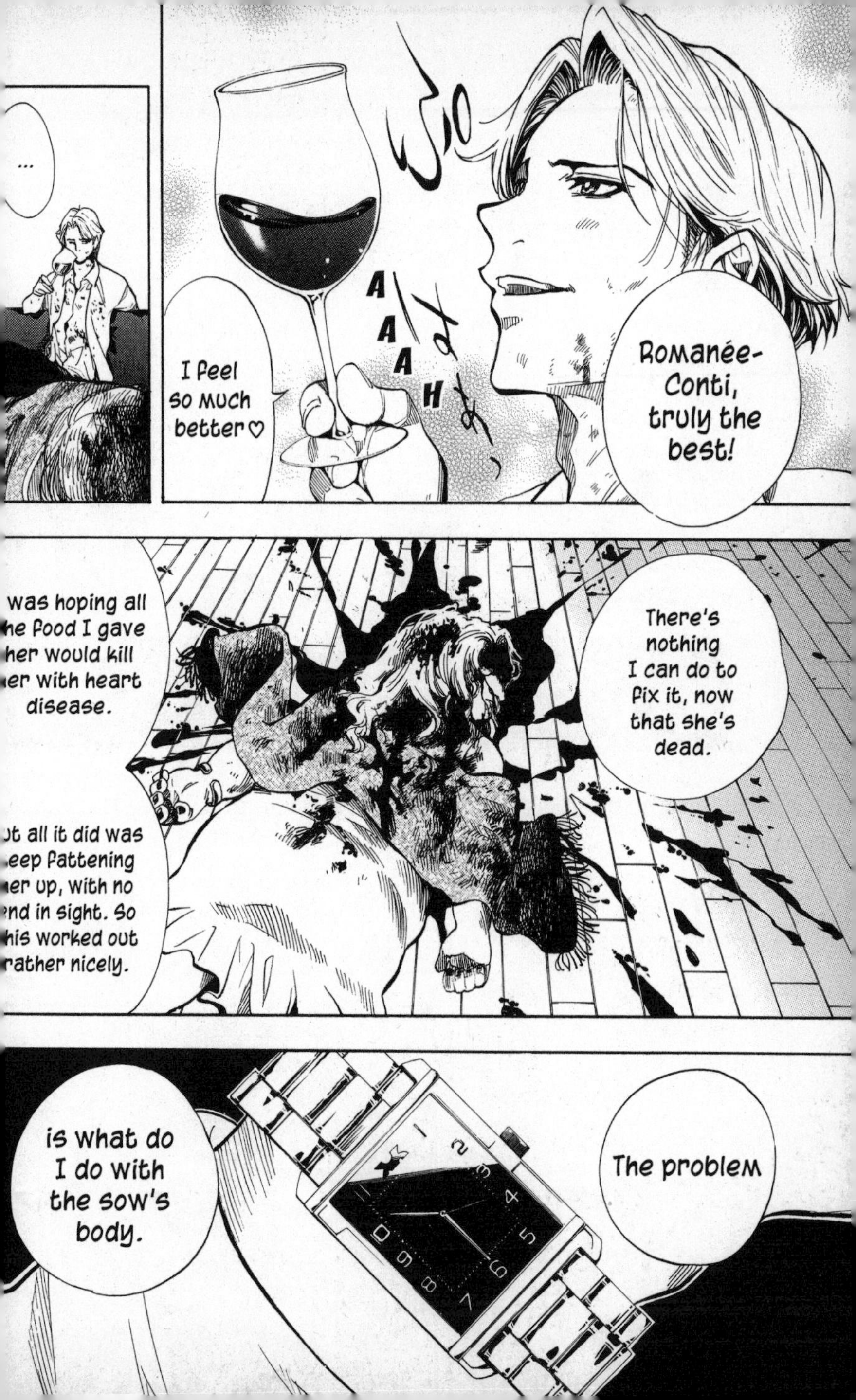
Romanée-Conti, truly the best!
AAAH
I feel so much better♡
...
There's nothing I can do to fix it, now that she's dead.
was hoping all he food I gave her would kill er with heart disease.
ut all it did was eep fattening er up, with no nd in sight. So his worked out rather nicely.
The problem
is what do I do with the sow's body.

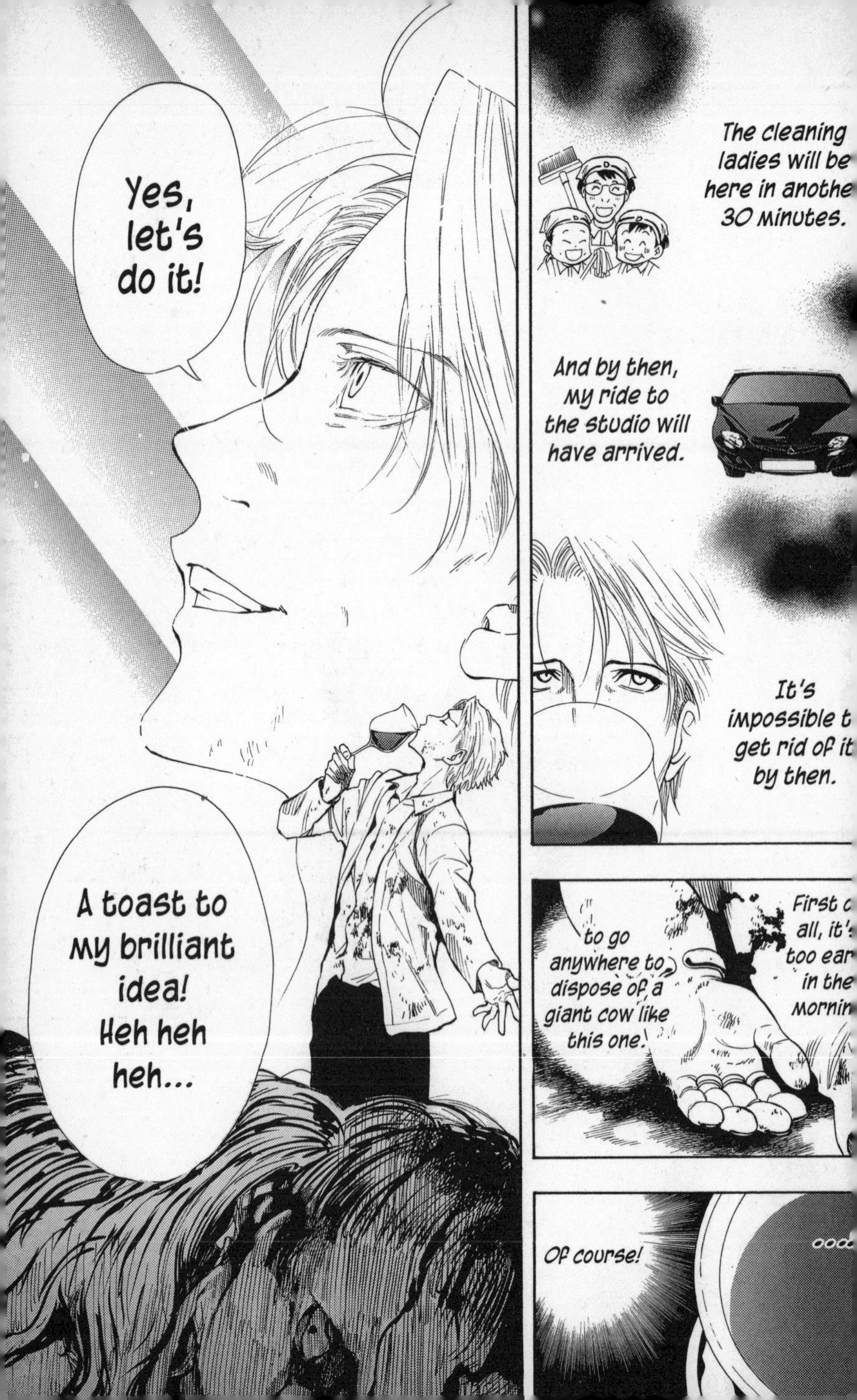
The cleaning ladies will be here in anothe 30 minutes.
And by then, my ride to the studio will have arrived.
It's impossible t get rid of it by then.
First o all, it's too ear in the mornin
to go anywhere to dispose of a giant cow like this one.
ooo
Of course!
Yes, let's do it!
A toast to my brilliant idea! Heh heh heh...

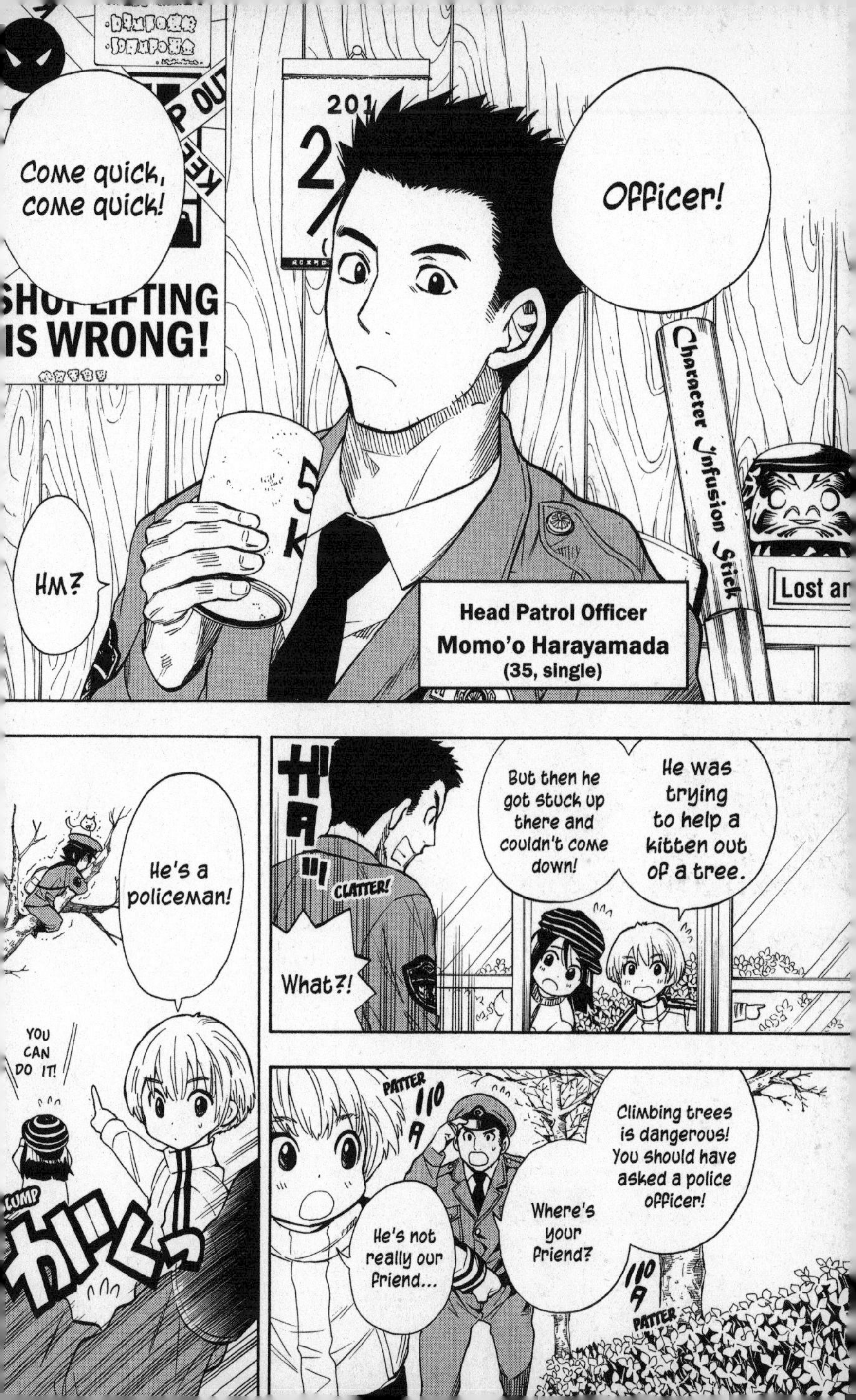
Officer!
Come quick, come quick!
Hm?
SHOPLIFTING IS WRONG!
Character Infusion Stick
Head Patrol Officer
Momo'o Harayamada
(35, single)
He was trying to help a kitten out of a tree.
But then he got stuck up there and couldn't come down!
CLATTER!
What?!
Climbing trees is dangerous! You should have asked a police officer!
PATTER
Where's your friend?
He's not really our friend...
PATTER
He's a policeman!
YOU CAN DO IT!

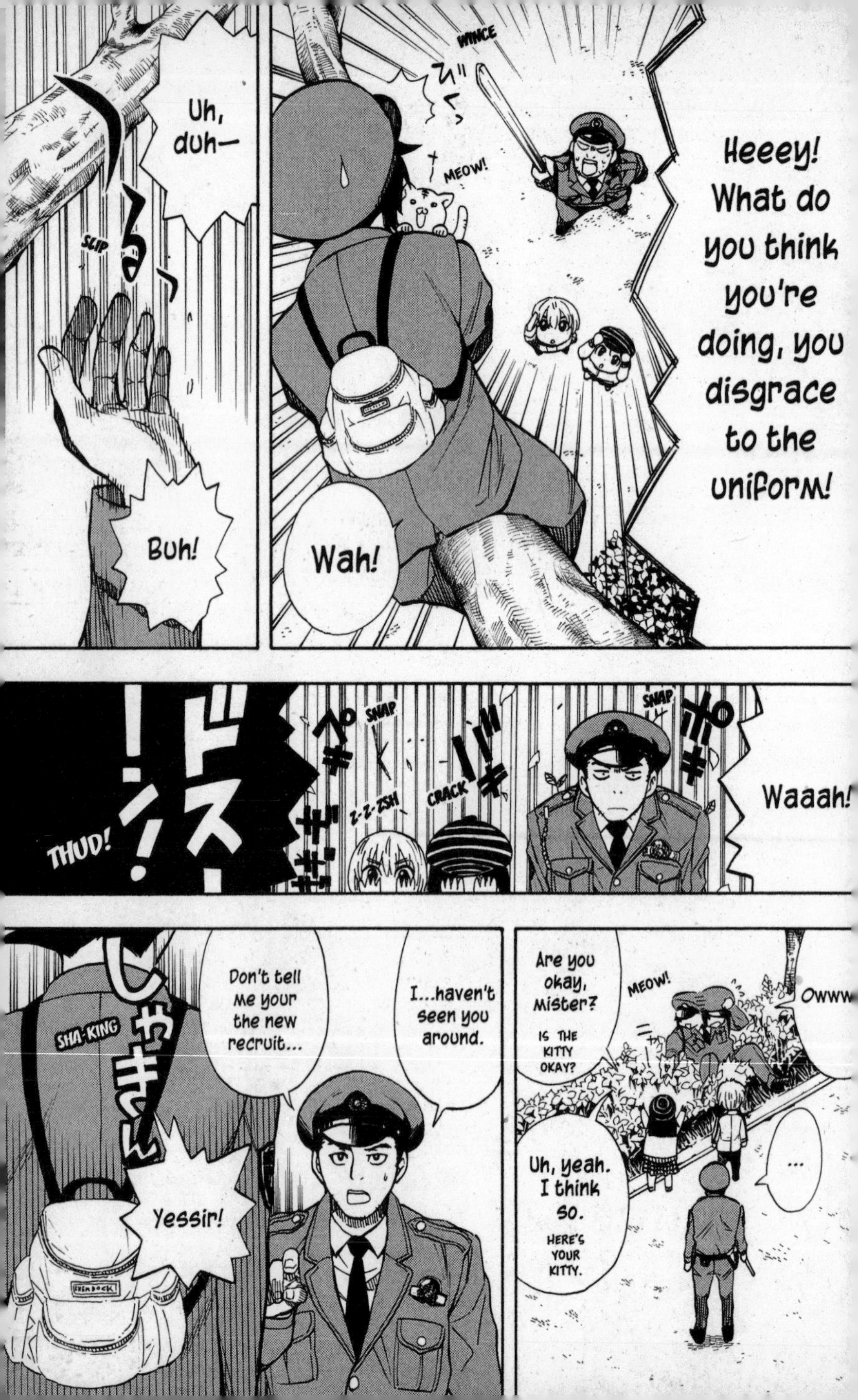
WINCE
MEOW!
Heeey! What do you think you're doing, you disgrace to the uniform!
Wah!
Uh, duh—
SLIP
Buh!
Waaah!
SNAP
CRACK
SNAP
Z-Z-ZSH
THUD!
Owww
MEOW!
Are you okay, Mister?
IS THE KITTY OKAY?
...
Uh, yeah. I think so.
HERE'S YOUR KITTY.
I...haven't seen you around.
Don't tell me your the new recruit...
SHA-KING
Yessir!

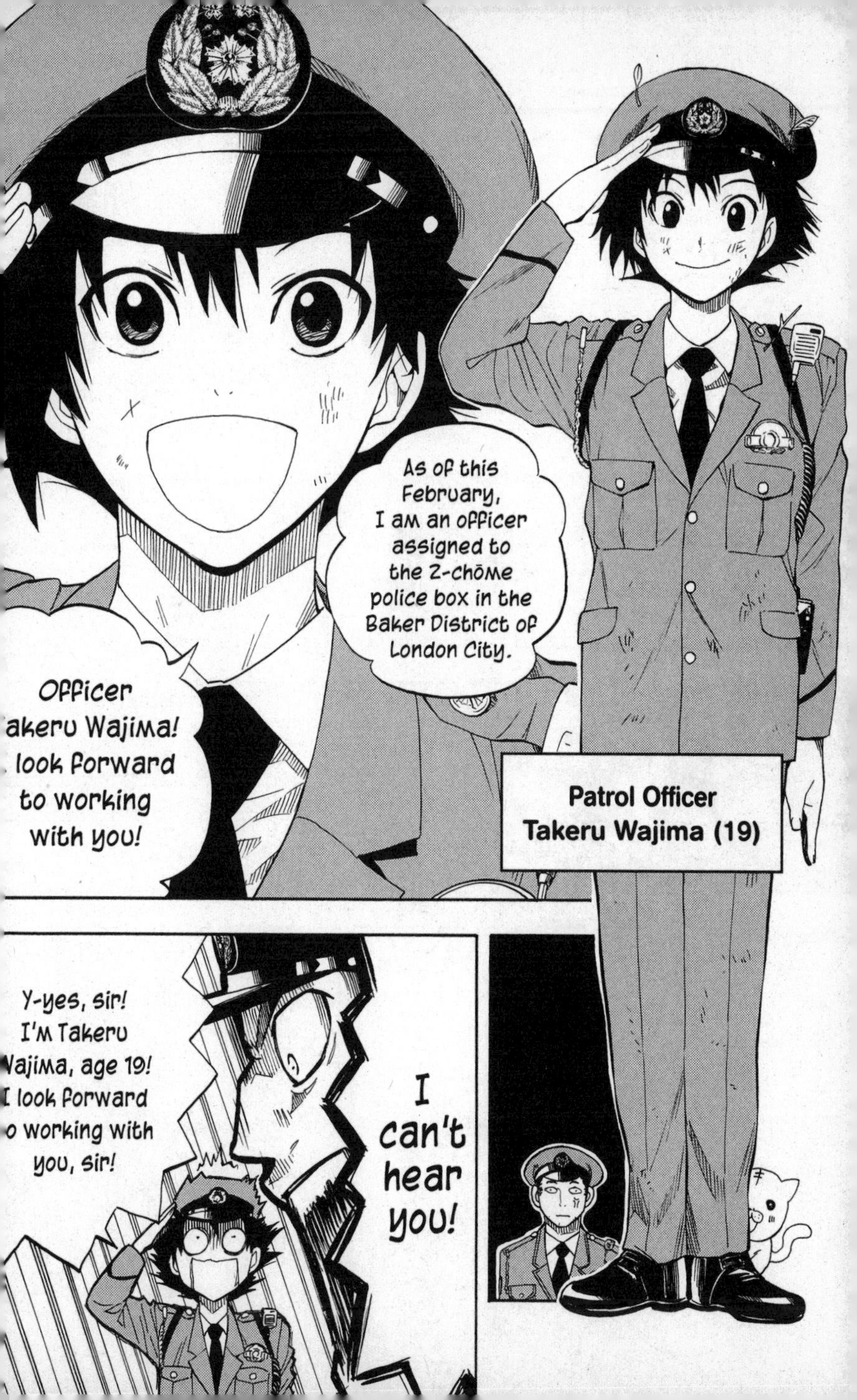
Patrol Officer
Takeru Wajima (19)
As of this February, I am an officer assigned to the 2-chōme police box in the Baker District of London City.
Officer akeru Wajima! look forward to working with you!
I can't hear you!
Y-yes, sir! I'm Takeru ajima, age 19! I look forward o working with you, sir!

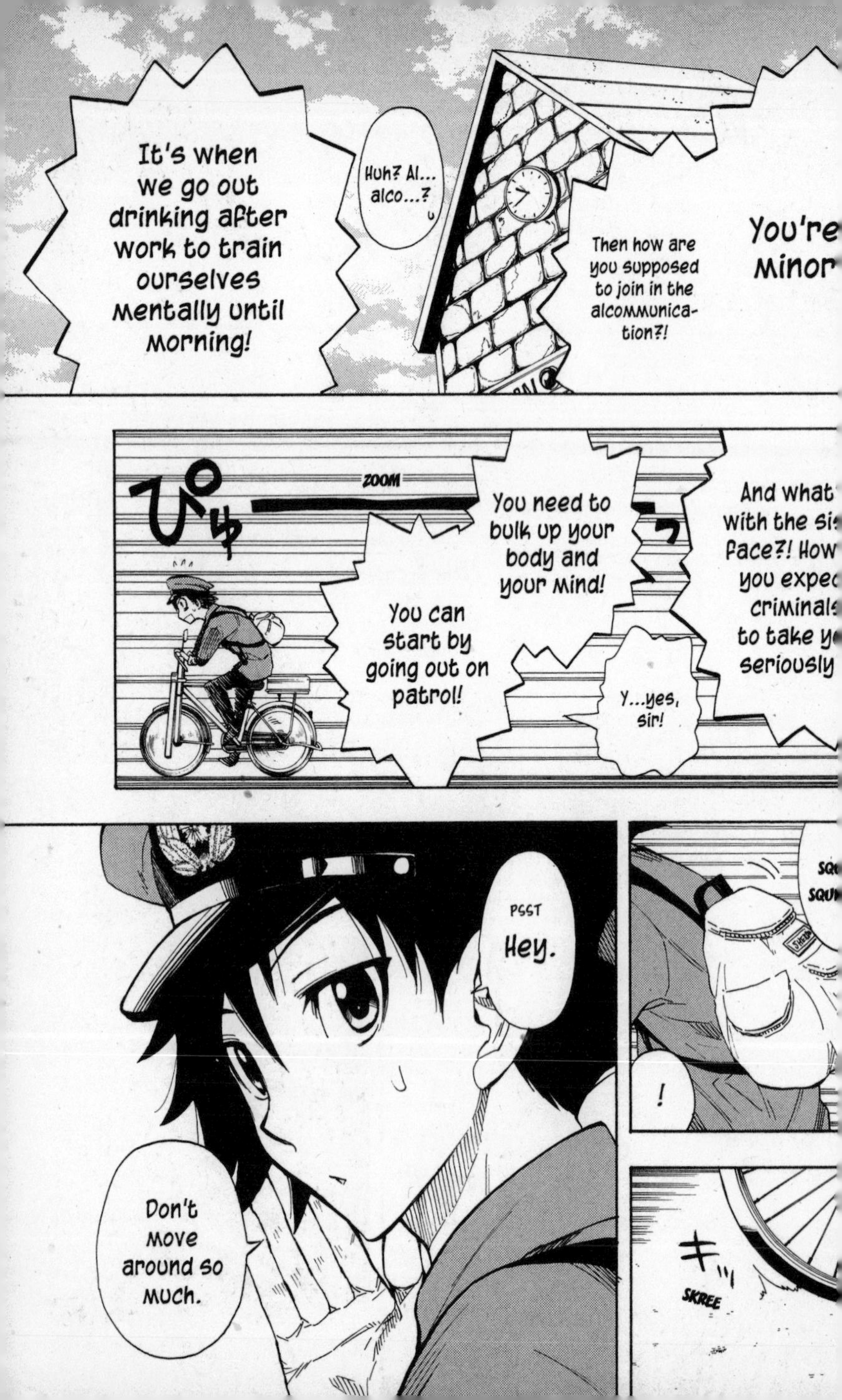
You're
Minor
Then how are you supposed to join in the alcommunication?!
Huh? Al... alco...?
It's when we go out drinking after work to train ourselves mentally until morning!
And what with the si face?! How you expec criminals to take y seriously
You need to bulk up your body and your mind!
ZOOM
ぴゅーっ
You can start by going out on patrol!
Y...yes, sir!
!
キ
SKREE
PSST
Hey.
Don't move around so much.

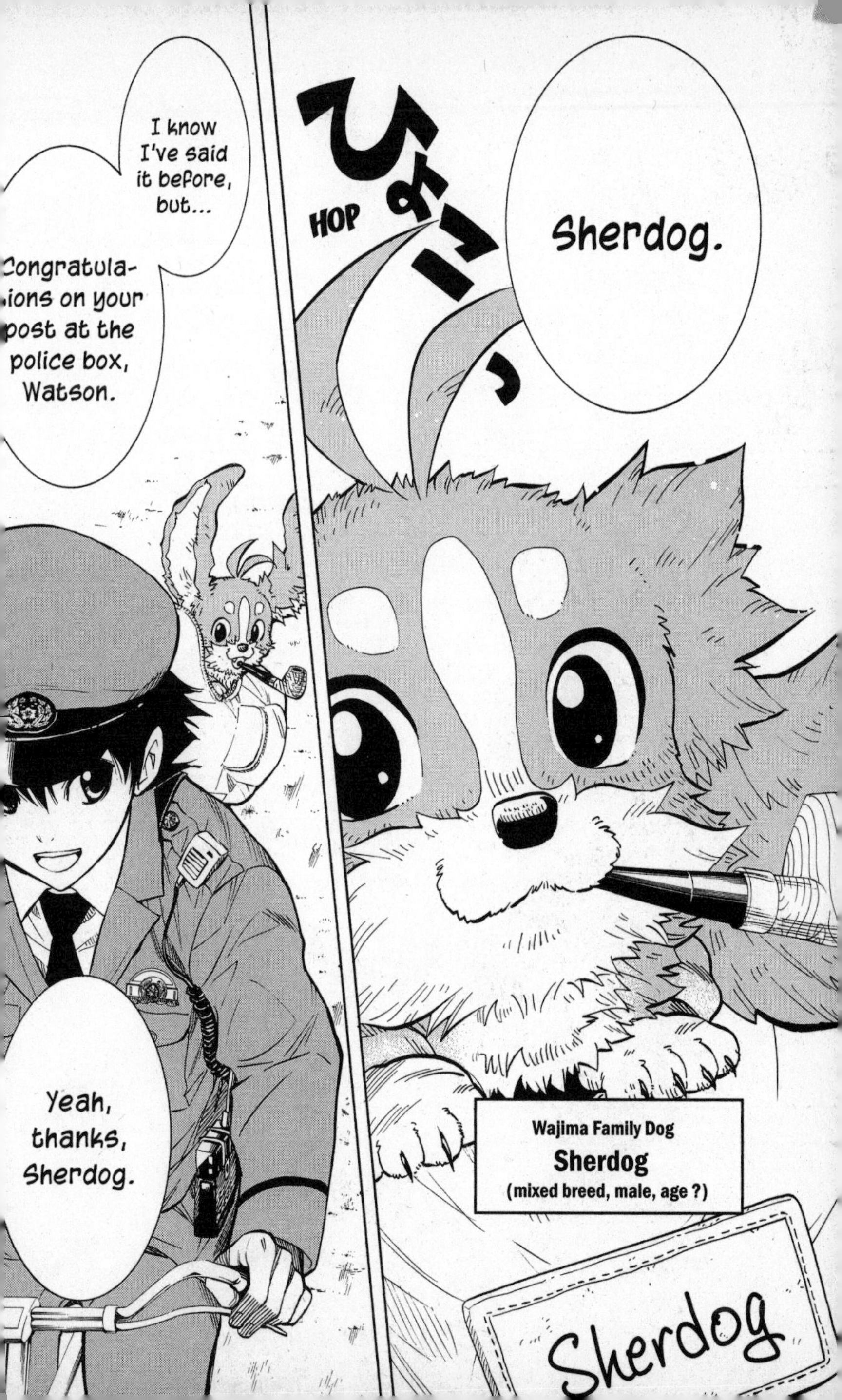
HOP
Sherdog.
Wajima Family Dog
Sherdog
(mixed breed, male, age ?)
Sherdog
I know I've said it before, but...
Congratulations on your post at the police box, Watson.
Yeah, thanks, Sherdog.

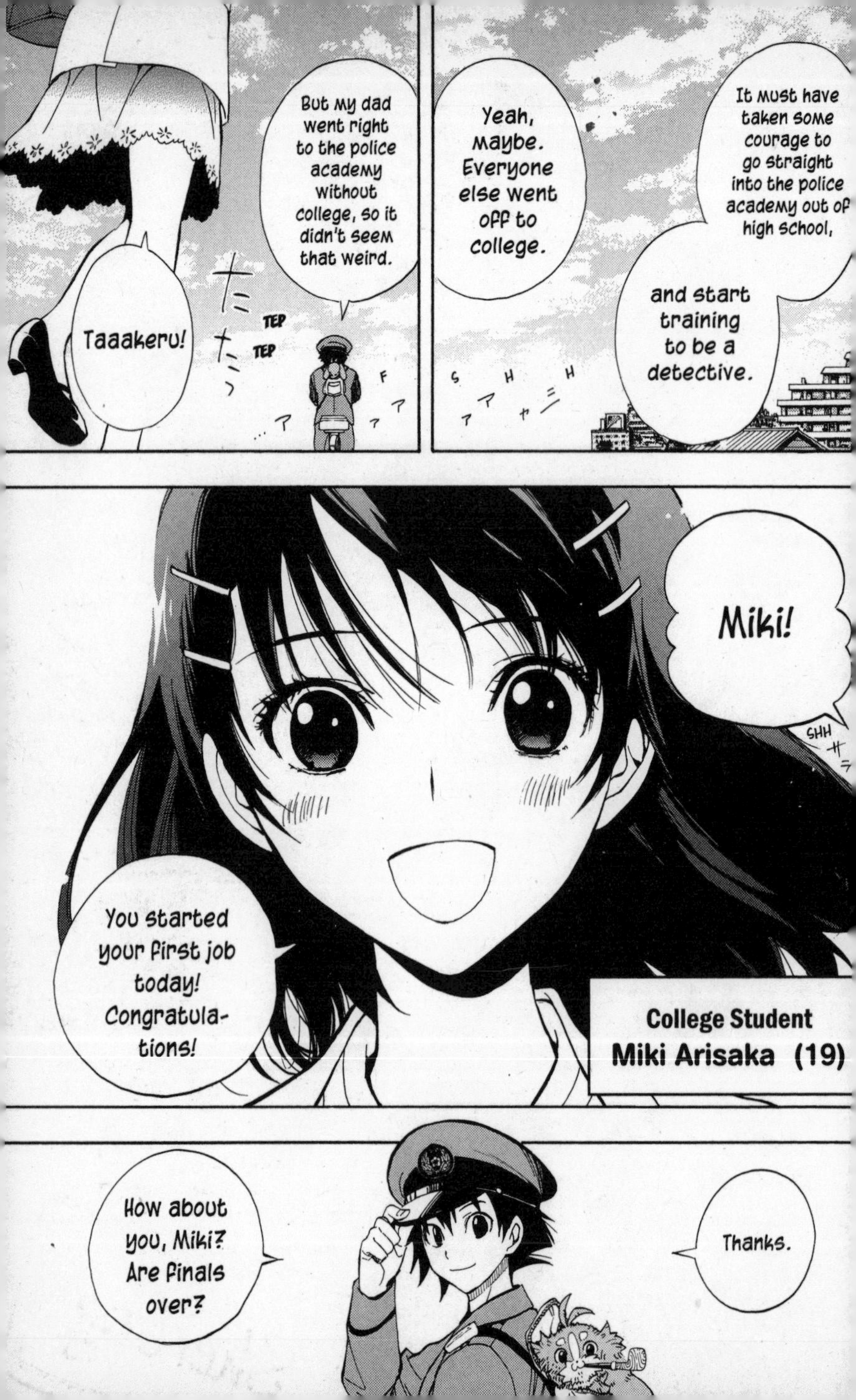
It must have taken some courage to go straight into the police academy out of high school,
and start training to be a detective.
Yeah, maybe. Everyone else went off to college.
SHH
But my dad went right to the police academy without college, so it didn't seem that weird.
F
TEP
TEP
Taaakeru!
Miki!
SHH
You started your first job today! Congratulations!
College Student
Miki Arisaka (19)
Thanks.
How about you, Miki? Are finals over?

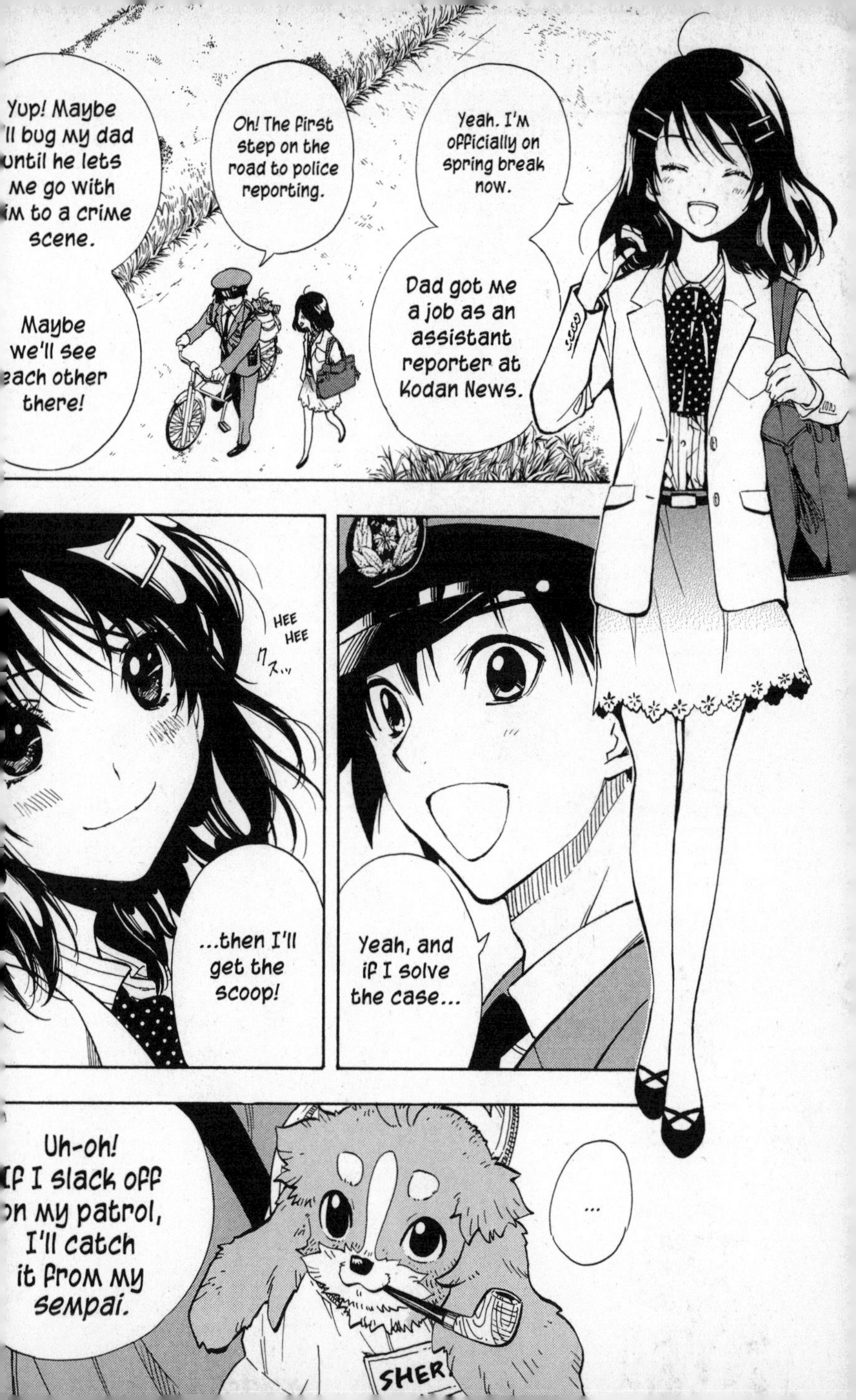
Yeah. I'm officially on spring break now.
Dad got me a job as an assistant reporter at Kodan News.
Oh! The first step on the road to police reporting.
Yup! Maybe 'll bug my dad until he lets me go with im to a crime scene.
Maybe we'll see each other there!
Yeah, and if I solve the case...
HEE HEE
クスッ
...then I'll get the scoop!
...
Uh-oh! f I slack off on my patrol, I'll catch it from my sempai.
SHER

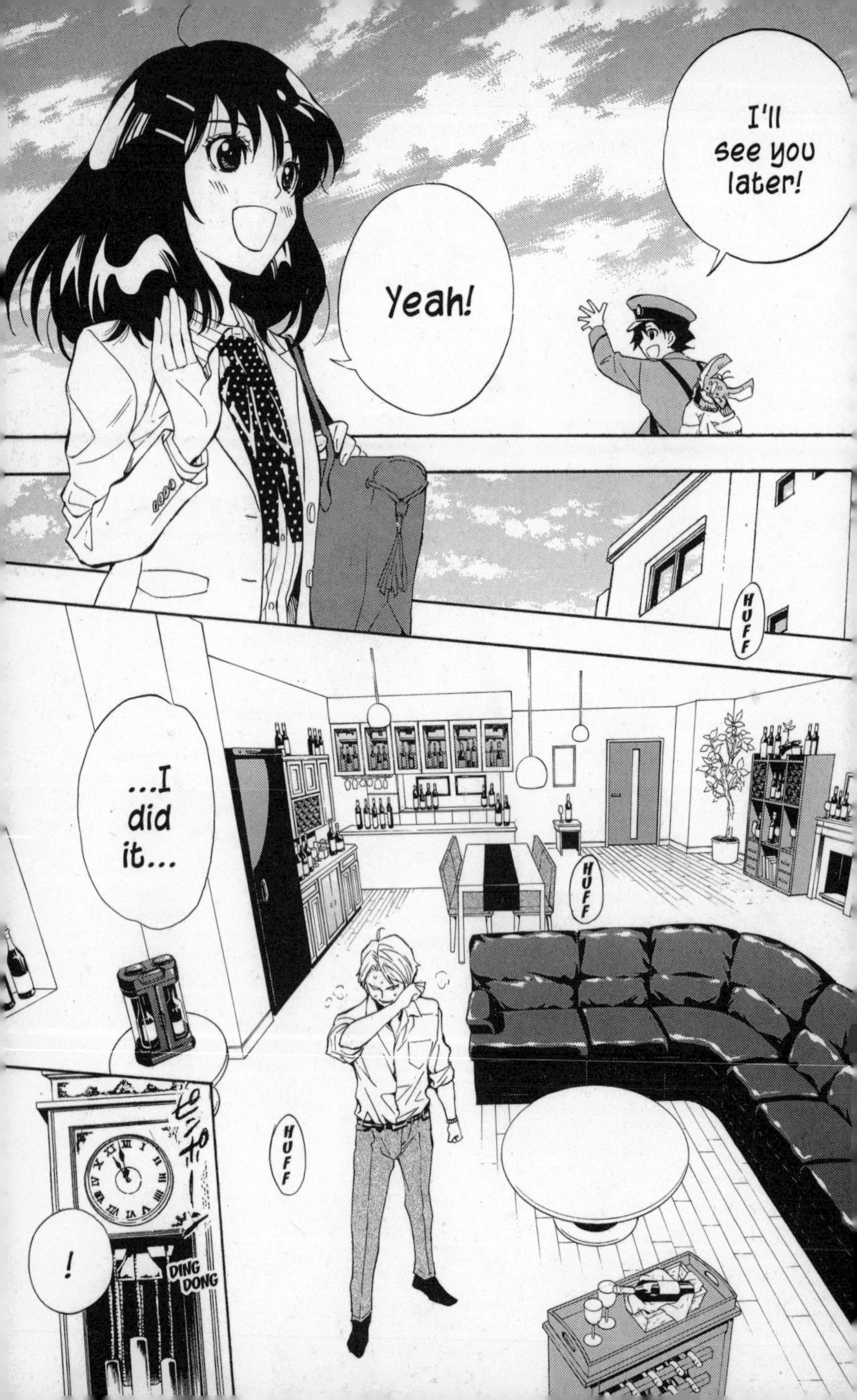
I'll see you later!
Yeah!
HUFF
HUFF
...I did it...
HUFF
DING DONG
!

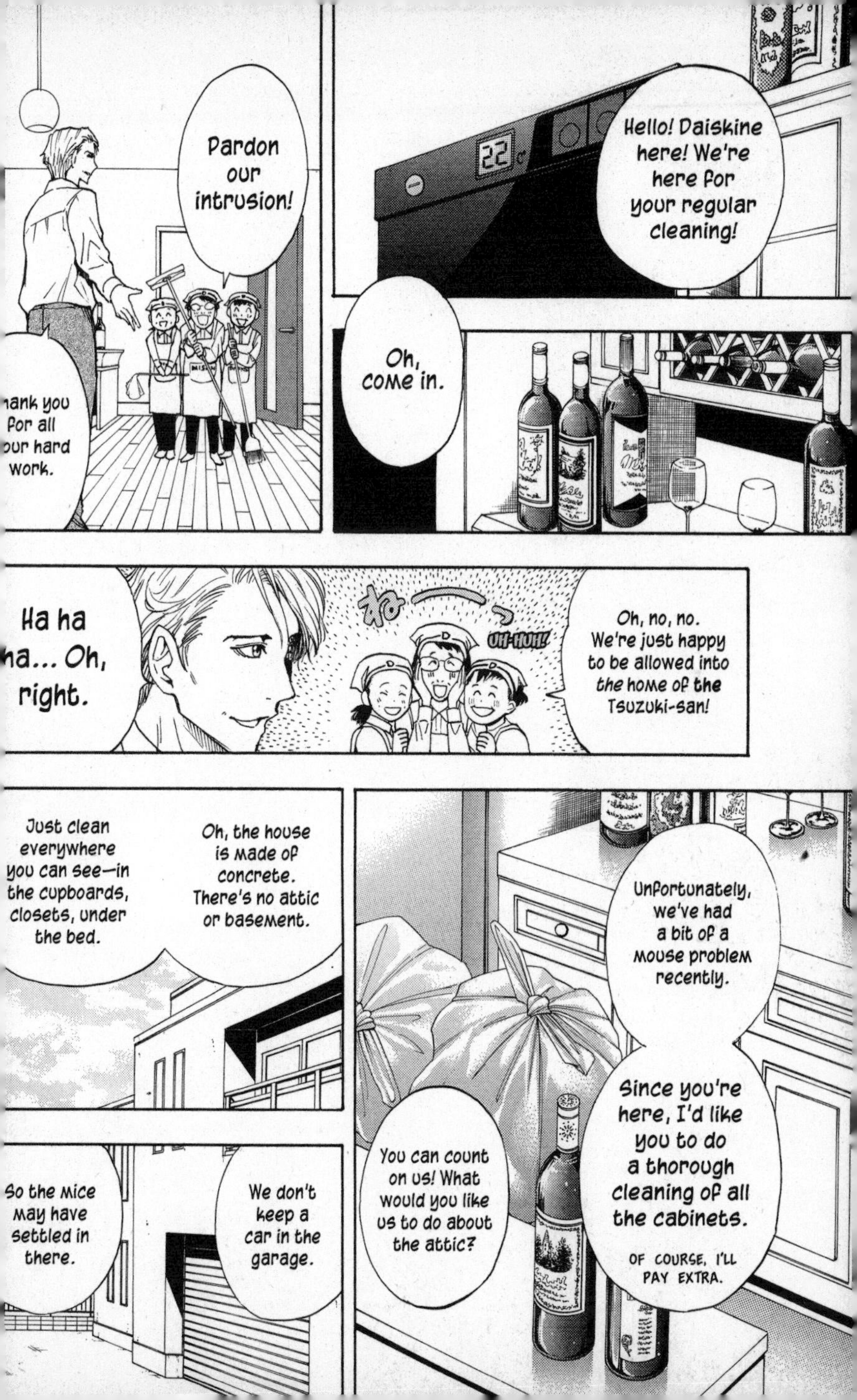
Hello! Daiskine here! We're here for your regular cleaning!
Oh, come in.
Pardon our intrusion!
hank you for all our hard work.
Oh, no, no. We're just happy to be allowed into the home of the Tsuzuki-san!
UH-HUH!
Ha ha a... Oh, right.
Unfortunately, we've had a bit of a mouse problem recently.
Since you're here, I'd like you to do a thorough cleaning of all the cabinets.
OF COURSE, I'LL PAY EXTRA.
You can count on us! What would you like us to do about the attic?
Oh, the house is made of concrete. There's no attic or basement.
Just clean everywhere you can see—in the cupboards, closets, under the bed.
We don't keep a car in the garage.
So the mice may have settled in there.

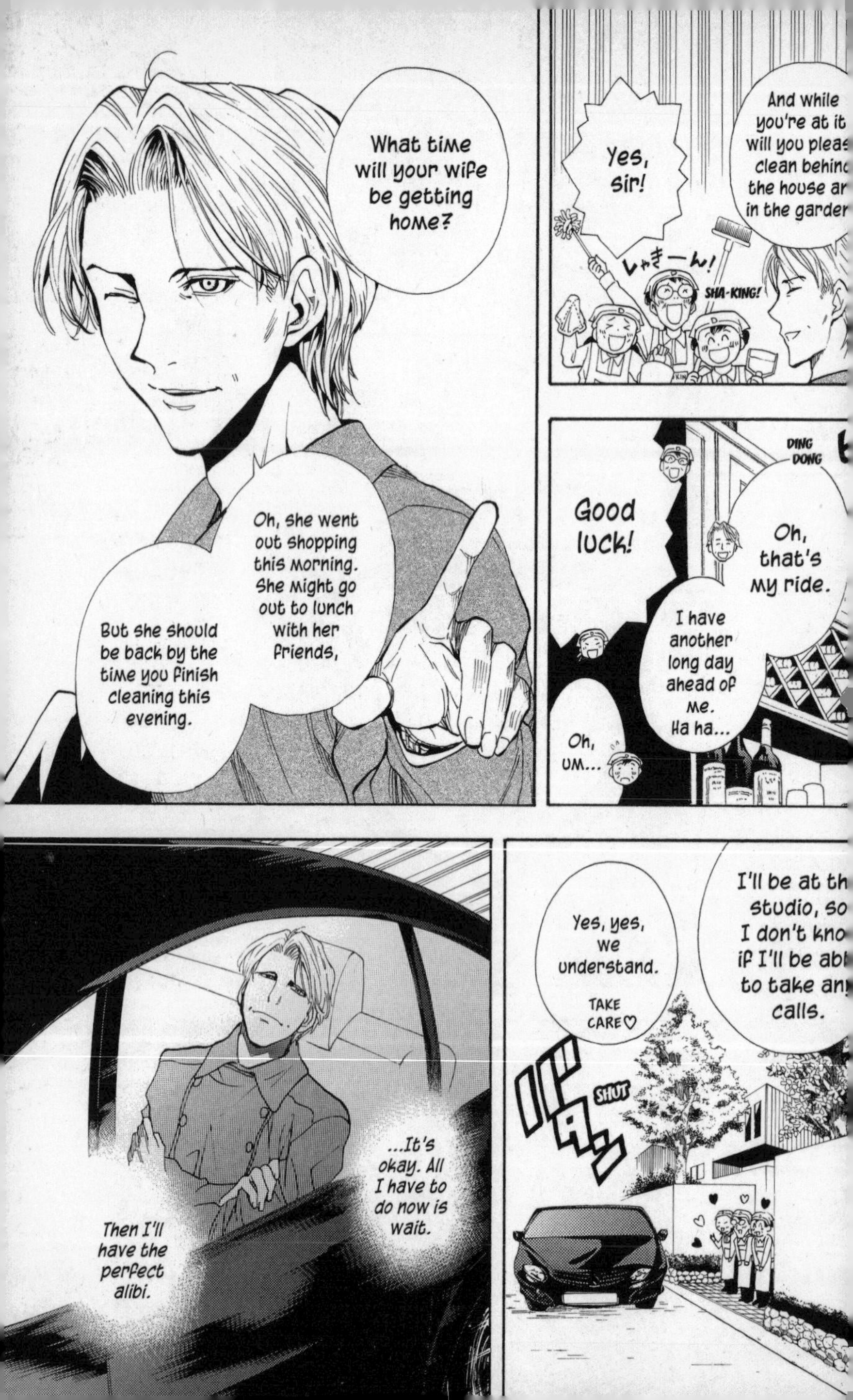
And while you're at it will you pleas clean behinc the house ar in the garder
Yes, sir!
しゃきーん!
SHA-KING!
DING DONG
Oh, that's my ride.
I have another long day ahead of me. Ha ha...
Good luck!
Oh, um...
What time will your wife be getting home?
Oh, she went out shopping this morning. She might go out to lunch with her friends,
But she should be back by the time you finish cleaning this evening.
I'll be at th studio, so I don't kno if I'll be abl to take an calls.
Yes, yes, we understand.
TAKE CARE♡
SHUT
...It's okay. All I have to do now is wait.
Then I'll have the perfect alibi.

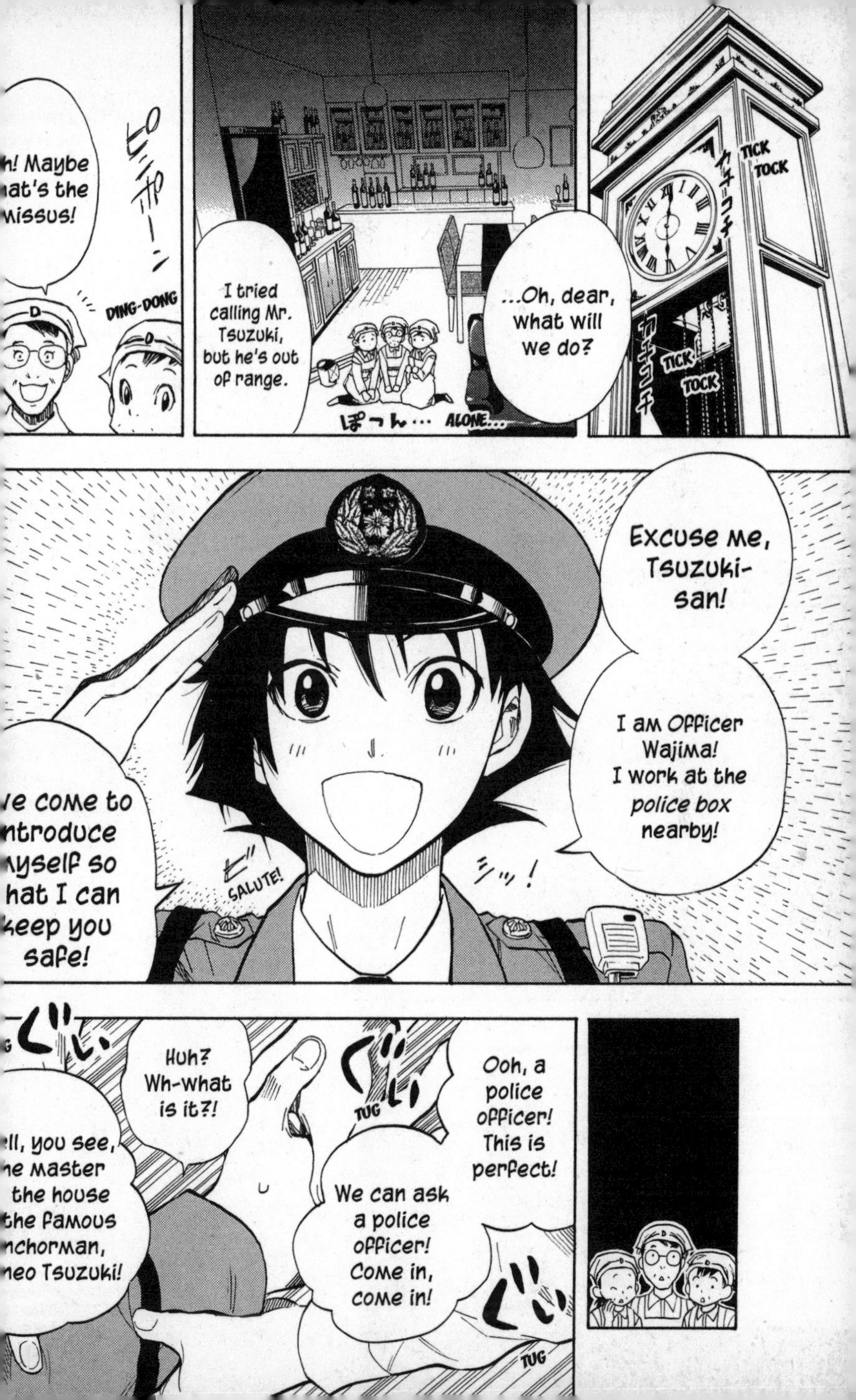
TICK
TOCK
TICK
TOCK
...Oh, dear, what will we do?
I tried calling Mr. Tsuzuki, but he's out of range.
ALONE...
h! Maybe ıat's the nissus!
DING-DONG
Excuse me, Tsuzuki-san!
I am Officer Wajima! I work at the police box nearby!
SALUTE!
ve come to ntroduce nyself so hat I can keep you safe!
Ooh, a police officer! This is perfect!
We can ask a police officer! Come in, come in!
TUG
TUG
Huh? Wh-what is it?!
ell, you see, ne master the house the famous nchorman, neo Tsuzuki!

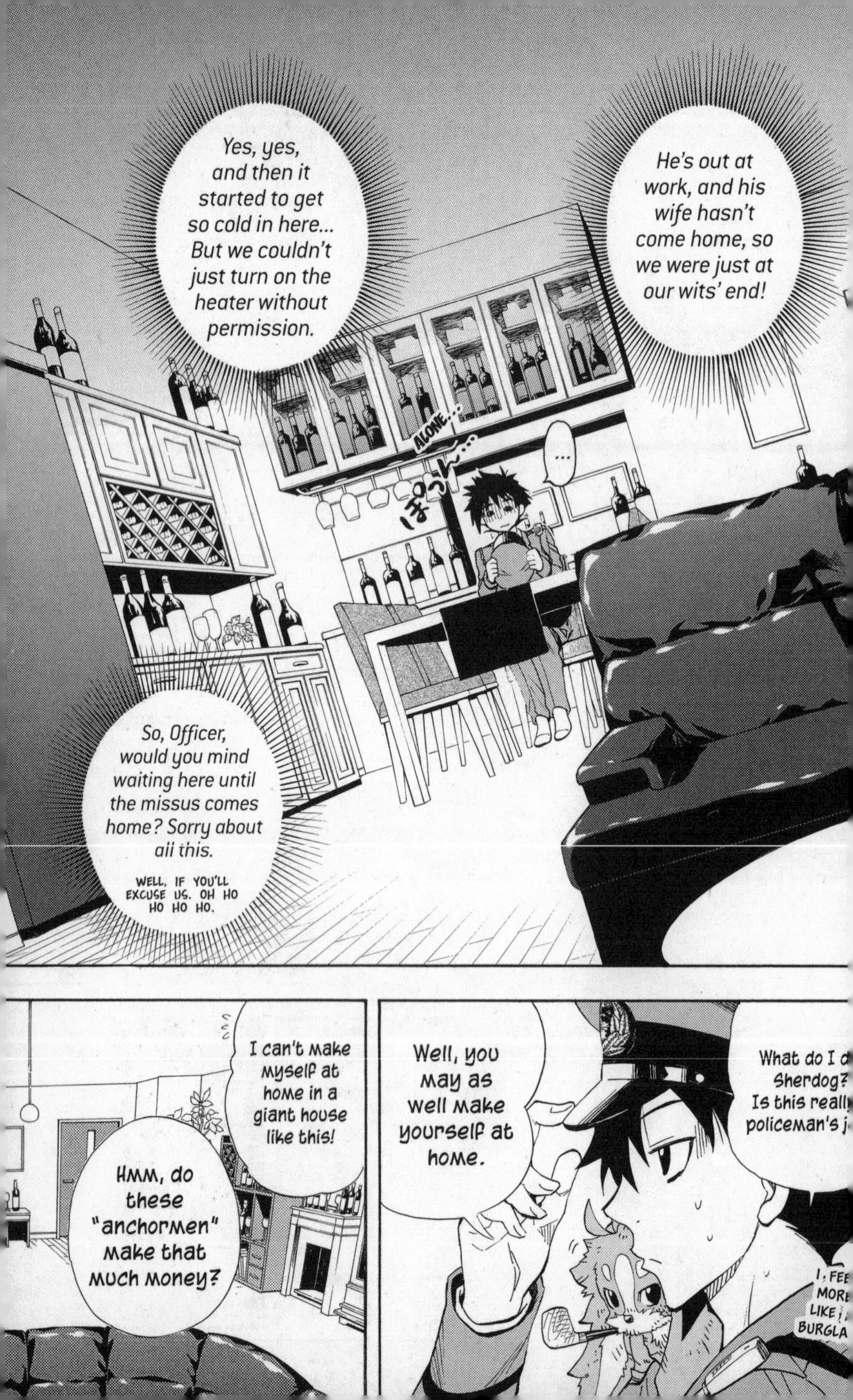
He's out at work, and his wife hasn't come home, so we were just at our wits' end!
Yes, yes, and then it started to get so cold in here... But we couldn't just turn on the heater without permission.
ALONE...
ぽつん
...
So, Officer, would you mind waiting here until the missus comes home? Sorry about all this.
WELL, IF YOU'LL EXCUSE US. OH HO HO HO HO.
What do I d Sherdog? Is this reall policeman's j
Well, you may as well make yourself at home.
I, FEE MORE LIKE BURGLA
I can't make myself at home in a giant house like this!
Hmm, do these "anchormen" make that much money?

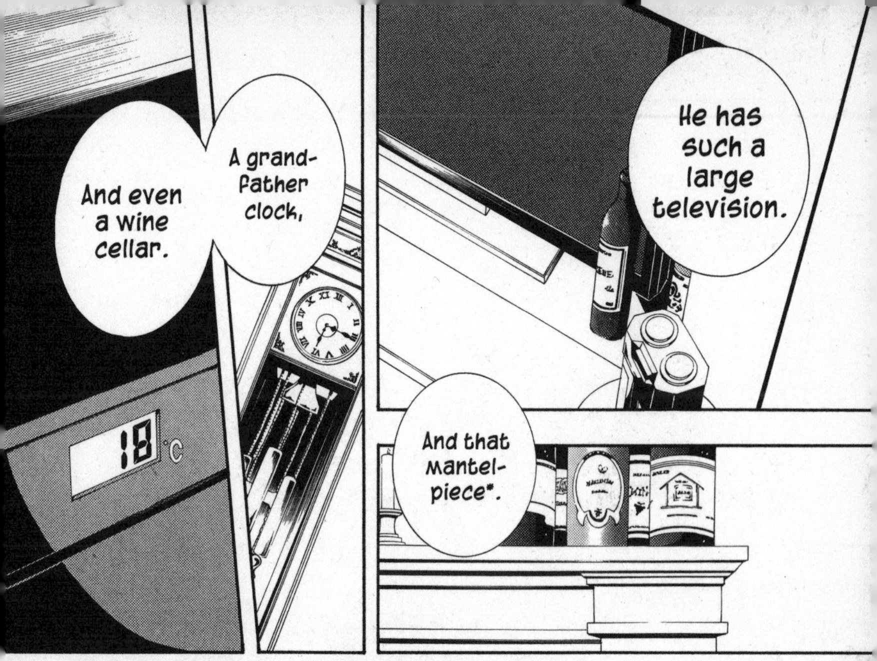
He has such a large television.
And that mantel-piece*.
A grand-father clock,
And even a wine cellar.
18 °C

*Decorative framework surrounding a fireplace, usually above the fireplace.

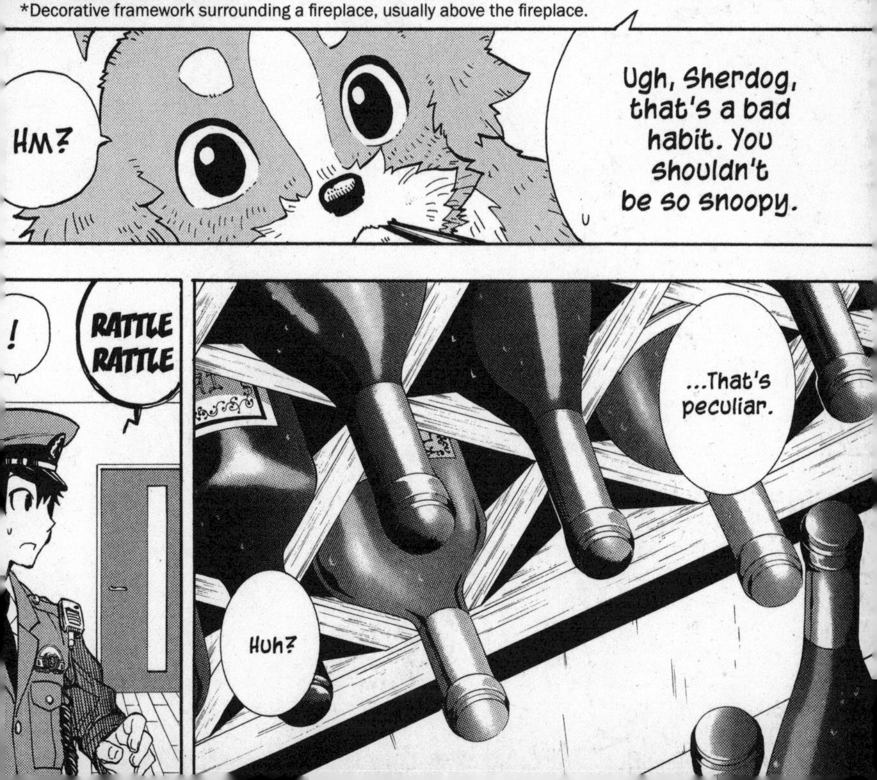
Ugh, Sherdog, that's a bad habit. You shouldn't be so snoopy.
Hm?
...That's peculiar.
Huh?
!
RATTLE RATTLE

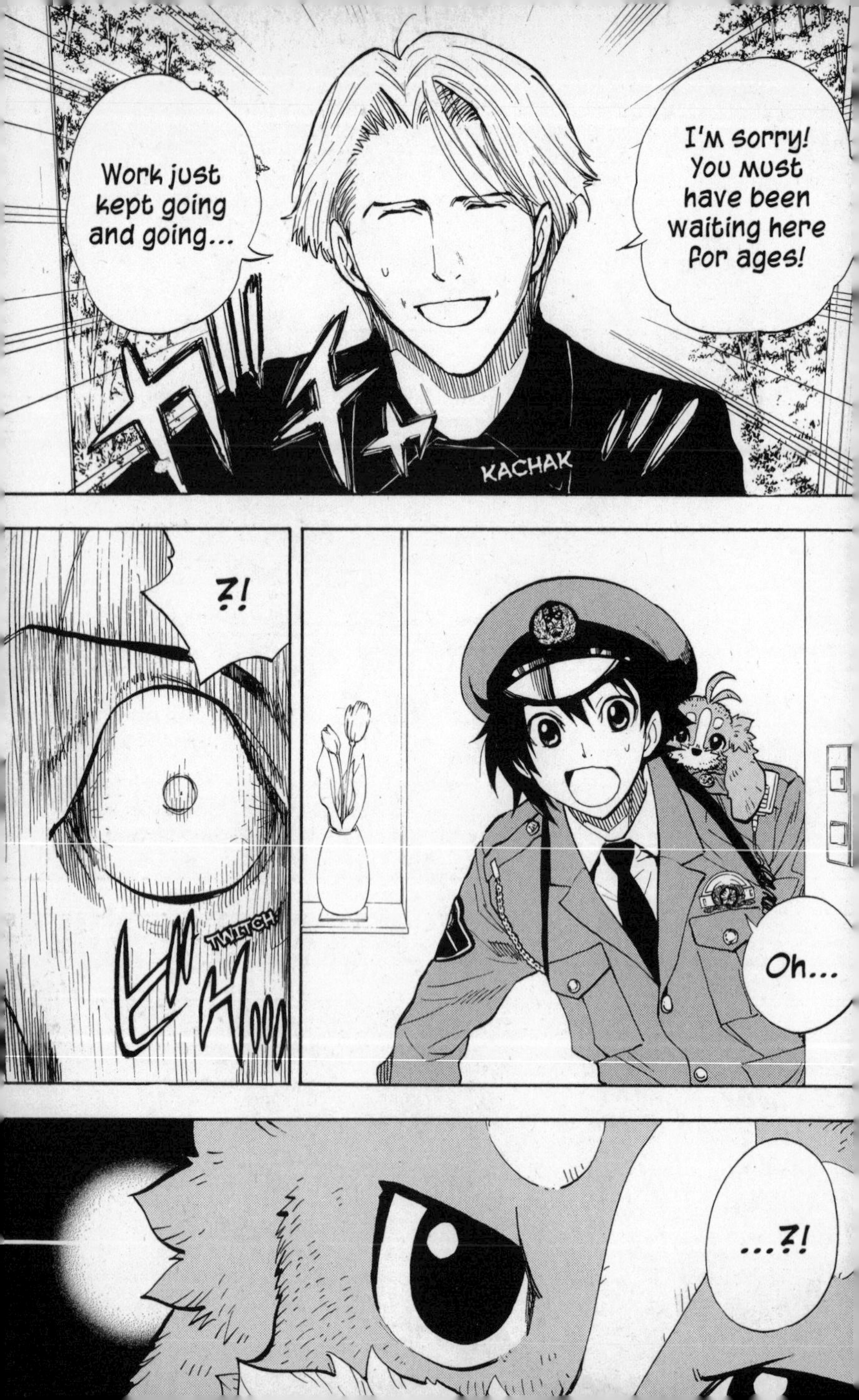
I'm sorry! You must have been waiting here for ages!
Work just kept going and going...
KACHAK
Oh...
?!
TWITCH
...?!

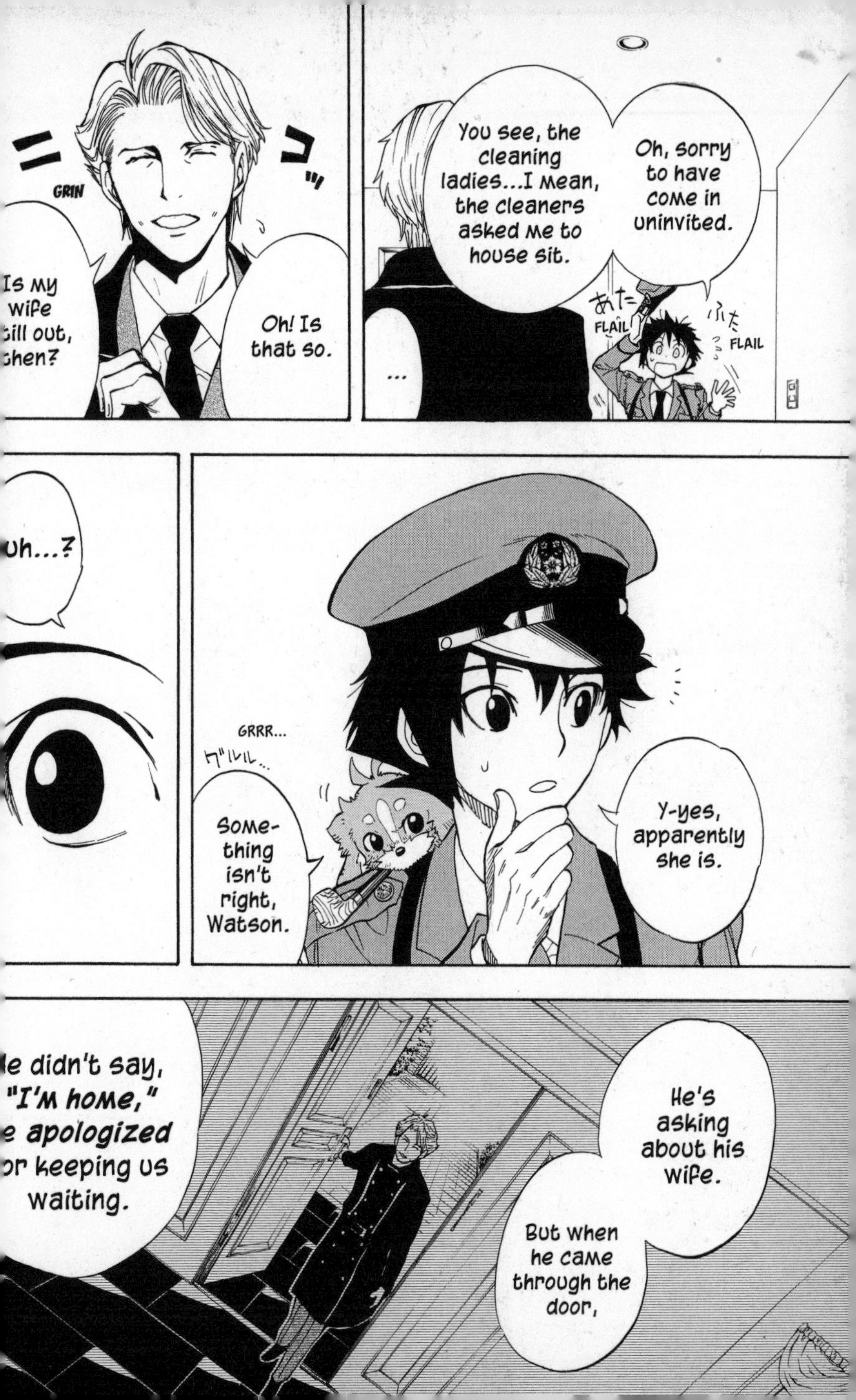

Oh, sorry to have come in uninvited.
You see, the cleaning ladies...I mean, the cleaners asked me to house sit.
あた FLAIL
ふた FLAIL
...
GRIN
Oh! Is that so.
Is my wife ill out, hen?
Y-yes, apparently she is.
GRRR...
グルル...
Some-thing isn't right, Watson.
uh...?
He's asking about his wife.
But when he came through the door,
e didn't say, "I'm home," e apologized or keeping us waiting.

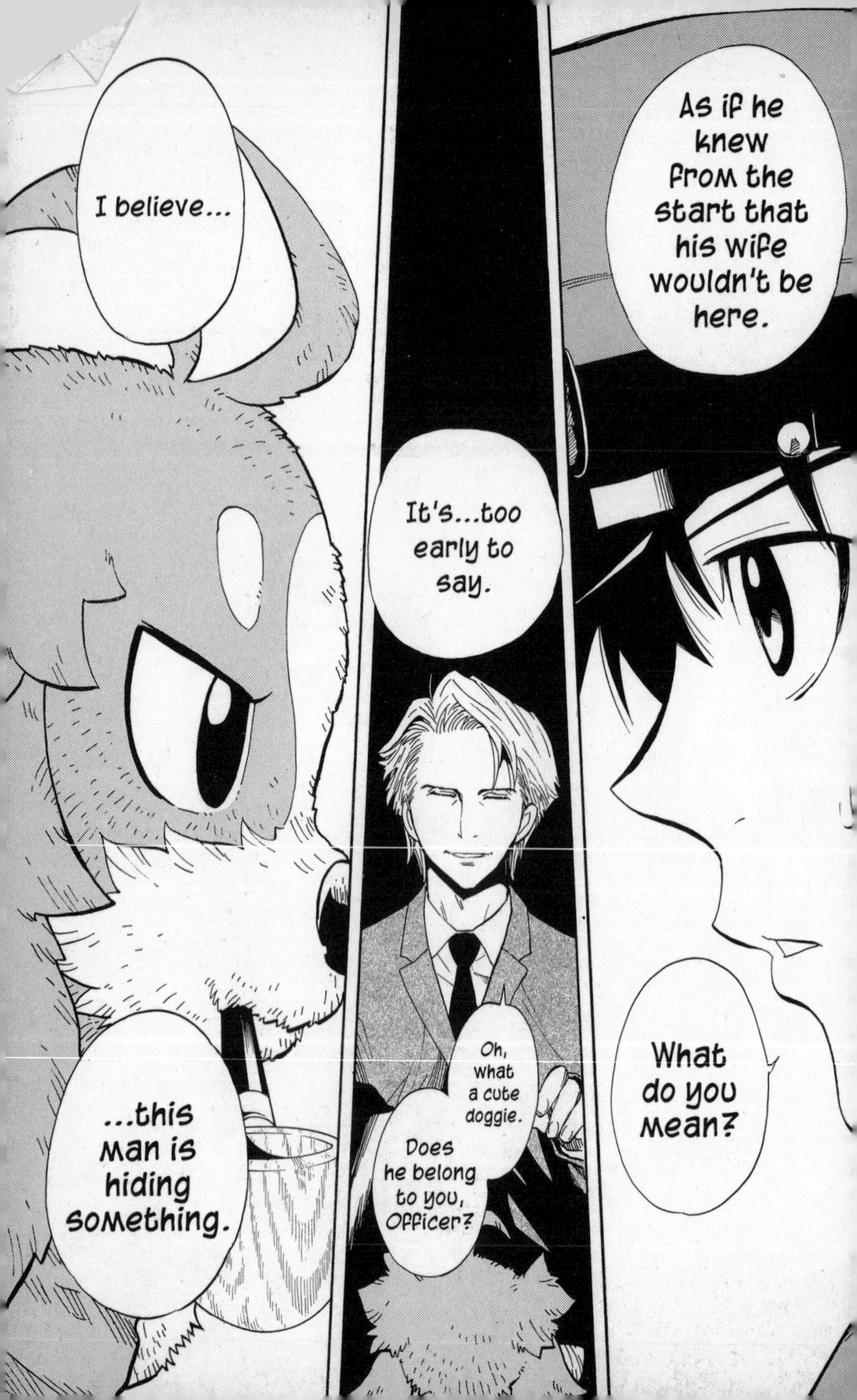
As if he knew from the start that his wife wouldn't be here.
What do you mean?
It's...too early to say.
Oh, what a cute doggie.
Does he belong to you, Officer?
I believe...
...this man is hiding something.

Sherlock Bones

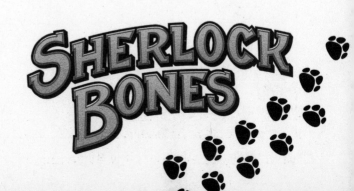

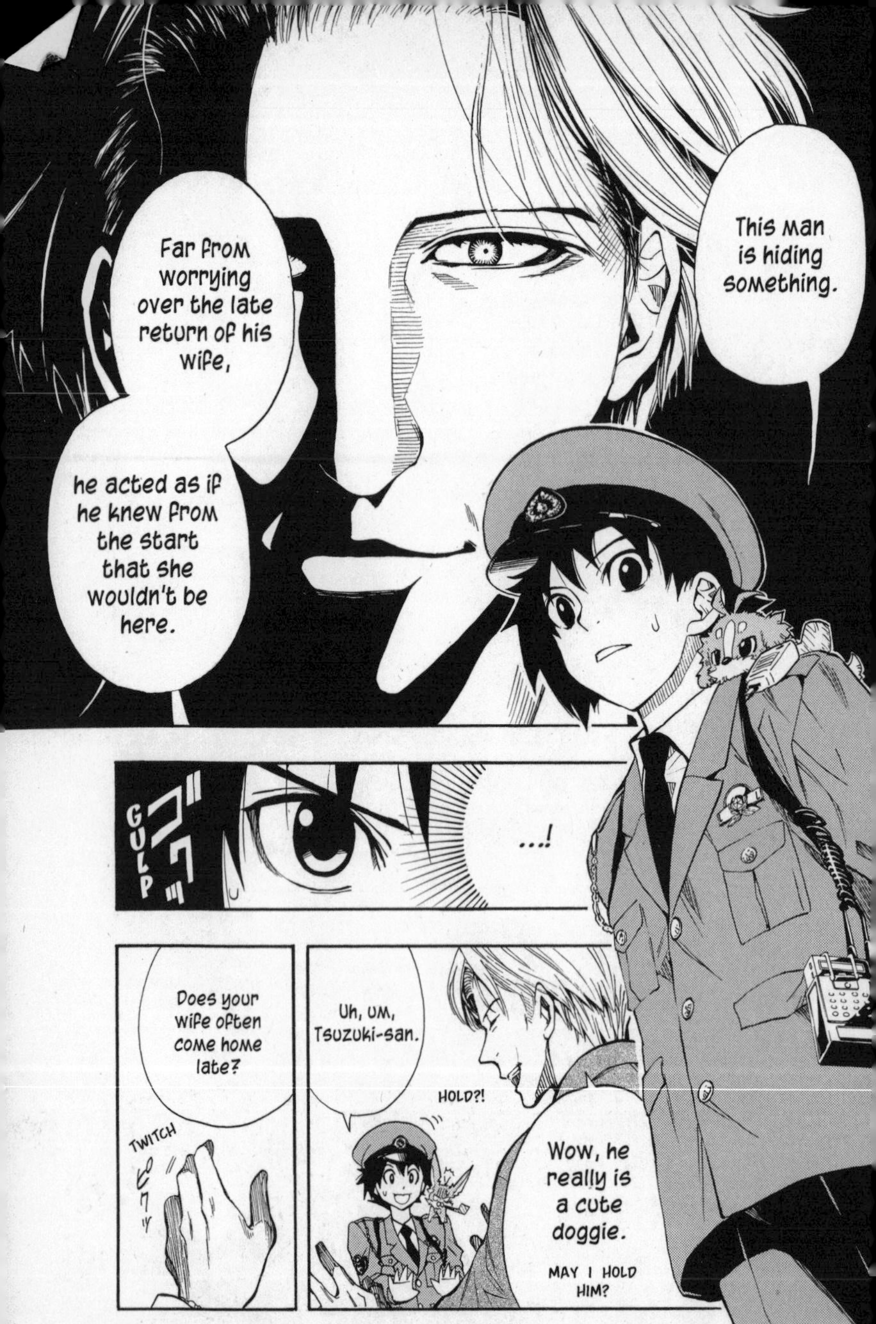
This man is hiding something.
Far from worrying over the late return of his wife,
he acted as if he knew from the start that she wouldn't be here.
GULP
...!
Wow, he really is a cute doggie.
MAY I HOLD HIM?
HOLD?!
Uh, um, Tsuzuki-san.
Does your wife often come home late?
TWITCH

Case 8: ⚜ Requiem for a New Beginning, Part 2

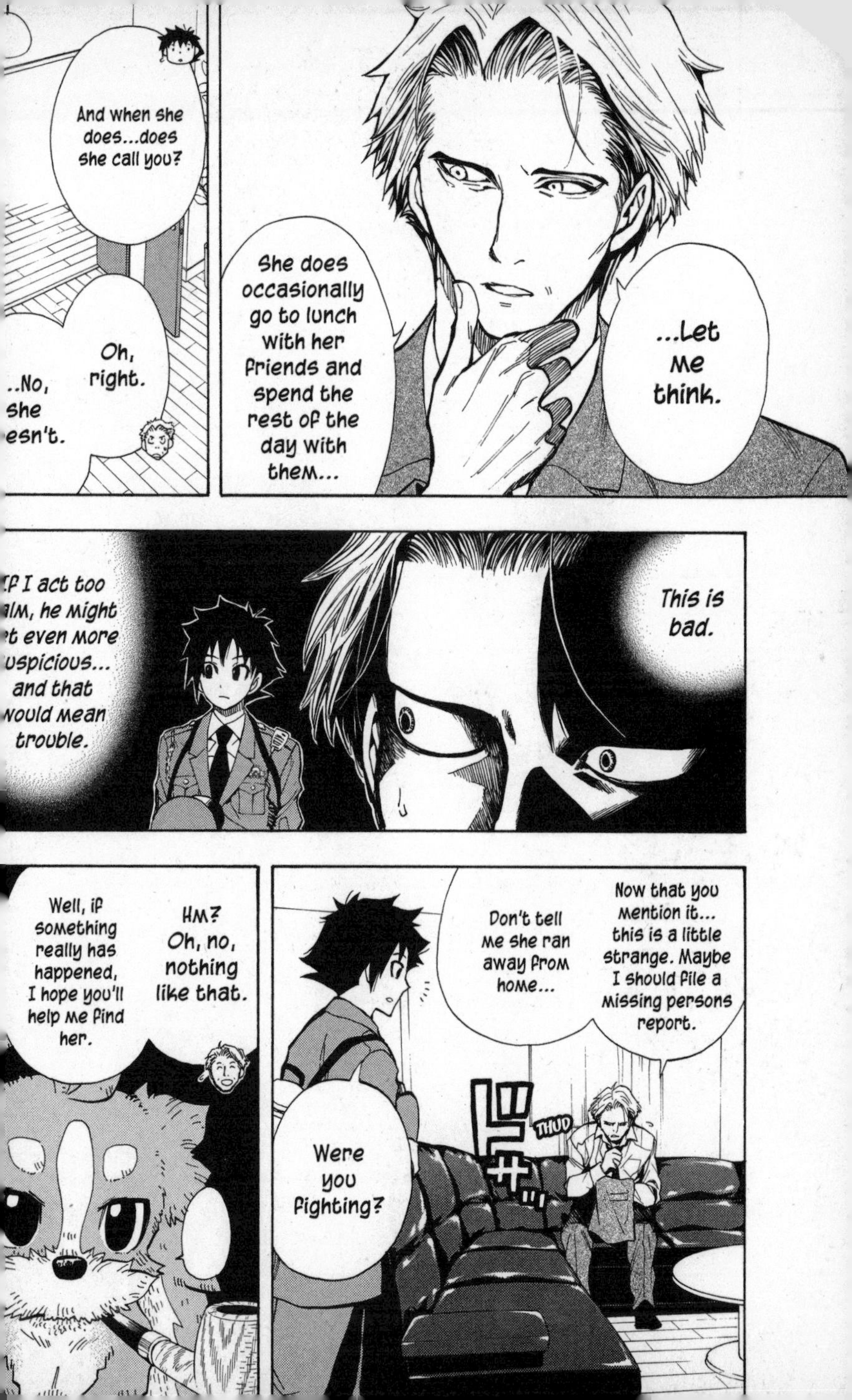
...Let me think.
She does occasionally go to lunch with her friends and spend the rest of the day with them...
And when she does...does she call you?
Oh, right.
..No, she esn't.
This is bad.
f I act too alm, he might t even more uspicious... and that ould mean trouble.
Now that you mention it... this is a little strange. Maybe I should file a missing persons report.
Don't tell me she ran away from home...
THUD
Were you fighting?
HM? Oh, no, nothing like that.
Well, if something really has happened, I hope you'll help me find her.

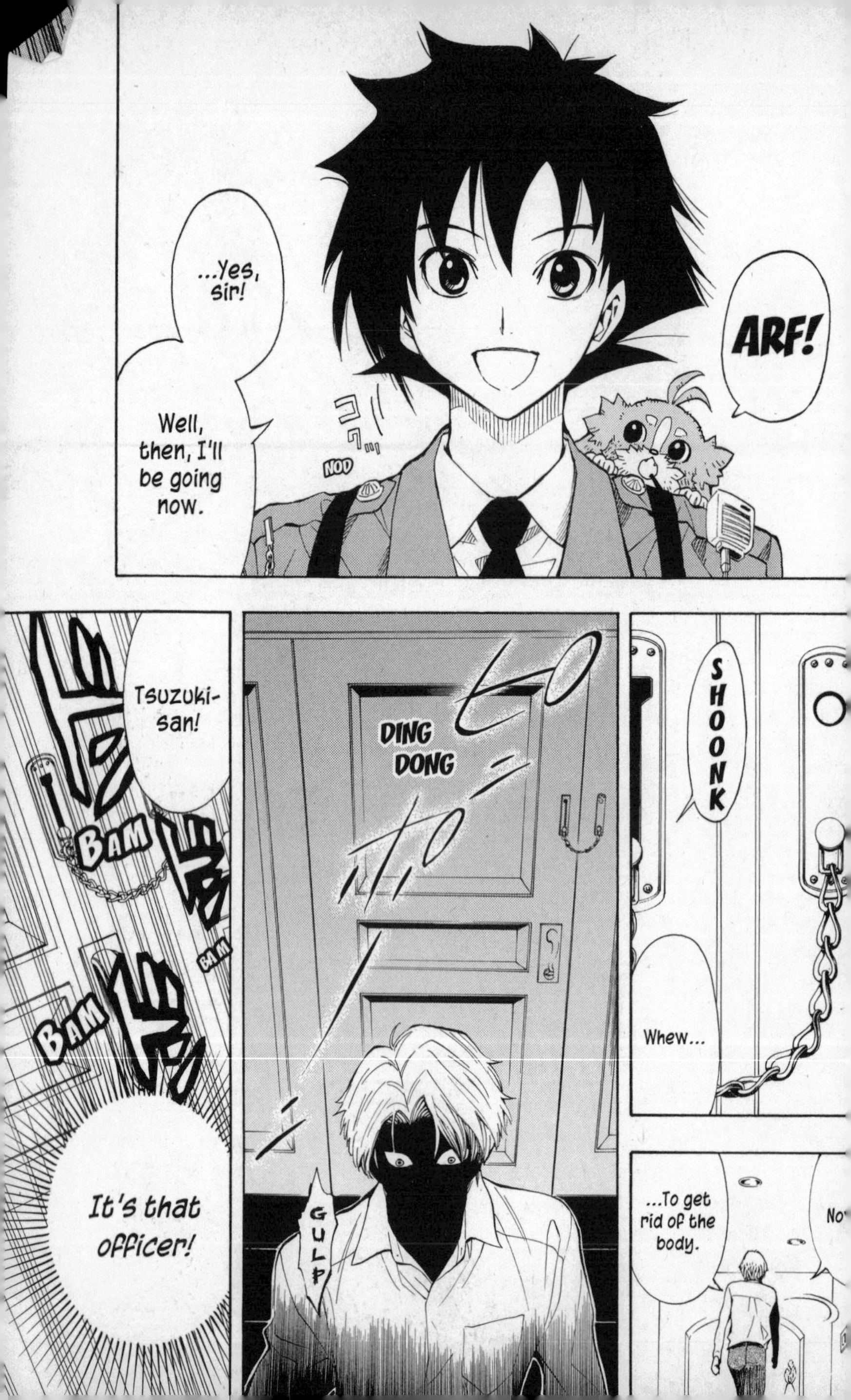
ARF!
...Yes, sir!
NOD
Well, then, I'll be going now.
SHOONK
Whew...
No
...To get rid of the body.
DING DONG
GULP
Tsuzuki-san!
BAM
BAM
BAM
It's that officer!

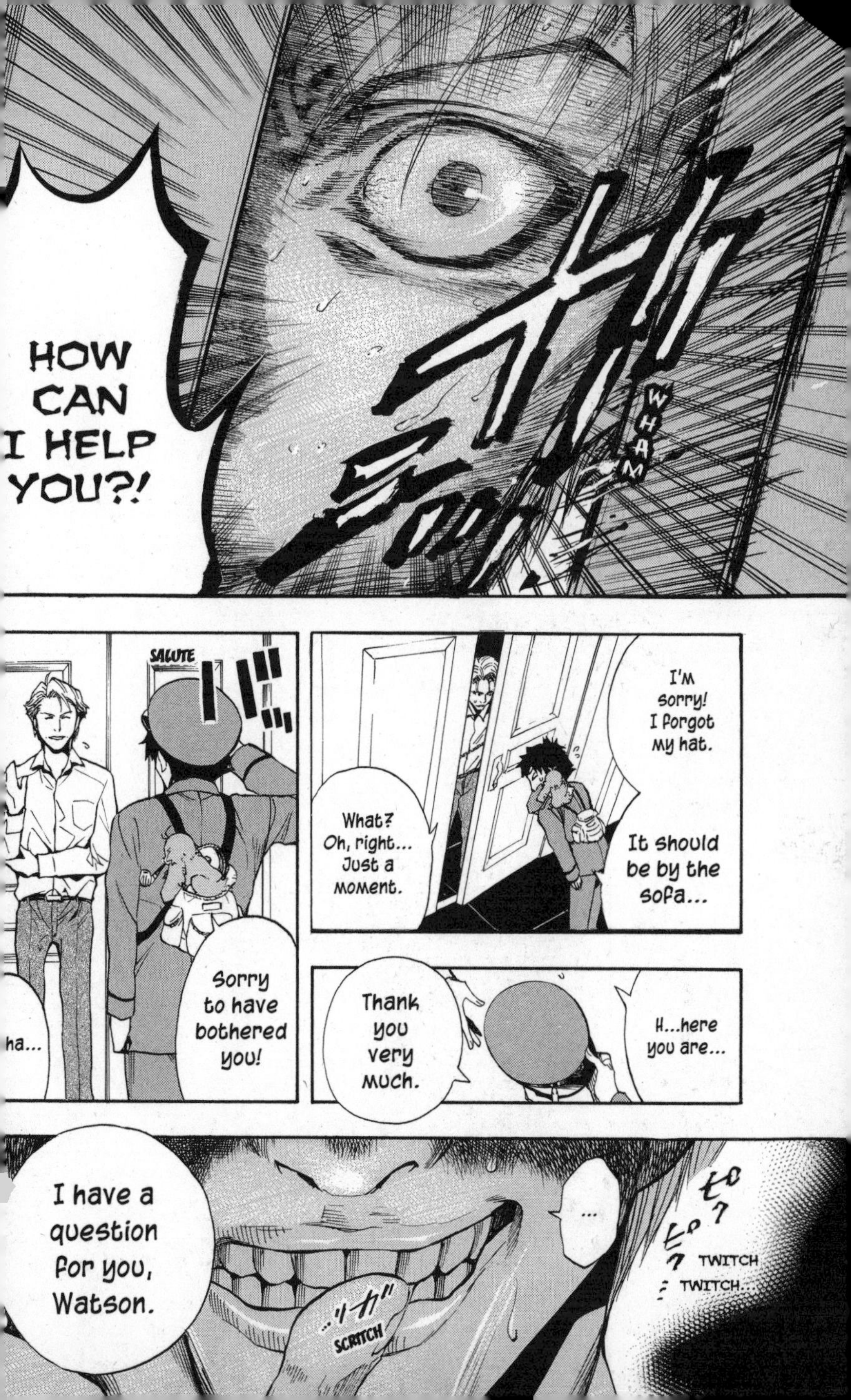
HOW CAN I HELP YOU?!
WHAM
I'm sorry! I forgot my hat.
It should be by the sofa...
What? Oh, right... Just a moment.
H...here you are...
Thank you very much.
SALUTE
Sorry to have bothered you!
ha...
...
TWITCH TWITCH...
I have a question for you, Watson.
SCRITCH

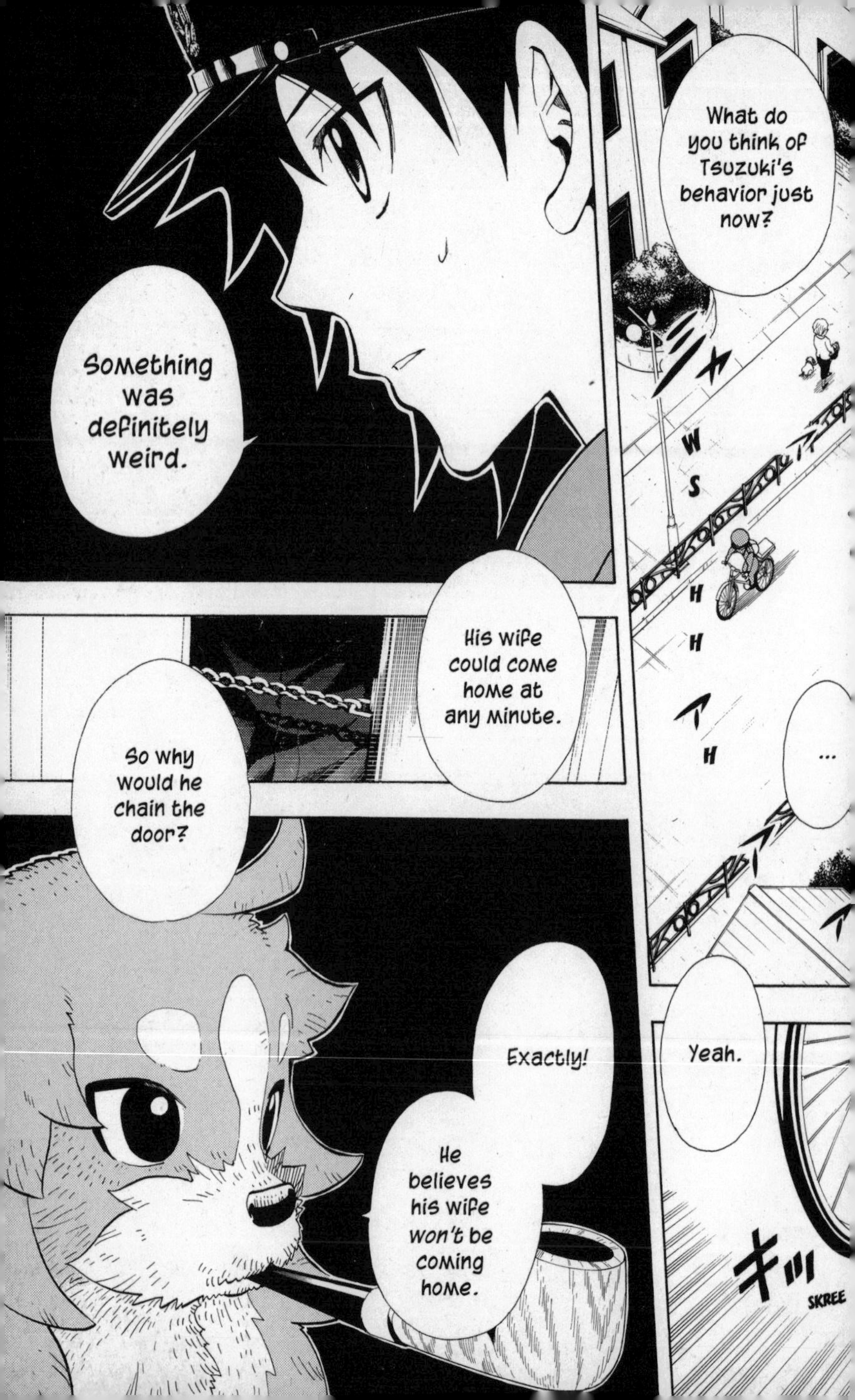
What do you think of Tsuzuki's behavior just now?
WSHHH
...
Yeah.
SKREE
Something was definitely weird.
His wife could come home at any minute.
So why would he chain the door?
Exactly!
He believes his wife won't be coming home.

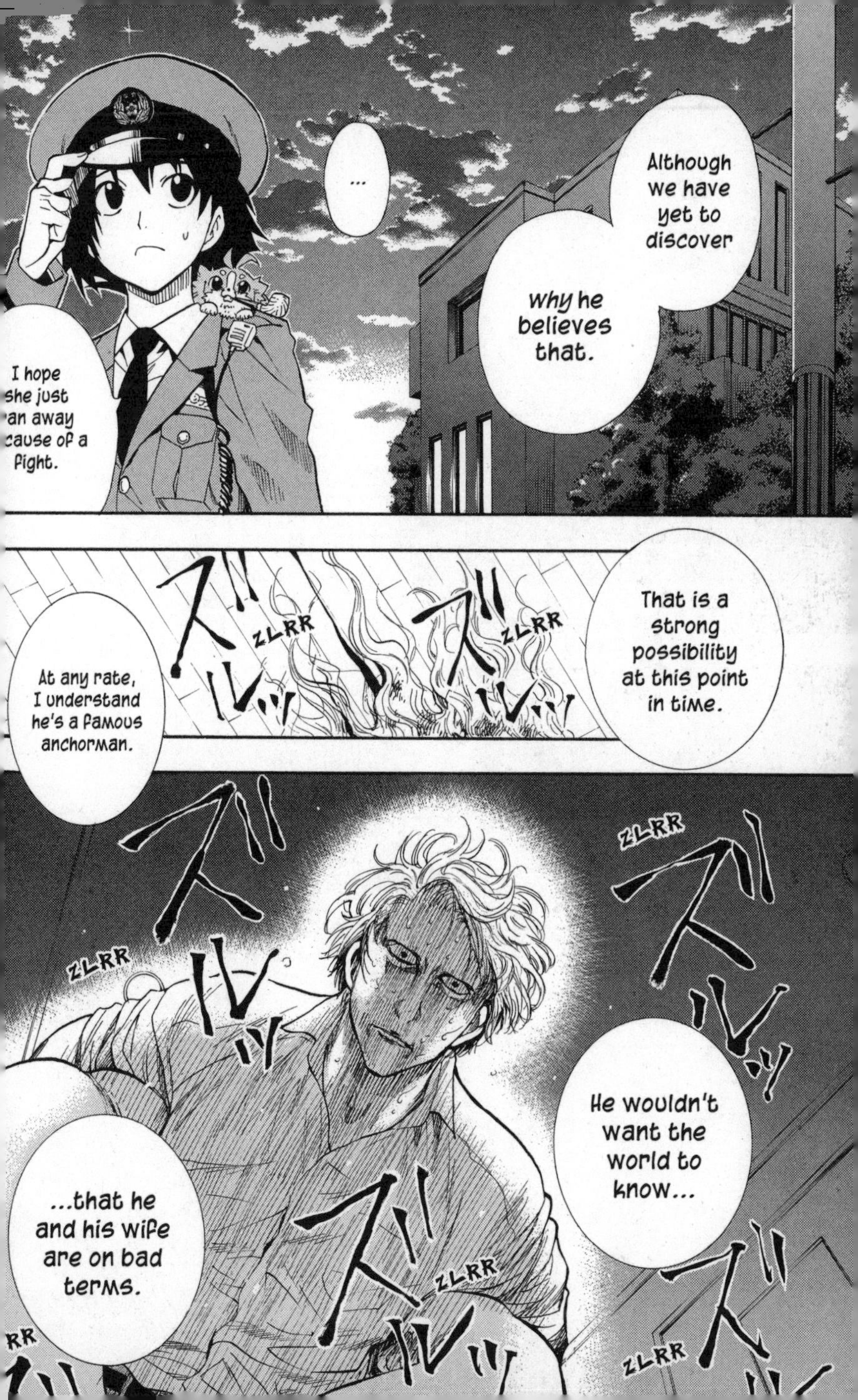

Although we have yet to discover
why he believes that.
...
I hope she just 'an away cause of a fight.
That is a strong possibility at this point in time.
ZLRR
ZLRR
At any rate, I understand he's a famous anchorman.
ZLRR
He wouldn't want the world to know...
ZLRR
ZLRR
ZLRR
...that he and his wife are on bad terms.
RR

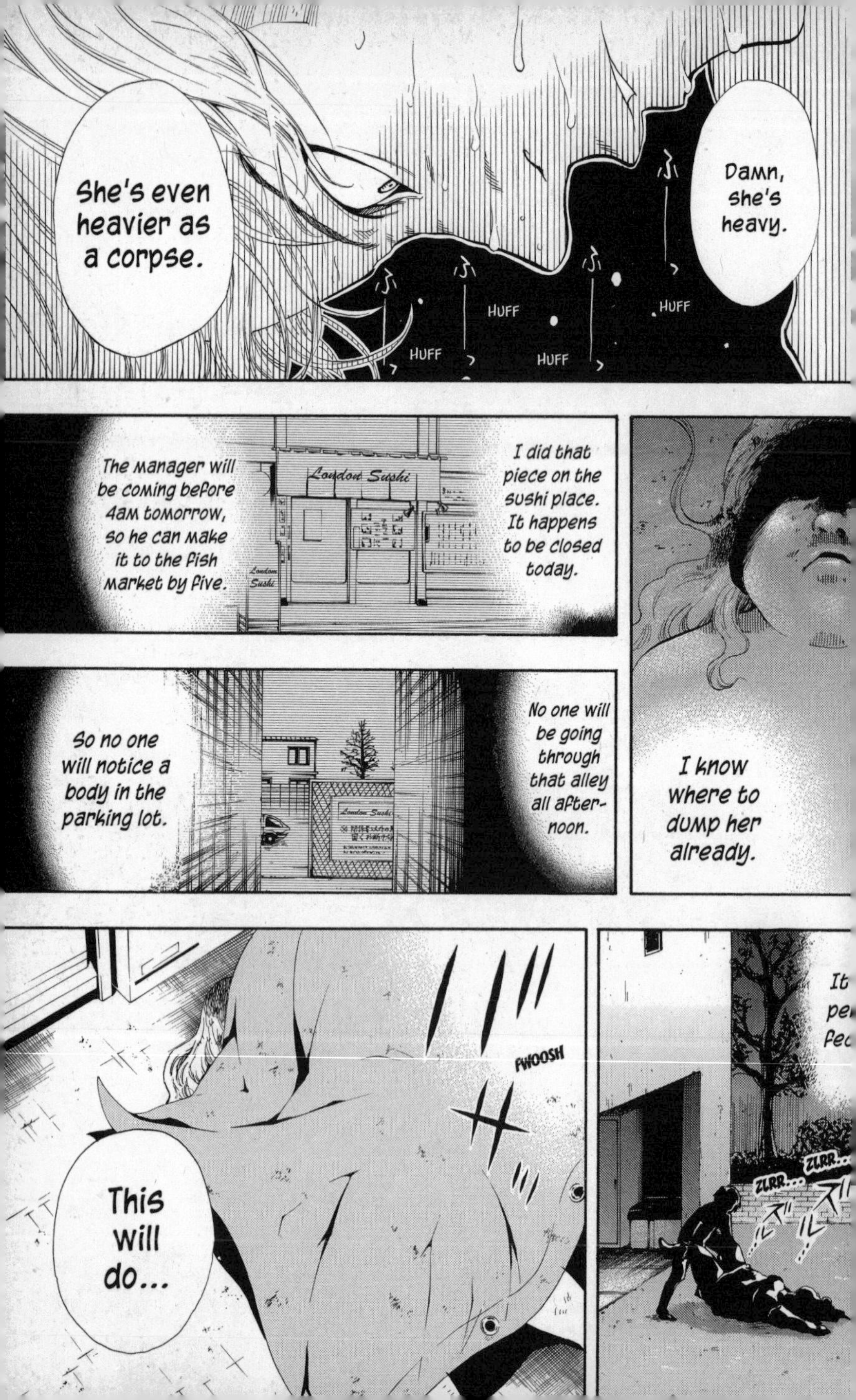
Damn, she's heavy.
HUFF
HUFF
HUFF
HUFF
She's even heavier as a corpse.
I know where to dump her already.
I did that piece on the sushi place. It happens to be closed today.
London Sushi
The manager will be coming before 4am tomorrow, so he can make it to the fish market by five.
No one will be going through that alley all afternoon.
London Sushi
So no one will notice a body in the parking lot.
It pe fec
ZLRR...
ZLRR...
PWOOSH
This will do...

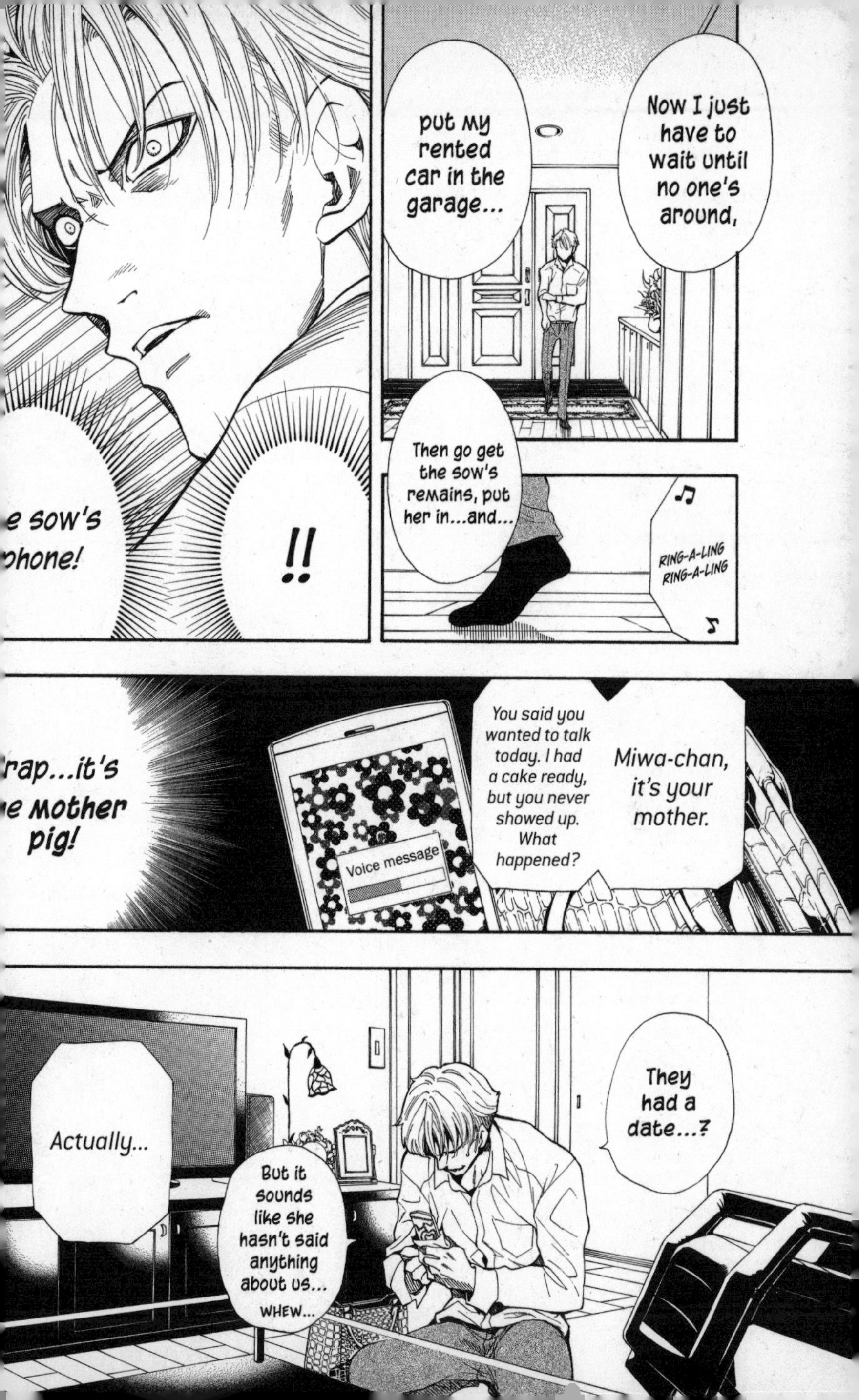
Now I just have to wait until no one's around,
put my rented car in the garage...
Then go get the sow's remains, put her in...and...
RING-A-LING RING-A-LING
!!
e sow's phone!
Miwa-chan, it's your mother.
You said you wanted to talk today. I had a cake ready, but you never showed up. What happened?
Voice message
rap...it's e mother pig!
They had a date...?
But it sounds like she hasn't said anything about us...
WHEW...
Actually...

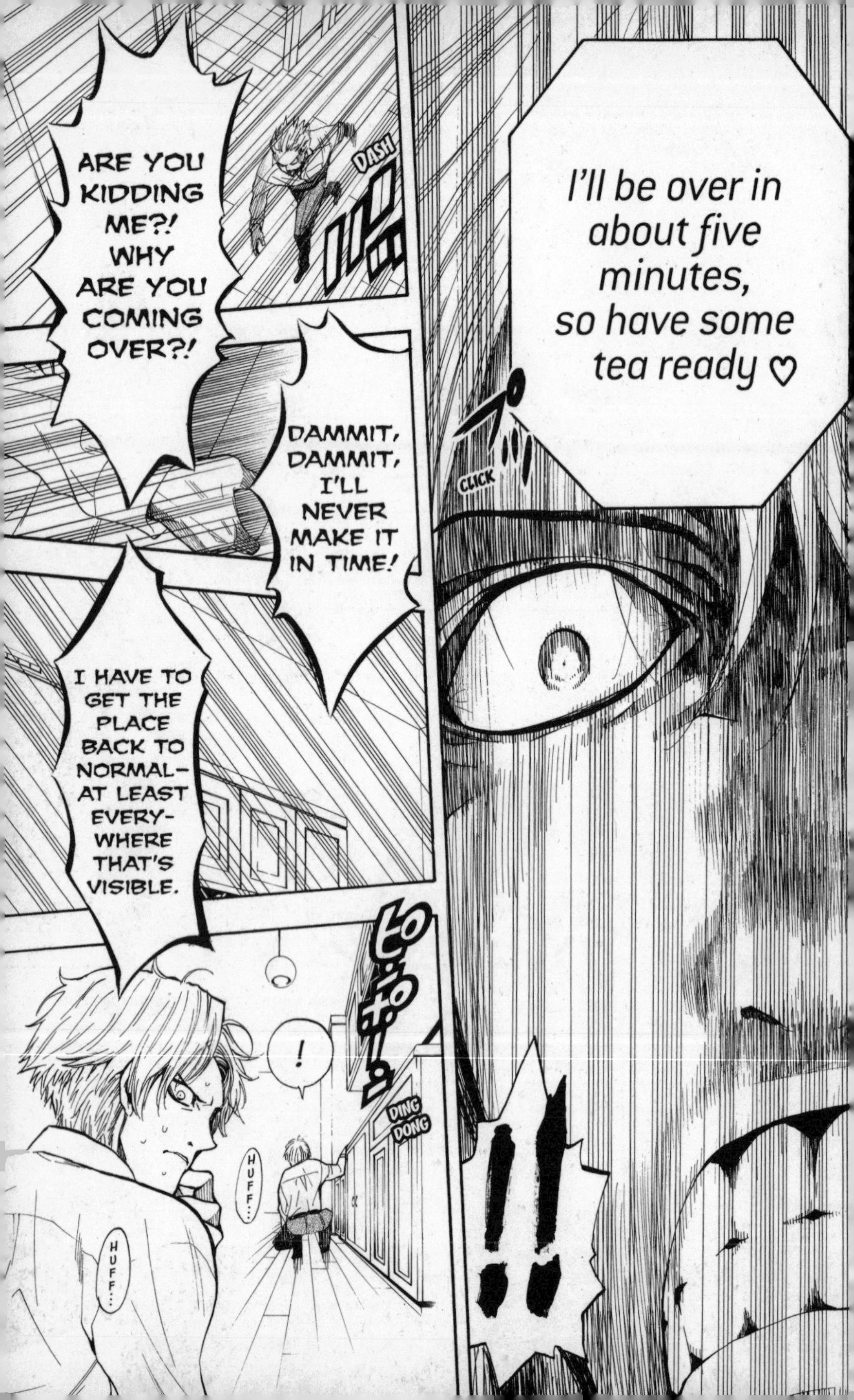
I'll be over in about five minutes, so have some tea ready ♡
CLICK
!!
ARE YOU KIDDING ME?! WHY ARE YOU COMING OVER?!
DASH
DAMMIT, DAMMIT, I'LL NEVER MAKE IT IN TIME!
I HAVE TO GET THE PLACE BACK TO NORMAL—AT LEAST EVERY-WHERE THAT'S VISIBLE.
DING DONG
!
HUFF...
HUFF...

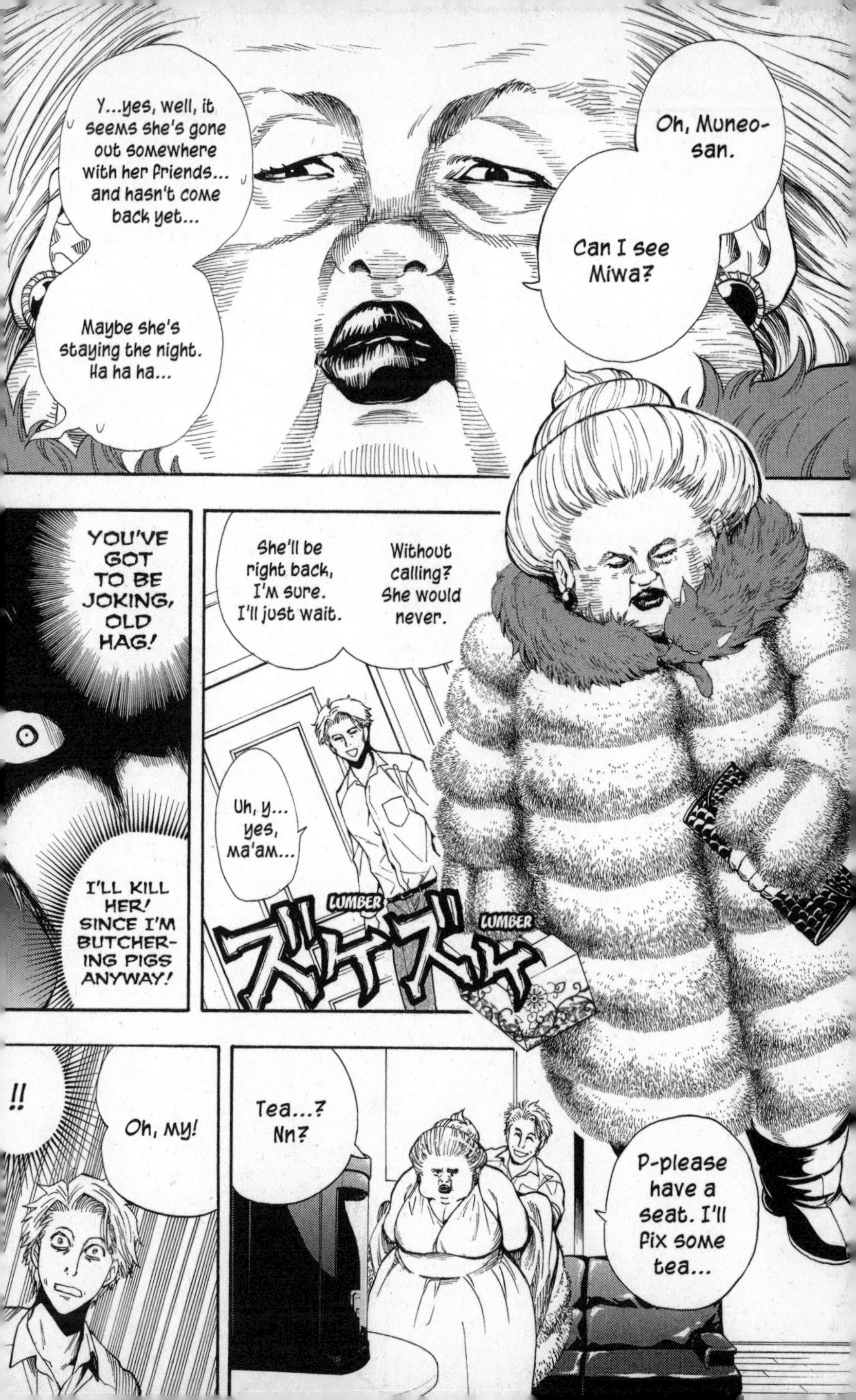
Oh, Muneo-san.
Can I see Miwa?
Y...yes, well, it seems she's gone out somewhere with her friends... and hasn't come back yet...
Maybe she's staying the night. Ha ha ha...
Without calling? She would never.
She'll be right back, I'm sure. I'll just wait.
Uh, y... yes, ma'am...
LUMBER
LUMBER
YOU'VE GOT TO BE JOKING, OLD HAG!
I'LL KILL HER! SINCE I'M BUTCHERING PIGS ANYWAY!
P-please have a seat. I'll fix some tea...
Tea...? Nn?
Oh, my!
!!

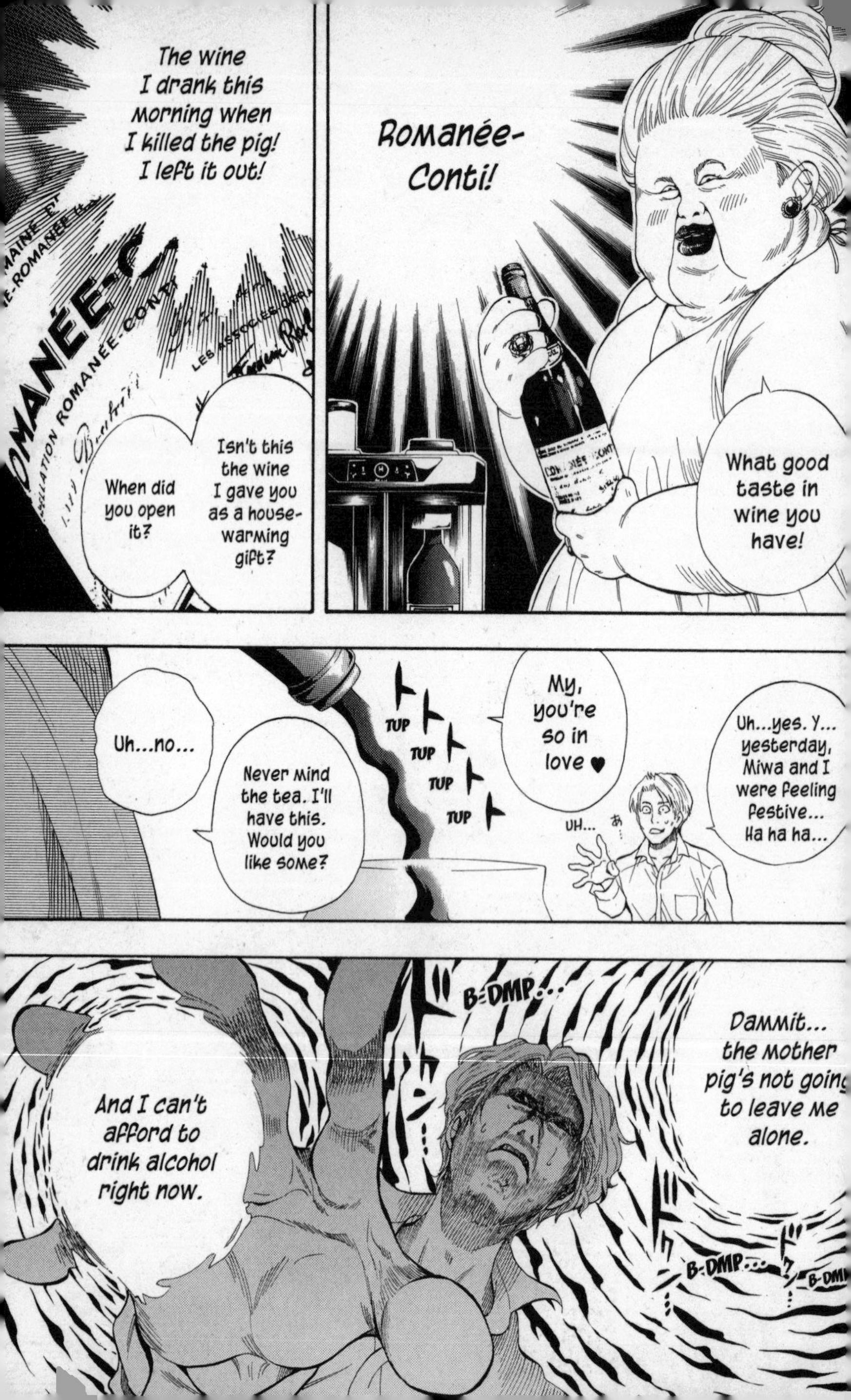

Romanée-Conti!
What good taste in wine you have!
The wine I drank this morning when I killed the pig! I left it out!
Isn't this the wine I gave you as a house-warming gift?
When did you open it?
ROMANÉE-CONTI
Uh...yes. Y... yesterday, Miwa and I were feeling festive... Ha ha ha...
UH... あ
My, you're so in love ♥
TUP TUP TUP TUP
Never mind the tea. I'll have this. Would you like some?
Uh...no...
Dammit... the mother pig's not going to leave me alone.
B-DMP...
B-DMP...
B-DMP...
And I can't afford to drink alcohol right now.

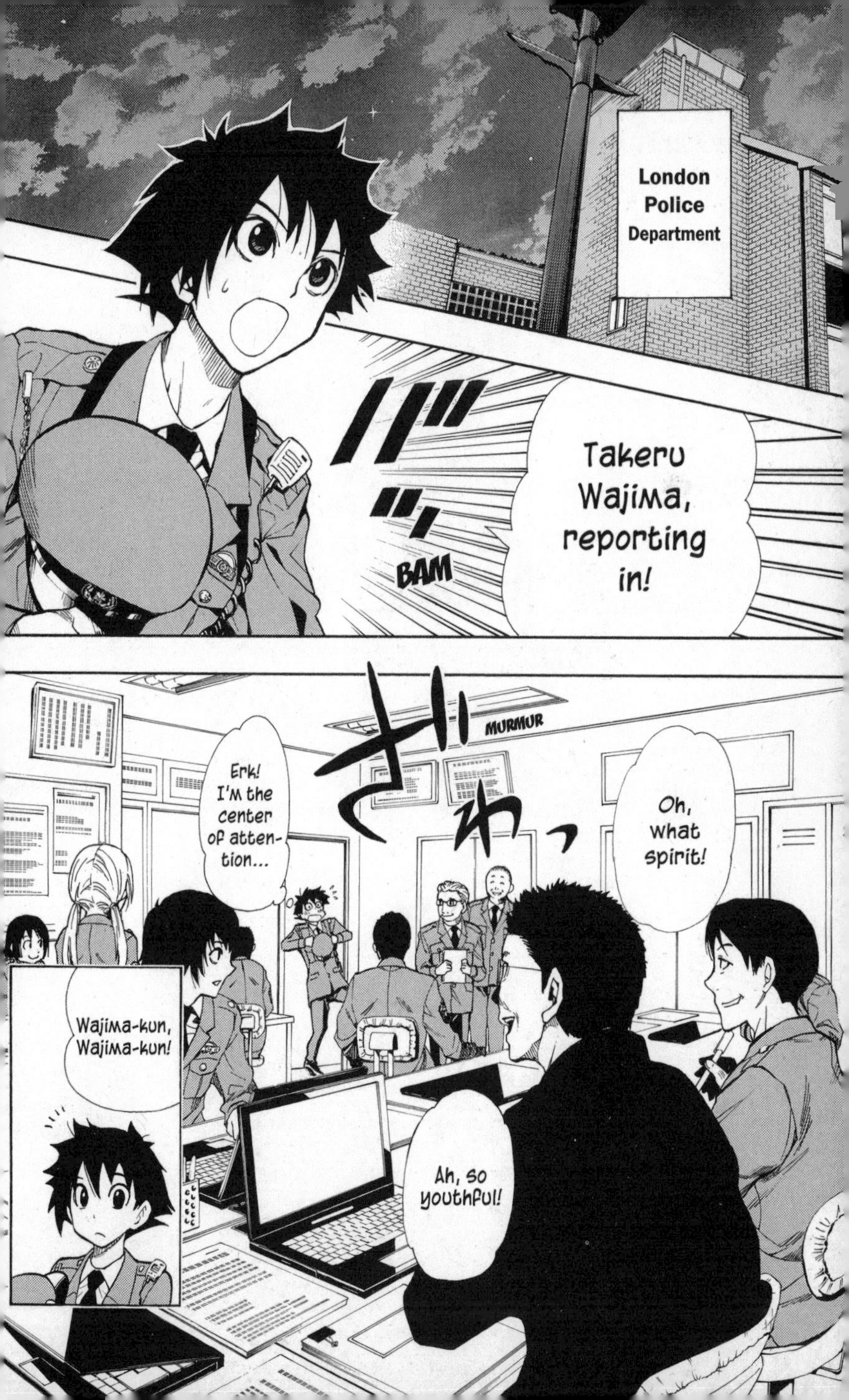
London Police Department
BAM
Takeru Wajima, reporting in!
MURMUR
Oh, what spirit!
Erk! I'm the center of atten-tion...
Ah, so youthful!
Wajima-kun, Wajima-kun!

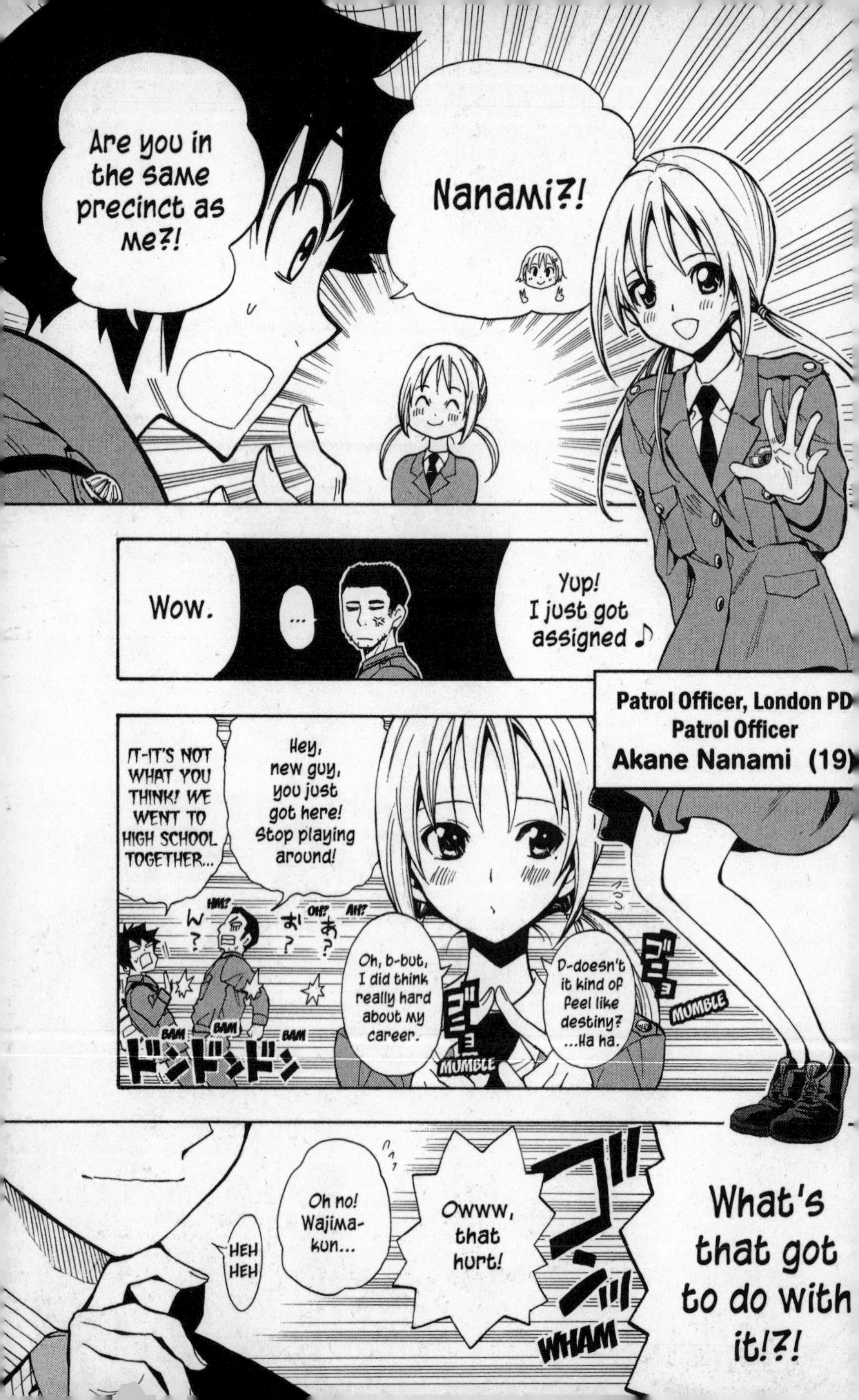
Nanami?!
Are you in the same precinct as me?!
Yup! I just got assigned ♪
...
Wow.
Patrol Officer, London PD
Patrol Officer
Akane Nanami (19)
D-doesn't it kind of feel like destiny? ...Ha ha.
MUMBLE
Oh, b-but, I did think really hard about my career.
MUMBLE
Hey, new guy, you just got here! Stop playing around!
IT-IT'S NOT WHAT YOU THINK! WE WENT TO HIGH SCHOOL TOGETHER...
AH?
OH?
HM?
BAM
BAM
BAM
ドンドンドン
What's that got to do with it!?!
WHAM
Owww, that hurt!
Oh no! Wajima-kun...
HEH HEH

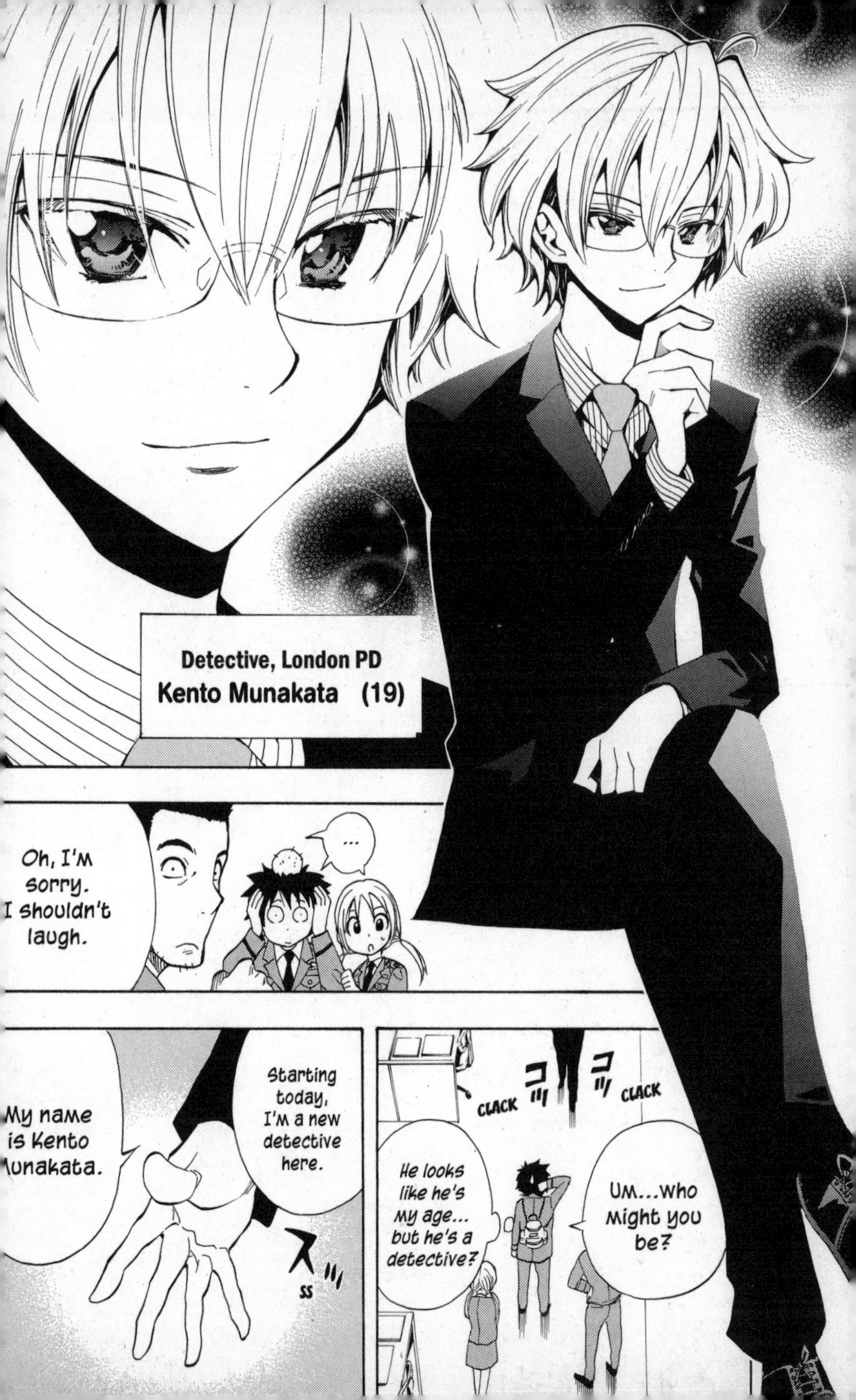

Detective, London PD
Kento Munakata (19)
...
Oh, I'm sorry. I shouldn't laugh.
CLACK
CLACK
Um...who might you be?
He looks like he's my age... but he's a detective?
Starting today, I'm a new detective here.
My name is Kento unakata.
SS

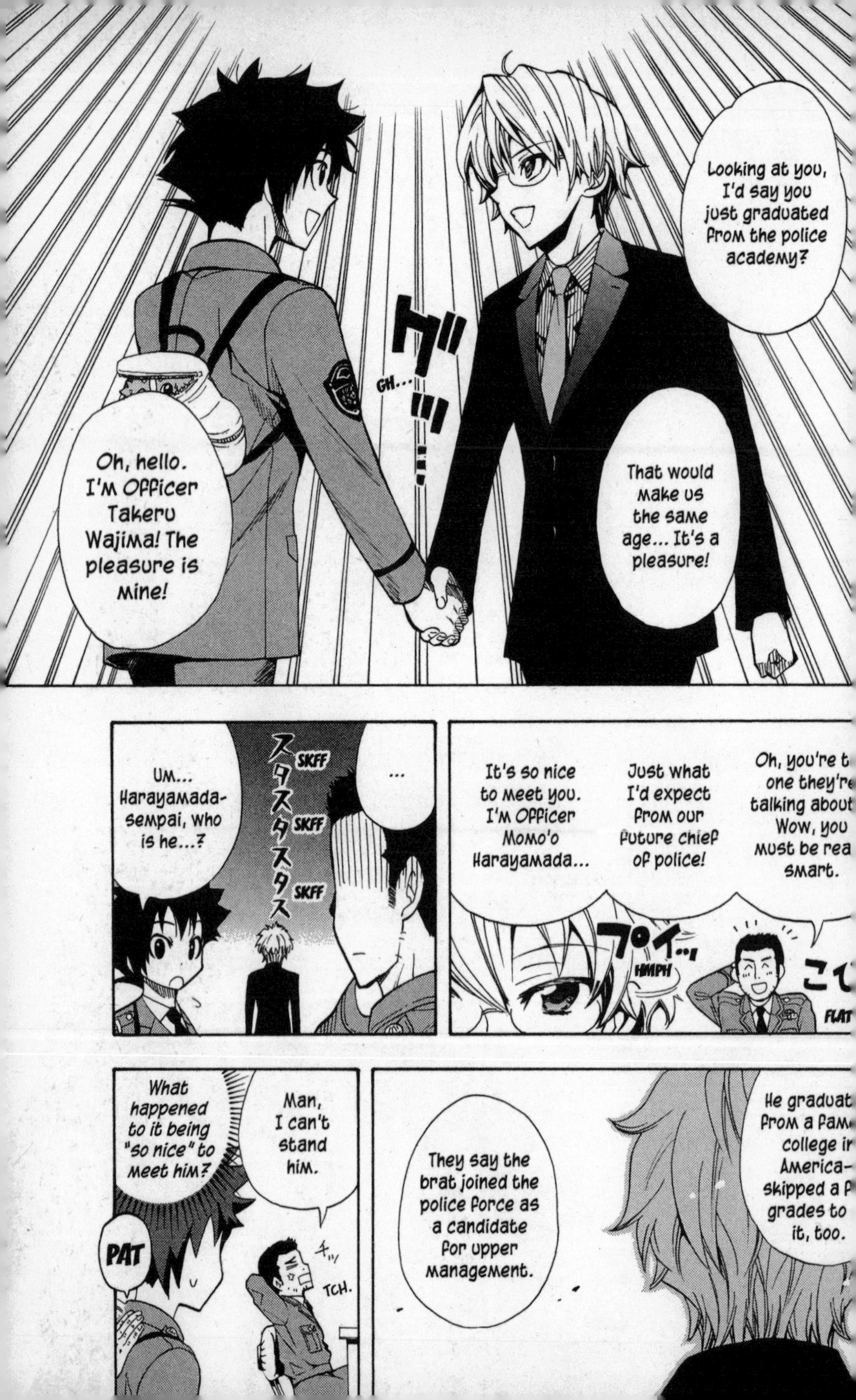
Looking at you, I'd say you just graduated from the police academy?
That would make us the same age... It's a pleasure!
GH...
Oh, hello. I'm Officer Takeru Wajima! The pleasure is mine!
Oh, you're t one they'r talking about Wow, you must be rea smart.
Just what I'd expect from our future chief of police!
It's so nice to meet you. I'm Officer Momo'o Harayamada...
プイ
HMPH
FLAT
...
スタスタスタ
SKFF
SKFF
SKFF
Um... Harayamada-sempai, who is he...?
He graduat from a fam college ir America- skipped a f grades to it, too.
They say the brat joined the police force as a candidate for upper management.
Man, I can't stand him.
TCH.
What happened to it being "so nice" to meet him?
PAT

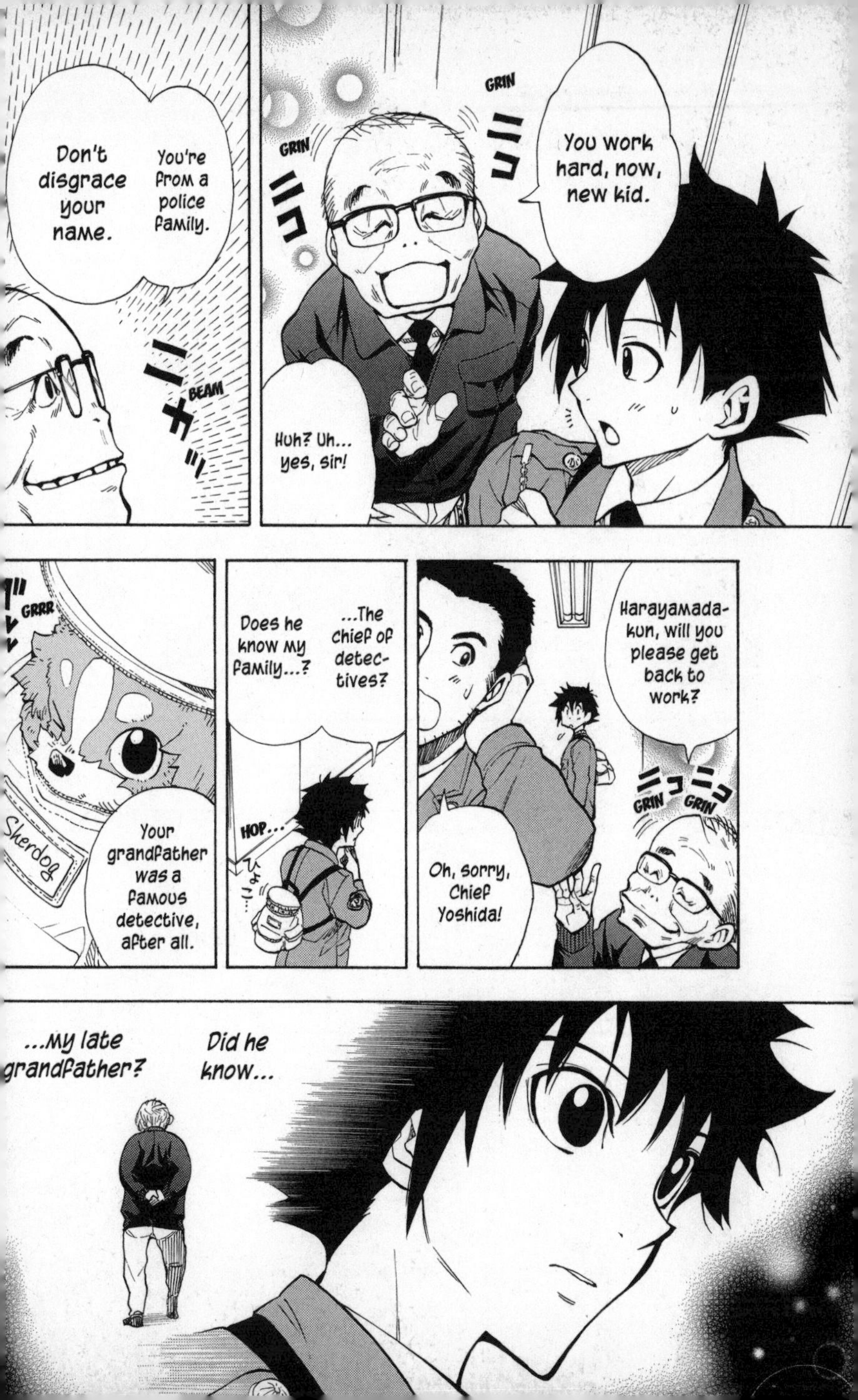
GRIN
ニコ
You work hard, now, new kid.
GRIN
ニコ
Huh? Uh... yes, sir!
You're from a police family.
Don't disgrace your name.
ニカッ
BEAM
Harayamada-kun, will you please get back to work?
ニコニコ
GRIN GRIN
Oh, sorry, Chief Yoshida!
...The chief of detectives?
Does he know my family...?
HOP...
GRRR
Sherdog
Your grandfather was a famous detective, after all.
Did he know...
...my late grandfather?

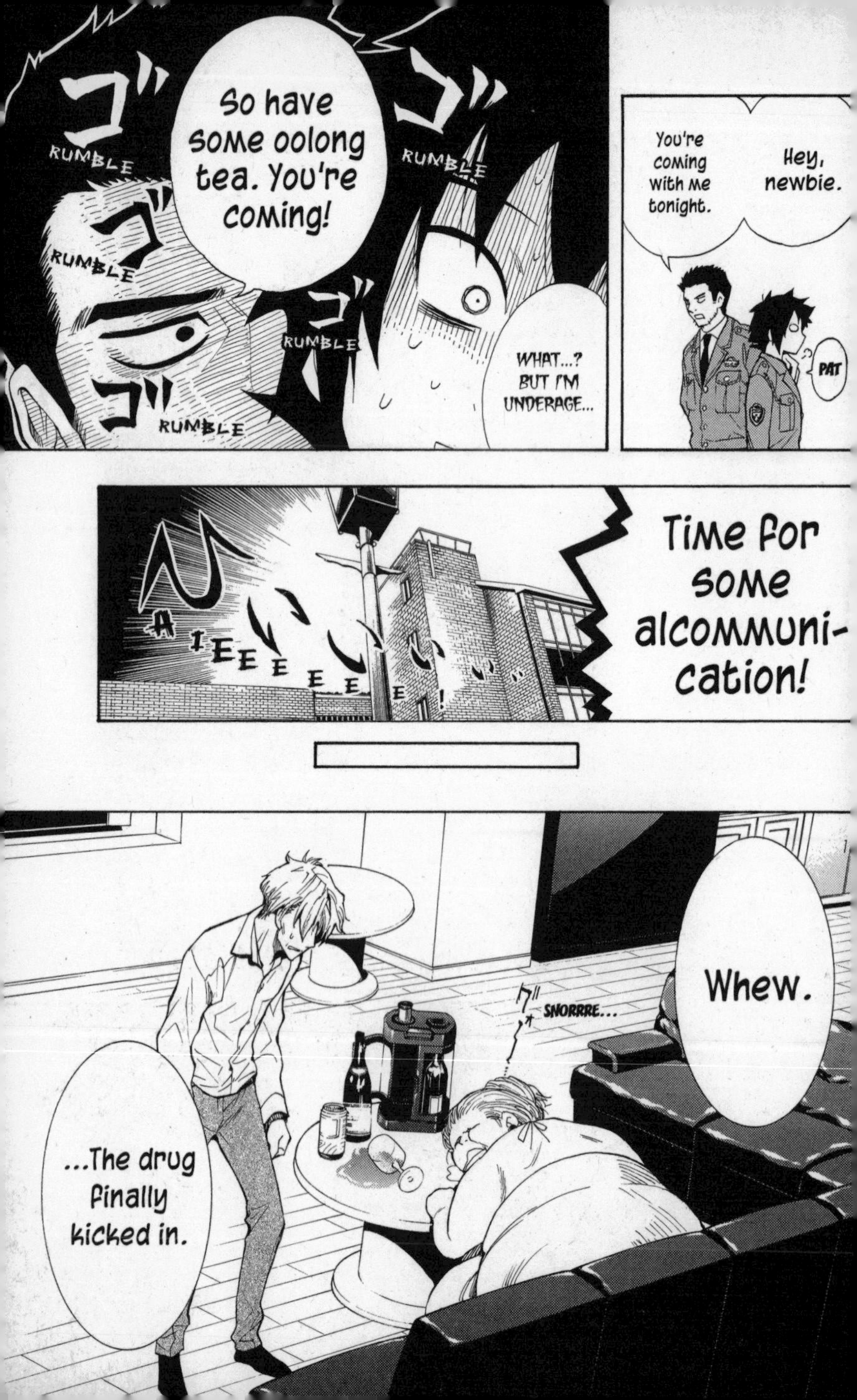
Hey, newbie.
You're coming with me tonight.
PAT
WHAT...? BUT I'M UNDERAGE...
So have some oolong tea. You're coming!
RUMBLE
RUMBLE
RUMBLE
RUMBLE
RUMBLE
Time for some alcommuni-cation!
AIEEEEEEE!
Whew.
SNORRRE...
...The drug finally kicked in.

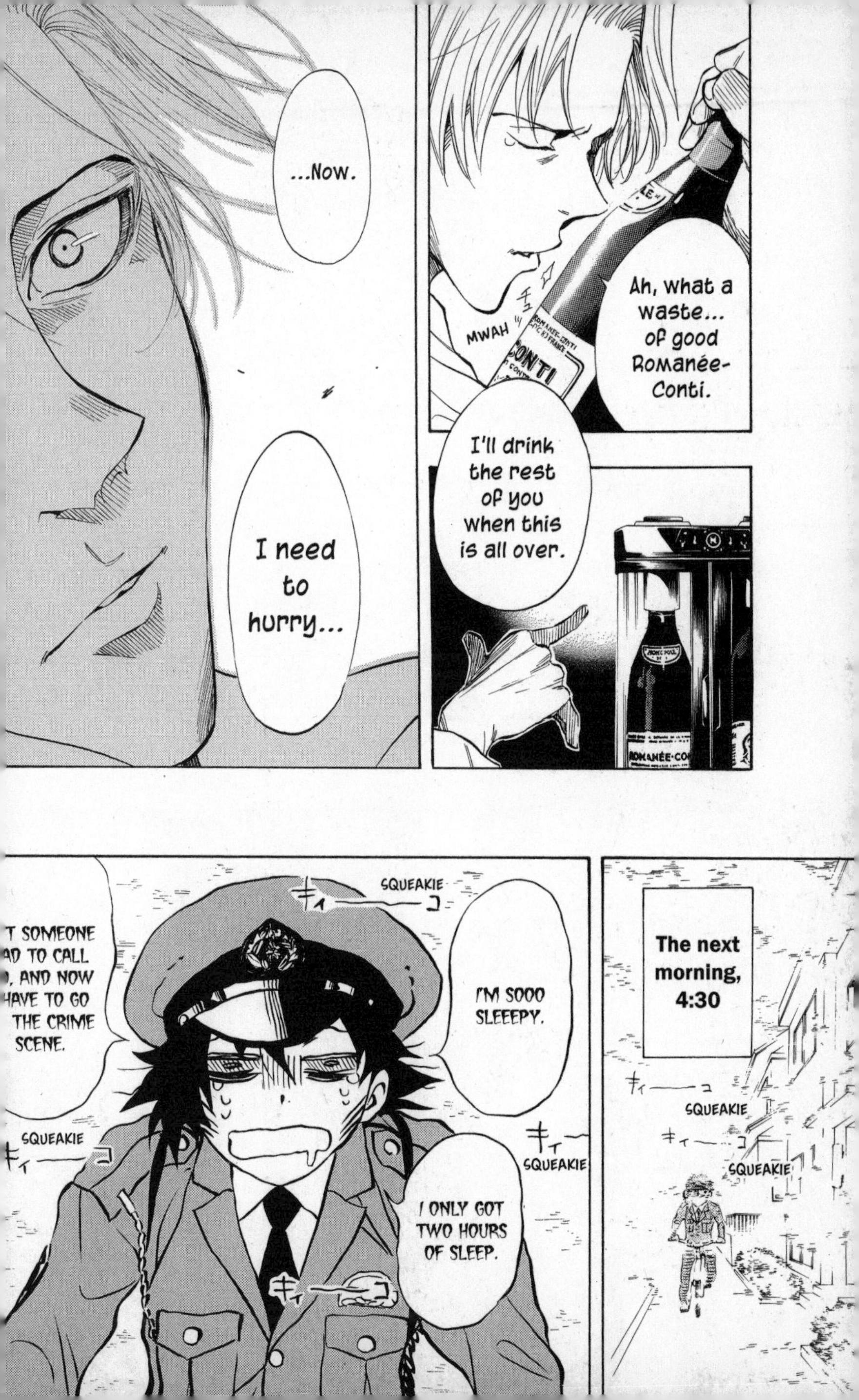
MWAH
Ah, what a waste... of good Romanée-Conti.
I'll drink the rest of you when this is all over.
...Now.
I need to hurry...
The next morning, 4:30
SQUEAKIE
SQUEAKIE
SQUEAKIE
I'M SOOO SLEEEPY.
SQUEAKIE
I ONLY GOT TWO HOURS OF SLEEP.
SQUEAKIE
T SOMEONE AD TO CALL , AND NOW HAVE TO GO THE CRIME SCENE.

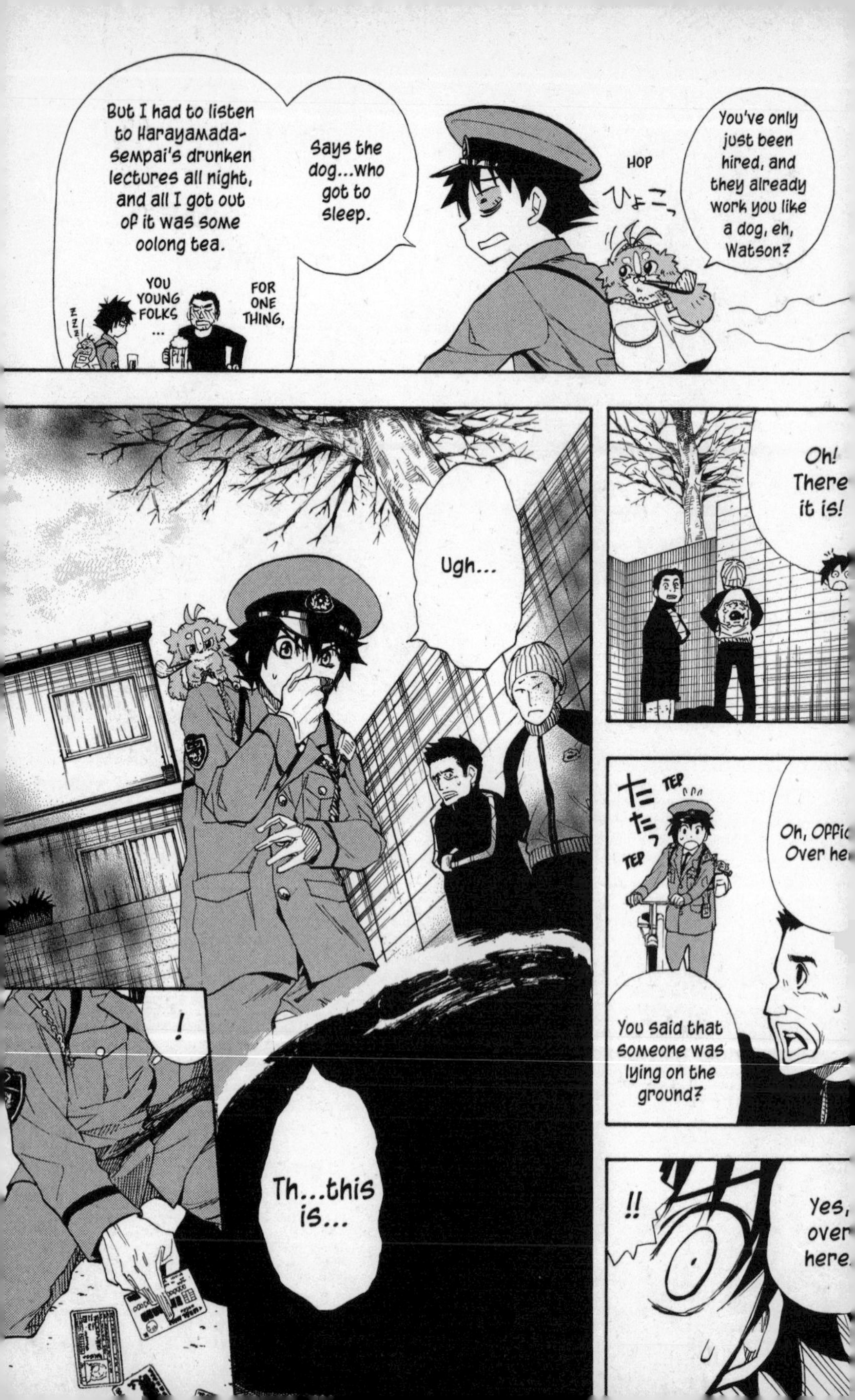
You've only just been hired, and they already work you like a dog, eh, Watson?
HOP
ひょこっ
Says the dog...who got to sleep.
But I had to listen to Harayamada-sempai's drunken lectures all night, and all I got out of it was some oolong tea.
FOR ONE THING,
YOU YOUNG FOLKS...
Oh! There it is!
Oh, Offic
Over he
たたっ
TEP
TEP
You said that someone was lying on the ground?
Yes, over here.
!!
Ugh...
!
Th...this is...

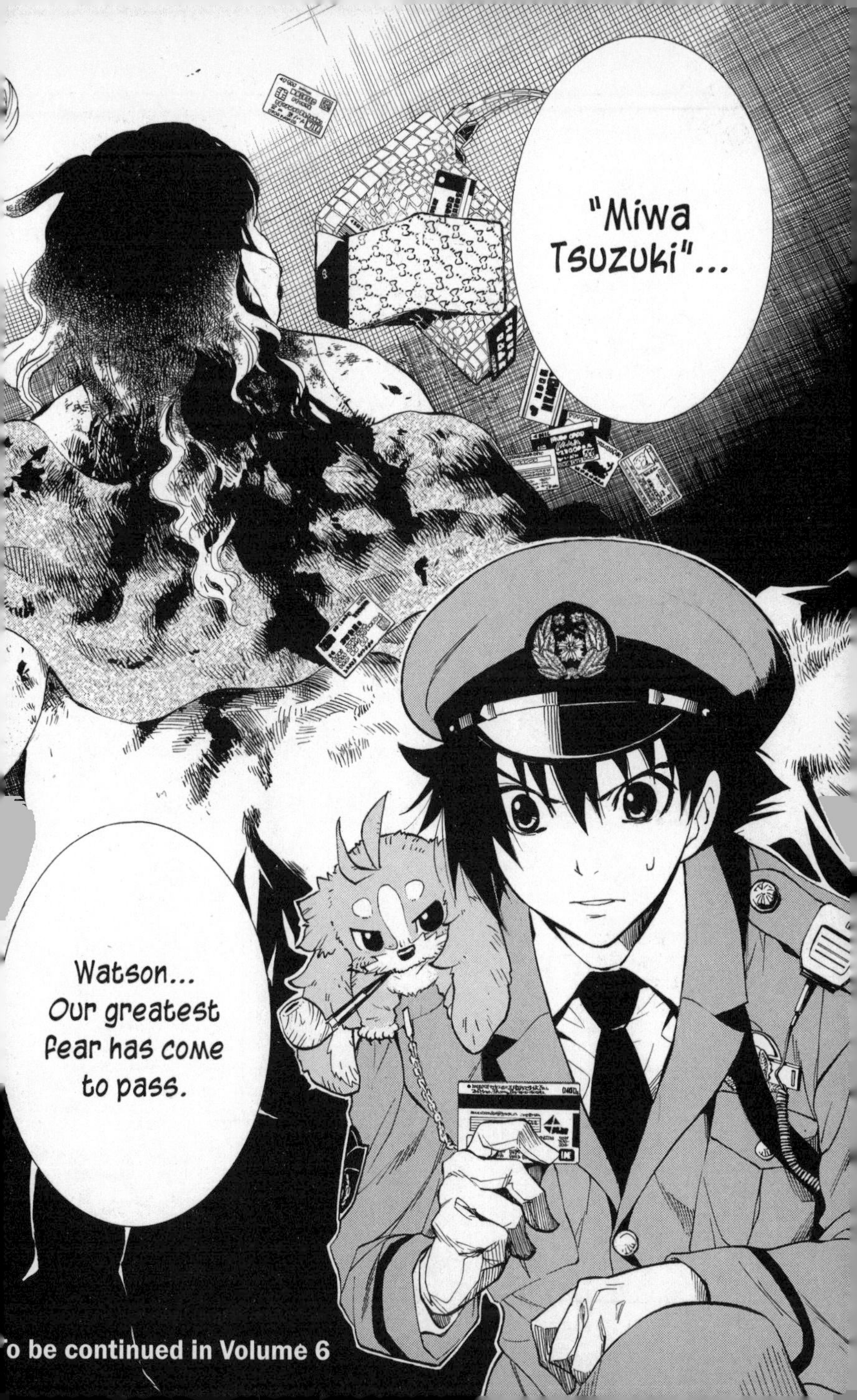
"Miwa Tsuzuki"...
Watson... Our greatest fear has come to pass.
o be continued in Volume 6

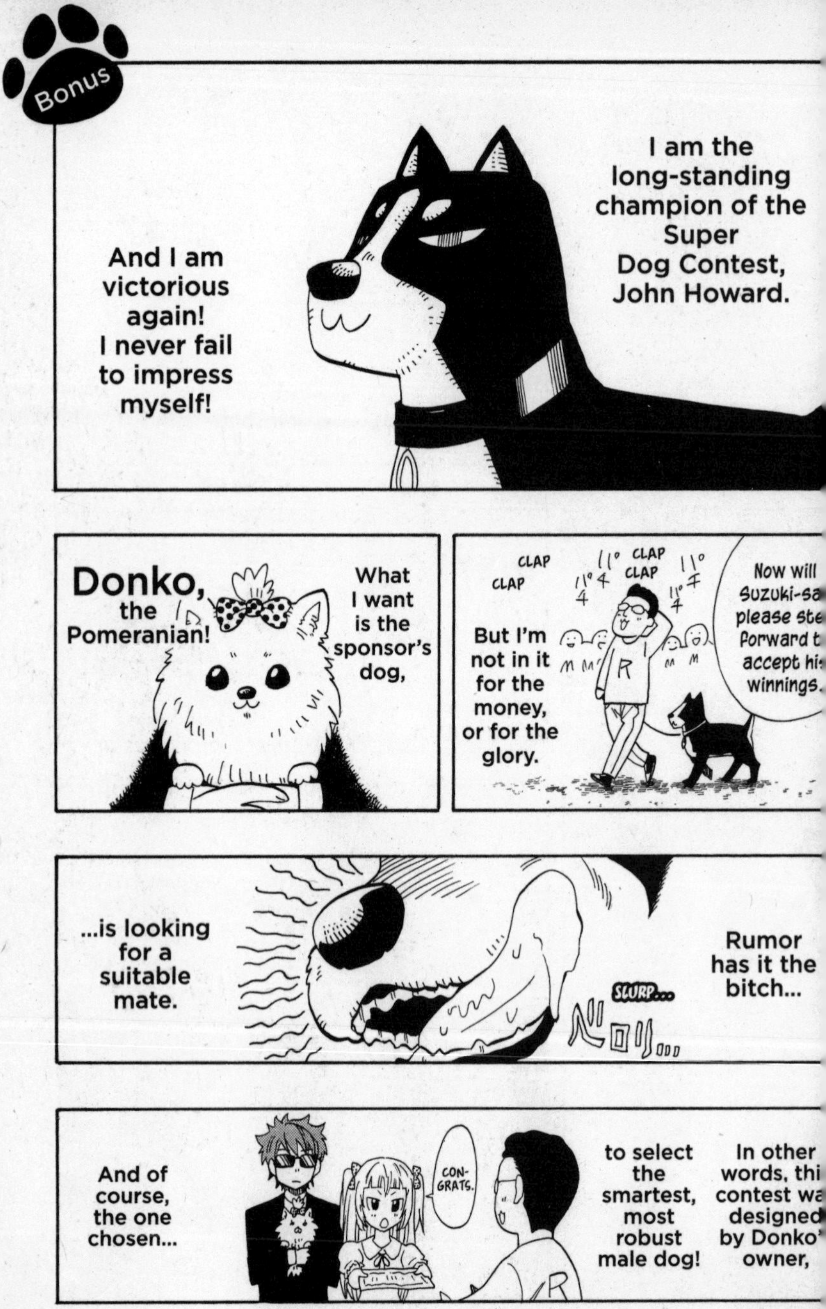
Bonus
I am the long-standing champion of the Super Dog Contest, John Howard.
And I am victorious again! I never fail to impress myself!
Now will Suzuki-sa please ste forward t accept hi winnings.
CLAP
CLAP
CLAP
CLAP
But I'm not in it for the money, or for the glory.
What I want is the sponsor's dog,
Donko, the Pomeranian!
Rumor has it the bitch...
SLURP...
...is looking for a suitable mate.
In other words, thi contest wa designed by Donko' owner,
to select the smartest, most robust male dog!
CON-GRATS.
And of course, the one chosen...

ANDO-SENSEI, EDITOR S-SAN, DESIGNER-SAN, PUBLISHING COMPANY-SAN, EVERYONE IN SALES, MY STAFF,
MY MENTOR, MY FRIENDS

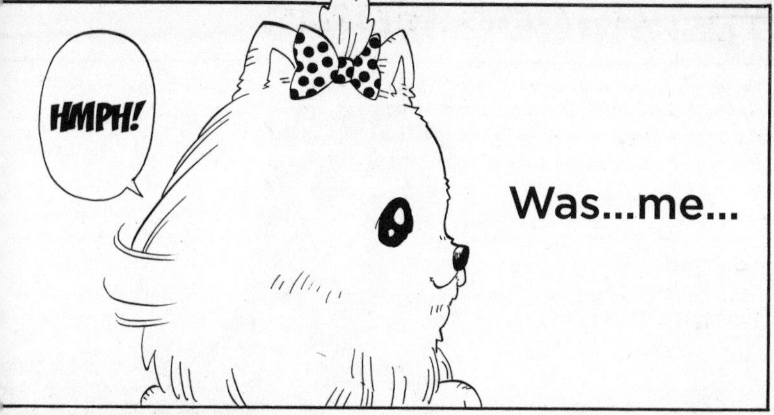
Was...me...
HMPH!

MY FAMILY, AND ALL MY READERS, THANK YOU SO MUCH! I'LL KEEP WORKING HARD. (^^)/ YUKI

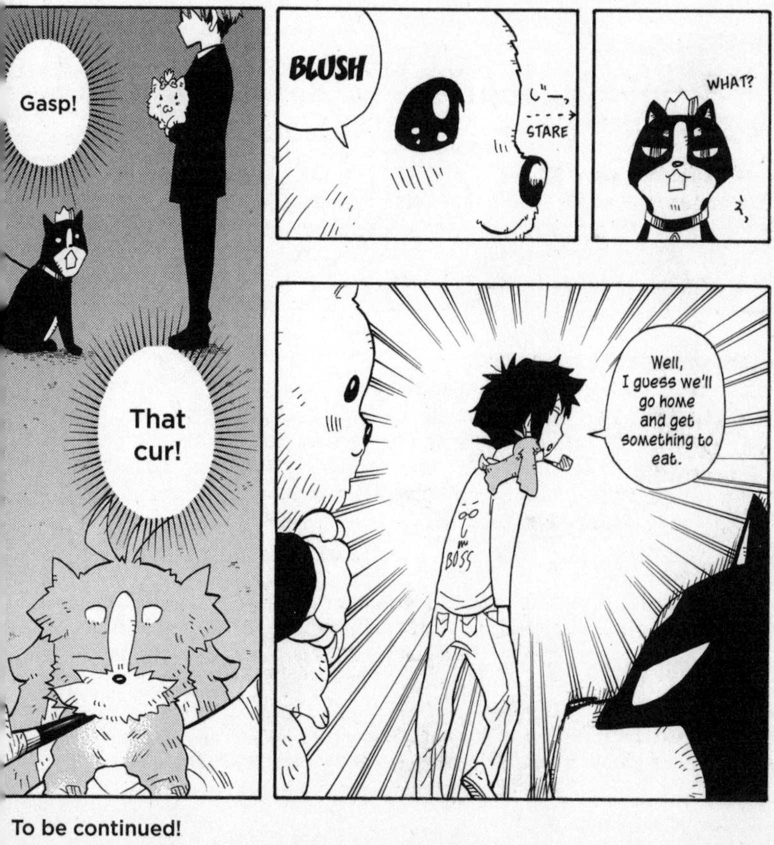
WHAT?
じー
STARE
BLUSH
Well, I guess we'll go home and get something to eat.
BOSS
Gasp!
That cur!

To be continued!

Translation Notes

Japanese is a tricky language for most Westerners, and translation is often more art than science. For your edification and reading pleasure, here are notes on some of the places where we could have gone in a different direction with our translation of the work, or where a Japanese cultural reference is used.

Mai-Mai Shimbun, page 18
This is a parody of Mainichi Shimbun, one of the major newspapers of Japan. Mainichi means "everyday," and mai-mai means "always." Shimbun, of course, means "newspaper."

Kuji TV, page 147
This is a parody of Fuji TV, one of the major Japanese television networks.

Lady killer, page 147
In the Japanese text, Miwa called her husband a "madame killer." The principle is the similar—it refers to a man who is good at charming women—but it specifically refers to more mature women.

2-chōme kōban, page 154
Kōban, loosely translates as "police box." Kōban are like miniature police stations, spread throughout the community, bringing the police close to the community so they can respond more readily to the citizens' needs. A chōme is a subsection of a city district, with 2-chōme being the second subsection of the Baker District.

Alcommunication, page 155
While it may seem like Officer Harayamada is making this up, the term nomication (a combination of nomu (to drink) and communication) is a real, though outdated, slang term in Japan. It refers to the bonding that occurs after work hours, when a group of coworkers or college classmates goes out drinking. The English translation, alcommunication, is a combination of the words "communication" and "alcohol."

Sempai, page 158
Sempai is a term of respect used to refer to someone who has more experience than the speaker. In this case, Takeru is referring to Officer Harayamada, who has been working at his kōban longer than he has.

Call 110, page 186
In Japan, there is more than one emergency phone number. 110 is the number for the police, while 119 is for medical emergencies or fire.

Sherlock Bones volume 5 is a work of fiction. N[illegible]aracters, places, and incidents are the products of the author's [illegible]n or are used fictitiously. Any resemblance to actual event[illegible]or persons, living or dead, is entirely coincidental.

A Kodansha Comics Trade Paperback Original.

Published in the United States by Kodansha Comics,
an imprint of Kodansha USA Publishing, LLC, New York.

Publication rights for this English edition arranged through Kodansha Ltd., Tokyo.

First published in Japan in 2012 by Kodansha Ltd., Tokyo, as *Tanteiken Sherdock* volume 5.

ISBN 978-1-61262-545-4

Printed in the United States of America.

www.kodanshacomics.com

9 8 7 6 5 4 3 2 1

Translator: Alethea Nibley and Athena Nibley
Lettering: Kiyoko Shiromasa